Media Freedom in the Age of Citizen Journalism

Media Freedom in the Age of Citizen Journalism

Peter Coe

Lecturer in Law, School of Law, University of Reading, UK

Cheltenham, UK • Northampton, MA, USA

© Peter Coe 2021

All rights reserved. No part of this publication may be reproduced, stored in a retrieval system or transmitted in any form or by any means, electronic, mechanical or photocopying, recording, or otherwise without the prior permission of the publisher.

Published by
Edward Elgar Publishing Limited
The Lypiatts
15 Lansdown Road
Cheltenham
Glos GL50 2JA
UK

Edward Elgar Publishing, Inc.
William Pratt House
9 Dewey Court
Northampton
Massachusetts 01060
USA

A catalogue record for this book
is available from the British Library

Library of Congress Control Number: 2021947959

This book is available electronically in the **Elgar**online
Law subject collection
http://dx.doi.org/10.4337/9781800371262

Printed on elemental chlorine free (ECF)
recycled paper containing 30% Post-Consumer Waste

ISBN 978 1 80037 125 5 (cased)
ISBN 978 1 80037 126 2 (eBook)
Printed and bound in the USA

Contents

Acknowledgements		vi
1	Introduction to *Media Freedom in the Age of Citizen Journalism*	1

PART I   THE MODERN MEDIA LANDSCAPE

2	A shackled institution: is the notion of the 'free press' a fallacy?	16
3	The internet, social media and citizen journalism	51

PART II   THEORETICAL CONSIDERATIONS

4	Unpacking media freedom as a distinct legal concept	95
5	The media-as-a-constitutional-component concept: a new theoretical foundation for media freedom	130
6	What the media-as-a-constitutional-component concept means for media freedom	178

PART III   LEGAL CHALLENGES

7	Anonymous and pseudonymous speech	203
8	Contempt of court and defamation	234
9	Reimagining regulation	261
Index		297

Acknowledgements

This book began its life in 2013 (as something very different to what you are reading now); it comes from my long-held fascination with the media, and how it can and does influence us as a society and as individuals. Consequently, it is the product of a number of things: of late nights and early mornings spent in my study, either after my wife Hayley and my daughter Annabelle had gone to bed, or before they had woken up; of long runs in the countryside, in all weathers, with my dog Luther, to think through problems or to overcome the agony of writer's block (he has still not forgiven me); of what seemed to be hours agonising over the editing of footnotes, of my infuriating quest for perfection, and therefore my hesitancy to send out chapters for review, and the fear I felt when each review was returned. Yet, despite all of this, ultimately it represents eight years (at the time I am writing these acknowledgments) of research and work that I have thoroughly enjoyed, and which have presented me with opportunities that, in 2013, I could never have envisaged. What this book does not represent, however, is the end of this journey, rather I see it as the start (I have not told Luther yet!). For me it has already been a catalyst for more research, and work, in this fascinating and ever-changing area that continues to give me so much pleasure. My hope for this book is that it will inspire others in the way that I have been inspired by so many brilliant scholars, a number of whom I am indebted to for their help and support, which I will come on to now.

One of the great joys of writing this book was the opportunity it gave me to work with outstanding scholars, who are also outstanding people, and to engage with their work. So much of them is in this book as it simply would not have been the book that it is without their input and their generosity. I am especially grateful to Paul Wragg, András Koltay, Daithí Mac Síthigh, David Rolph and Rebecca Moosavian. I owe them all so much for the time they took to provide such valuable, constructive and challenging feedback on various drafts of chapters, their enthusiasm for the project and their inspiration and encouragement (especially at the times when my enthusiasm was waning and I wondered whether I would ever finish what I had started, and when I was experiencing doubt in my own ability). Without wanting or intending to embarrass him, I want to extend a special thank you to Professor Wragg. Paul has been with me every step of the way (I am sure he has mixed feelings about this book!), and at every step he has been a mentor and a friend. He has supported and inspired me in more ways than I am sure he knows.

Acknowledgements vii

I am thankful to colleagues, and former colleagues, who have supported me since 2013. They include Alastair Mullis, James Devenney, Simon Brown, Sarah Fox, Eglė Dagilytė, Ryan Murphy, James Brown and Laura Scaife. I am also extremely grateful for the support I have been given by the team at Edward Elgar, especially my editor, Amber Watts.

And, of course, there are so many others, who probably have no idea of their contribution to this book but have influenced my thinking, and who are, therefore, very much part of it. They include, to name but a few: David Acheson, Eric Barendt, Tom Bennett, Paul Bernal, Ian Cram, José Van Dijck, Mark Frankel, Tom Gibbons, Jonathan Heawood, Lexie Kirkconnell-Kawana, Andrew Kenyon, David Mangan, Dario Milo, Andrew Murray, Jan Oster, Gavin Phillipson, Ed Procter, Megan Richardson, Jake Rowbottom, Hugh Tomlinson QC, Russell Weaver and Hilary Young.

Finally, and most importantly, from the bottom of my heart, I want to thank my wonderful family, and in particular Hayley and Annabelle (and of course, Luther). Without their support and encouragement (and their abundance of patience) I would not have been able to contemplate writing this book, let alone complete it. This book is as much theirs as it is mine.

Peter Coe
Bodicote
May 2021

1. Introduction to *Media Freedom in the Age of Citizen Journalism*

1 THE MEDIA PARADIGM, BUT NOT AS WE KNOW IT

Journalism has changed. The internet and social media have permanently altered the media ecology and have shifted the media paradigm beyond recognition by enabling new actors to enter the media marketplace, and by changing the way that news is generated, published and consumed.[1]

On the one hand, these changes have had a profound effect on the viability of the traditional institutional press and on the extent to which journalists operating within the industry's typical corporate institutional structure are able to discharge their 'watchdog' role and contribute positively to public discourse and the public sphere. In the ways that are explored in Chapter 3, the internet and social media have contributed to the pressures that are generated by corporate ownership of the institutional press.[2] These pressures encourage journalists operating within this structure to publish content that appeals to mass audiences and attracts advertisers, rather than engage in high-quality, yet expensive and time-consuming, diverse public interest journalism.[3]

To the contrary, the internet and social media do not only remove the technological and financial barriers to producing and disseminating content by allowing anybody with a mobile device (we do not even need a computer) to communicate instantaneously with a mass audience.[4] They also enable journalists to circumvent the structure and some of the 'norms' of, in particular, the institutional press, but also the institutional broadcast media (television and radio), and, in a sense, they liberate those journalists from some of the constraints and pressures imposed on the press by the dominant proprietor and corporate ownership models.[5] Consequently, it has been suggested that

---

[1]　See Chapter 3 section 3.
[2]　Ibid and see Chapter 2 section 3.3.2.
[3]　Ibid.
[4]　Chapter 3 section 6.2.1.
[5]　Ibid sections 6.2.2 and 6.2.3.

2   *Media freedom in the age of citizen journalism*

the internet's dismantling of these obstacles has contributed to the democratisation of the public sphere[6] by making the emergence of more voices in the public space possible;[7] a contention that is animated by the ascendance of citizen journalism.[8] The internet, and particularly the growth of social media, which has seen it emerge as arguably the dominant infrastructure for speech, have facilitated this by creating the ideal environment for citizen journalism to flourish, with citizen journalists tending to publish their content on social media platforms. Indeed, the role played by social media in citizen journalism's ascendance was observed by Leveson LJ in his *Inquiry into the Culture, Practices and Ethics of the Press* (*Inquiry*),[9] in which he referenced the ability of citizen journalists, operating through social media, to reach vast numbers of people almost instantly.[10] Another related phenomenon that has

---

[6]   See generally J. Balkin, 'Digital Speech and Democratic Culture: A Theory of Freedom of Expression for the Information Society' (2004) 79 *New York University Law Review* 1, 54; I. Cram, *Citizen Journalists: Newer Media, Republican Moments and the Constitution* (Edward Elgar Publishing, 2015) 3.

[7]   A. Koltay, *New Media and Freedom of Expression: Rethinking the Constitutional Foundations of the Public Sphere* (Hart Publishing, 2019) 74; E. Volokh, 'Cheap Speech and What It Will Do' (1995) 104 *Yale Law Journal* 1805, 1833; P. Schwartz, 'Privacy and Democracy in Cyberspace' (1999) 52 *Vanderbilt Law Review* 1609; J. Rowbottom, 'Media Freedom and Political Debate in the Digital Era' (2006) *Modern Law Review* 489.

[8]   Cram (n 7) 37–72; J. Oster, 'Theory and Doctrine of "Media Freedom" as a Legal Concept' (2013) 5(1) *Journal of Media Law* 57–78, 63; J. Oster, *Media Freedom as a Fundamental Right* (Cambridge University Press, 2015); C. Calvert and M. Torres, 'Putting the Shock Value in First Amendment Jurisprudence: When Freedom for the Citizen-Journalist Watchdog Trumps the Right of Informational Privacy on the Internet' (2011) *Vanderbilt Journal of Entertainment and Technology Law* 323, 344; A. Cohen, 'The Media That Need Citizens: The First Amendment and the Fifth Estate' (2011) 85 *Southern Californian Law Review* 1; T. Gibbons, 'Conceptions of the Press and the Functions of Regulation' (2016) 22(5) *Convergence: The International Journal of Research into New Media Technologies* 484, 486.

[9]   Leveson LJ's *Inquiry* did no more than 'observe' the ascendance of citizen journalism as it was, perhaps rather short-sightedly, exclusively concerned with the printed press. Although it may be defensible that his *Inquiry* was limited in this way as the institutional press were the 'wrongdoers' in the context within which he was reporting, arguably his regulatory solution to press malfeasance ought to have recognised the increasing influence that citizen journalists are having on the public sphere and what this means for the future of press regulation. This is discussed in Chapter 9.

[10]   In relation to blogs, Leveson LJ refers to *Guido Fawkes*, which, according to its founder, Paul Staines, can be visited by up to 100,000 people per hour when big stories are being broken (see section 2 below for more discussion on *Guido Fawkes*). Leveson LJ also makes specific reference to the usage of social media sites, such as Facebook and Twitter: Lord Justice Leveson, *An Inquiry into the Culture, Practices and Ethics of the Press: Report*, HC 780, November 2012, 168, [4.3]–[4.4], 173, [5.2] respectively.

Introduction 3

been stimulated by social media's growth is a symbiosis with, in particular, the institutional press, but also the broadcast media, in which citizen journalists (and social media content generally) increasingly act as a 'source' of news.[11] By providing the technological architecture and the environment for citizen journalists to publish the diverse content that journalists operating within a corporate structure may be reluctant or unable to provide, the internet and social media allow them to regularly contribute to the robustness of the public sphere by performing a 'watchdog' role that is typically associated with the institutional press.[12]

2   CITIZEN JOURNALISM

The origins of citizen journalism can be found in the civic and public journalism reform movement of the late 1980s.[13] This movement, which aimed to encourage public interest and participation in public affairs,[14] advocated that news media should 'go beyond the mere reporting of information to act as a catalyst and as a forum for the revitalization of democracy'.[15] Despite these early origins, however, as discussed above it was the internet and the emergence of social media that really provided the means for journalism to be opened up to 'citizens'. Yet, even with this technological infrastructure in place, it took the tragic events that unfolded on 11 September 2001 to provide

---

The role that social media now plays in how we communicate was summed up by the Criminal Court of the City of New York in *New York v Harris* 2012 N.Y. Misc. LEXIS 1871 *3, note 3 (Crim. Ct. City of N.Y. N.Y. County, 2012): 'The reality of today's world is that social media, whether it be Twitter, Facebook, Pinterest, Google+ or any other site, is the way people communicate.'

[11] A 'side-effect' of this symbiotic relationship is that false information published by citizen journalists can have an even greater impact as it is often 'recycled' by the traditional media. In turn, the fact that the traditional media has published it serves to justify and support the false information. Thus, the cycle becomes self-fulfilling. This is discussed in detail in section 5.3 of Chapter 3.

[12] See Chapter 3 section 6.2.3.

[13] T. Flew and J. Wilson, 'Journalism as Social Networking: The Australian Youdecide Project and the 2007 Federal Election' (2010) 11(2) *Journalism* 131; F. Kperogi, 'Cooperation with the Corporation? CNN and the Hegemonic Cooperation of Citizen Journalism through IReport.Com' (2011) 13(2) *New Media & Society* 314; B. Massey and T. Haas, 'Does Making Journalism More Public Make a Difference? A Critical Review of Evaluative Research on Public Journalism' (2002) 79(3) *Journalism & Mass Communications Quarterly* 559.

[14] Massey and Haas (n 13).

[15] M. McDevitt, B. Gassaway and F. Perez, 'The Making and Unmaking of Civic Journalists: Influences of Professional Socialization' (2002) 79(1) *Journalism & Mass Communications Quarterly* 87, 87.

a stimulus for the exponential growth of citizen journalism and its morphosis into what it is associated with today.[16] As planes struck each of the Twin Towers of the World Trade Center in New York, and as another plane was flown into the Pentagon in Virginia, citizen journalists began blogging content about what they were witnessing, some of which would eventually be used by the press and broadcast media.

Because of the wide spectrum of activity that it covers, citizen journalism is not easy to define. At one end, at it its most primal and crudest, it could be an individual providing some sort of one-off 'content' on an event that contributes to public discourse, such as some of the commentary provided by bloggers during and after the 2001 terrorist attacks. However, for some of these bloggers this event triggered the beginning of a journey in which their journalistic activity became increasingly 'professionalised' and important to the public sphere.[17] Thus, at the opposing end of the spectrum, at its most sophisticated, citizen journalism can include actors operating outside of the institutional media structure as 'professional' journalists in all but name, and it can arguably even encapsulate professional journalists blogging in an individual capacity rather than as part of the institutional press and broad-cast media.[18] Citizen journalists at this end of the spectrum contribute to the robustness of the public sphere in a myriad of different and impactful ways from countries all over the world. For instance, the blog *Night Jack*, which is discussed in more detail in Chapter 7 in the context of the *Author of a Blog v Times Newspapers Ltd*[19] litigation, won the 2009 Orwell Blogger Prize for citizen journalism.[20] The blog's author, Richard Horton, was a serving police officer, who used it to pseudonymously discuss his work and criticise govern-ment ministers and police operations.[21] According to the judges who awarded

---

[16]   D. Gillmor, *We the Media: Grassroots Journalism By the People, For the People* (O'Reilly Media, 2004) 18–22.

[17]   Ibid. Gillmor cites early bloggers such as Dave Farber and his 'Interesting People' mailing list and Glenn Reynolds, who used his blog, Instapundit.com, to write about the attacks and their aftermath. The site now has a 'massive following'. Meg Hourihan, who was one of the co-founders and co-creators of *Blogger*, produced content about the events using the tool. At the time, the site was in its infancy but in 2003, after Hourihan had left its parent company Pyra Labs, it was sold to Google. Hourihan has since gone on to co-author (with Paul Bausch and Matthew Haughey) *We Blog: Publishing Online with Weblogs* (John Wiley & Sons, 2002) and, in 2004, co-founded *Kinja.com*, a news aggregator for online news publishers.

[18]   Gillmor (n 16) ch. 6. See Chapter 3 section 4.2 for a discussion on how job cuts in the press industry have led to a growth in independent non-institutional journalists, and the impact this has had on the institutional media.

[19]   [2009] EMLR 22.

[20]   https://www.orwellfoundation.com/blogger/jack-night/.

[21]   For further examples of citizen journalism, see Gillmor (n 16) ch. 7.

Introduction   5

the prize to *Night Jack*, the blog's whistleblowing content provided a valuable 'insight into the everyday life of the police' which took the audience 'to the heart of what a policeman has to do'.[22] The content produced by the political blog *Guido Fawkes*, which is authored by Paul Staines, has also been the subject of critical acclaim. In 2005 it won the Political Commentary category of The Backbencher Political Weblog Awards, run by *The Guardian*,[23] and in 2006 *The Independent* placed Staines at number 36 in the 'Top 50 newsmakers of 2006'.[24] In 2011 *GQ Magazine* ranked him as joint-28th in the magazine's list of the 100 Most Influential Men in Britain.[25] The blog's extensive reach was the subject of evidence presented to Leveson LJ during his *Inquiry*.[26]

Arguably, however, the positive impact of citizen journalism on the public sphere is most obvious in conflict or crisis situations that present significant dangers and/or accessibility challenges to the institutional media and their reporters. The SARS-CoV-2 (COVID-19) pandemic generated disturbing examples of this. In July 2020 the BBC's *Panorama* reported on how Chinese citizen journalists living in Wuhan were resisting state censorship by using 'foreign social media platforms banned in China' to inform the rest of the world of the *actual* scale of the spread of the disease and the 'rising numbers of dead' in the city, and how this was being covered up by the Chinese government. Both of the citizen journalists featured in the programme seem to have paid the ultimate price for providing hugely valuable content that defied China's intolerance of a free media: they stopped reporting in early February 2020 and have 'vanished', with neither being seen since.[27]

Because of the dangers posed to journalists when reporting on conflicts, and the challenges associated with deploying them in these situations, citizen journalists provide valuable content from war zones, as was the case during the Arab Spring uprising,[28] and as continues to happen during the ongoing

---

[22]   M. Hughes, 'Online and under cover: The award-winning NightJack blog is a gritty and addictive insider's view of modern-day policing', *Independent*, 21 May 2009.

[23]   'My Life in Media: Guido Fawkes', *The Independent*, 5 November 2007.

[24]   'The top 50 newsmakers of 2006', *The Independent*, 18 December 2006.

[25]   'GQ Give Guido Oxygen of Publicity', *Guido Fawkes*, 28 November 2011.

[26]   See n 10.

[27]   BBC, *Panorama: China's Coronavirus Cover-Up*, BBC 1, 27 July 2020.

[28]   See generally D. McGoldrick, 'The Limits of Freedom of Expression on Facebook and Social Networking Sites: A UK Perspective' (2013) 13 *Human Rights Law Review* 125; N. Miladi, 'Social Media and Social Change' (2016) 25(1) *Digest of the Middle East* 36. This issue is also discussed in Chapter 4 section 5.3 and Chapter 5 section 6.1.

Iraq conflict, which began in 2003.[29] In conflict situations such as these, by being able to provide 'real time', 'on the ground' coverage of events as they unfold from areas that are often inaccessible to 'professional' reporters, citizen journalists have not only provided alternative content to what the mainstream media is able to publish or broadcast, but also, perhaps more importantly, they have covered events that would have been, or have been, missed entirely by institutional media outlets.[30] Thus, in these circumstances, if it were not for citizen journalism, the public would be unaware that certain events had even taken place.

OhmyNews.com provides an alternative and interesting model as it is an example of a professional/citizen journalism hybrid that makes regular contributions to public discourse. The South Korean publication relies on stories supplied by citizen journalists, which are subject to an editorial process. According to the newspaper's founder, Oh Yeon Ho, '[e]very citizen's a reporter ... Journalists aren't some exotic species, they're everyone who seeks to take new developments, put them into writing, and share them with others.'[31] Probably the most high-profile example of the newspaper's importance to public discourse is the influential role it played in the election of the country's former President, Roo Moo Hyun, in 2003, who granted his first post-election interview to the publication rather than to one of the three major conservative newspapers that had dominated the country's print journalism.[32]

According to Dan Gillmor, citizen journalism has helped to make the institutional media more transparent by virtue of blogs such as Jim Romenesko's Poynter Institute MediaNews,[33] which, in his view, is a 'water cooler not just for journalism but for people who observe journalism'.[34] Thus, in addition to acting as a public watchdog by producing important and diverse public interest content, citizen journalists are performing another vital democratic function:

---

[29]   D. Tapscott and A.D. Williams, *Wikinomics: How Mass Collaboration Changes Everything* (Atlantic Books, 2008) 308–309.

[30]   Gillmor (n 16) 136–137. For example, on 10 December 2003, thousands of Iraqis protested in Baghdad against bombings by insurgents that had caused far more civilian than military casualties. The major media outlets failed to cover the march and missed its significance. Rather, the most prominent coverage of the march came from a citizen journalist named Zeyad through his blog, *Healing Iraq*, which has become a key channel for anyone wanting to learn more about the conflict.

[31]   Ibid 110.

[32]   Ibid. See 125–129 for a case study on OhmyNews.com. See also C.E. Baker, *Media Concentration and Democracy: Why Ownership Matters* (Cambridge University Press, 2007) 111.

[33]   https://www.poynter.org/media-news/. Romenesko retired from the Poynter Institute in 2011.

[34]   Gillmor (n 16) 61–64.

Introduction 7

they are making 'professional' journalists and the institutional media more accountable[35] by exposing unfair and inaccurate reporting.[36]

3   THE PURPOSE OF THIS BOOK

The examples in the previous section are just a snapshot of how citizen journalism contributes to public discourse. Thus, because citizen journalism, and its symbiotic relationship with the institutional media[37] has not only permanently altered the media ecology, but has also shifted the media paradigm, citizen journalists are no longer an outlier of free speech. Rather, they are central to how we receive and impart information and ideas.

In this book I claim that the enhanced right to media freedom attaches to actors defined as 'media', and that this right is a freedom which serves specific positive goals for democratic participation. Therefore, it affords media entities privileged protection over and above non-media actors but, as a result, it carries with it concomitant responsibilities and obligations. Consequently, in Chapter 4 I advance the notion that there are two categories of free speech: (i) the personal right to freedom of expression and (ii) media freedom, and that the latter ought to be treated differently from the former. In a world where citizen journalists are making an important and positive contribution to the public sphere by reporting on matters of public interest, being able to identify the beneficiaries of media freedom is critical to the effective operation of the right. However, in the current categorisation of who belongs to which group there is a gap as there is a definable category of actors who are, as citizen journalists, effectively 'media', but are not recognised as such. This is because the methods that have traditionally been used to define media, and therefore who should be subject to the enhanced right to media freedom, at best lack merit and are, at worst, redundant.[38] Because of the vital role played by citizen journalists in the newsgathering process and in the publication of public interest news, both as publishers in their own right and as sources of news used by the institutional media, this situation is problematic. It therefore presents four fundamental questions that this book addresses: (i) At what point do individuals who are publishing information become 'media' and therefore to be treated as journalists? (ii) Because citizen journalists are not necessarily socialised into the norms of professional journalism, should they be subject to the same

---

[35]   Baker (n 32) 111.
[36]   Gillmor (n 16) 61–64.
[37]   This symbiosis is explained in section 1.
[38]   These methods are the 'press-as-technology model', the 'mass audience approach' and the 'professionalised publisher approach'. They are discussed in detail in Chapter 4 section 5.

law and regulation as 'institutional professional' journalists, or should the law and regulation treat them differently? (iii) If we accept the existence of certain 'duties and responsibilities' in the case of institutional journalists, should the same or similar 'burdens' apply to citizen journalists? (iv) (a) If they should be treated differently, to what extent should the law and regulation differ for them as compared to their institutional counterparts? (b) If they should be subject to the same law and regulation as institutional journalists, should the nature of citizen journalism, and the needs of citizen journalists, at least be considered for the purposes of implementing law and regulation?

This difficult situation that we find ourselves in with citizen journalists is understandable. The dominant philosophical theories that underpin free speech and media freedom are John Stuart Mill's argument from truth[39] and, particularly in the context of online expression,[40] the marketplace of ideas, which was laid down by Justice Oliver Wendell Holmes in *Abrams v United States*.[41] However, these libertarian[42] arguments are based on nineteenth- and early twentieth-century means of communication. They are not suitable for twenty-first-century speech, and the modern media,[43] of which the internet and social media, and citizen journalism are central components.[44] As it stands, the law relating to the operation of free speech and media freedom is lagging behind reality. Consequently, the law's treatment of media freedom as a normative concept needs to be modernised, but for the law to catch up, so must its theoretical foundations. Thus, the purpose of this book is to offer an alternative normative framework that deals with the problems posed in the four questions above and understands media freedom within the context of twenty-first-century means of receiving and imparting information and ideas and the legal challenges this creates and which, ultimately, improves access to the public sphere.

To facilitate this modernisation (and in relation to the first question) Chapter 5 advances a new functional definition of the media that delineates media from non-media actors. I call this the media-as-a-constitutional-component concept,

---

[39] J. Mill, *On Liberty and Other Essays* (Oxford University Press, 1991).

[40] D. Weiss, 'Journalism and Theories of the Press' in S. Littlejohn and K. Foss (eds), *Encyclopedia of Communication Theory Volume 2* (Sage, 2009) 574–579, 579; L. Dahlberg, 'Cyber-libertarianism 2.0: A Discourse Theory/Critical Political Economy Examination' (2010) 6(3) *Cultural Politics* 331, 332–333.

[41] 250 US 616 (1919).

[42] Libertarianism is discussed in detail in Chapter 5. Its meaning and origins are explained in section 2.2 of that chapter.

[43] See Chapter 5 sections 2 and 3.

[44] P. Coe, '(Re)embracing Social Responsibility Theory as a Basis for Free Speech: Shifting the Normative Paradigm for a Modern Media' (2018) 69(4) *Northern Ireland Legal Quarterly* 403–431.

Introduction 9

and it is underpinned by social responsibility theory and the argument from democratic self-governance. I argue in that chapter that although the conditions created by the internet have meant that libertarianism has become the dominant normative paradigm for online speech,[45] in reality social responsibility theory provides a more appropriate normative foundation for the modern media. Essentially, the theories differ in that libertarianism dictates that free speech is absolute and, as a result, does not propagate duties and responsibilities that attach to the right to freedom of expression and media freedom, whereas, under social responsibility theory, this freedom carries concomitant responsibilities and obligations to society, employers and the market.[46] This normative foundation provided by social responsibility theory supports the concept's premise that who or what is media should be defined functionally, rather than institutionally. Therefore, the performance of a constitutional function, and the dissemination of speech that is of value to the public sphere, such as reporting on a matter of public interest, and adherence to certain standards of professional behaviour, should define the beneficiaries of media freedom (and therefore those subject to the responsibilities and obligations attached to this enhanced right), rather than the fact that the actor is already contributing to public opinion or their education, training or employment. In making this claim I argue that although the media-as-a-constitutional-component concept shares similarities with Robert Post's participatory theory of democracy,[47] it overcomes problems with it relating to access to the public sphere.[48]

In respect of the second and third questions posed above, I suggest that citizen journalists should be subject to the responsibilities associated with the 'professional' media in an equivalent yet, depending on the circumstances, potentially different way to their institutional counterparts. Therefore, the concept underpins a framework for a modified regulatory scheme that is advanced in Chapter 9, which is applicable, and it is argued would be attractive, to citizen journalists, and which allows for the fact that they are not necessarily socialised into the norms of professional journalism.

---

[45] Chapter 5 section 2.1.

[46] Social responsibility theory, and how it differs from libertarianism, is discussed in detail in section 4 of Chapter 5.

[47] R. Post, 'Participatory Democracy and Free Speech' (2011) 97 *Virginia Law Review* 477; R. Post, 'Democracy and Equality' (2005) 1 *Law, Culture and the Humanities* 142.

[48] Chapter 5 section 4.2.1.

4 PARAMETERS AND STRUCTURE

The book's parameters are set by its focal point. As stated above, this relates to the application of the normative paradigms and philosophical foundations underpinning free speech, and the concept of media freedom, to citizen journalism and its symbiotic relationship with the 'traditional institutional' media. Thus, it is necessary to properly frame this examination of the broader issues relating to communication doctrine, and the nature and operation of freedom of expression and media freedom, from both practical and theoretical perspectives. For instance, as explained in section 3, this book explores libertarian and social responsibility theory; it analyses the conceptual distinction between freedom of expression and media freedom; it unpacks the contents of media freedom; and it considers the standards and responsibilities attached to the operation of media.

At this point it is important for me to clarify that when I refer to the traditional institutional media this, as I have suggested in the previous sections, includes the press and the broadcast media. The term press is used when I am referring to that industry specifically. Therefore, although this book considers, and takes into account, news journalism in its broader sense, to encapsulate journalists working for other news media organisations that are predominantly found on television, radio or online, it is undoubtedly more acutely focussed on the implications of the relationship that citizen journalists and social media platforms have with the press than it is on the broadcast media. This is because it is my contention that the impact of the internet and social media, including their facilitation of citizen journalists, has been most greatly felt by the institutional press, which has had a profound impact on its health and viability and on the public sphere more broadly (in particular, see Chapters 2 and 3).

In overview, this book is separated into three parts. In Part I, Chapters 2 and 3 provide context for the rest of the book by setting out the current media landscape. Specifically, Chapter 2 examines whether the concept of the free press, and the institutional media generally, is a fallacy. In doing so it considers how ownership of the press generates pressures that contribute to the curtailment of press freedom and access to the public sphere, thereby creating serious challenges to democracy. By looking at these arguments in the context of the internet, social media and citizen journalism, Chapter 3 forms the other half of this initial investigation. On the one hand it considers how the internet and social media undermine the viability of the press, and how social media in particular has distorted the public sphere in other interrelated ways that may indirectly impact upon the ability of journalists to positively contribute to public discourse. On the other hand, it looks at how they provide the ideal environment for citizen journalism to flourish by facilitating three factors that have enabled it to make an important contribution to the robustness of the public sphere. However, because of the challenges created for the public sphere by the internet and social media, this chapter recognises that these factors are not without limitations that prevent citizen journalists from playing what could be an even greater role in the public sphere's democratisation. It is ultimately suggested that some of these limitations can be overcome, or at least alleviated, by the application of the media-as-a-constitutional-component concept and the framework that it provides.

Part II advances the media-as-a-constitutional-component concept. It begins with Chapter 4, which lays the foundations for the chapters that follow in this Part, and in Part III. It begins by distinguishing media freedom from individual freedom of expression, and establishes that the former provides enhanced protection, over and above the right to freedom of expression, for actors operating as part of the media. In doing this, it compares the jurisprudence of the European Court of Human Rights (ECtHR) with United States (US) scholarship and jurisprudence from the US Supreme Court. The dominant, although not the only view in the US, is based upon the press-as-technology model, which rejects the notion that the media has any constitutional privileges in excess of other speakers. This comparison with the diametrically opposed position of the ECtHR is useful as it forms the foundation for section 5 of that chapter, which, inter alia, discredits the press-as-technology-model as a method for distinguishing media from non-media actors in the current media environment. The chapter goes on to analyse the concept of media freedom. First, it explains its role and why the right is conceptually important to media actors. Secondly, it sets out what the right means in reality to its beneficiaries in respect of the protection it affords media speech and the media institution-ally. Finally, it identifies the shortfalls of the traditional methods adopted by courts and scholars for distinguishing between media and non-media actors (including, as alluded to above, the press-as-technology model), and therefore who/what is subject to media freedom.

As explained in the previous section, Chapter 5 introduces a definition of the media that is based on the functions that are per-formed by the actor, rather than institutional status. This definition is based on the media-as-a-constitutional-component concept, which essen-tially offers an alternative means of interpreting free speech that recognises twenty-first-century methods of communication. In doing so, it discredits libertarianism as a normative paradigm for underpinning media and, instead, argues that social responsibility theory and the argument from democratic self-governance provides a sound foundation for the re-conceptualisation of the media and media freedom. It is explained in this chapter how this new normative framework could better deal with some of the legal challenges that arise from the media operating within the current libertarian paradigm (some of these challenges form the subject of Part III of the book, in Chapters 7 to 9). In doing this, and in setting the scene for Chapter 9, it outlines how the concept seeks to resolve the shortcomings of social responsibility theory in relation to its dogmatic resistance to anything other than the blunt and self-serving scheme of voluntary self-regulation we currently have in the United Kingdom (UK).

Chapter 6 begins by setting out the parameters that are imposed by the media-as-a-constitutional-component concept on media freedom. This leads into a discussion as to the standards attached to media discourse and conduct by the concept. Specifically, it explores the notion of public interest, media conduct and the media's requirement to act in good faith pursuant to the concept. In respect of public interest, it argues that the concept, and the social responsibility and argument from democratic self-governance rationales underpinning it, align it clearly with the jurisprudence of the ECtHR: a position that is diametrically opposed to a divergent line of English and Welsh case law supporting a 'role model' principle. As a result, it advances three factors to be considered in providing guidance on what is in the public interest in line with the constitutional norms and values inherent within the concept.

In Part III, Chapters 7 to 9 explore specific legal challenges first visited in Chapter 5. The overarching purpose of these chapters is to explain how the media-as-a-constitutional-component concept offers an alternative, and it is argued preferable, way of dealing with these challenges than is currently the case under the libertarian paradigm. Chapter 7 considers two ways of communicating that, although not confined to the online arena, have become synonymous with the internet and social media: anonymous and pseudonymous speech. This chapter looks at how the concept enables a better balance to be struck between speaker and audience interests in the context of anonymity and pseudonymity. Chapter 8 looks at contempt of court and defamation. It argues that the adoption of the concept would go some way to address an imbalance between the state or claimants and the media, particularly in respect of the principle of open justice and the operation of the various defences available to defamation defendants. Finally, Chapter 9 concludes the book by advancing principles for a modified self-regulatory scheme which could, if implemented, effectively regulate citizen journalists and the institutional press.

At this juncture it is important to mention that this book could have concerned itself with a multitude of challenges arising from citizen journalism and online communication. For instance, it does not consider wider conceptual perspectives of media freedom, free speech policy and regulation in respect of

Introduction 13

the internet generally.[49] Nor does it deal with certain discrete issues, such as: the interaction between new media companies and competition law and anti-trust law, and how this impacts on free speech policy[50] (although competition law in respect of media mergers is considered in detail in Chapter 2); criminal activity on social media,[51] in a broad sense at least; online expression in the workplace;[52] intermediary liability;[53] and children's rights, child protection and digital literacy. Data protection is dealt with, but only incidentally. This is because these issues either fall outside the scope of the book, or there is already extensive coverage of them, or both. Rather, the legal challenges dealt with in this book are not only currently very topical but are particularly acute in respect of citizen journalism and/or are relatively underrepresented in the canon of free speech scholarship.

Finally, citizen journalism and media freedom have global scope and signifi-cance. The benefits they bring to the facilitation of free speech and democracy, and the challenges they create, are not confined by borders. Unsurprisingly, the jurisprudence and scholarship pertaining to them are equally international and, in respect of some countries, such as the US, more developed than the UK. Thus, throughout the book, a comparative approach is taken to the formulation and application of the media-as-a-constitutional-component concept[54] and to the legal challenges presented by citizen journalism that it attempts to meet. In respect of domestic law, at times I refer to laws applying to the UK, and at

---

[49]   For detailed discussion on these issues, see A. Murray, 'Mapping the Rule of Law for the Internet' in D. Mangan and L. Gillies (eds), *The Legal Challenges of Social Media* (Edward Elgar Publishing, 2017) 13–33; D. Weisenhaus and S. Young (eds), *Media Law and Policy in the Internet Age* (Hart, 2017).

[50]   For analysis of this issue, see M. Ammori, 'The "New" New York Times: Free Speech Lawyering in the Age of Google and Twitter' (2014) 127 *Harvard Law Review* 2259.

[51]   For example, see J. Rowbottom, 'Crime and Communication: Do Legal Controls Leave Enough Space for Freedom of Expression' in Mangan and Gillies (n 49) 37–60; P. Coe, 'The Social Media Paradox: An Intersection with Freedom of Expression and the Criminal Law' (2015) 24(1) *Information & Communications Technology Law* 16.

[52]   For example, see D. Mangan, 'Social Media in the Workplace' in Mangan and Gillies (n 49) 201–221; P. Wragg, 'Free Speech at Work: Resolving the Difference Between Practice and Liberal Principle' (2015) 44(1) *Industrial Law Journal* 1.

[53]   For example, see A. Scott, 'An Unwholesome Layer Cake: Intermediary Liability in English Defamation and Data Protection Law' in Mangan and Gillies (n 49) 222–248; J. Oster, 'Communication, Defamation and Liability of Intermediaries' (2015) 35(2) *Legal Studies* 348.

[54]   For example, the book draws on scholarship and jurisprudence from the United States, Australia and New Zealand. It also applies jurisprudence from the ECtHR, the Inter-American Court of Human Rights and the Human Rights Committee in relation to the European Convention on Human Rights, the American Convention on Human Rights and the International Covenant on Civil and Political Rights respectively.

other times I refer to the law of England and Wales (for ease, hereinafter I will use the law of England or English law). This is not a lack of consistency but rather an attempt to ensure that I discuss the application and extent of certain laws accurately.

PART I

The modern media landscape

2. A shackled institution: is the notion of the 'free press' a fallacy?

1 INTRODUCTION

In the Preface to his book *The Illusion of the Free Press*[1] John Charney describes Orson Welles' adaptation of H.G. Wells' science-fiction novel *The War of the Worlds*,[2] which was aired over the Columbia Broadcasting System on 30 October 1938, and the differences of opinion as to the level of public panic that ensued as a result.[3] The reason for beginning his book in this way is because Welles' experiment had two profound implications on public perception of the media; it showed the power that new communication technology could exert over its audiences, and it demonstrated how the media is able to influence the public. According to Charney, '[b]y describing a non-reality, opening a chasm between media descriptions of reality and the reality they describe, Welles revealed the distance that separates these two realms and exposed the fragility of one of the central institutions of liberal democracies' and, in doing so, he unveiled the 'illusion of the free press'.[4]

Charney's claim that the idea of the free press is an epistemological illusion reflects the arguments advanced by the influential body of research known as the critique of the political economy of the press (CPEP).[5] The purpose of this chapter is to examine whether the concept of the free press, and the traditional

---

[1]   J. Charney, *The Illusion of the Free Press* (Hart Publishing, 2018).

[2]   H.G. Wells, *The War of the Worlds* (Penguin, 1898).

[3]   According to Charney, some sceptics claimed that fewer than 20 per cent of listeners believed that the Earth was being attacked by Martians. To the contrary, the *New York Times* reported the following day that a 'wave of mass hysteria seized thousands of listeners ... and disrupted households, interrupted religious services, created traffic jams and clogged communications systems' Charney (n 1) vii; 'Radio Listeners in Panic, Taking War Drama as Fact', *New York Times* (31 October 1938).

[4]   Charney (n 1) vii–viii.

[5]   CPEP includes, among other commentators: R.W. McChesney, *The Political Economy of the Media: Enduring Issues, Emerging Dilemmas* (Monthly Review Press, 2008); N. Chomsky and E.S. Herman, *Manufacturing Consent: The Political Economy of the Mass Media* (Vintage, 1994); B.H. Bagdikian, *The New Media Monopoly* (7th edn., Beacon Press, 2004); H. Marcuse, 'Repressive Tolerance' in A. Feenberg and W.

institutional media generally, is a fallacy. Thus, section 2 sets out the premise of the arguments advanced by the CPEP. This forms the foundation for section 3, which considers how ownership of the press and other forms of traditional media generates pressures that contribute to the curtailment of press freedom and access to the public sphere, thereby creating serious challenges to democracy. In doing so, it looks at competition law and the dominant proprietor and corporate ownership models.

This chapter feeds into Chapter 3, which looks at how the internet and social media have evolved into important arenas for speech to occur. It asks whether, as platforms for speech, the internet and social media's creation of an audience and producer convergence,[6] which has facilitated citizen journalism and other new types of news publishers, has overcome the problems that are considered in this chapter that have typically been associated with the press.

2   THE 'FREE' PRESS: IS IT ALL JUST AN ILLUSION?

Prior to the internet and the advent of social media, the traditional media, and particularly the press, was the only institution that had the ability to reach mass audiences through regular publication or broadcasts.[7]

The theoretical origins of the press industry, and the traditional institutional media generally, are founded on freedom of expression philosophy[8] and the notion that, as 'the Fourth Estate', its primary function is to act as a 'public watchdog',[9] in that it operates as the general public's 'eyes and ears' by investigating and reporting abuses of power.[10] Thus, pursuant to the liberal theory of the media, the press is free and independent; it is committed to the discovery and reporting of truth, the advancement of knowledge and,

---

Leiss (eds), *The Essential Marcuse: Selected Writings of Philosopher and Social Critic Herbert Marcuse* (Beacon Press, 2007).

[6]   See generally A. Bruns, *Blogs, Wikipedia, Second Life and Beyond: From Production to Produsage* (Peter Lang Publishing, 2008).

[7]   See generally J. Van Dijck, *The Culture of Connectivity A Critical History of Social Media* (Oxford University Press, 2013) 3–23.

[8]   See Chapter 4 for a discussion on the distinction between freedom of expression and media freedom and Chapter 5 for analysis of the philosophical foundations of free speech.

[9]   *Observer and Guardian v United Kingdom* (1992) 14 EHRR 153, [59].

[10]   *Attorney-General v Guardian Newspapers Ltd (No. 2)* [1990] 1 AC 109, 183 per Sir John Donaldson MR; see also E. Barendt, *Freedom of Speech* (2nd edn., Oxford University Press, 2005) 418; D. Weiss, 'Journalism and Theories of the Press' in S. Littlejohn and K. Foss (eds), *Encyclopedia of Communication Theory Volume 2* (Sage, 2009) 574–579, 577.

ultimately, to strengthening democracy.[11] This liberal ideal is reflected in the observations made by Leveson LJ in his *Inquiry*, that in recent years the press has played a critical role in informing the public on matters of public interest and concern.[12] The *Inquiry* cites a number of examples of valuable public interest journalism, relating to a wide variety of stories, submitted by Associated Newspapers Limited,[13] *The Guardian*, Northern & Shell,[14] *The Sun, The Times* and *Sunday Times* and *The Telegraph*.[15] These include, among others: the *Daily Mail's* Stephen Lawrence campaign;[16] *The Guardian's* investigation into tax avoidance by Barclays, GlaxoSmithKline and Shell;[17] *Daily Star Sunday* articles on the PIP breast implants scandal and the dangers posed by them;[18] *The Sun's* undercover investigation revealing that a Magistrates' Court clerk was offering to wipe clean convicted drivers' licences for a £500 fee;[19] *The Sunday Times'* Thalidomide Campaign against Distillers[20] and its investigation that exposed corruption in the FIFA voting process for determining which nation will host the football World Cup;[21] and *The Telegraph's* series of articles on the MPs' expenses scandal.[22] This type of journalism, which is driven by a commitment to professionalism and the public interest, is undoubtedly adopted and replicated by many journalists, newspapers and other traditional media outlets around the world and has led to the communication of some of the most important stories of our time.[23] In this respect the value of journalists,

---

[11] Charney (n 1) 3.

[12] Lord Justice Leveson, *An Inquiry into the Culture, Practices and Ethics of the Press: Report*, HC 780, November 2012, 451–455.

[13] Associated Newspapers Limited has been known as DMG Media since 2013. It publishes the *Daily Mail, Mail on Sunday, MailOnline, Metro* and *Metro.co.uk*. DMG Media is part of Daily Mail and General Trust plc (DMGT). In November 2019, DMGT purchased JPI Media Publications Limited and, in doing so, the *'i'* newspaper. The takeover was cleared by the government in March 2020.

[14] Northern & Shell published the *Daily Express, Sunday Express, Daily Star* and *Daily Star Sunday*, and the magazines *OK!, New!* and *Star* until these were sold to Trinity Mirror in February 2018. Northern & Shell also owned three entertainment television channels: Channel 5, 5* and 5USA until 2015.

[15] Leveson (n 12) 455–470.

[16] Ibid 455.

[17] Ibid 457.

[18] Ibid 458.

[19] Ibid 459–460.

[20] Ibid 460.

[21] Ibid 461.

[22] Ibid 463–470.

[23] For examples from the US, see the Pulitzer Prize winners: https://www.pulitzer .org/prize-winners-by-year. For further examples from the UK, see *The Cairncross Review*, 'A sustainable future for journalism', 12 February 2019, 19 (Cairncross).

A shackled institution

in so far as they play a critical role in free speech and democracy by engaging in this type of activity, is undeniable.

However, in contrast to these examples of high-quality public interest journalism, an increasing number of traditional institutional media outlets choose to engage with 'sexy' stories that sell, as opposed to reporting on matters of public concern.[24] Thus, a number of commentators, many of whom have contributed to the CPEP,[25] have argued that the press's (and media's) public watchdog role gradually diminished towards the end of the twentieth century as its focus shifted onto commercially viable, and often self-serving, stories.[26] Media ownership, and the power derived from it, and the expectations placed on the modern mass media, such as the need for rolling 24-hour news,[27] means that there is a constant conflict between the traditional media's role as a watchdog, or gatekeeper, and commercial reality.[28] Indeed, it has been observed that during the twentieth and twenty-first centuries investigative journalism has been detrimentally affected by increased concentration of news media ownership,[29] which is now vested in a relatively small number of large and powerful

---

[24] Numerous examples are provided by Leveson LJ in his *Inquiry*: Leveson (n 12) 539–591.

[25] See n 5.

[26] For example, see T. Aalberg and J. Curran (eds), *How Media Inform Democracy: A Comparative Approach* (Routledge, 2012); C. Calvert and M. Torres, 'Putting the Shock Value in First Amendment Jurisprudence: When Freedom for the Citizen-Journalist Watchdog Trumps the Right of Informational Privacy on the Internet' (2011) 13(2) *Vanderbilt Journal of Entertainment and Technology Law* 323, 341; J. Curran and J. Seaton, *Power Without Responsibility – Press, Broadcasting and the Internet in Britain* (7th edn., Routledge, 2010) 96–98; T. Gibbons, 'Building Trust in Press Regulation: Obstacles and Opportunities' (2013) 5(2) *Journal of Media Law* 202, 214; T. Gibbons, 'Freedom of the Press: Ownership and Editorial Values' (1992) 5(2) *Public Law* 279, 296; T. Gibbons, 'Conceptions of the Press and the Functions of Regulation' (2016) 22(5) *Convergence: The International Journal of Research into New Media Technologies* 484, 485; R. McChesney, *Rich Media, Poor Democracy Communication Politics in Dubious Times* (University of Illinois Press, 1999) 275; A. Kenyon, 'Assuming Free Speech' (2014) 77(3) *Modern Law Review* 379, 387–391.

[27] Gibbons, 'Building Trust in Press Regulation' (n 26) 214.

[28] C. Edwin Baker, *Human Liberty and Freedom of Speech* (Oxford University Press, 1989) 250.

[29] Gibbons 'Freedom of the press' (n 26) 286; S.L. Carter, 'Technology, Democracy, and the Manipulation of Consent' (1983–1984) 93 *Yale Law Journal* 581, 600–607; P. Garry, 'The First Amendment and Freedom of the Press: A Revised Approach to the Marketplace of Ideas Concept' (1989) 72 *Marquette Law Review* 187, 189; O.M. Fiss, 'Free Speech and Social Structure' (1985) 71 *Iowa Law Review* 1405, 1415. See also Leveson LJ's assessment of the commercial pressures on the press: Leveson (n 12) 93–98; Media Reform Coalition, *Who Owns the UK Media?* 12 March 2019.

companies,[30] and the commercial pressures imposed by this corporate ownership model,[31] which has resulted in the proliferation of 'churnalism'[32] – the recycling of news from other sources by journalists.[33] From a UK perspective, at the time of writing this increase in ownership concentration is demonstrated by Daily Mail and General Trust plc's (DMGT) purchase of JPI Media Publications Limited (JPI Media) and the *'i'* newspaper,[34] which has reduced the number of national newspaper owners from seven to six.[35] In a public statement following the acquisition, DMGT's Chairman, Lord Rothermere,[36] was clear that the rationale for the acquisition was based on commercial reasons:

> The acquisition of the *'i'* is both strategically and financially compelling for DMGT and there is scope for potential synergies in the future, notably from dmg media's existing infrastructure and in advertising sales. The business will benefit from DMGT's long-term approach and commitment to investing in editorial content. We also see good opportunities to develop inews.co.uk, a growing digital media asset. Financially, the *'i'* will be a strong cash generator for the Group as we continue to invest across the portfolio, both organically and through acquisitions.[37]

As we will see in Chapter 3, the internet and the emergence of social media have, theoretically at least (although, as is discussed in that chapter, perhaps not in reality), increased access to the public sphere, by enabling individuals, and those operating as citizen journalists, to instantaneously communicate

---

[30] P. Thomas, 'Media Democracy' in S. Littlejohn and K. Foss (eds), *Encyclopedia of Communication Theory Volume 2* (Sage, 2009) 627–630, 628; Media Reform Coalition (n 29). Media ownership and the impact that the dominant proprietor and corporate ownership models have had on press freedom are discussed in section 3.3.

[31] N. Fenton, 'Regulation Is Freedom: Phone Hacking, Press Regulation and the Leveson Inquiry – The Story So Far' (2018) 23(3) *Communications Law* 118, 119. The corporate ownership model is discussed in detail in section 3.3.2.

[32] See generally N. Davies, *Flat Earth News* (Vintage, 2009).

[33] Churnalism is discussed in more detail in section 3.3.2. The symbiotic relationship that now exists between 'traditional' institutional journalists and citizen journalists is discussed throughout this book (however, see Chapter 3 section 5.3 in particular).

[34] As stated at n 13, DMGT acquired JPI Media and the *'i'* newspaper in November 2019 for £49.6 million. It was approved by the government in March 2020. This purchase is considered again at section 3.3.2.

[35] Ofcom, 'Public interest test of the completed acquisition by Daily Mail and General Trust plc of JPI Media Publications Limited and thus the *'i'* newspaper', 10 March 2020, [5.6].

[36] The Rothermere media dynasty is considered in section 3.1.

[37] Daily Mail and General Trust plc Acquisition of the *'i'* newspaper and website, 29 November 2019, https://www.dmgt.com/~/media/Files/D/DMGT/investors/Oculus%20Nov19/DMGT%20acquisition%20of%20the%20i%20newspaper%20and%20website.pdf. See also Ofcom (n 35) [3.10]. Similarly, Ofcom found that the purchase would be good for the long-term stability of the *'i'* newspaper: [6.4], [6.6].

with millions of people, meaning that the ability to reach mass audiences is no longer reserved to the press and other traditional media institutions. Before this relatively recent communication phenomenon, however, the public were, to a great extent, limited as to what they were exposed to reading or seeing by what large proportions of the institutional news media chose to communicate.[38] As discussed in more detail in section 3, such decisions made by newspapers, both in the past and today, may come down to editorial bias or control, based on, for instance, the owner's social, political[39] or business agenda,[40] commercial revenue,[41] or a combination of all of these factors, rather than being based on the results of sound investigative journalism.[42]

Thus, according to Bernard Cohen, although the press cannot determine what people think, it is 'stunningly successful' in influencing what they think about.[43] Even though Cohen said this in the early 1960s it holds true today, as demonstrated by the press's reporting of COVID-19[44] (perhaps, at times, to

---

[38] Arguably this remains the case with the press and other forms of traditional media today.

[39] Rodolfo Leyva has argued that in respect of the UK's Conservative newspapers, such as *The Sun* and the *Daily Mail*, 'their reporting – particularly on socio-political issues – is very often ideologically biased, emotionalised, and misleading'. See R. Leyva, 'Media Ethics, Regulations, and Effects: How the British Right-wing Press Disregards All Three and Undermines Democratic Deliberations' (2020) 25(2) *Communications Law* 79, 79. Similarly, from a US perspective, in citing *The Courier-Journal's* explicit Democratic and liberal bias as an example, Russell Weaver has stated that '[t]he gatekeeper role of editors and owners of newspapers and magazines, and the evidence of their potential biases, continues even today'. See R.L. Weaver, *From Gutenberg to the Internet: Free Speech, Advancing Technology, and the Implications for Democracy* (2nd edn., Carolina Academic Press, 2019) 37.

[40] Bagdikian (n 5) xxvii–xxxi; McChesney (n 26); N. Chomsky, *Media Control* (2nd edn., Seven Stories Press, 2002); J. Curran and M. Gurevitch, *Mass Media and Society* (Edward Arnold, 1991) 88; Gibbons, 'Conceptions of the Press' (n 26) 485; Media Reform Coalition (n 29).

[41] Gibbons, 'Building Trust in Press Regulation' (n 26) 214; E. Barendt, *The First Amendment and the Media* in I. Loveland (ed), *Importing The First Amendment Freedom of Speech and Expression in Britain, Europe and the USA* (Hart Publishing, 1998) 30–31.

[42] This criticism is advanced by Eric Barendt with regard to the marketplace of ideas theory (see Chapter 5 section 3.2): Barendt (n 10) 12; see also Gibbons, 'Freedom of the Press' (n 26) 296.

[43] B.C. Cohen, *The Press and Foreign Policy* (Princeton University Press, 1963) 13.

[44] According to Ofcom's *Covid-19 News and Information: Consumption and Attitudes*, at the time of writing '[t]raditional media was the most-used source of news and information about the coronavirus', https://www.ofcom.org.uk/research-and -data/tv-radio-and-on-demand/news-media/coronavirus-news-consumption-attitudes -behaviour, 23 February 2021.

the detriment of other important and newsworthy stories),[45] and its role in the dissemination of false news about the virus.[46] CPEP has therefore advanced the countervailing argument to the liberal theory of the media that the notion of the free press is an illusion[47] or a myth,[48] and that, in fact, the press, and the traditional news media generally, is shackled by ownership, and ownership concentration,[49] which creates a predominantly self-serving industry.[50] In turn, this not only affects the way in which the press disseminates information, and therefore how it portrays social reality and consequently distorts our understanding of the world,[51] but it also limits our access to the public sphere and our ability to engage in public discourse.[52]

Two of the main proponents of this view are Noam Chomsky and Edward Herman, whose propaganda model 'describes the forces that cause the mass media to play a propaganda role, the process whereby they mobilize bias, and the patterns of news choices that ensue'.[53] They argue that the model demonstrates that the mass media are 'effective and powerful ideological institutions that carry out a system-supportive propaganda function by reliance on market forces, internalized assumptions and self-censorship'[54] and that it 'suggests that the "societal purpose" of the media is to inculcate and defend the economic, social, and political agenda of privileged groups that dominate the

---

[45]   Although, at the time of writing, there are no statistics to support this presumption, it certainly seemed to me that at times certain elements of the press chose to publish COVID-19-related information (including repeating information) of relatively minor significance, rather than reporting on other, more significant, and more newsworthy stories, such as the UK's withdrawal from the European Union.

[46]   See the discussion in section 3.3.2. It is also animated by the effect that the press industry's increased reliance on advertising has had on journalism, and the type of reporting that is favoured by newspapers. This is discussed in section 3.3.2 and again in Chapter 3 section 4.3.

[47]   For instance, see D. Berry, 'Radical Mass Media Criticism, History and Theory' in J. Klaehn (ed), *The Political Economy of Media and Power* (Peter Lang, 2010) 324.

[48]   McChesney (n 5) 306.

[49]   See generally (n 5).

[50]   T. Gibbons, '"Fair Play to All Sides of the Truth": Controlling Media Distortions' (2009) 62(1) *Current Legal Problems* 286, 289. See also J. Curran, 'Mediations of Democracy' in J. Curran and M. Gurevitch (eds), *Mass Media and Society* (4th edn., Hodder Arnold, 2005) 129.

[51]   Gibbons (n 50).

[52]   Chomsky and Herman (n 5) xi–xii. See also C. Edwin Baker, *Media Concentration and Democracy: Why Ownership Matters* (Cambridge University Press, 2007) ch. 1; Gibbons, 'Freedom of the Press' (n 26) 286–287; Weaver (n 39) 32–38; Kenyon (n 26) 385–386; C.E. Baker, *Media, Markets, and Democracy* (Cambridge University Press, 2002) 4.

[53]   Chomsky and Herman (n 5).

[54]   Ibid 306.

A shackled institution

domestic society and the state'.[55] James Curran has said much the same. He has argued that the contribution of the popular press to political enlightenment and scrutiny has been grossly misrepresented;[56] rather than working *for* the public as their watchdog and champion, the press had set itself *against* the interests of citizens: 'much of the press chose to side with privilege, and in some cases to actively bully the vulnerable.' Consequently, concentrated ownership, and the sanctity attributed to laissez-faire principles of press behaviour and speech,[57] conspired against viewpoint diversity within the public sphere.[58] As discussed below, this argument is, to an extent, borne out by the use in the UK of discretionary competition law powers by politicians and the perceived bias this can create.[59] Similar criticisms of the role played by the media in making access to the public sphere, at the very least, difficult for certain groups or members of society, have been advanced by other commentators. For instance, Herbert Marcuse has argued that by blocking unorthodox and minority views, the press and media generally contribute to a mentality 'for which right and wrong, true and false are predefined wherever they affect the vital interests of the society'.[60] Thus, in the opinion of Ben Bagdikian, the institutional bias of the media 'does more than merely protect the corporate system. It robs the public of a chance to understand the real world.'[61] This reflects the view of the author and investigative journalist Nick Davies, who says that 'we are deep into a third age of falsehood and distortion, in which the primary obstacles to truth-telling lie inside the newsrooms, with the internal mechanics of an industry which has been deeply damaged'.[62] More recently, Charney has suggested that the 'list' of commentators sharing this description of the media, and its effect on audiences, goes 'on and on', yet, particularly in the case of the press, they share a common element: the 'ability to select, produce, censor and spread information that contributes to reproducing existing social practices and aligning public opinion with the tenets of prevailing ideologies'.[63]

The remainder of this chapter will consider how the constraints and pressures imposed on the press, and to an extent the news media generally, by

---

[55] Ibid 298.

[56] J. Curran, 'Press History' in J. Curran and J. Seaton, *Power Without Responsibility: The Press, Broadcasting and New Media in Britain* (8th edn., Routledge, 2018) 1–192.

[57] See Chapter 5 section 2.2.

[58] J. Curran, 'Introduction' in J. Curran (ed), *The British Press: A Manifesto* (Macmillan, 1978) 1–11.

[59] See section 3.2.

[60] Marcuse (n 5) 42.

[61] Bagdikian (n 5) xviii.

[62] Davies (n 32) 23.

[63] Charney (n 1) 3–4.

24   *Media freedom in the age of citizen journalism*

3   OWNERSHIP AND THE MEDIA MARKET PLACE

3.1   Why Does Ownership Matter? The Main Arguments for Opposing Ownership Concentration and Promoting Plurality

The purpose of this section is to set out the central (negative) argument for limiting ownership concentration and the (positive) arguments for promoting plurality. These arguments form the framework for the remainder of the chapter, which considers them within the contexts of competition law and the dominant proprietor and corporate ownership models.[64]

The central *negative* argument for limiting the concentration of media ownership is that it allows for a more democratic distribution of communicative power. Its premise is that the ideal in democracy is political egalitarianism, in which there is a 'very wide dispersal of power and ubiquitous opportunities for people to present preferences, views and visions'[65] and influence collective decisions, including state 'will formation'.[66] This democratic distribution principle determines that democracy implies the widest possible dispersal of power within public discourse, which, when applied to media ownership, can be interpreted as requiring the maximum dispersal of media ownership.[67] It is important to note that this principle does not require a completely equal distribution of communicative resources as this would destroy the mass media and would instead leave a large number of individual speakers.[68] Rather, the aim of the principle is to keep media concentration within reasonable limits and at a level that is most consistent with democratic goals.[69]

A related hypothetical *positive* case for promoting plurality is that the widest possible dispersal of media ownership provides a democratic safeguard against the possibility of an individual using their newspaper or other media outlets to

---

[64]   The Trust model adopted by *The Guardian* is also briefly considered. This chapter focusses on the dominant proprietor and corporate ownership models as they are the most common and they overlap. See Mediatique, Department for Digital, Culture, Media & Sport, 'Overview of recent dynamics in the UK press market', April 2018, [2.16]; for detailed analysis of the not-for-profit and public ownership models, see J. Rowbottom, *Media Law* (Hart Publishing, 2018) 288–306.

[65]   Baker, *Media Concentration and Democracy* (n 52) 7.

[66]   See J. Habermas, *Between Facts and Norms* (MIT Press, 1996).

[67]   Baker, *Media Concentration and Democracy* (n 52) 7.

[68]   Ibid 11.

[69]   Rowbottom (n 64) 290.

A shackled institution 25

exercise enormous, unequal, unchecked and therefore undemocratic, power[70] to serve their own needs and advance their own political, social and business agendas. Accordingly, the 'widest possible dispersal of media power reduces the risk of the abuse of communicative power in choosing or controlling the government'.[71] Dispersal of ownership structurally prevents what C. Edwin Baker has referred to as 'the Berlusconi effect':[72] despite having no connection with a recognised political party, Silvio Berlusconi, who at the time was Italy's richest individual, and who owned Mediaset, which controlled approximately 45 per cent of Italy's national television, as well as newspapers and other print media, used his media power to secure election as the country's Prime Minister in 1994 and then again in 2001. In doing so he became Italy's longest-serving Prime Minister since World War II.[73] Another final *positive* argument in favour of plurality is that a wide dispersal of media ownership is more likely, on the whole, to provide a range of views on events and, as a result, is able to better serve the needs of citizens within a democracy. Baker has cast this argument in slightly different terms in that a more fragmented market means the media is more likely to be representative of the entire population so that every significant group in society has a means of expressing its views in its own terms.[74]

Notwithstanding the force of these arguments, they can be met with convincing rejoinders.[75] For instance, a wide dispersal of media ownership does not, necessarily, mean that more views will be heard or that the 'risk of abuse of communicative power' will be prevented, or that the quality of journalism will improve. This is because, so the counter-argument goes, regardless of how many owners there are, and how many outlets they own, ultimately they are owners of a *business* that will be driven by profits, its shareholders and market forces. If those forces dictate that a particular ideological or political view will sell more newspapers, or that 'the most profitable market is in low value sensationalist journalism, then that is where owners will drive the business'.[76] Conversely, plurality can be achieved with very limited ownership dispersal in that a single owner could, in theory at least, own multiple outlets all offering a different view or even, as Paul Wragg suggests, one owner could own

---

[70] Baker, *Media Concentration and Democracy* (n 52) 16.

[71] Ibid.

[72] Ibid.

[73] P. Ginsborg, *Silvio Berlusconi: Television, Power and Patrimony* (Verso, 2004).

[74] Baker, *Media Concentration and Democracy* (n 52) 11.

[75] For a more detailed analysis of these arguments, and others, see P. Wragg, *A Free and Regulated Press. Defending Coercive Independent Press Regulation* (Hart Publishing, 2020) 71–75.

[76] Ibid 73. Indeed, Owen Fiss has said that it is nonsense that the public gets what it wants from the market; rather it gets what is on offer. O.M. Fiss, *Liberalism Divided* (Westview Press, 1996) 144.

a single title that provides separate columns labelled 'fact' and 'opinion' that captures the 'broadest range of opinions'.[77] Moreover, even if greater ownership dispersal, or increased plurality, or both, resulted in multiple perspectives on an issue, it does not mean that those viewpoints will be read and a greater range of voices heard. It is conceivable that nobody reads them.

As we will see later in the chapter, the arguments for limiting concentration of ownership and promoting plurality are difficult to reconcile with the current state of the media market, which not only reflects the first rejoinder set out above, but in essence tells us the following: (i) Despite contentions to the contrary from Benjamin Compaine, an assessment of the historic and modern media marketplace suggests that media ownership is anything but widely dispersed and is in fact becoming increasingly concentrated.[78] Arguably, this situation is not helped in the UK by competition laws and a media mergers regime based on discretionary powers.[79] (ii) The dominant proprietor model, which is most commonly associated with the press barons of the nineteenth and twentieth centuries[80] who used their newspapers to further their own interests[81] is still very much in existence, as demonstrated by the likes of Rupert Murdoch.[82] (iii) The dominant proprietor model overlaps with what is now the most common model of ownership – corporate ownership. This model imposes pressures on newspapers and other media outlets related to revenue and profit generation that favour activities that will appeal to the largest possible audiences and the most lucrative commercial and advertising partners. Consequently, the model can significantly impact on the ability of journalists to undertake investigative journalism and can limit content diversity and therefore restrict, or even prevent, minority voices from being heard.[83]

---

[77]   Ibid 75. It is acknowledged that although the existence of a limited set of benevolent owners, or even one benevolent owner, could, in theory, achieve the ideals of pluralism, in reality, as discussed in sections 3.3.1 and 3.3.2, most (although not all) owners are in the Rupert Murdoch mould.

[78]   See section 3.3.2.

[79]   See section 3.2.

[80]   See section 3.3.1.

[81]   Of course, this was not the case with all newspaper owners, such as John Edward Taylor, who founded what was *The Manchester Guardian* and became *The Guardian*, and his nephew C.P. Scott and great-nephew John Russell Scott, who succeeded him. See 'History of the Guardian and the Observer', *The Guardian*, 16 November 2017.

[82]   See section 3.3.2.

[83]   See section 3.3.2.

3.2 The Press and Competition Law

The press, and the media generally, are subject to universal and media-specific competition laws. In respect of the former, they are intended to do two things: first, to protect consumers from leading companies abusing their dominant position within their respective market, such as the markets for newspapers or broadcasting services; and secondly, to ensure that potential competitors can enter the market by, for instance, setting up a new newspaper or establishing a new television or radio station. Thus, the chief concern of these laws is preventing monopolies from driving up prices. Examples of the latter are stricter controls on press mergers than those governing mergers in other industries, and statutory limits on the accumulation of radio and television licences.[84] Unlike universal competition laws, which are driven by price, as we shall see below, media-specific competition laws are predominantly concerned with content.

The theoretical foundation for governments to intervene in media ownership to promote free speech through the imposition of media-specific competition laws is underpinned and justified by the concept of 'pluralism' and the value of 'media plurality' or 'information pluralism', the objective of which is to ensure that citizens are able to access the widest possible variety of sources of information and opinion.[85] As Joseph Raz has stated, 'freedom of expression can be supported as part of a pluralist argument for using the law to promote pluralism in the society'.[86] Thus, in theory at least, these laws should contribute to the freedom of the press, and the media generally, and increase access to the public sphere, by preventing the media being owned and controlled by a limited number of proprietors who may use their ownership of media enterprises to further their own political, business or social agendas.

The most explicit expressions of national courts requiring the enactment and application of competition laws to safeguard media plurality, particularly in the context of the print media,[87] come from the decisions of the French Conseil constitutionnel.[88] For example, the Conseil has ruled that a law limiting newspaper holdings to 15 per cent of the market, and requiring transparency

---

[84]   Barendt (n 10) 429–430.

[85]   Ibid 430.

[86]   J. Raz, 'Free Expression and Personal Identification' (1991) 11 *Oxford Journal of Legal Studies* 303, 323.

[87]   For commentary on the decisions of constitutional courts using competition laws to safeguard pluralism in the broadcasting media, see Barendt (n 10) ch. 12, section 5.

[88]   The Conseil constitutionnel (Constitutional Council) was established by the Constitution of the Fifth Republic, which was adopted on 4 October 1958. It is a court vested with various powers, including, in particular, the review of the constitutionality of legislation. See https://www.conseil-constitutionnel.fr/en/general-overview.

concerning their ownership and financing, did not inhibit media freedom and commercial freedoms. In doing so it found that Parliament is entitled to regulate freedom of communication to make its exercise more effective and to balance it with other constitutional rules and values, including pluralism. In coming to its decision, the Conseil stressed that Article 11 of the Declaration of the Rights of Man conferred on readers rights of choice, which must not be subordinated to private interests or public control or left to the market.[89] The Italian[90] and German Constitutional Courts[91] have also adopted an approach in line with the Conseil.

Similar decisions have been reached in the US. For instance, as demonstrated by *Federal Communications Commission v National Citizens Committee for Broadcasting*,[92] the Supreme Court has approved media-specific concentration laws that have restricted cross-media mergers or 'common ownership'[93] between newspaper and broadcasting companies. In this case the Court unanimously upheld a Commission regulation that prevented the common ownership of a radio or television broadcast station and a daily newspaper located in the same community.[94]

Of significance to the UK is the landmark US case of *Associated Press v United States*,[95] which influenced its position on limiting press mergers to protect plurality. The Supreme Court held that general antitrust laws could be applied to the press, with Black J stating that '[f]reedom of the press from governmental interference ... does not sanction repression of that freedom from private interests'.[96] The judgment, which determined that media freedom does not provide immunity to newspapers, press agencies or, by extension,

---

[89]   For example, in Decision 84-181 of 10–11 October 1984, Rec. 73, [35]–[38].

[90]   The Italian Constitutional Court used the concept of pluralism in its decisions upholding the constitutionality of restrictions imposed on the freedom of the owners of private commercial television channels to limit the number of channels that one company can control. For example, see 420/1994 [1994] *Giur cost* 3716, in which the Court held that provisions allowing one group to control 25 per cent of national broadcasting licences, or three channels, were incompatible with Articles 3 and 21 of the Italian Constitution. See generally E. Barendt, *Broadcasting Law* (Oxford University Press, 1995) 24–28.

[91]   The German Constitutional Court has said that *Pressefreiheit* imposes a duty on the state to take steps to avert the dangers arising from media monopolies. See 20 BVeerfGE 162, 176 (1966).

[92]   436 US 775 (1978).

[93]   Ibid per Marshall J at 436.

[94]   *Rules Relating to Multiple Ownership of Standard, FM, and Television Broadcast Stations, Second Report and Order*, 50 F.C.C.2d 1046 (1975) as amended by 53 F.C.C.2d 589 (1975) and codified in 47 CFR §§ 73.35, 73.240, 73.636 (1976).

[95]   326 US 1 (1945).

[96]   Ibid 20.

A shackled institution 29

other media outlets, from any general legislation intended to safeguard that freedom,[97] was cited by the 1962 Royal Commission on the Press to support its corresponding conclusion that introducing legislation to regulate press mergers was unobjectionable on the grounds of media freedom.[98] Mergers of 'media enterprises'[99] are now subject to special discretionary[100] mergers control pursuant to the Enterprise Act 2002. Under the legislation, if a merger involving a newspaper or broadcaster meets a prescribed threshold[101] the Secretary of State for Business, Energy and Industrial Strategy has the power to make a 'public interest intervention',[102] in which Ofcom will make an initial investigation into the impact of the merger.[103] Depending on the outcome of the investigation, the Secretary of State *may* refer the merger to the Competition and Markets Authority[104] for a full assessment of the impact of the merger on the public interest.[105] This requires consideration of whether specified public interest considerations are present, including whether there is a 'need for accurate presentation of the news and[106] free expression of opinion',[107] and the need, so far as is reasonably practicable, for a 'sufficient plurality of views in each market for newspapers in the [UK] or a part of [it]'.[108] If the Authority determines that the merger would be contrary to the public interest, then the

---

[97]   Barendt (n 10) 431.

[98]   Royal Commission on the Press 1962 (Cmnd. 1811), [337].

[99]   Which explicitly include 'newspaper enterprises'. See section 58A(2) and (3) Enterprise Act 2002.

[100]   The primary approach taken in the UK has been to regulate media ownership via the discussed discretionary power. However, an example of a fixed rule restricting media ownership is the '20/20 rule' pursuant to paragraph 1 of Part 1 of Schedule 14 to the Communications Act 2003. This determines that a newspaper company with a 20 per cent market share cannot purchase more than a 20 per cent share in a company holding an ITV licence. See Rowbottom (n 64) 292–295 for commentary on fixed rules and discretionary powers.

[101]   Pursuant to section 23(1) of the Enterprise Act 2002 the Secretary of State's power to intervene arises where the annual turnover of the enterprise being taken over exceeds £70 million and/or where the merger meets the share of supply threshold in section 23(2). Where these conditions are not met, under section 59, the Secretary of State can still intervene in 'special merger situations' where one of the companies meets a share of supply threshold for newspapers (section 59(3C)) or broadcasters (section 59(3D)).

[102]   Ibid section 42.

[103]   Ibid section 44A.

[104]   The Competition and Markets Authority was formerly known as the Competition Commission and, prior to that, the Monopolies and Mergers Commission.

[105]   Enterprise Act 2002 section 45.

[106]   Ibid section 58(2A)(a).

[107]   Ibid section 58(2A)(b).

[108]   Ibid section 58(2B).

Secretary of State can impose a remedy, including imposing conditions on the merger, or blocking it entirely.[109]

The UK's preference for a media mergers regime that is based on discretionary powers creates practical challenges relating to how plurality is defined.[110] As we have seen, the application of the regime's standards is predominantly left to the regulators and the Secretary of State, which is largely determined on a case-by-case basis. The uncertainties created by this approach, and by the standards themselves, have led Rachael Craufurd Smith and Damian Tambini to argue that the vagueness of the public interest test is 'patently unsatisfactory'.[111] As Rowbottom states, although '[m]ost people know a powerful media baron when they see one',[112] pursuant to the standards, for a public interest intervention to be justified, evidence will need to be adduced showing that the merger will detrimentally affect the quality of content or the diversity of views or the level of plurality. To demonstrate the detrimental impact of the merger on the free expression of opinion in a newspaper, or broadcast standards in a television or radio enterprise, the regulator will have to look at the acquiring company's past conduct, which assumes that it can identify inappropriate owner influence.[113] This would be relatively easy where, for example, a proprietor has a track record of failing to meet professional standards,[114] such as engaging in phone hacking. However, to the contrary, in many merger situations, it will be practically very difficult for the regulator to accurately determine the effects that it will have on content and quality.[115]

The use of the discretionary powers also creates something far more insidious than these practical challenges. Although, as discussed above, pluralism provides the conceptual foundation for governments to impose competition laws to promote media plurality in order to protect free speech, contribute to the freedom of the press and increase access to the public sphere, paradoxically discretionary powers could be used by the government, or individual politicians, to serve their own agendas, which may not align with the advancement of these principles and, in doing so, undermine the purpose of the competition legislation. This is because, although the Secretary of State must

---

[109] Ibid sections 55 and 66 and paragraphs 9 and 11 of Schedule 7.

[110] For detailed discussions on defining media plurality, see K. Karppinen, *Rethinking Media Pluralism* (Fordham University Press, 2013); Rowbottom (n 64) 295–298.

[111] R. Craufurd Smith and D. Tambini, 'Measuring Media Plurality in the United Kingdom: Policy Choices and Regulatory Challenges' (2012) 4 *Journal of Media Law* 35, 49.

[112] Rowbottom (n 64) 296.

[113] Ibid.

[114] Ibid.

[115] Ibid.

follow published guidance in making their decision and, pursuant to sections 55(3) and 66(7) of the 2002 Act, must take account of the Competition and Markets Authority report when deciding on appropriate remedies, ultimately these powers involve a politician deciding when to trigger the public interest investigation and what, if any, action should follow. As Rowbottom observes, this can create suspicion and the perception of bias 'where the minister is seen to be sympathetic or hostile to a particular proprietor', particularly given the 'political benefits that can flow from certain distributions of communicative power and the risk of the discretion being used to secure good relations with a particular media company'.[116] Political bias in this context, both for and against a proprietor, was evident during News Corporation's failed attempt to purchase a larger share of British Sky Broadcasting in 2010. Statements made by the former Business Secretary, Vince Cable, that he had 'declared war on Rupert Murdoch' were caught by undercover *Daily Telegraph* journalists,[117] which resulted in Cable transferring responsibility for any public interest intervention to the then Culture Secretary Jeremy Hunt. However, it subsequently transpired that Hunt's special adviser had been in regular contact with a News Corporation lobbyist,[118] which, according to Leveson LJ in his *Inquiry*, had generated a 'perception of bias'[119] in favour of News Corporation.[120]

3.3   Ownership Models

As discussed above, media-specific competition laws should contribute to freedom of press and our access to the public sphere by protecting and promoting media plurality by preventing the media being owned and controlled by a handful of people or organisations who may use their outlets as organs to further their own agendas. This section considers the extent to which ownership, and how the pressures generated by the dominant proprietor and corporate ownership models, negatively impact upon media plurality and contribute to the problems identified by the CPEP. In doing so it assesses both the historic pre-competition law era and the current state of media ownership.

---

[116]   Ibid 293–294.

[117]   R. Winnett, 'Vince Cable: I have declared war on Rupert Murdoch', *The Telegraph*, 21 December 2010.

[118]   P. Lunt and S. Livingstone, *Media Regulation* (SAGE, 2012) 73–74.

[119]   Leveson (n 12) 1407.

[120]   Rowbottom (n 64) 293–294. Because of this issue there have been calls for the decision to be entirely Ofcom's responsibility or, at the very least, for there to be a strong assumption that the Secretary of State will follow the regulator's advice: Leveson (n 12) 1476.

3.3.1   The early press barons and the dominant proprietor model

In the fifteenth century Johannes Gutenberg invented the printing press: a technological breakthrough that had the potential to increase access to the public sphere by enabling significant numbers of people to engage in mass communication.[121] However, Gutenberg's invention was never readily accessible to ordinary people. In its early days, access to the printing press was repressed and tightly controlled in countries around the world by 'state gatekeepers'[122] in the form of monarchs, the Church and governments, who were fearful of allowing ordinary people to propagate their own ideas and to communicate with each other.[123] Accordingly, in *First National Bank of Boston v Bellotti*[124] the US Supreme Court stated:

> Soon after the invention of the printing press, English and continental monarchs, fearful of the power implicit in its use and the threat to Establishment thought and order – political and religious – devised restraints, such as licensing, censors, indices of prohibited books, and prosecutions for seditious libel, which generally were unknown in the pre-printing press era. Official restrictions were the official response to the new, disquieting idea that this invention would provide a means for mass communication.[125]

Although, in recent history, state repression of the press has subsided in many countries,[126] arguably access to the public sphere for ordinary people did not, and as we will see, has not, increased to the extent that printing, publishing and

---

[121]   D. Crowley and P. Heyer, *Communication in History: Technology, Culture, Society* (5th edn., Pearson, 2007) 82. According to Crowley and Heyer, some commentators believe that printing 'was the major cultural/technological transformation in the history of the West' and that 'printing, along with numerous other developments, marked the transition between the end of Middle Ages and the dawn of the modern era'.

[122]   For a history of state repression of the press from around the world, see Weaver (n 39) 21–32.

[123]   Exceptions to this included Italy and Germany, which allowed newspapers more leeway in reporting foreign news than in discussing domestic politics. Crowley and Heyer (n 121) 2.

[124]   435 US 765 (1978).

[125]   Ibid 800–801. See generally W.T. Mayton, 'Seditious Libel and the Lost Guarantee of a Freedom of Expression' (1984) 84 *Columbia Law Review* 91, 97–98; N.L. Rosenberg, *Protecting the Best Men: An Interpretive Theory of the History of Libel* (The University of North Carolina Press, 1986); M.L Kaplan, *The Culture of Slander in Early Modern England* (Cambridge University Press, 1997).

[126]   Although, of course, this is not true of all countries. There are many countries around the world where the media is subject to strict state controls. See Weaver (n 39) 25–26.

A shackled institution 33

communication technology would allow,[127] as state gatekeepers have largely been replaced by 'private gatekeepers'.[128] Historically, the number of people who could own, and therefore use, the printing press was small due to the equipment required and the costs involved. Consequently, according to Russell Weaver, those who did not own printing presses had 'limited options available for accessing print technology to communicate their views'.[129] Rather, they were 'subject to the whims' of the owners and operators of the presses who, by controlling and limiting access to their presses, could also exert significant influence over mass communication.[130]

In the UK and the US, these early private gatekeepers became known as press 'barons', 'lords' and 'titans' because of the number of newspapers they owned, the control they exerted over their own outlets and the press industry generally, and the power this gave them to advance their own political, social and business agendas. This type of ownership represents the classic model of the 'dominant proprietor'.[131] Although it is most commonly associated with the press barons of the late nineteenth and twentieth centuries, as we will see in the following section, it still exists today. Because of the behaviour that is symptomatic of this model, it is democratically concerning[132] due to the opportunity it presents for press freedom and access to the public sphere to be undermined and curtailed by wealthy owners using their media enterprises as instruments to promote their own agendas.

It is exemplified by the UK's early press barons, who included the likes of Alfred and Harold Harmsworth, who later became Lord Northcliffe and Lord Rothermere respectively. The brothers launched and owned the *Daily Mail*[133] and *Daily Mirror*, and Northcliffe later bought *The Observer*, *The Times* and *The Sunday Times*. In Northcliffe's case, his ownership of these newspapers,

---

[127] In Chapter 3 I consider whether social media and its facilitation of citizen journalism has overcome this problem and has increased access to the public sphere.

[128] This is not the case in all countries. For example, in countries such as China and Russia hybrid state/private gatekeepers exist, where 'private' commercial media companies are subject to state control.

[129] Weaver (n 39) 34.

[130] Ibid.

[131] See generally J. Turnstall, *Newspaper Power* (Oxford University Press, 1996) ch. 5.

[132] Rowbottom (n 64) 298.

[133] The paper was launched by the brothers in 1896. When Northcliffe died in 1922, Rothermere acquired his brother's controlling interest in Associated Newspapers Limited, which is now known as DMG Media (see n 13) and is owned by DMGT, the Chairman of which is his great-grandson, the 4th Viscount Rothermere, Jonathan Harmsworth.

34 *Media freedom in the age of citizen journalism*

and their vast circulation, gave him 'unrivalled power',[134] as the *Daily Mail* became, in the early part of the twentieth century, the UK's highest-selling newspaper, while *The Times* 'gave him a direct line to the British establishment'.[135] Thus, according to Piers Brendon, 'by attracting massive investments of capital [Northcliffe] created the greatest press confederacy in the world. His enemies named him Northoleon.'[136] Northcliffe provides an excellent example of how the press barons used, and continue to use, their publications to influence UK politics.[137] Northcliffe's support for the Conservative Party by, for example, investing large sums of money into Conservative organs such as the *Manchester Courier*, was rewarded with a peerage in 1905. In 1909, the secretary to Arthur Balfour, who was the Tory Prime Minister at the time, remarked on 'how admirably our Party is served by the *Daily Mail*. It is the most potent auxiliary. Everyone reads it.'[138]

The power of the press barons is demonstrated further by the separate campaigns that Rothermere and William Maxwell Aitken (who became Lord Beaverbrook), the owner of the *Daily Express*, ran against the former Conservative leader and Prime Minister Stanley Baldwin. Both barons wanted the British Empire to become a free trade bloc, whereas Baldwin favoured protectionism. The confrontation between the barons and the Prime Minister led to Baldwin's famous speech at the Queen's Hall in London on 17 March 1931, in which he stated:

> Their newspapers are not newspapers in the ordinary acceptance of the term, they are engines of propaganda for the constantly changing policies, desires, personal wishes, personal likes and personal dislikes of two men ... What the proprietorship of these papers is aiming at is power, but power without responsibility, the prerogative of the harlot throughout the ages.[139]

The dominant proprietor model, and the early press barons' sphere of influence, were not confined to the UK; rather the barons from the UK and the US were inextricably linked in that they 'reacted on each other and the Atlantic was no bar to the flow of influence'.[140] Northcliffe's *Daily Mirror*, for instance, inspired Joseph Patterson's *Daily News* and, in 1929, William

---

[134] P. Jackson and T. de Castella, 'Clash of the press titans', *BBC*, 14 July 2011.

[135] Ibid.

[136] P. Brendon, *The Life and Death of the Press Barons* (Secker & Warburg, 1982) 110.

[137] Their modern-day equivalents are discussed below.

[138] Brendon (n 136) 116.

[139] T. Driberg, *Beaverbrook: A Study in Power and Frustration* (Weidenfeld & Nicolson, 1956) 213.

[140] Brendon (n 136) 109.

Randolph Hearst urged his editors to adopt Northcliffe's style of journalism.[141] Hearst was known as the 'super-Northcliffe of America'[142] and was the inspiration for the character Charles Foster Kane in Orson Welles' *Citizen Kane*. Consequently, it has been suggested that it is from Hearst that the press baron blueprint truly originates.[143] Regardless of whether or not this is correct, in terms of media power, influence and, at the time, reach, few newspaper owners anywhere in the world, both past and present, could rival Hearst's empire.[144] It included, among others,[145] the *San Francisco Examiner*,[146] *The New York Morning Journal*, the *Los Angeles Examiner*, the *Detroit Times*, the *Boston Herald American*, the *Washington Times* and the *Houston Chronicle*. Like his UK press baron counterparts, Hearst used his newspapers 'aggressively' to campaign for causes that he supported[147] and to promote his preferred views and positions.[148] This led to US Congressman Sherman Minton's denouncement of Hearst as the greatest menace to the freedom of the press that exists in this country, because instead of using the great chain of newspapers he owns, and the magazines and news agencies ... to disseminate the truth to the people, he prostitutes them to the propaganda that pursues the policies he dictates'.[149]

Other than Northcliffe's 'confederacy', perhaps the only other media empire that could rival Hearst's was the Medill dynasty, which began when Joseph Medill purchased the *Chicago Tribune* in 1855. Other family members followed in Medill's footsteps, which eventually led to the family owning *The Daily Post*[150] in New York and *The Washington Herald*,[151] which was later combined with the *Washington Times* to create the *Washington*

---

[141] Ibid.

[142] *The Britannia and Eve*, 5 October 1928, accessible via https://www.britishnewspaperarchive.co.uk/search/results/1928-10-05?NewspaperTitle=Britannia%2Band%2BEve&IssueId=BL%2F0001849%2F19281005%2F&County=London%2C%20England; see also Brendon (n 136) 126.

[143] Jackson and de Castella (n 134).

[144] Weaver (n 39) 34.

[145] Other newspapers owned by Hearst included the *Das Morgan Journal*, the *Seattle Post-Intelligencer*, the *Washington Herald*, the *San Antonio Light* and the *Baltimore News American*.

[146] William Hearst took over the running of this newspaper from his father, George Hearst, in 1887 when Hearst senior was elected to the US senate.

[147] W.A. Swanberg, *Citizen Hearst* (Prentice Hall, 1981) 100, 119–127.

[148] J.A. Barron, 'Access to the Media – 1967 to 2007 and Beyond: A Symposium Honoring Jerome A. Barron's Path-Breaking Article "Access Reconsidered"' (2008) 76 *George Washington Law Review* 826, 832. See generally Brendon (n 136) ch. 8.

[149] G. Seldes, *Lords of the Press* (Julian Messner Incorporated, 1938) 234.

[150] Owned by Joseph Medill Patterson, a grandson of Joseph Medill.

[151] Eleanor Medill Patterson, Joseph Medill's granddaughter, was the editor and eventual owner of the newspaper.

Times-Herald, meaning that, at one point in history, the Medills owned the three largest-circulation daily newspapers in the three most important cities in the US.[152] Again, like Northcliffe and Hearst et al, the Medills used their newspapers to advance their own agendas. As Joseph Epstein has commented, the 'Medill grandchildren viewed journalism as purveying entertainment while enhancing their social positions and spreading their political views'.[153] For example, during World War II the Medills advocated for an isolationist position that was attributed to their dislike of President Roosevelt.[154]

As we shall see in the following section, the dominant proprietor ownership model, and the democratic challenges that it poses, are not confined to the press barons of the past. Rather, elements of it are still very evident in today's media,[155] albeit with many modern-day press barons there is undoubtedly an overlap with the corporate ownership model, which brings its own problems for democracy.

3.3.2 Today's media, the corporate ownership model and advertising

Benjamin Compaine has argued that modern media ownership does not present a concentration problem because the media is owned by 'thousands of large and small firms and organizations ... controlled, directly and indirectly, by hundreds of thousands of stockholders, as well as by public opinion'.[156] Consequently, in his view, the media, if viewed as a whole, is not concentrated and, regardless, competition and antitrust laws provide an appropriate remedy for any problems that may be caused by a lack of plurality.[157]

Compaine's position on media ownership can be attacked on three fronts. First, we have seen that, in respect of UK competition laws at least, because of their discretionary nature, they can in fact contribute to media concentration as opposed to alleviating it. Secondly, as we will see, the corporate ownership model, within which many media companies are owned by 'hundreds of

---

[152] Additionally, Robert Rutherford, another grandson of Joseph Medill, became the publisher of the *Chicago Tribune*, and Alicia Patterson, Joseph Medill's great-granddaughter, became the editor of *Newsday*.

[153] J. Epstein, 'Dynasts of the Daily Press', reviewing M. McKinney, *The Magnificent Medills: America's Royal Family of Journalism During a Century of Turbulent Splendor*, *The New York Times* Book Review Section, 16 October 2011, 14.

[154] Ibid.

[155] Weaver (n 39) 37.

[156] B.M. Compaine and D. Gomery, *Who Owns the Media?: Competition and Concentration in the Mass Media Industry* (3rd edn., Routledge, 2000) 578. Compaine and Gomery take explicitly opposing views and are therefore the primary authors of each of their respective chapters. Where I refer to Compaine I am referring to chapters written exclusively by him.

[157] Ibid ch. 8. See also Baker, *Media Concentration and Democracy* (n 52) 55.

A shackled institution 37

thousands of stockholders', can severely limit the freedom of the press and access to the public sphere, and in so doing presents a significant challenge to democracy. However, before considering this model, we will look at the third rejoinder to Compaine's argument as it feeds into, and provides context for, the arguments relating to the democratic challenges posed by corporate ownership of the media.

Compaine's contention that objectionable ownership concentration within the modern media is a myth conflicts with the democratic distribution principle[158] and the arguments raised by the CPEP and other commentators who have suggested that despite competition and antitrust laws, vast swaths of 'the world's most lucrative media real estate'[159] is owned by a relative handful of media giants,[160] whose print and online publications are read, and whose television and radio stations are watched and listened to, by audiences around the world. In arguing that this level of ownership concentration is dangerous for democracy,[161] Bagdikian has likened the media conglomerates discussed below to a cartel who 'find ways to cooperate so that [they] can work together to expand their power', which he suggests has become a 'major force' in shaping contemporary life.[162] This is a view shared by Robert McChesney, who has said that despite the

> seeming excess of 'competition,' the media system is anything but competitive ... Not only are all of the markets oligopolies, where almost all of the main players are owned by a handful of firms, the media giants also tend to work quite closely together ... these interactions bear many of the hallmarks of a cartel, or at least a 'gentleman's club'.[163]

Consequently, he argues that the 'wealthier and more powerful the corporate media giants have become, the poorer the prospects for participatory democracy'.[164]

In 2007 Baker wrote that 'despite Compaine's rhetorical claim' he knows of 'no evidence that the mergers since 1997 have reversed the trend toward increased concentration'.[165] An assessment of the current media market provides evidence that supports Baker's earlier contention and the arguments advanced by Bagdikian and McChesney, and undermines those advanced

---

[158] See section 3.1 and nn 65 and 66.
[159] Thomas (n 30) 628.
[160] Ibid. See also Weaver (n 39) 35; Media Reform Coalition (n 29).
[161] Bagdikian (n 5) xvi, 4–28.
[162] Ibid 3–6.
[163] McChesney (n 26) 28.
[164] Ibid 2.
[165] Baker, *Media Concentration and Democracy* (n 52) 55.

by Compaine. Within the UK market the dominant companies include Lord Rothermere's DMGT,[166] News UK[167] and Reach Plc.[168] According to the Media Reform Coalition, at the time of writing, these companies account for 83 per cent of the national newspaper market.[169] This is borne out by Mediatique's *Overview of recent dynamics in the UK press market* for the Department of Digital, Culture, Media & Sport, which found that the press industry had 'witnessed a period of significant consolidation'.[170] As previously discussed, DMGT's purchase of the '*i*' newspaper means that newspaper ownership in the UK is now in the hands of just six companies.[171] Prior to the acquisition DMGT's titles reached more adults in the UK than any other newspaper group. With its purchase of the '*i*' DMGT has strengthened its position as the largest newspaper group in the UK, by increasing its readership from 13.2 million to 14.6 million readers, which is equivalent to 28 per cent of UK adults.[172] News UK has the second-largest reach, with 6.9 million readers.[173]

This does not tell the full 'News UK story', however, as the company is a subsidiary of Rupert Murdoch's News Corporation, which is one of the largest media conglomerates in the world with revenues in excess of $1 billion a year.[174] As well as News UK's publications, it owns a huge variety of other media enterprises in Australia and the US.[175] News Corporation, and the other global media conglomerates, which include WarnerMedia Group,[176] The Walt

---

[166] See section 2.

[167] News UK's publications include *The Sun, The Times, The Sunday Times*. See https://www.news.co.uk/.

[168] Reach Plc owns the *Daily Express,* the *Sunday Express*, the *Mirror* and the *Daily Star* as well as a number of other local newspapers and radio stations. See https://www.reachplc.com/our-newsbrands.

[169] Media Reform Coalition (n 29).

[170] Mediatique (n 64). Similarly, a Reuters Institute study in 2018 into increased collaboration among news publishers on investigative journalism projects cited the severe economic pressures on newsrooms as a reason for pooling resources: Reuters Institute for the Study of Journalism, Richard Sambrook, 'Global Teamwork: The Rise of Collaboration in Investigative Journalism', 2018, 1.

[171] See Ofcom (n 35) [5.6].

[172] Ibid [5.8].

[173] Ibid [5.7].

[174] Weaver (n 39) 35.

[175] See https://newscorp.com/about/our-businesses/. It also previously owned 20th Century Fox (and later 21st Century Fox), which it sold to Walt Disney Studios, a subsidiary of the Walt Disney Company, in 2019.

[176] See https://www.warnermediagroup.com/.

Disney Company,[177] ViacomCBS,[178] Bertelsmann,[179] Meredith,[180] Gannett[181] and the Hearst Corporation, which continues to control scores of newspapers, radio and television outlets, cable television systems and book publishers, as well as businesses in sectors such as property, transport and health,[182] demonstrate that although ownership may be associated with a particular industry and country, it is now undoubtedly a diversified and global business that transcends traditional geographical boundaries. Unlike the press barons of the past, whose businesses tended to be confined to one type of medium – the press – these companies are truly multi-media. The range of mediums they own, their utilisation of media convergence[183] and their portfolios of other non-media businesses means that their reach and influence can permeate into every aspect of our lives and therefore far exceeds any press baron that has come before.

Within this modern media market, different ownership models exist and, as we shall see, the dominant proprietor and corporate ownership models overlap considerably. Contemporary press barons include the likes of Jeff Bezos, the founder and Chief Executive Officer of Amazon, who acquired the *Washington Post* in 2013 for $250 million, Evgeny Lebedev, the owner of the *Independent*, the *Independent on Sunday*[184] and the *Evening Standard*,[185] and Sir David and Frederick Barclay, who own *The Daily Telegraph* and *The Sunday Telegraph*. However, the control and influence that Rupert Murdoch exerts over his media enterprises arguably provides the best example of the endurance of the dominant proprietor model, and how it continues to undermine the democratic safeguard argument,[186] within a modern context. He is undoubtedly an archetypal press baron in the mould of Northcliffe and Hearst et al. However, because of the array of media outlets, across a variety of mediums, that he controls, combined with their global reach and the proliferation of convergence, Murdoch has even greater social, political and business agenda-setting powers than his predecessors. He has used, and continues to use, his newspapers, and other media outlets, as instruments to influence public opinion to align with,

---

[177] See https://thewaltdisneycompany.com/.

[178] See https://www.viacbs.com/.

[179] See https://www.bertelsmann.com/#st-1.

[180] See https://www.meredith.com/national-media/brands.

[181] See https://www.gannett.com/brands/. Gannett's UK subsidiary is NewsQuest Media Group: https://www.newsquest.co.uk/news-brands.

[182] See https://www.hearst.com/home.

[183] For example, in June 2020 News UK launched *Times Radio* as a joint venture between *The Times*, *The Sunday Times* and Wireless Group Limited.

[184] Purchased in 2010.

[185] Purchased in 2009 and owned jointly with his father, Alexander Lebedev.

[186] See n 70.

and advance, his own ideological and socio-political views.[187] For instance, in evidence given by Andrew Neil to the House of Lords Select Committee on Communications, the former editor of *The Sunday Times* described Murdoch as the 'editor-in-chief' of *The Sun*[188] and Nick Davies has said that '[f]irst and foremost [Murdoch] uses his media outlets to build alliances with politicians who, in return, will help him with his business'.[189]

To the contrary, the professional culture of journalists cannot be underestimated. As we have seen, journalists have been, and continue to be, responsible for providing us with valuable information and important and ground-breaking stories.[190] Consequently, this culture can constrain and limit proprietor influence,[191] as demonstrated by the statements provided to Ofcom from the editors of the *Daily Mail*, the *Mail on Sunday* and *Metro* to support DMGT's purchase of JPI Media and the *'i'* newspaper, all of which assert that they make the editorial decisions for their newspapers without interference from Lord Rothermere, DMGT's commercial management or the wider group.[192] For example, Ted Verity, the *Mail on Sunday's* editor, stated that he alone made the decision to change the newspaper's position on Brexit.[193]

---

[187] Leyva (n 39) 79. Similarly, Pradip Thomas has argued that 'News Corporation's ownership of 60 to 70 per cent of newspaper circulation in the [UK] and Australia, its close association with conservative politics and social agendas, and its anodyne or noncontroversial and soothing content is often cited as a contemporary example of dumbing down.' Thomas (n 30) 628.

[188] House of Lords Select Committee on Communications, *The ownership of the news* (HL 2007-08, 122-II) 339.

[189] Davies (n 32) 17. At the time of writing, former Australian Prime Minister, Kevin Rudd, launched a petition calling for a Royal Commission into News Corporation's dominance of Australian media. According to the petition the company employs tactics that 'chill free speech and undermine public debate' and that its business models 'encourage deliberately polarising and politically manipulated news'. Echoing the statements made by Baldwin and Minton in respect of Lords Rothermere and Beaverbrook and Hearst respectively (see nn 139 and 149) according to Rudd, Murdoch 'has become a cancer, an arrogant cancer, on our democracy'. E. Visontay, 'Kevin Rudd petition calls for royal commission into News Corp domination of Australian media', *The Guardian*, 11 October 2020.

[190] See nn 13 to 23.

[191] Rowbottom (n 64) 299.

[192] Ofcom (n 35) [6.26]. Ofcom itself found that DMGT does not have 'a financial incentive to alter the current editorial line of the *'i'* [6.19]. These statements correspond with the Competition Commission's findings in its report to the Secretary of State for Business, Enterprise and Regulatory Reform on the acquisition by British Sky Broadcasting Group Plc (BSkyB) of 17.9 per cent of the shares of ITV Plc: Competition Commission, *Acquisition of BSkyB Group Plc of 17.9% of the Shares in ITV Plc* (December 2007), [5.65]–[5.70].

[193] Ibid.

A shackled institution 41

From a normative legal perspective, Verity's decision does not present a problem. Editorial freedom relating to the media generally is well established in the jurisprudence of, for example, the ECtHR and the US Supreme Court.[194] From an epistemological perspective, however, editorial freedom is potentially problematic. Taking Verity's decision as an example, it may be so that he alone decided the *Mail on Sunday's* Brexit policy, but any editor is ultimately appointed and employed by their respective newspaper's owner (in this case DMGT), or individuals or editorial appointment boards that *may*, in some cases, be influenced by the owner. Indeed, according to Lesley Hitchens, journalists working for rival newspapers, let alone the same outlets, often share the same values as a result of their training and previous employment.[195] In the same way that we frequently see academics moving universities with their Head of School, there is often a flow of staff from one media company to another, as new senior newspaper employees regularly bring their preferred journalists and other staff with them.[196] Therefore, it is conceivable that any appointment, particularly a key appointment such as an editor, will reflect the overall culture and biases of the company and the people who control it. As Jacob Rowbottom has observed, '[a] strong proprietor will make senior appointments that are largely sympathetic to his own agenda and will reward those that are loyal'.[197] This can even be the case where 'independent' boards are responsible for approving editorial appointments, where those boards are not sufficiently independent of the newspaper owner:[198] in Neil's evidence to the House of Lords Select Committee on Communications[199] he described the Independent Board at his newspaper, and at *The Times*, as 'a bunch of establishment worthies and Murdoch policeman'.[200] Moreover, in Verity's case, even though *he* exercised editorial control that was prima facie independent of DMGT, his *unilateral* decision represents editorial bias as his view on the matter ultimately dictated the stance that his journalists were to take on the UK leaving the European Union.[201]

---

[194] See Chapter 4 section 3.2.2.1.

[195] L. Hitchens, *Broadcasting Pluralism and Diversity* (Hart Publishing, 2006) 135.

[196] Rowbottom (n 64) 291.

[197] Ibid 299. Rowbottom goes on to say that the proprietor's 'views and interests may also be widely known on a few key issues, so that staff know which stories to pursue and which lines to take without instruction from [them]'.

[198] Ibid 294.

[199] See House of Lords Select Committee on Communications (n 188).

[200] Ibid 344.

[201] In the US, at least, it has been held by the Supreme Court that newspapers can discharge journalists who do not comply with the editorial line. See *Associated Press v National Labor Relations Board* 301 US 103 (1937) per Roberts J, 133.

As previously explained, today's dominant ownership model is corporate ownership.[202] It overlaps considerably with the dominant proprietor model as most modern-day press barons, including the likes of Rupert Murdoch, Lord Rothermere and the Barclay brothers, operate within a corporate system. However, these barons have effective control over the shares or over their company, and/or, as illustrated by Murdoch, they operate as a dominant chief executive or chairman exerting considerable personal influence over their media enterprises.[203] Alternatively, the companies operating within this model that do not have a dominant press baron figure at the helm are still shareholder led in the typical sense in that their main purpose is to return a profit to their shareholder-owners. Thus, this model is primarily driven by profit, either for the owners themselves, shareholders or both.[204] It has been suggested that it effectively commoditises news,[205] as illustrated by a statement given to Leveson LJ's *Inquiry* by *The Sun's* then associate editor, Trevor Kavanagh, in which he said 'news is as saleable a commodity as any other. Newspapers are commercial, competitive businesses, not a public service.'[206] As we have seen, this is a situation that is often exploited by owners such as Rupert Murdoch through their relationships with politicians and political parties, who in turn embrace the opportunity to ally with media outlets that will act as their political organ.[207]

The commoditisation of news generates a number of problems that contribute to undermining the free press, limiting access to the public sphere and therefore creating challenges to democracy. First, as discussed above, it encourages churnalism.[208] During the last two decades an increasing number of news outlets have begun to operate within the corporate model.[209] The model's growth, combined with the emergence of citizen journalists and other new types of news publishers, the increase in free newspapers, which has led to more competition for decreasing advertising revenue, and the need for news outlets to provide news on a rolling 24-hour-a-day basis at a faster pace than ever before across multiple platforms, has created a frenetically competitive profit-driven environment, which has resulted in commercial reality being

---

[202]   See n 64 and sections 3.1 and 3.3.1.

[203]   Turnstall (n 131) ch. 5; Rowbottom (n 64) 299.

[204]   See section 2 and n 37 for Lord Rothermere's speech on the commercial and financial rationale behind DMGT's acquisition of the '*i*' newspaper.

[205]   Fenton (n 31) 119.

[206]   'Trevor Kavanagh's speech to the Leveson inquiry: full text', *The Guardian*, 6 October 2011.

[207]   See n 189; Fenton (n 31) 119–120.

[208]   See nn 32 and 33.

[209]   Fenton (n 31) 119.

prioritised over the democratic functions of the press.[210] It has been suggested that this 'faster and shallower corporate journalism',[211] which requires media outlets to attract readers for commercial rather than journalistic reasons, encourages journalists to 'quickly cast aside' the values of professional journalism, including appropriate source and fact checking,[212] and to 'indulge in sensationalism, trade in gratuitous spectacles and deal in dubious emotionalism'.[213] Regardless of whether this is true or not, within this hyperactive environment it is undoubtedly a constant challenge to maintain profit margins and provide adequate dividends for shareholders without employing fewer journalists.[214] But, as Fenton suggests, 'fewer journalists with more space to fill means doing more work in less time', the result of which is an increase in churnalism: the recycling of news by journalists through the 'cut and paste practice' of using news from other sources,[215] such as unattributed rewrites of press agency or public relations material[216] and social media.[217]

At the time of writing we are in the midst of the COVID-19 pandemic, which has served to amplify the problems caused by the corporate model and its encouragement of the recycling of information by journalists working for established newspapers and other mainstream media outlets. The requirement for the media to constantly produce news means that journalists do not have the luxury of time when it comes to source and fact checking at the best of times, let alone during a rapidly evolving international crisis. Rather, they are

---

[210] See nn 27 and 28.

[211] See generally A. Phillips, *Journalism in Context: Practice and Theory for the Digital Age* (Routledge, 2014).

[212] Weaver points out that 24-hour news coverage has contributed to this as it creates accuracy problems that are attendant to quicker publication: Weaver (n 39) 202.

[213] Fenton (n 31) 119. At the time of writing, an example of this type of behaviour in respect of the COVID-19 pandemic was provided by the *Daily Mirror*. On 2 April 2020 it tweeted 'UK's deadliest day set to be Easter Sunday when government fear 50,000 will die'. However, the article headline was actually 'Coronavirus "could kill 50,000" in UK with Easter Sunday "to be deadliest day"'. The article goes on to say that '[a] worst case scenario for Britain would see a coronavirus death toll of 50,000 for the entire pandemic if people ignore the lockdown and social distancing laws, while a so-called best case scenario would be 20,000 deaths' and that '[a]s it stands the UK is not on course [for] a death toll of that [50,000] scale'. See the discussion at section 4.3 of Chapter 3 on how online advertising promotes greater reliance on low-quality journalism.

[214] Fenton (n 31) 119. As discussed in section 4.2 of Chapter 3 our shift to online news consumption has contributed to a significant decline in journalists and a 'brain drain' within the profession.

[215] See n 31– n 33.

[216] Fenton (n 31) 119; Baker, *Media Concentration and Democracy* (n 52) 117.

[217] M. Frankel, 'Social Media Communities and Reporting of the COVID-19 Pandemic', Reuters Institute for the Study of Journalism, 30 July 2020.

having to make decisions quickly on whether to publish or broadcast information coming from a huge variety of sources on an esoteric topic that most people know a limited (at best) amount about.[218] For instance, in January 2020, *The Washington Times* incorrectly reported that the virus may have originated from the Wuhan Institute of Virology in China as part of a covert biological weapons programme.[219] The article sparked conspiracy theories and the spread of further misinformation on the virus's origin around the world,[220] including being repeated in the UK by the *Mail Online*,[221] and published, and then later amended, by the *Daily Star*.[222] Throughout the pandemic there has also been a huge amount of false news published on social media, some of which has been re-published by mainstream newspapers and other media.[223] The fact that 'trusted' sources recycled the information justified and supported it, creating a self-fulfilling cycle which in some instances contributed to a spiral of panic.[224] From a UK perspective, even before the pandemic the public's trust in the press was very low, with journalists languishing towards the bottom of the league table of the country's trusted professions.[225] The scale of this distrust is demonstrated by the latest European Broadcasting Union survey,

---

[218] P. Coe, 'The Good, The Bad and The Ugly of Social Media During the Coronavirus Pandemic' (2020) 25(3) *Communications Law* 119–122.

[219] B. Gertz, 'Coronavirus may have originated in lab linked to China's biowarfare program', *The Washington Times*, 26 January 2020.

[220] BBC Monitoring, 'China coronavirus: Misinformation spreads online about origin and scale', *BBC*, 30 January 2020.

[221] B. Thomson, 'China "appoints its top military bio-warfare expert to take over secretive virus lab in Wuhan", sparking conspiracy theories that coronavirus outbreak is linked to Beijing's army', *Mail Online*, 14 February 2020.

[222] A. Blair, 'Claims Coronavirus "started in secret lab" for world's deadliest diseases dismissed', *Daily Star*, 30 January 2020.

[223] Journalists using social media and other online platforms as a source of news, the symbiotic relationship this has created with citizen journalists, and how this has contributed to the spread of false news is discussed in more detail in Chapter 3 section 5.3. As discussed in that section, the UK government's 'Online Harms White Paper: Full government response to the consultation' confirmed that upon the enactment of the Online Safety Bill online misinformation and disinformation will come under the remit of Ofcom: 'Online Harms White Paper: Full government response to the consultation', 15 December 2020, [2.80]–[2.88]. See clause 98 of the Online Safety Bill.

[224] Coe (n 218); Axel Bruns et al, 'When a virus goes viral: pros and cons to the coronavirus spread on social media' *Inforrm*, 22 March 2020. Bruns et al suggest that the panic buying of food and other essentials was partly caused by elements of the mainstream media amplifying social media trends relating to empty shelves in supermarkets (some of which were entirely misleading). This made the problem appear much worse than it was, which in turn caused the irresponsible behaviour that led to the shortage of food and other essentials.

[225] Ipsos Mori Veracity Index 2019, 'Trust in professions survey'.

which reported that the UK ranks lowest out of 33 European Union countries in respect of the trust that citizens have in their press.[226] Although the UK's press seems to be the subject of particular distrust amongst its own public, it reflects a global trend in falling trust in the media generally.[227] Arguably, this worldwide crisis of trust has been exacerbated further by the reporting of the pandemic.[228] Consequently, in April 2020, Google announced $6.5m (£5.2m) worth of grants to support fact-checking groups and non-profits worldwide battling misinformation on coronavirus. In the UK a proportion of the money will go towards the fact-checking charity *Full Fact* and the independent organisation *First Draft*, which offers guidance to journalists on verifying content on social media. The effectiveness of this initiative remains to be seen.[229]

Secondly, the corporate model can generate pressure to attract the most profitable audiences and advertisers, which in turn can influence a newspaper's editorial line and the decisions made by its journalists. Although some institutions separate their commercial and editorial departments to safeguard against this pressure directly impacting on journalistic decisions, the effectiveness of this measure is questionable.[230] This is illustrated by the political journalist Peter Oborne's resignation from *The Daily Telegraph* in 2015, which he claims was a result of the newspaper's editorial line being influenced by its relationship with its commercial partners.[231] It seems that Oborne was not alone in being troubled by his employer's behaviour. It transpired that a number of the newspaper's other journalists had voiced their

---

[226] European Broadcasting Union, 'Market Insights: Trust in Media 2020', April 2020.

[227] According to the Reuters Institute for the Study of Journalism, at the outset of the pandemic levels of trust in the news globally were at their lowest point since it started to track that data. In a direct comparison with 2019, its Digital News Report 2020 found that fewer than four in ten (38%) people trust most news most of the time – down four percentage points. Less than half (46%) said they trust the news that they themselves use. See Reuters Institute, 'Digital News Report 2020', 5.

[228] S. Cushion et al, 'Coronavirus: fake news less of a problem than confusing government messages – new study', *The Conversation*, 12 June 2020.

[229] Coe (n 218). In November 2020 it was announced that *Full Fact* will coordinate the collaboration of *YouTube*, *Facebook* and *Twitter*, along with governments and research bodies, to combat the spread of misinformation about potential COVID-19 vaccines: 'YouTube, Facebook and Twitter align to fight Covid vaccine conspiracies', *BBC*, 20 November 2020.

[230] Rowbottom (n 64) 299.

[231] Oborne resigned because he claimed an investigation into HSBC had not been published to protect the newspaper's commercial interests. See P. Oborne, 'Why I have resigned from the Daily Telegraph', *opendemocracy.net*, 17 February 2015. The newspaper's response can be found in 'The Daily Telegraph's promise to our readers', *The Daily Telegraph*, 19 February 2015.

46   *Media freedom in the age of citizen journalism*

concerns that they too were being discouraged from writing unfavourable stories about advertisers and other commercial partners, and that 'commercial matters were affecting editorial output'.[232] The journalists also provided examples to *Newsnight* of how commercial concerns impacted upon coverage of China and Russia.[233] Furthermore, regardless of any overt safeguards, such as a distinction between commercial and editorial functions, the key financial interests of a newspaper, such as its investments and commercial partnerships, 'may be sufficiently internalised among its staff to influence content without direction',[234] either in the form of the editorial line adopted or from those who control or own the newspaper. Thus, even with functional separations in place, these examples demonstrate how editors and journalists may be reluctant to produce and publish content that will alienate advertisers or undermine the commercial interests of the company or be discouraged from doing so.[235] Indeed, as demonstrated by the contentions made by Oborne and his colleagues, it has been suggested that the media's reliance on advertising revenue can create an 'immunity from bad publicity' for advertisers as newspapers, and other media outlets, will think twice before publishing negative stories linked to advertising partners.[236]

Even where editorial and journalistic decisions are not influenced by the sort of *direct* advertiser pressure reported by *The Daily Telegraph* journalists, those working for newspapers and other media companies operating within the corporate model will need to have their company's profitability, and therefore its ability to generate revenue and its relationship with its commercial and advertising partners, at the forefront of their minds when they make general editorial and journalistic choices. For example, in determining how resources are used, there may be little incentive to encourage, produce and publish expensive and time-consuming investigative journalism that may only attract a limited audience.[237] Rather, quick and inexpensive journalistic activities that appeal to the largest possible audience and will therefore provide bigger revenues and

---

[232]   C. Cook, 'More Telegraph writers voice concern', *BBC*, 19 February 2015.

[233]   Ibid.

[234]   Rowbottom (n 64) 299.

[235]   Ibid 300. See also Wragg (n 75) 74.

[236]   Charney (n 1) 5.

[237]   According to *The Cairncross Review*, '[i]nvestigative journalism is easily the riskiest and most expensive activity that most publishers undertake' and, although this type of reporting 'presents an enormous challenge ... it is also at the heart of the journalist's role as guardian of public probity'. Despite the importance attached to investigative journalism the *Review* saw no evidence of newspapers being able to recoup the costs of producing such stories. Rather, 'it seems likely that much investigative journalism is undertaken by the mainstream press as an investment in reputation'. Indeed, according to Richard Sambrook, the severe economic pressures on newsrooms has led

attract more advertisement financing may be prioritised. Indeed, it has been argued that the fact that newspapers now have an online presence in addition to their print circulation has contributed to, rather than remedied, the problems identified by the CPEP.[238] Newspaper revenues have significantly decreased because of free access to online news.[239] This, combined with increased competition from the likes of Gumtree and Craigslist over classified advertisements, which historically was one of the press's most important sources of revenue (particularly local newspapers),[240] have resulted in the press becoming increasingly dependent on commercial advertisers,[241] to the detriment of investigative journalism.[242] One only has to look at most newspapers' websites to see they are saturated by advertisements. Yet, despite this, according to the *Cairncross Review*, '[f]ew print publishers imagined how dramatically their share of the advertising market would shrink, or how little online advertising revenue they would capture'.[243] Thus, it seems that newspapers are fighting over an increasingly diminishing source of advertising income,[244] a situation

---

to an increase in collaboration among news publishers on investigative journalism projects. See *Cairncross* (n 23) 19 and Sambrook (n 170).

[238] *Cairncross* (n 23) 42–44. The *Review* recognises that in an attempt to increase online advertising revenue, newspapers have encouraged the sensationalisation of news and the prioritisation of low-quality 'clickbait' over high-quality, investigative and minority publications. This is considered in more detail in Chapter 3 section 4.3. E. Bell and T. Owen, 'The Platform Press; How Silicon Valley Re-engineered Journalism', *Tow Centre*, 29 March 2017; L. Andrews, *Facebook, The Media and Democracy: Big Tech, Small State?* (Routledge, 2020) 58; D. Boyer, *The Life Informatic: Newsmaking in the Digital Era* (Cornell University Press, 2013).

[239] For example, see M. Sweney, 'Daily Mail owner's print advertising revenues plunge by 70%', *The Guardian*, 28 May 2020.

[240] *Cairncross* (n 23) 47, 79.

[241] Ibid 40, 60: *The Cairncross Review* acknowledges that in recent years there has been a collapse of revenues from print advertising: 'In 2007, advertising in the national and local press brought in £4.6 billion, and accounted for 40% of total UK advertising spend. In 2017, the share of advertising appearing in the printed press had fallen from 40% to 12%, and generated £1.4 billion in expenditure – a fall of 70% compared to 2007.' This has coincided with a decline in revenue from print circulation: 'In 2007, sales brought in an estimated £2.2 billion of revenue. The estimated sales revenue for 2017 had dropped to £1.7 billion. Overall, revenues from advertising and sales of printed newspapers have dropped by 50% between 2007 and 2017.' See also Andrews (n 238) 59; R. Kaiser, 'The Bad News about News' (2014) *The Brookings Essay*, http://csweb.brookings.edu/content/research/essays/2014/bad-news.html.

[242] See nn 237 and 238.

[243] Ibid 41.

[244] Ibid.
By 2017, digital advertising expenditure with the press was £487 million. This was less than 5% of total online advertising spend and nowhere near comparable to the revenue that publishers had generated from print advertising in the past.

48   *Media freedom in the age of citizen journalism*

that has led Charney to suggest that while the 'old problems of the political economy have been sharpened, [the press's] watchdog role has weakened'.[245]

In the 1940s Max Horkheimer and Theodor Adorno claimed that advertising is the cause of the 'production of sameness' within the press because content needs to appeal to mass audiences to attract advertisers. Consequently, they argued that the press needs to lower its standards to find a common denominator which will appeal to largely heterogeneous groups of people with different interests.[246] Despite Horkheimer's and Adorno's claim being over 70 years old it is arguably even more applicable today than it was when it was made. The fact that newspapers and other media outlets are competing to attract the same large audiences to help them secure advertising contracts not only means that standards are lowered, but also contributes to 'competitive duplication', where the content published or broadcast by each news provider tends to be replicated by their competitors.[247] It dictates that media companies will only cater for minority tastes if they are able to exhaust the revenue they can generate from the publication or broadcasting of content that appeals to mass audiences, and pursuing minority audiences becomes more profitable than making marginal gains with the majority.[248] This means that in reality media content has a tendency to look very similar regardless of the existence of a multiplicity of providers.[249] Furthermore, the flow of staff from one media company to another discussed earlier in this section means that the type of content among the media is unlikely to be radically different.[250] Although competitive duplication is common across all forms of media, the press is particularly affected. This is because advertisers usually prefer to promote their products on platforms that can reach massive audiences, which the press is generally able to supply in abundance. Accordingly, Charney has argued that in these circumstances not only does news content 'tend to be relatively homogenous across the spectrum', but as discussed above in relation to churnalism[251] and advertising

---

    Including digital and non-digital, advertising in the press declined from £7.6 billion in 2007 to £2.7 billion in 2017, a 65% reduction.
See also Ofcom (n 35) [4.10], [4.12].

[245]   Charney (n 1) 6.

[246]   T.W. Adorno and M. Horkheimer, *Dialectic Enlightenment* (Verso Books, 1997) 124 (first published in 1947).

[247]   G. Doyle, *Understanding Media Economics* (Sage Publications, 2002) 74.

[248]   Ibid.

[249]   J. Rowbottom, *Democracy Distorted* (Cambridge University Press, 2010) 188; House of Lords Communication Committee, *Media Plurality* (HL 2013–14, 120), [57]–[63]; Charney (n 1) 4.

[250]   Rowbottom (n 64) 291.

[251]   See n 208 and Davies (n 32).

revenue,[252] serious journalism is also 'usually eclipsed by [publications and broadcasts] designed to amuse and entertain rather than inform the public'.[253] Similarly, in Baker's view, commercial media, and public media to the extent that it relies on advertising as well as public funding, plays a limited role in supporting political equality as it 'disfavours ... media focusing on political ideology, non-market-valued ethnic and cultural divisions, economically poorer groups, or any life-style needs and interests not easily exploitable for marketing purposes'.[254] Ultimately, the corporate ownership models' commoditisation of news means that access to the public sphere is largely limited to those that produce content that appeals to the largest audience possible. Although this may mean that the media operating within this model is more responsive to consumers, by giving them content that they *want*, this contributes to a democratic deficit as this is not necessarily the same as what they *need* as citizens in a democracy.[255]

Chomsky and Herman have argued that this reliance on advertising has meant that advertisers have become the patrons of the media. In their view advertisers do not just encourage the production and distribution of content that will appeal to mass audiences, they also act as 'normative reference organizations, whose requirements and demands the media must accommodate if they are to succeed'.[256] This is illustrated by advertisers choosing to promote their products in 'friendly' media, in that they will only subsidise organisations that do not damage their interests and, as discussed above, by the idea of 'immunity from publicity' that stems from newspapers and other media outlets being mindful of what they publish so as not to prejudice their advertising and commercial partners. Thus, the fact that advertisers are effectively operating as a 'normative compass', by virtue of the financial support they choose to provide or not to provide, enables them to control dissident views, meaning that the 'radical press, which canalises dissidence and is generally antagonistic to the interests of big corporations, is one of the victims of a media system heavily reliant on advertisement'.[257]

Although perhaps to a lesser extent, these arguments relating to the commoditisation of news even apply to The Guardian Media Group, which is owned by the Scott Trust, a company which is committed to upholding the

---

[252] See nn 233–237.

[253] Charney (n 1) 5. In particular, see *Cairncross* (nn 237 and 238).

[254] Baker, *Media, Markets, and Democracy* (n 52) 184. See also Kenyon (n 26) 385–386.

[255] Rowbottom (n 64) 300; Baker, *Media Concentration and Democracy* (n 52) 29.

[256] Chomsky and Herman (n 5) 16.

[257] Charney (n 1) 5.

financial and editorial independence of *The Guardian* newspaper.[258] The Trust is responsible for appointing the newspaper's editor and does not distribute dividends to its shareholders. Rather, its purpose is to ensure that the company's commercial activities serve the needs of its journalism, as opposed to the opposite.[259] However, regardless of this 'ideal' the newspaper is not immune from the same market pressures that affect all newspapers. Even though the company prioritises journalistic over commercial goals, it still needs to attract audiences, advertisers and sponsors to make it viable. Indeed, although the articles published on *The Guardian's* website are free to access, at the bottom of every article is a request for a financial donation. Thus, its journalistic activity, and the editorial decisions that are made, cannot ignore, and must react, at least to an extent, to the pressures imposed by the market.[260]

4   CONCLUSION

The dominant proprietor and corporate ownership models, which are the two most common models of news media ownership, clearly pose significant challenges to democracy that lend support to the CPEP's claim that the notion of the free press is a fallacy. Arguably the fact that the models' commoditisation of news has created a commercial necessity to treat audiences as consumers, and therefore a bias for giving audiences content that they *want* rather than what they *need* as citizens, has created a democratic deficit: as opposed to being organs for journalists to discharge their watchdog role, and increasing access to the public sphere by acting as conduits for different groups within society to express their views, large parts of the press and news media generally are owned by a relatively limited number of individuals or multinational conglomerates, meaning that journalists are often constrained by corporate shackles such as the whims of owners or the need to generate profits for shareholders or appease advertising and commercial partners. As we have seen, in the UK this is a position that is not helped by competition laws and a mergers regime based on discretionary powers.

Chapter 3 builds on what we have discussed in this chapter. It considers, inter alia, whether the democratic challenges we have considered in relation to the press have, or can be, overcome by social media and its facilitation of citizen journalists. In doing so, it asks what the barriers are to social media and citizen journalism increasing access to the public sphere, and where the challenges may lie in the future.

---

[258]   'The Scott Trust: values and history', *The Guardian*, 26 July 2015.
[259]   Ibid.
[260]   Rowbottom (n 64) 300.

3. The internet, social media and citizen journalism

1 INTRODUCTION

The previous chapter considered the CPEP's contention that the notion of the free press is a fallacy. In doing so it looked at how ownership of the press and other forms of traditional media generates pressures that contribute to the curtailment of press freedom and access to the public sphere, thereby creating serious challenges to democracy. By looking at these arguments in the context of the internet, social media and citizen journalism, this chapter forms the other half of this investigation.

As alluded to in Chapter 2,[1] the shift to online news consumption has had a profound impact on the fortunes of the press in particular.[2] For instance, as we shall see in section 4, it has arguably led to a decrease in print circulation and newspaper sales,[3] a reduction in the breadth and depth of news reporting[4] and ultimately a decline in newspapers and journalists,[5] while at the same time it has increased competition for advertising revenue.[6] Despite these 'effects', whether the changes wrought by the internet and its symbiosis with social media platforms (which have been made available via the internet) have actually increased access to the public sphere and solved the other problems identified by the CPEP in respect of the press and the traditional media is a difficult, if not impossible, question to answer with a simple 'yes' or 'no'. An assessment of the many and varied arguments and data on this subject (which could fill a number of books, let alone one chapter), and the different interpretations

---

[1] See Chapter 2, section 3.3.2.

[2] Mediatique, Department for Digital, Culture, Media & Sport, 'Overview of recent dynamics in the UK press market', April 2018, 4–5.

[3] Ibid; *The Cairncross Review*, 'A sustainable future for journalism', 12 February 2019, 24 (Cairncross); Ofcom, 'Public interest test of the completed acquisition by Daily Mail and General Trust plc of JPI Media Publications Limited and thus the '*i*' newspaper', 10 March 2020, [4.12] (Ofcom).

[4] Cairncross, (n 3) 14–15; Ofcom (n 3) [4.14]).

[5] Cairncross (n 3) 15; Ofcom (n 3) [4.14]–[4.15]). See also Mediatique (n 2) [4.4].

[6] Cairncross (n 3) 4; Ofcom (n 3) [4.10], [4.12]; Mediatique (n 2) 4–5.

of this information that lead to different conclusions, tells us that there is no commonly agreed upon answer to this question. Consequently, attempting to quantify or say with certainty what the effects of something so amorphous, complex and constantly evolving as the internet and social media are on the public sphere and democracy, which are equally as amorphous and complex, is, in my view, doomed to fail.[7] Rather, as this chapter will go on to suggest, the answer to the question can probably be found somewhere between 'yes' and 'no', in that the internet and social media have solved some of the problems (by, for example, being a catalyst for citizen journalism) and not others (at least to the extent that many early commentators predicted they would), and they have undoubtedly created new challenges (such as online filter bubbles and the amplification of false news) or added to existing ones (for instance, by creating a new breed of corporate owners and increasing reliance on, and competition for, advertising revenue).[8]

What is not in doubt, however, is that the internet and social media platforms have altered the media ecology and shifted the media paradigm, which has led to democratically significant *transformative* effects on the public sphere.[9] They have altered its *structure*[10] by providing an abundance of new loci for public discourse that have not only changed the way in which news is generated, published, communicated and consumed, but have also contributed to the growth of citizen journalism,[11] which, as we shall see in section 6, is

---

[7]   Indeed, both András Koltay and Jacob Rowbottom have commented that the contribution made to democracy in Western countries by the internet remains unclear: A. Koltay, *New Media and Freedom of Expression: Rethinking the Constitutional Foundations of the Public Sphere* (Hart Publishing, 2019) 70; J. Rowbottom, *Democracy Distorted: Wealth, Influence and Democratic Politics* (Cambridge University Press, 2010) 243.

[8]   Baker has suggested that the 'Internet changes the communication order – in some ways for the better and in others may be for the worse', C.E. Baker, *Media Concentration and Democracy: Why Ownership Matters* (Cambridge University Press, 2007) 112.

[9]   Ibid 98.

[10]   Koltay (n 7) 147.

[11]   They have also contributed in other ways. For example, in January 2019 Facebook announced that it will invest $300 million (around £229 million) in local news globally, over three years. As part of this fund, Facebook launched a Local News Partnership in the UK, between Facebook, the National Council for Training Journalists (NCTJ) Archant and Reach Plc, in which Facebook will invest £4.5 million to train journalists and 'widen the talent pool' for journalism. This two-year pilot scheme, which started in January 2019, will make available around 80 places and is being overseen by a newly established charitable organisation called the 'Community News Project'. Facebook will fund the scheme, but the NCTJ will be responsible for finding and training the journalists – Facebook will have no further input aside from the provision of some training around the use of digital tools. There will be no obligation upon

making an increasingly important contribution to the robustness of the democratic public sphere.[12]

The internet and social media have enabled citizen journalists to communicate with mass audiences, an ability that was once reserved to traditional media institutions. The implications of this communication facilitation for how we distinguish between media and non-media entities, and therefore the beneficiaries of media freedom, are, as explained in Chapter 1, part of the problem that this inquiry seeks to address and are dealt with in later chapters.[13] The purpose of this chapter is to consider how citizen journalism contributes to the public sphere. However, providing useful analysis of this cannot be achieved in a vacuum; it needs to be framed within the broader context of the internet and social media as they provide the mechanisms through which citizen journalism occurs. Consequently, this chapter begins by setting out the early hopes for the transformative effect that the internet and social media would have on the democratisation of the public sphere. Section 3 looks at how the internet and social media have altered the media ecology by changing the way in which we consume news. It also asks whether social media platforms are now, in reality, operating as both technology *and* media companies. Section 4 deals with the impact that our transition to online news consumption has had on the viability of the press and what this means for the public sphere, and section 5 considers how social media in particular has *distorted* the public sphere. Finally, in section 6 I consider the positive impact of the internet and social media on the public sphere, in that they have facilitated citizen journalism. However, this section argues that there are limitations to this, some of which can be remedied by the adoption of the media-as-a-constitutional-component concept.

2 THE INTERNET AND SOCIAL MEDIA: PROPHECIES OR PIPE DREAMS?

In the earlier days of the internet and social media bold and optimistic predictions were made by commentators as to their potentially dramatic impact on our access to the public sphere and how, as a result, they would help us to meet the challenges to democracy and solve the problems advanced by the CPEP that were considered in the previous chapter. As we shall see during this chapter, some of these predictions were prophetic, whereas others were pipe dreams.

---

journalists to put their work on Facebook, nor will Facebook 'up rank' or favour their articles above other content in its News Feed. See Cairncross (n 3) 83.

[12] Ibid 18–19; Baker (n 8) 98, 110.

[13] See Chapters 4 and 5.

54 *Media freedom in the age of citizen journalism*

In 2000 Benjamin Compaine asserted that 'there can be little disagreement that there is more competition than ever among media players', and that this point is obvious on the basis of 'a single word, Internet'.[14] At the time, in his assessment, the internet would be entirely transformative in that it would be the catalyst for the democratisation of the public sphere by breaking up the concentrated power enjoyed by certain entities in the mainstream media.[15] Other commentators shared Compaine's view that, as a result of this democratisation process, the internet (and by extension social media) would bring an abrupt end to concentrated media ownership and power,[16] and in doing so would fuel greater media plurality. Five years earlier, for example, the cyber-libertarian and political activist John Perry Barlow commented that large media conglomerates are 'merely arranging deck chairs on the Titanic' and that the internet would be the 'iceberg'.[17] In a similar vein to Barlow, Eli Noam suggested that in the 'cyber-media future ... it is unlikely that media conglomerates combining all aspects of media will be successful in the long term'.[18] In the same year that Barlow made his comments, Nicholas Negroponte accurately predicted that the internet would usher in a once-in-a-millennium period of fundamental social change that would alter human social life and cognition and would give individuals far greater power over their own lives than was ever previously anticipated.[19] With equal foresight, in 1998 the political commentator and author Thomas Friedman, said:

> The Internet will change how people live, work, play and learn ... And it will have every bit as much impact on society as the Industrial Revolution. It will promote globalization at an incredible pace. But instead of happening over 100 years, like the Industrial Revolution, it will happen over 7 years.[20]

---

[14] B.M. Compaine and D. Gomery, *Who Owns the Media? Competition and Concentration in the Mass Media Industry* (3rd edn., Routledge, 2000) 574.

[15] Ibid 579. See also Koltay (n 7) 71.

[16] See Robert W. McChesney's detailed assessment of some of these views, and the impact of the internet on the media: R.W. McChesney, *Rich Media, Poor Democracy: Communication Politics in Dubious Times* (University of Illinois Press, 1999) ch. 3.

[17] Cited in E. Herman and R.W. McChesney, *Global Media: The New Missionaries of Global Capitalism* (Bloomsbury, 1997) 107.

[18] E. Noam, 'Media Concentration in the United States: Industry Trends and Regulatory Responses', cited in Baker (n 8) 28, although, as is discussed in section 4, in later years Noam's opinion on this changed significantly.

[19] See N. Negroponte, *Being Digital* (Albert A. Knopf, 1995). See also W.M. Bulkeley, 'Peering Ahead', *Wall Street Journal*, 16 November 1998, R4.

[20] T. Friedman, 'The Internet Wars', *New York Times*, 11 April 1998, 25.

The internet, social media and citizen journalism

One only has to point to the exponential growth of companies like Amazon for an emphatic vindication of Friedman's comment.[21] It was envisaged that in having this transformative effect the internet (and social media) would erode the existing bottlenecks to accessing the public sphere, blur the lines among the media and create convergence, thereby making 'conventional industry classifications decreasingly relevant', which would lay the foundations for 'diversity, accessibility and affordability'.[22] By being a mechanism that enables the dissemination of information and opinions easily, quickly and relatively inexpensively to potentially vast numbers of people and which, theoretically, has unlimited content storage capacity, it was hoped that the internet and social media would encourage a more plural media and expand the public sphere by accommodating a greater diversity of voices and opinions. Additionally, it was anticipated that they would remove the institutional (in the sense that the press and other traditional media institutions no longer monopolise the ability to reach mass audiences), financial and technological barriers to entering the public sphere that had hitherto limited mass communication to the mainstream media and had restricted the expression of independent and minority voices.[23] Thus, it was said that the internet would become the 'Fifth Estate', by connecting people to each other, and would therefore enable citizens to take more control than ever before over the government and politics.[24]

The *potential* for the internet and social media to meet, and even surpass, these predictions is supported by their usage figures and by the broader impact they have had on how we interact and communicate with each other as individuals and as societies. In the UK alone, 87 per cent of adults aged 16 and above used the internet in 2019,[25] with social media reaching 98 per cent of this digital population.[26] Globally it is estimated that 4.13 billion people accessed the internet in the same year, meaning that internet usage has more than

---

[21] Amazon was founded by Jeff Bezos in 1994. At the time of writing Amazon was worth $1 trillion, with Bezos' net worth being $171.6 billion (more than the current GDP of Hungary or Algeria). See B. Hoyle, 'Bezos breaks his own wealth record', *The Times*, 4 July 2020, 14. For a detailed history of Amazon, see B. Stone, *The Everything Store: Jeff Bezos and the Age of Amazon* (Bantam Press, 2013).

[22] Compaine and Gomery (n 14) 541, 575.

[23] Koltay (n 7) 71.

[24] W.H. Dutton, 'The Fifth Estate Emerging through the Network of Networks' (2009) 27(1) *Prometheus* 1.

[25] Ofcom, 'Online Nation 2020 Report', 24 June 2020, 7.

[26] Ibid 16. According to the report, Facebook (including Facebook Messenger, WhatsApp and Instagram) alone reaches 96 per cent of online adults in the UK. See page 13.

doubled since 2010.[27] In almost the same period the growth in social media use is even more startling: in 2010 97 million people used social networks worldwide; by 2020 this had increased to 3.8 billion, and by 2023 it is projected that social media use will have grown to 3.43 billion people.[28] Currently, more than 3.2 billion images and 720,000 hours of video are shared daily on social media platforms.[29] Thus, in becoming an indispensable part of everyday life for most of us, the internet and social media have 'penetrated every fibre of culture today' by creating an 'online layer through which people organise their lives ... [that] influences human interaction on an individual and community level, as well as on a larger societal level'.[30] This profound impact that they have had on the media ecology by changing how we interact with each other was summed up by the Criminal Court of the City of New York in *New York v Harris*, which stated that '[t]he reality of today's world is that social media, whether it be Twitter, Facebook, Pinterest, Google+ or any other site, is the way people communicate'.[31]

As is discussed in the following sections, by going some way to dismantling some of the institutional, financial and technological barriers to entry to the public sphere that were typically associated with the press and other forms of traditional media, in *certain contexts* the internet and social media do provide the *means* for more actors to enter the media market, and for a greater diversity of voices to speak and be heard, a situation that we shall see in section 6 is exemplified by the ascendance of citizen journalism and its contribution to the robustness of the public sphere. However, whether in providing these means they have fulfilled the initial hopes invested in them is debatable.[32] The following sections will consider the extent to which they have, in reality, increased the scope of the democratic public sphere, or whether in some situations they have merely *distorted* it.

---

[27] In 2010 it was estimated that there were 2.035 billion users worldwide. Statista, 'Number of internet users worldwide from 2005 to 2019', https://www.statista.com/statistics/273018/number-of-internet-users-worldwide/.

[28] Ibid.

[29] T.J. Thomson, D. Angus and P. Dootson, '3.2 billion images and 720,000 hours of video are shared online daily. Can you sort real from fake?' *Inforrm*, 13 November 2020.

[30] J. Van Dijck, *The Culture of Connectivity A Critical History of Social Media* (Oxford University Press, 2013) 4.

[31] *New York v Harris*, 2012 N.Y. Misc. LEXIS 1871 *3, note 3 (Crim. Ct. City of N.Y., N.Y. County, 2012).

[32] Baker (n 8) 122.

3   A CHANGED MEDIA ECOLOGY

3.1   News Consumption

The internet and social media have not altered the media ecology by just changing our communication habits,[33] they have also changed the way that news is generated and how it is consumed. Media convergence means that the press and other forms of traditional media are now largely operating online in addition to their 'staple' method of communication,[34] while outlets such as the *Independent*,[35] *Huffington Post*, *Buzzfeed* and *The Ferret* in the UK, and *ProPublica* in the US, which may be classed as 'traditional professional' press, operate exclusively online.[36] As was discussed in Chapter 2, social media and other internet platforms are increasingly used as a source of news by the press and other traditional institutional media entities.[37] This situation has been amplified by the emergence of citizen journalism, which has seen the formulation of a symbiotic relationship with the press and other traditional media, who often recycle content produced by citizen journalists.[38] The facilitation of citizen journalism by the internet and social media, and citizen journalism itself, has added to the disruption to the media paradigm as the press and other traditional media organisations no longer monopolise the news-gathering, -generation and -publication process.[39]

This shift in the paradigm is demonstrated by evidence relating to trends in how news is consumed from both the US and the UK. In September 2012 the

---

[33]   See Van Dijck (n 30) and *New York v Harris*, 2012 N.Y. Misc. LEXIS 1871 *3, note 3 (Crim. Ct. City of N.Y., N.Y. County, 2012).

[34]   As discussed in Chapter 2 at section 3.3.2, media convergence has meant that newspapers have moved into other forms of media, as well as operating online. For example, News UK launched *Times Radio* in June 2020 as a joint venture between *The Times*, *The Sunday Times* and Wireless Group Limited.

[35]   The *Independent* became digital-only in 2016.

[36]   See generally Cairncross (n 3) 18.

[37]   See Chapter 2 section 3.3.2.

[38]   See generally Baker (n 8) 111; L. Durity, 'Shielding Journalist-"Bloggers": The Need to Protect Newsgathering Despite the Distribution Medium' (2006) 5 *Duke Law & Technology Review* 1; J.S. Alonzo, 'Restoring the Ideal Marketplace: How Recognizing Bloggers as Journalists Can Save the Press' (2006) 9 *New York University Journal of Legislation and Public Policy* 751, 754; J. Oster, 'Theory and Doctrine of "Media Freedom" as a Legal Concept' (2013) 5(1) *Journal of Media Law* 57, 63; M. Frankel, 'Social Media Communities and Reporting of the COVID-19 Pandemic', Reuters Institute for the Study of Journalism, 30 July 2020.

[39]   Citizen journalism, its contribution to the public sphere and how the internet and social media have contributed to its ascendance are discussed in more detail in section 6.

Pew Research Centre published a report that analysed trends in news consumption by US citizens between 1991 and 2012.[40] The report confirmed that print newspaper sales were declining[41] and that a younger demographic of news consumers, comprised of adults under 30 years old, were turning to citizen journalists, operating online, rather than television news. Indeed, between 2010 and 2012, the percentage of US citizens, across all age groups, receiving their news from social media increased from 9 per cent to 19 per cent. Accordingly, the report states that social media platforms were the preferred source of news for 33 per cent of the under-30s age group; with just 13 per cent of this group obtaining their news from either the print or digital newspaper formats. These figures are reflected in a further report from the Pew Centre,[42] which confirms that 'millennials' (persons born between 1981 and 1996) were most likely to obtain information about the 2016 presidential election via social media, with Facebook the most used platform, followed by Twitter and YouTube.[43] The report states that of the 91 per cent of all US adults who 'learned' about the election between the 12 and 27 January 2016, 14 per cent claimed social media was the 'most helpful' source of information. Similarly, 13 per cent stated that news websites and mobile applications were the most helpful. However, in comparison, only 3 per cent and 2 per cent felt that local and national print newspapers respectively fell into the 'most helpful' source category. Despite the Facebook and Cambridge Analytica scandal, the Pew Centre has confirmed the continuation of this trend, from a US perspective at least. According to research published in December 2018, online platforms continue to 'outpace' print newspapers as a source of news.[44]

The Pew Centre's figures are indicative of trends outside the US and, significantly, in the UK. According to Ofcom's most recent *News Consumption*

---

[40] Pew Research Centre, 'In Changing News Landscape, Even Television is Vulnerable', 27 September 2012.

[41] This trend has been detected by the Pew Research Centre in a report which considers the diminishing financial viability of newspapers in the US over a period of two decades. This has coincided with regular occurrences of ownership change as successive owners tried and failed to prevent declining circulation levels. In turn, this led to less advertising revenue. See Pew Research Centre, 'The declining value of US newspapers', 22 May 2015; see generally I. Cram, *Citizen Journalists: Newer Media, Republican Moments and the Constitution* (Edward Elgar Publishing, 2015) 1.

[42] Pew Research Centre, 'The 2016 Presidential Campaign – a News Events That's Hard to Miss', 4 February 2016; see also Pew Research Centre, 'News Habits on Facebook and Twitter', 14 July 2015.

[43] This is concerning when one considers the use of 'junk news' during the 2016 election. See n 96 for an explanation of junk news, and section 5.3 for further discussion.

[44] Pew Research Centre, *Social media outpaces print newspapers in the US as a source of news*, 10 December 2018.

Survey, the internet is used by 65 per cent of adults as a source of news (by way of comparison, it was 66 per cent in 2019, and 64 per cent in 2018). Although television remains the most popular method of consumption, with 75 per cent of adults using it for news (as was the case in 2019), its use for this purpose has decreased from 79 per cent in 2018. Similarly, adults using radio to listen to the news has fallen from 44 per cent in 2018 to 42 per cent in 2020, and in the same period, newspapers, which were used by 40 per cent of adults in 2018, and 38 per cent in 2019, are now used by 35 per cent.[45] The internet's symbiosis with social media is reflected in the fact that, like the internet, and unlike newspapers and radio in particular, its popularity as a source of news remains steady in respect of its use by adults to consume news, and continues to grow as a source of news for 16 to 24-year-olds. Of the 65 per cent of adults who go online for news, 45 per cent use social media as an internet news source (this is a 4 per cent decrease from 2019, when 49 per cent of adults used social media for consuming news, but it represents a 1 per cent increase from 2018),[46] which increases to 79 per cent for 16 to 24-year-olds (a 3 per cent increase from 2019).[47] Although sourcing news from multiple platforms is now a widespread practice, with people using seven different sources on average, doing so through social media platforms such as Facebook[48] and other news aggregators such as Apple and Google News is becoming increasingly common, particularly amongst 16 to 24-year-olds.[49] As we will see in section 5, this trend is not only pertinent because citizen journalists tend to publish through social media platforms, but also because of the potential for distortion presented by social media platforms and news aggregators.

Section 4 will consider what these statistics, and the changes to our news consumption habits that they represent, mean in reality to the viability of the press and the health of the democratic public sphere. Before that, however,

---

[45]   Ofcom, 'News Consumption in the UK: 2020', 13 August 2020, 12; Ofcom (n 25) 21–22.

[46]   Ofcom, News Consumption in the UK: 2020 (n 45) 8; Ofcom, 'News Consumption in the UK: 2019', 24 July 2019, 7–17.

[47]   Ofcom, News Consumption in the UK: 2020 (n 45) 14, 20, 41.

[48]   L. Andrews, *Facebook, The Media and Democracy: Big Tech, Small State?* (Routledge, 2020) ch. 5. At the time of writing, Facebook has announced the launch of a new Facebook News function. The platform has said that it will pay UK news publishers for content that is not already on the platform and that it will prioritise 'original reporting'. The curation of the news content for the function will be outsourced to Upday, which will be tasked with surfacing 'reliable' and 'relevant' news. 'Facebook News will pay UK outlets for content in 2021', *BBC*, 1 December 2020. Facebook News is discussed further in section 5.1.

[49]   Ofcom (n 3) [4.8]; Ofcom (n 45) 8, 56; Ofcom, 'News Consumption in the UK: 2019' (n 46) 61.

the following section will turn to an incidental question that stems from the changes wrought by the internet and social media on the media ecology – whether social media platforms are technology companies *and* media companies. Social media is returned to again in section 5, which looks at other ways it (and the internet more broadly) has contributed to the digital distortion of the public sphere.

3.2 Are Social Media Platforms Technology Companies *and* Media Companies?

In addition to changing the way in which we consume news, whether social media platforms have altered the media ecology and disrupted the paradigm in another way – by becoming media companies in their own right, and therefore subject to the enhanced right to media freedom and the obligations and responsibilities that this brings – is the source of ongoing debate. Although delving deeply into these arguments is beyond the scope of this book, sketching them here provides context for the discussion in section 5 on how the news aggregation and editing practices of social media platforms can further distort the public sphere.

Facebook is at the epicentre of this argument, largely because it continues to publicly resist being defined as a media company or publisher despite its actions to the contrary. In 2016, during an announcement that the company was entering the market for original and licensed video content with the launch of Facebook Watch, Mark Zuckerberg stated that 'Facebook is a new kind of platform. It's not a traditional technology company. It's not a traditional media company ... We don't write the news that people read on the platform. But at the same time we also know that we do a lot more than just distribute news, and we're an important part of the public discourse.'[50] Although the statement appeared to move Facebook away from its corporate line that it is simply a technology company that distributes content created by its users using an impersonal and objective algorithm, and is certainly not a censor or arbiter of truth,[51] it has since gone to lengths to reiterate this message to the

---

[50] S. Gibbs, 'Mark Zuckerberg appears to finally admit Facebook is a media company', *The Guardian*, 22 December 2016.

[51] P. Coe, '(Re)embracing Social Responsibility Theory as a Basis for Media Speech: Shifting the Normative Paradigm for a Modern Media' (2018) 69(4) *Northern Ireland Legal Quarterly* 403, 405.

The internet, social media and citizen journalism 61

US Congress[52] and in interviews and speeches.[53] Despite this the company has made other statements, and continues to engage in news generation, publication and editorial-related activities that conflict with this message, and which suggest that it is in fact operating in similar ways to a traditional media company.

For instance, in 2013, when announcing changes to Facebook's News Feed, Zuckerberg said, 'What we're trying to do is give everyone in the world the best personalised newspaper we can', and in 2017 Facebook announced its journalism project 'to establish stronger ties between Facebook and the news industry'.[54] In 2018 it consolidated its position as a sports broadcaster by adding the rights to show every La Liga football match to Asian audiences for three years in addition to it broadcasting Major League Baseball games to US audiences.[55] However, arguably the most significant contradiction to Facebook's corporate message occurred in 2018 during the ongoing *Six4Three v Facebook* litigation[56] and came from the company's own lawyers. They argued that Facebook's right to deny data to Six4Three and other application developers was 'a quintessential publisher function'. In doing so, the platform's lawyers compared this to the right of a newspaper, and repeatedly stated that Facebook is a publisher that makes editorial decisions and is therefore protected by the First Amendment to the US Constitution.[57]

The argument made by Facebook's legal team correlates with how its algorithms, and the algorithms of other social media platforms, curate news content

---

[52]   See 'Zuckerberg: We're a tech company, not a publisher', 10 April 2018, https://www.youtube.com/watch?v=4HTae-X757g.

[53]   For example, Facebook's Chief Operating Officer Cheryl Sandberg said in 2017 that 'at our heart we're a tech company ... we don't hire journalists'.

[54]   The programme consists of three components: (i) new collaborative tools for news journalism; (ii) training and tools for journalists; and (iii) training tools for everyone else. See Andrews (n 48) 60.

[55]   D. Lee, 'Another big sports deal for Facebook', *BBC*, 14 August 2018. Facebook is not the only online platform to enter the sports broadcasting market. For instance, in the past few years Amazon has won the rights to the ATP Finals, and in the 2019/2020 football season Amazon Prime began broadcasting live Premier League fixtures (the current contract runs to the 2021/2022 season). This followed an agreement in the US with the NFL to stream ten Thursday-night games (taking over the deal from Twitter, which had previously streamed the matches). In 2015, YouTube reached an agreement with BT to show the UEFA Champions League final. See generally D. Geey, *Done Deal: An Insider's Guide to Football Contracts, Multi-Million Pound Transfers and Premier League Big Business* (Bloomsbury Sport, 2019).

[56]   https://digitalcommons.law.scu.edu/historical/1750/.

[57]   S. Levin, 'Is Facebook a publisher? In public it says no, but in court it says yes', *The Guardian*, 3 July 2018.

and influence what users see.[58] As is discussed in more detail in section 5, these algorithms shape how news is aggregated, presented and distributed, and how users consume news by producing a personalised news feed for each and every user using settings that are dependent on, but not entirely under the control of, the respective user.[59] By presenting content in a particular way, or by removing material due to statutory requirements imposed by national governments, or because the content conflicts with the respective platform's business goals or ideology,[60] or contravenes its own policies, Facebook, Twitter and other social media are playing an editorial-like role;[61] a situation recognised by the Australian Competition and Consumer Commission (ACCC): 'Digital platforms like Google and Facebook are more than mere distributors or pure intermediaries in the supply of journalism ... They increasingly perform similar functions as news media businesses such as selecting, publishing and ranking content, including significant amounts of news media content.'[62]

Regardless of the corporate messages coming from the likes of Facebook and Twitter, clearly social media platforms are no longer playing a passive role in the curation and dissemination of news content. Consequently, the argument for greater legal responsibilities to be placed on social media and other digital platforms to protect the public sphere[63] has gained traction in

---

[58] Although Twitter gives more control to its users over the curation of their news feeds, it still makes editorial decisions by, for example, removing content that infringes legislation or its own policies.

[59] Koltay (n 7) 158; Andrews (n 48) 60.

[60] See the discussion in section 5.1 relating to the 2016 Facebook 'Trending Topics' scandal.

[61] Because of this Natalie Helberger has argued that Facebook is a 'new breed of social editor'. N. Helberger, 'Facebook is a new breed of editor: a social editor', *LSE Media Policy Project*, 16 June 2017. In respect of Facebook, Tarleton Gillespie has argued that its switch from a chronological news feed to an algorithmically curated one meant that it began to produce 'a media commodity': T. Gillespie, *Custodians of the Internet: Platforms, Content Moderation, and the Hidden Decisions That Shape Social Media* (Yale University Press, 2018) 43. Similarly, Timothy Berners-Lee has argued that Facebook is making billions of editorial decisions every day: T.B. Lee, 'Mark Zuckerberg is in denial about how Facebook is harming our politics', *Vox*, 10 November 2016.

[62] ACCC, 'Examining the impact of digital platforms on competition in media and advertising markets', 27 February 2019. See nn 125, 131, 145, 146 and 196 for further discussion on the ACCC's 'News media and digital platforms mandatory bargaining code' brought into force in February 2021 by the Treasury Laws Amendment (News Media and Digital Platforms Mandatory Bargaining Code) Act 2020, and the 'minimum standards' for the treatment of news on digital platform services that it imposes on Facebook and Google.

[63] For example, see Andrews (n 48) 60–61; R. Foster, 'News Plurality in a Digital World', Reuters Institute for the Study of Journalism, July 2012, 48; P.M. Napoli

different jurisdictions, albeit in different legal contexts. For instance, in the US, this is illustrated by the controversy surrounding section 230 of the 1996 Communications Decency Act, which provides immunity for digital intermediaries for civil liability resulting from the content of third-party users.[64] It has been argued that platforms should lose this protection because, rather than being passive conveyors of user-generated content, they are actively soliciting, algorithmically sorting and repurposing content.[65] Although at the time of writing section 230 remains in force, Twitter's high-profile disagreement with former US President Donald Trump over its adding of 'fact-check links' to his tweets about fraudulent postal ballots in US elections[66] resulted in the former President making an 'Executive Order on Preventing Online Censorship', which, in theory at least, narrows the protection that section 230 provides to social media companies.[67] In the UK Ofcom has been installed as a new 'online harms regulator' which will oversee and enforce a statutory duty of care placed on social media companies to take responsibility for the safety of their users and tackle harm caused by content published on their platforms.[68] However, according to the government's response to the Online Harms White Paper

---

and R. Caplan, 'Why Media Companies Insist They're Not Media Companies, Why They're Wrong, and Why It Matters' (2017) 22(5) *First Monday*.

[64] Section 230 does not just apply to the likes of Facebook, Google and Twitter. For example, it also applies to, and protects, news organisations that allow user comments to be published on their sites.

[65] Andrews (n 48) 67. Section 230(c)(2) provides that sites are not liable for their moderation choices.

[66] R. Cellan-Jones, 'Trump threatens to shut down social media companies', *BBC*, 27 May 2020.

[67] For analysis of what the Order means for section 230, see E. Bechtold, 'Donald Trump's attacks on social media threaten the free speech rights of all Americans', *Inforrm*, 2 June 2020; M. Douglas, 'Trump's Twitter tantrum may wreck the internet', *Inforrm*, 29 May 2020.

[68] Department for Digital, Culture, Media & Sport and Home Office, 'Online Harms White Paper: Full government response to the consultation', 15 December 2020. In its response to the consultation, the government confirmed that the legislation (currently the Online Safety Bill) will name Ofcom as the regulator [2] (clause 1 of the Bill). Under the legislation, Ofcom will issue codes of practice which will outline the systems and processes that companies need to adopt to fulfil their duty of care [31]–[32] (clause 29 of the Bill). It will have the power to fine companies up to £18 million, or 10 per cent of annual global turnover, whichever is higher, if they are failing in their duty of care (clause 85(4) of the Bill). Ofcom will also be given the power to block non-compliant services from being accessed in the UK [38] (clause 91 of the Bill). The response also suggests that Ofcom will be empowered via secondary legislation to impose criminal sanctions against individual executives or senior managers at technology firms, for example if they do not respond fully, accurately and in a timely manner to information requests by the regulator [38].

consultation, due to concerns raised by stakeholders 'about how the legislation will impact journalistic content online and the importance of upholding media freedom', content published by a news publisher on its own site will not be in scope of the regulatory framework, and user comments on that content will be exempted.[69] In addition, the government says that to protect media freedom, once the Online Safety Bill is enacted it 'will include robust protections for journalistic content shared on in-scope services'.[70] These statements clearly suggest that the government does distinguish between 'in-scope' technology companies, such as Facebook, TikTok, Instagram and Twitter, and exempted 'news publishers'.[71] In Australia, in the Supreme Court of Victoria case of *Defteros v Google LLC*,[72] Justice Richards found that Google is a publisher because its search engine is 'not a passive tool' as it is 'designed by humans who work for Google to operate in the way it does, and in such a way that identified objectionable content can be removed, by human intervention'.[73]

---

[69] Ibid [22]. Compare this to the Australian case of *Fairfax Media v Voller* [2020] NSWCA 102, in which the New South Wales Court of Appeal held that media companies are not just responsible for the content written by their journalists. According to the judgment they are also 'publishers' of comments made by readers on their social media accounts. The decision means that those who encourage engagement on social media – including media companies, journalists and 'internet famous' people – can be held responsible for things said by random people who 'engage' by commenting on content produced by others. In December 2020, the High Court of Australia granted the defendant permission to appeal.

[70] Ibid [23]. Clause 13 of the Online Safety Bill sets out 'duties to protect content of democratic importance' and clause 14 provides 'duties to protect journalistic content'. However, these duties (which are in addition to the clause 12 general duty applicable to all services to 'have regard to protecting users' right to freedom of expression' and 'protecting users from unwarranted infringements of privacy') only apply to 'Category 1 services'. Pursuant to clause 59(6) these are regulated user-to-user services that will be included in a register to be established by Ofcom. The clause 14 duty is discussed in section 5.3.

[71] In its response the government says that it 'will continue to engage with a range of stakeholders to develop our proposals' [23].

[72] [2020] VSC 219.

[73] Ibid [40]. In the UK the leading case on platforms being publishers is *Tamiz v Google Inc* [2013] 1 WLR 2151. It was held by the Court of Appeal that on the facts Google was not a publisher *prior* to being notified of the existence of defamatory material on its *Blogger* platform unless it knew or ought by the exercise of reasonable care to have known that the publication was likely to be defamatory. However, the Court considered that it could be inferred that, after notification of the presence of the offending material on the blog, Google had made itself responsible for the continued publication by not removing it. This inference of responsibility did not arise until Google had had a 'reasonable time within which to act to remove the defamatory comments'. See [26] and [33]–[35] per Richards LJ.

Policy makers, the judiciary, academics and politicians from around the world are taking notice of the traditional media-like functions that are being carried out by social media companies. This recognition has gone hand in hand with an increasing appetite to make social media platforms more legally accountable for their actions within this arena, as illustrated by the examples above. If social media platforms were classed as media, it would confer on them the benefit of being subject to the enhanced right to media freedom but, of course, as discussed in Chapter 4, this freedom, and the privileged protection it provides to the media, carries with it concomitant responsibilities and obligations that are likely to conflict with the commercial aims of most platforms. Thus, so long as social media companies refuse to concede (publicly at least) that they are effectively operating as media companies, it seems that this is a debate that is destined to go on for some time yet.

4   UNDERMINING THE VIABILITY OF THE PRESS AND REINFORCING THE ARGUMENTS MADE BY THE CPEP

It is clear from the statistics in section 3.1 that the internet and social media have had a profound effect on our news consumption habits. This section will turn to the contention touched upon in Chapter 2: that by turning a considerable proportion of the public away from the press and other forms of traditional media, the internet and social media have undermined the economic viability of the press in particular; and rather than expanding the scope of the public sphere in this context, they have instead contributed to the problems identified by the CPEP, which has led to its further contraction.[74]

One consequence of our move away from the press and other forms of traditional media to online news consumption has been a precipitous decline in print circulation. Between 2008 and 2018 weekday national newspaper sales fell from 11.5 million to 5.8 million copies a day. During the same period, the drop in circulation for Sunday national newspapers was even greater, falling from 11.2 million copies per issue to less than 5 million. In a similar period (2007 to 2017) local and regional newspaper sales decreased from 63.4 million to 31.4 million per week.[75] Unsurprisingly, this decline in newspaper sales correlates with the figures in the previous section relating to the steady fall in people using newspapers to consume news,[76] a trend that, according to *The*

---

[74]   See Chapter 2 section 3.2.2.
[75]   Cairncross (n 3) 25–26; Mediatique (n 2) 43–45; Ofcom (n 3) [4.10].
[76]   See n 45.

66 *Media freedom in the age of citizen journalism*

Cairncross Review, has hit local and regional newspapers particularly hard as they are now only read by one person in ten in the UK.[77]

The drop in sales caused by our increasing preference for online news consumption has affected the newspaper industry in a number of interrelated ways that have adversely impacted upon the press's ability and willingness to engage in high-quality public interest journalism.[78] In turn, this has undermined the functioning of our democracy by narrowing the scope of the public sphere. Some of the ways in which the press has been affected by this change in our news consumption habits were briefly touched upon in Chapter 2 in the context of newspapers operating within the corporate model of ownership. The remainder of this section will dive deeper into the challenges created for the press, the public sphere and democracy by our digital transition.

4.1 Increased Consolidation and Its Impact on Media Plurality and Content Diversity

As we saw in the previous chapter[79] the loss in revenue from falling sales, and the economic pressure that this has put on newspapers, has led to an increase in consolidation within the industry through mergers[80] or the pooling of newsroom resources,[81] which has ultimately resulted in greater ownership concentration and reduced plurality.[82] Thus, although the internet could contribute to widening the scope of the democratic public sphere as, in theory at least, it provides the *means* for a more balanced playing field between small and large

---

[77] Cairncross (n 3) 27.

[78] Ibid 77.

[79] See Chapter 2 section 3.3.2.

[80] In addition to DMGT's purchase of the '*i*' newspaper discussed in Chapter 2 (see sections 2 and 3.2.2) other examples of consolidation activity within the UK press industry include Reach Plc (then Trinity Mirror) taking full control of *Local World* in 2015, and in 2018, the company acquiring the publishing assets of Northern & Shell, including the *Daily Star* and *Daily Express* newspapers. See Ofcom (n 3) [4.15].

[81] For example, since July 2019, *The Times* and *Sunday Times* can share journalistic resources after the Department for Digital, Culture, Media and Sport accepted new undertakings to protect the editorial independence of both titles: DCMS, July 2019, 'Notice of acceptance on the proposed undertakings by News Corp UK and Ireland Ltd (News UK)'. See also Mediatique (n 2) 5; Reuters Institute for the Study of Journalism, Richard Sambrook, 'Global Teamwork: The Rise of Collaboration in Investigative Journalism', 2018, 1.

[82] According to the Media Reform Coalition, 83 per cent of the national newspaper market is taken up by DMGT, News UK and Reach Plc. As discussed in Chapter 2 (section 3.3.2) DMGT's purchase of the '*i*' newspaper means that there are now only six newspaper owners in the UK: Media Reform Coalition, *Who Owns the UK Media?* 12 March 2019.

The internet, social media and citizen journalism   67

media companies and for enabling a greater diversity of voices to be heard through the press and other content creators from whom the public can choose, it does not in any way guarantee this.[83] Rather, in reality it is contributing to the opposite. This is due to the financial pressure that it has placed on the press, as greater consolidation means fewer owners, which in turn contributes to corporate dominance by increasing the reach that those fewer owners have and the opportunity this gives them to advance their own agendas. At the same time it decreases the opportunity for smaller media companies to enter and survive in the market[84] and for alternative and minority voices to be heard. Consequently, in almost direct conflict with his own early predictions as to the potential positive impact of the internet on media plurality and the diversity this would offer,[85] Noam has since stated that the 'fundamental economic characteristics of the internet' suggest that 'when it comes to media pluralism, the internet is not the solution but it is actually becoming the problem'.[86]

4.2   A Reduction in the Number of Journalists Within the Institutional Press and Its Impact on Competition, Quality and Trust

The drop in revenue combined with increased consolidation and cost-cutting measures has led to a significant reduction of journalistic and non-journalistic staff within the UK's institutional press, which in turn has curtailed public interest reporting.[87] Between 2007 and 2019 the number of frontline full-time journalists fell from an estimated 23,000 to 17,000.[88] Indeed, at the time of writing, Reach Plc announced that it was cutting 550 jobs, equating to 12 per cent of its workforce, as a result of a 30 per cent reduction in revenue caused

---

[83]   Baker (n 8) 101.

[84]   J. Curran, 'The Internet of Dreams: Reinterpreting the Internet' in J. Curran, N. Fenton and D. Freedman (eds), *Misunderstanding the Internet* (2nd edn., Routledge, 2016) 5–6; J. Curran, N. Fenton and D. Freedman, 'The Internet We Want' in *Misunderstanding the Internet*, 204; M. Hindman, *The Internet Trap. How the Digital Economy Builds Monopolies and Undermines Democracy* (Princeton University Press, 2018).

[85]   Noam (n 18).

[86]   See transcript of Internet Governance Forum 2012 session on 'Media Pluralism and Freedom of Expression in the Internet Age', http://www.intgovforum.org/cms/transcripts. See also: P.M. Napoli and K. Karppinen, 'Translating Diversity to Internet Governance' (2013) 18(12) *First Monday*.

[87]   Cairncross (n 3) 77.

[88]   Ibid; Mediatique (n 2) 5; Ofcom (n 3) [4.14].

68 *Media freedom in the age of citizen journalism*

by falling sales and decreased advertising income.[89] These job cuts across the industry have had the following knock-on effects.

First, they have acted as a catalyst for more independent journalists. In being forced to leave the corporate institutional press many 'professional' journalists have re-entered the profession in a non-corporate and non-institutional capacity – as independent journalists, often operating exclusively online. Thus, the fact that some of these journalists may well have lost their jobs on the premise that cuts were needed to improve their respective newspaper's financial efficiency and secure its long-term future is ironic as, by doing this, many of the newspapers operating within the corporate ownership model have inadvertently increased their competition, which has contributed to the demise in their fortunes.[90] The reduction in the number of journalists masks the potentially greater problem of 'brain drain' within the profession as, in recent years, newspapers (particularly local and regional titles) have replaced 'senior, experienced reporters with less expensive, young reporters'.[91] Consequently, *The Cairncross Review* found that 'there may be 6,000 fewer journalists, but an even greater loss of experienced journalists'.[92]

Secondly, the reduction in journalists overall, and within that the loss of experienced journalists, has, in different ways, contributed to a decline in the quality of content published by newspapers. As discussed in detail in Chapter 2, the effect of media hyperactivity in the form of 'faster and shallower corporate journalism', including the need for newspapers to provide news 24 hours a day across multiple platforms, combined with fewer journalists, has encouraged churnalism,[93] and can lead to professional values and appropriate source and fact checking to be cast aside,[94] which results in more mistakes,[95] including the inadvertent dissemination of disinformation, misinformation, junk news[96]

---

[89] 'Daily Mirror owner Reach to cut 550 jobs as sales fall', *BBC*, 7 July 2020.

[90] R.L. Weaver, *From Gutenberg to the Internet: Free Speech, Advancing Technology, and the Implications for Democracy* (2nd edn., Carolina Academic Press, 2019) 187–188.

[91] Cairncross (n 3) 77.

[92] Ibid.

[93] N. Fenton, 'Regulation Is Freedom: Phone Hacking, Press Regulation and the Leveson Inquiry – The Story So Far' (2018) 23(3) *Communications Law* 118, 119. See Chapter 2 section 3.2.2.

[94] Ibid.

[95] Weaver (n 90) 202

[96] According to Philip N. Howard, 'junk news' differs from 'fake news' in that rather than simply being fabricated news, junk news is political news and information that is sensational, extremist, conspiratorial or severely biased, or is commentary presented as news. See P.N. Howard, *Lie Machines* (Yale University Press, 2020) 86–87.

The internet, social media and citizen journalism

and false news.[97] Perhaps even more worryingly for the health of the public sphere and the functioning of democracy is that both *The Cairncross Review* and Ofcom have acknowledged that as a result of these job losses and other cost reduction measures newspapers have 'cut back on the breadth and depth of their reporting',[98] with increasing emphasis being placed on publishing stories that can be produced quickly and inexpensively using inexperienced journalists or shared resources, while appealing to the largest possible audiences and attracting the biggest advertising revenues.[99] Unsurprisingly, this has led to a decrease in investigative and other public interest journalism 'that are more important for the democratic process'[100] due to the time, skill and experience that are needed, and the expense that is often incurred, to investigate stories that do always not appeal to mass audiences.[101] All of these factors have combined to undermine the trust placed in the press by the public[102] and media sources.[103] This has turned the public and sources away from the press[104] and towards other news providers, such as citizen journalists,[105] which has fuelled the decline in sales and revenue discussed above.

---

[97] See Chapter 2 section 3.3.2; P. Coe, 'The Good, The Bad and The Ugly of Social Media During the Coronavirus Pandemic' (2020) 25(3) *Communications Law* 119. The dissemination of misinformation, junk news and fake news is discussed in more detail in section 5.3.

[98] Cairncross (n 3) 14–15; Ofcom (n 3) [4.14].

[99] See Chapter 2 section 3.3.2.

[100] Cairncross (n 3) 15.

[101] Ibid 19, 77.

[102] See the discussion on trust in Chapter 2 section 3.3.2.

[103] For example, Edward Snowden disclosed information regarding American surveillance programmes to blogger Glenn Greenwald as he did not trust the *New York Times* to publish the material. For detailed commentary on this case, see P. Coe, 'National Security and the Fourth Estate in a Brave New Social Media World' in L. Scaife (ed), *Social Networks as the New Frontier of Terrorism: #Terror* (Routledge, 2017) 165–192, 175–179. See also M. Ammori, 'The "New" New York Times: Free Speech Lawyering in the Age of Google and Twitter' (2014) 127 *Harvard Law Review* 2259, 2265.

[104] Indeed, during the *Leveson Inquiry*, Alastair Campbell, the former Labour government's chief press secretary, gave evidence that 'people are going elsewhere to find information they can trust', www.levesoninquiry.org.uk/wp-content/uploads/2011/11/Witness-Statement-of-Alastair-Campbell.pdf, 28. From a US perspective this is supported by the findings of the Knight Foundation, which found that, generally, readers are disillusioned with the press and think it is untrustworthy: https://www.knightfoundation.org/reports/indicators-of-news-media-trust.

[105] However, see the discussion in sections 6.2.1 to 6.2.3 for a discussion on the trust and credibility issues affecting citizen journalists.

4.3 Greater Reliance on Online Advertising Which Promotes Low-quality Journalism[106]

In Chapter 2 we saw how the press industry's increasing reliance on commercial and advertising partners was putting pressure on newspapers to prioritise content that appeals to mass audiences, rather than engaging in investigative and other public interest or minority journalism.[107]

This situation has been exacerbated by our transition away from printed newspapers to online news consumption, which has seen the industry's print advertising revenue decline from just over £1.8 billion in 2010 to £607 million in 2019.[108] To the contrary, from 2007 to 2017 online advertising went from 16 per cent to 48 per cent (or £10.6 billion) of total UK advertising spend,[109] and by 2019 it had reached £15.7 billion.[110] For the press, however, this increase in online advertising has not offset the fall in print advertising. By 2017 digital advertising expenditure with newspapers was £487 million, which equated to just 5 per cent of total online advertising spend,[111] a figure that is 'nowhere near comparable to the revenue that publishers had generated from print advertising in the past'.[112]

The majority of advertising revenue is being swallowed up by Google and Facebook, who, because of their control over the advertising supply chain,[113] captured an estimated 78 per cent of all UK online advertising revenues in

---

[106] How platforms such as Facebook and Google distribute news publishers' content, and their role in news aggregation, are discussed in section 5.1.

[107] See section 3.3.2.

[108] Ofcom (n 3) [4.10]. As stated in Chapter 2 section 3.3.2, increased competition from the likes of Gumtree and Craigslist within the classified advertisements market, which was once a staple source of revenue for the press (particularly local and regional newspapers), has contributed to this sharp fall in revenue. Cairncross (n 3) 47, 79.

[109] Cairncross (n 3) 41; Mediatique (n 2) 39–40.

[110] Ofcom (n 25) 52.

[111] Mediatique (n 2) 6.

[112] Cairncross (n 3) 41.

[113] Ibid 62; Competition & Markets Authority, 'Online platforms and digital advertising: Market study final report', 1 July 2020, 65.

2019.[114] This 'superiority' in the online advertising market[115] means that newspapers are competing for an increasingly smaller pot of advertising income. According to *The Cairncross Review*, most 'legacy' newspapers[116] adopted the strategy of prioritising lower-quality 'mass-market' content or 'clickbait' to pursue 'scale' to compensate for these low yields.[117] *Cairncross* heard evidence that the competition for 'scale and reach' has contributed to the sensationalisation of news content, which has led journalists and publishers to favour clickbait and sensationalist headlines in order to generate a higher number of clicks, which in turn makes them more attractive to online advertisers.[118] The *Daily Mirror's* reporting of the COVID-19 pandemic provides an excellent example of this. On 2 April 2020, the newspaper tweeted 'UK's deadliest day set to be Easter Sunday when government fear 50,000 will die'. However, the article headline was actually 'Coronavirus "could kill 50,000" in UK with Easter Sunday "to be deadliest day"'. The article, when read in full, provides more context, and actually undermines the statement made in the tweet and the article's own headline, as it goes on to say that '[a] worst case scenario for Britain would see a coronavirus death toll of 50,000 for the entire pandemic if people ignore the lockdown and social distancing laws, while a so-called best case scenario would be 20,000 deaths' and that '[a]s it stands the UK is not on course [for] a death toll of that [50,000] scale'.[119] This propensity for using clickbait as a way of attracting readers and generating advertising income has been particularly harmful to the provision of local public interest news because local and regional newspapers simply cannot compete with the scale and reach of their national counterparts. Indeed, according to one submission to *Cairncross* from a local journalist, '[the online advertising market] ... forces us into either "clickbait" headlines or content. There will always

---

[114] Ibid 9. The Competition & Markets Authority estimate that of the approximately £14 billion that was spent on digital advertising in the UK in 2019, around 80% was captured by Google and Facebook. See also Ofcom (n 110) 53–54. This is a situation that is replicated in other countries. For instance, in Australia it is estimated that in 2018 for every A\$100 spent by Australian advertisers, A\$49 went to Google and A\$24 to Facebook. 'Facebook and Google news law passed in Australia', *BBC*, 25 February 2021.

[115] Cairncross (n 3) 61–62; Australian Competition and Consumer Commission, Digital Platforms Enquiry Preliminary Report, 10 December 2018, 4–5.

[116] Including *The Guardian*, *The Sun*, the *Independent* and the *Daily Mail*.

[117] Cairncross (n 3) 42. See also Andrews (n 48) 58.

[118] Cairncross (n 3) 42–43.

[119] G. Faulconbridge, 'Coronavirus "could kill 50,000" in UK with Easter Sunday "to be deadliest day"', *The Mirror*, 2 April 2020; Coe (n 97) 119–122.

be more stories about "WAGS" or TV shows because they guarantee clicks. Local council reports do not.'[120]

Despite this reliance on clickbait it does not appear to have guaranteed the long-term financial success of the press.[121] Consequently, newspapers are being driven towards mining valuable user data[122] to compete with the likes of Google and Facebook.[123] However, because of the sophisticated ways that these platforms accumulate, use, manage and protect data,[124] newspapers are 'fighting a losing battle ... on the data front'.[125] Again, this has hit local newspapers particularly hard as their potential to increase advertising revenues in this way is limited by their smaller and less influential audiences, and by not having the financial resources and technological capabilities to collect, utilise and ultimately monetise audience data.[126] The fact that newspapers, and particularly the local and regional press, cannot compete with online platforms within the digital advertising arena, and are therefore likely to see a continued reduction in their advertising revenues, means that their ability to invest in high-quality journalism and minority or alternative content will continue to diminish.[127]

The reliance on digital advertising has not just encouraged newspapers to use clickbait and to pursue lower-quality 'mass-market' journalism. As discussed in detail in Chapter 2, the need for publishers to produce material that appeals to the largest possible audiences, and which is therefore more attractive to advertisers, results in the production and consumption of the same *type* of content.[128] Online news consumption has further compounded the pressures placed on newspapers operating within the corporate ownership model,[129] which has not just contributed to lower-quality journalism, but has also led to less variety, and in particular a reduction in minority and alternative content.[130]

---

[120] Cairncross (n 3) 43. See also Competition & Markets Authority (n 113) 9.

[121] Ibid. A contributing factor in this is the use of ad-blockers: the more popular they become the greater number of clicks publishers will need to generate revenue.

[122] Competition & Markets Authority (n 113) 15–16.

[123] Cairncross (n 3) 45.

[124] Ibid 62–63; Competition & Markets Authority (n 113) 15–16.

[125] Cairncross (n 3) 47, 63. The ACCC's 'News media and digital platforms mandatory bargaining code's' 'minimum standards' will require Google and Facebook to provide information about how and when they make available user data collected through users' interactions with news content. See nn 62, 131, 145, 146 and 196.

[126] Ibid 47.

[127] Competition & Markets Authority (n 113) 9.

[128] See Chapter 2 section 3.3.2.

[129] Ibid.

[130] T.W. Adorno and M. Horkheimer, *Dialectic Enlightenment* (Verso Books, 1997) 124; G. Doyle, *Understanding Media Economics* (Sage Publications, 2002) 74.

4.4 A Vicious Circle for the Public Sphere?

Our shift from print to online news consumption has created a vicious circle. Its contribution to falling print circulation has led to a sharp fall in income, both from newspaper sales and advertising revenue, which has resulted in the implementation of cost-cutting measures across the industry at local, regional and national levels. These measures have included consolidation and cutting large swathes of the journalistic workforce. The former has increased ownership concentration and has reduced the number of alternative and minority voices within the media market, and ultimately the public sphere. The latter has significantly impacted upon the quality of journalism on offer, while inadvertently increasing competition for the institutional press by creating more independent or non-institutional journalists. It has also undermined our trust in the press, turning ever more people away from it and towards online news sources, which in turn contributes to falling sales and the resulting loss of advertising revenues. To attempt to offset this the press has increased its reliance on digital advertising, but because of the dominance of online platforms within this arena, the lean of newspapers towards lower-quality journalism, which was already a symptom of the commercial pressures generated by the corporate ownership model, has been compounded by their being driven to use clickbait to attract larger audiences that will appeal to advertisers, rather than engaging in investigative and other public interest or minority journalism.

The effect of this vicious circle is worrying, not only for the health and prosperity of newspapers and journalism at all levels (although it has been particularly damaging for regional and local publications), but also for the scope of the public sphere and the functioning of democracy. The Competition & Markets Authority (CMA) was particularly concerned with this in its *Online platforms and digital advertising* report, where, within the context of the impact of digital advertising on the press, it noted the 'wider social, political and cultural harm' that is symptomatic of the 'decline of authoritative and reliable news media' and 'the decline of the local press which is often a significant force in sustaining communities'.[131]

---

[131] Competition & Markets Authority (n 113) 9. See nn 62, 125, 145, 146 and 196 for discussion on the ACCC's introduction of a 'News media and digital platforms mandatory bargaining code' to address the bargaining power imbalance between Australian news media businesses and digital platforms, specifically Google and Facebook. At the time of writing the CMA announced the creation of a Digital Markets Unit (to be launched in April 2021), which will be empowered to write and enforce a new code of practice on technology companies which will set out the limits of acceptable behaviour. The code will seek to mediate between platforms and news publishers, for instance, to try to ensure that publishers are able to monetise their content. See A. Hern, 'New UK

74 *Media freedom in the age of citizen journalism*

The next section looks at how the internet and social media have *distorted* the public sphere in other ways, whereas in the final section of this chapter we will consider the *positive* role played by the internet and social media in the democratisation of the public sphere by looking at how citizen journalism has contributed to its robustness.

5 DIGITALLY DISTORTING THE PUBLIC SPHERE?

In the previous section we looked at how our changing news consumption habits have impacted upon the viability of the press and its ability to positively influence the scope of the public sphere. The purpose of this section is to consider how the internet and social media have distorted the public sphere in other interrelated ways, including those that do not necessarily relate directly to the press and citizen journalists, but may inadvertently affect their ability to positively contribute to the public sphere.

5.1 The Online Aggregation and Distribution of Content by Digital Gatekeepers: Editing and Ideology

As discussed in section 3.1, although we are increasingly going to 'multiple sources' for our news this does not tell the full story. It masks a problem for the public sphere because it is often achieved through platforms operating as news aggregators, such as Facebook and Google, and technology companies such as Apple,[132] who effectively filter the news we see by algorithmically pulling together content from multiple news outlets to disseminate via their own platforms (for example, via Facebook's News Feed or Google News, and the new Facebook News function or Google News Showcase). In this sense, these companies are operating as gatekeepers,[133] as although the content that is disseminated through their sites is controlled by algorithms, which also determine how prominently these stories are displayed,[134] the algorithms are programmed by a human 'editor',[135] who is likely to be working towards

---

tech regulator to limit power of Google and Facebook', *The Guardian*, 27 November 2020.

[132] Ofcom (n 3) [4.8]; Ofcom (n 45) 8, 56; Ofcom (n 46) 61.

[133] Koltay (n 7) 82.

[134] Cairncross (n 3) 71; Competition & Markets Authority (n 113) 319.

[135] P. Bernal, *The Internet, Warts and All. Free Speech, Privacy and Truth* (Cambridge University Press, 2018) 71–101; Koltay (n 7) 84–87, 195. This is illustrated by Facebook's new Facebook News function, which was launched in February 2021 and operates alongside its existing News Feed. The platform will pay certain pub-

commercial goals,[136] as opposed to journalistic professional standards.[137] Thus, the process of news distribution by platforms 'is not a neutral or value-neutral activity', rather it is likely to reflect the business and ideological interests of the respective platform.[138] Indeed, Paul Bernal has said that the supposed neutrality of these 'gatekeepers' is a 'myth'.[139] In itself this is not necessarily a problem, however when considering that most users will be unfamiliar with the underlying interests and values of the particular news aggregator they are using, combined with our increasing reliance on them, which means that we are less likely to see content we are not shown,[140] it presents an opportunity for the public sphere to be distorted.

This is animated by the concerns expressed in *The Cairncross Review* as to the control that platforms have over news distribution generally, and the often (seemingly) arbitrary way that they change their algorithms to affect news dissemination and presentation. In respect of the former, *Cairncross* cites a dispute between the German publisher Axel Springer and Google. The publisher told Google News that it could no longer publish snippets of text and images from their publications. Google complied and ran only head-lines of articles. Over the following two weeks, Axel Springer experienced a 40 per cent reduction in website traffic from Google, and an 80 per cent drop in traffic from Google News. Consequently, the publisher agreed to be re-indexed by Google News.[141] *The Cairncross Review's* concern over the use of algorithms[142] is reflected in Greg Piechota's research on how Facebook utilises algorithms. Like the *Review*, Piechota acknowledges the platform's

---

lishers for content that is not already on the site, and 'will prioritise original reporting'. Facebook has outsourced the curation of the function's content to Upday, which will be tasked with surfacing 'reliable' and 'relevant' news to feature. What is classed as 'reliable' and 'relevant', however, will be determined by an 'on-the-day editor'. Facebook News is discussed further below: 'Facebook News will pay UK outlets for content in 2021', *BBC*, 1 December 2020. Similarly, also in February 2021, Google launched Google News Showcase, which has seen it sign licensing agreements with a number of publishers and will mean users can see selected paywalled content – more than they would normally see on the respective publishers' websites without signing up. See C. Tobitt, 'Google begins UK roll-out of news showcase paying publishers for paywalled content', *Press Gazette*, 10 February 2021.

[136] Koltay (n 7) 195.

[137] See the arguments relating to the professional culture of journalists in Chapter 2 section 3.3.2.

[138] Koltay (n 7) 195.

[139] Bernal (n 135) 71–101.

[140] Ibid.

[141] Cairncross (n 3) 69–70. For a similar discussion relating to Facebook see Andrews (n 48) 59.

[142] Cairncross (n 3) 71–72.

opacity when it comes to providing reasons to publishers for changing its algorithms. Additionally, and of arguably greater concern for the public sphere, his research found that Facebook seems to privilege some publishers over others.[143] The CMA has echoed these concerns, stating in its *Online platforms and digital advertising* report that it had heard evidence from several newspapers about unexpected changes to the Google Search and Facebook News Feed algorithms 'that resulted in dramatic reductions in traffic to certain newspapers overnight'[144] and, incidentally, that even a small change to an algorithm by these platforms 'can have very significant consequences for the ongoing viability of a particular publisher'.[145] The CMA's findings are reflected in the ACCC's introduction of a 'News media and digital platforms mandatory bargaining code' discussed above.[146] The code's minimum set of standards for the treatment of news on digital platform services require Google and Facebook to provide advance notice of changes to algorithmic ranking and presentation of news.[147] The reasons behind making algorithmic changes such as these are almost certainly financial. As discussed below, although they do not actually produce any content, the likes of Facebook and Google are competing with newspapers over audience figures and, ultimately, advertising income, while at the same time they are seeking to maximise the revenues they generate from the newspapers themselves for presenting their content through their platforms to their users.[148]

A related issue that comes from news aggregation is that it has enabled platforms such as Facebook and Google to become the 'primary domain of news services', which has given them a 'dominant role in online media distribution markets without actually collecting any news'.[149] Thus, because news aggregation means that platforms profit from the content produced by journalists without any real effort on their part, they have disrupted the press's business

---

[143] G. Piechota, 'The Facebook-Media Relationship: It's Complicated', International News Media Association, 27 September 2016. It seems that that this trend is likely to continue with the platform's launch of its new Facebook News function (discussed below), which will see it paying certain publishers for original content. At the time of writing the Hearst Corporation, the Guardian Media Group, JPI Media and the Midland News Association had all agreed deals with Facebook, with more expected to join. See nn 135 and 150.

[144] Competition & Markets Authority (n 113) 17.

[145] Ibid 319. See n 131 for the CMA's creation of a new Digital Markets Unit.

[146] See nn 62, 125, 131, 146 and 196 .

[147] Ibid; ACCC, Q&As: Draft news media and digital platforms mandatory bargaining code, July 2020, 3.

[148] Koltay (n 7) 196.

[149] Ibid 158; F. Filoux, 'How Facebook and Google Now Dominate Media Distribution', *Monday Note*, 19 October 2014.

model.[150] The recent launch of Facebook News and Google Showcase, which will see Facebook and Google paying certain publishers for original content, may appear to redress this balance by providing some short-term financial relief to the publishers that it partners with.[151] However, in reality it is likely to only further undermine their viability and tighten Facebook's and Google's grip on the market as they are able to pay for original content that will in turn attract more readers and advertising revenue. They will undoubtedly prioritise content from their partner publishers (whom they are paying), which will drive readers and advertising income away from other publishers, placing more pressure on them to agree to similar deals. Moreover, the fact that platforms such as Facebook and Google drive news dissemination puts them in control of audience data, which means that they have access to data sets that are increasingly valuable to advertisers. Consequently, it enables them to exponentially increase their advertising revenues to the detriment of newspapers that do not have the financial and technological resources to keep up.[152] Ultimately, these factors, combined with how platforms are using algorithms to aggregate and distribute news, have directly impeded the ability of newspapers to develop successful business strategies,[153] which, in turn, as we saw in the previous section, has affected their capacity for engaging in journalistic activities that benefit the public sphere.

In addition to achieving their business goals, platforms may also adapt their news feeds in line with their ideology, particularly their social and political objectives.[154] A high-profile example of this is the 2016 story from technology blog, Gizmodo, which reported accusations made by former Facebook employees that conservative topics and sources had been deliberately and systematically suppressed by the platform, with staff being instructed to select topics based on political considerations. Specifically, the report alleged that links to certain conservative websites were not allowed in the platform's now defunct 'Trending Topics' section, despite their being amongst the most frequently shared content on the platform. These allegations directly conflicted with the platform's previous claims that the content of Trending Topics was

---

[150] Koltay (n 7) 74; B. Rossi, 'The Reinvention of Publishing; Media Firms Diversify to Survive', *The Guardian*, 30 January 2017.

[151] See nn 135 and 142.

[152] See the discussion in section 4.3.

[153] Cairncross (n 3) 72.

[154] The impact of the proposed Online Safety Bill in relation to this issue is discussed in section 5.3.

compiled by algorithms and determined solely by user activity rather than with any human intervention.[155]

Undoubtedly this scandal is concerning because although Trending Topics no longer exists, it is conceivable that similar news editing practices might be used by the platform's other services, or outside of the US.[156] Indeed, it reflects a broader trend amongst similar companies, such as Google and Apple, who have also engaged in ideologically based content selection.[157] However, perhaps its greatest significance lies in what it revealed, or at least confirmed, to the world: that the news items that were featured and widely discussed on Facebook – in other words the topics that were 'Trending' at the time – were not being selected and distributed by neutral algorithms, but by human editors, or 'news curators'[158] operating within Facebook's ideological parameters. Section 3.2 discussed the editorial-like activities being carried out by platforms such as Facebook, and how it, and other social media companies, are increasingly performing functions typically associated with the traditional media. Thus, this scandal provides further evidence of a badly kept secret, namely the transition of platforms, such as Facebook and Google, from technology companies to actual news editors akin to the traditional media. In doing so, it demonstrates that although the owners and leaders of these companies may exercise their own free speech, by doing this through their platforms, very often to their own ends,[159] they have the power to significantly distort the democratic public sphere by, for instance, exerting direct political influence

---

[155] Koltay (n 7) 196–197; P. Bump, 'Did Facebook Bury Conservative News? Ex-Staffers Say Yes', *Washington Post* 9 May 2016; M. Nunez, 'Former Facebook Workers: We Routinely Suppressed Conservative News', *Gizmodo*, 9 May 2016.

[156] Koltay (n 7) 196–197.

[157] C. Parshall, 'The Future of Free Speech, Free Press, and Religious Freedom on Facebook, Google, Apple, etc' (2013) *National Religious Broadcasters*. A survey from political scientists at Stanford University found that the technology companies established in Silicon Valley hold liberal, cosmopolitan and globalist political views and support the extension of human rights to the extent that they do not interfere with their own business interests. However, they tend to agree with conservative libertarians in relation to government regulation, labour and employment policies. In respect of Facebook, this political ideological bias is reflected in Zuckerberg's 2017 manifesto, which sets out a political agenda to build a global community above and beyond nation states. See F. Manjoo, 'Silicon Valley's Politics: Liberal, With One Big Exception', *New York Times*, 6 September 2017; M. Zuckerberg, 'Building a Global Community', *Facebook*, 16 February 2017.

[158] S. Thielman, 'Facebook news selection is in the hands of editors not algorithms, documents show', *The Guardian*, 12 May 2016.

[159] Bernal (n 135) 127.

through the manipulation of our news consumption using obscure means and based on opaque ideological principles.[160]

Ideological neutrality is a fundamental requirement of a healthy and functioning democratic public sphere. By surrendering this neutrality to platforms, and by embracing their biases, the public sphere can become distorted. Therefore, the non-neutrality of platforms gains a completely new, and more sinister, quality if the editorial decisions made by platforms that influence our news consumption are value laden and guided by an ideology, or for the purpose of achieving certain social objectives, over and above the open discussion of public affairs or a free and democratic public sphere.[161]

5.2 User Preferences, the Creation of Trends and 'Filter Bubbles'[162]

Users of social media platforms, such as Facebook, consume aggregated news items via its News Feed (or a similar service depending on the platform) which is personalised to the user based upon the aggregation of their news preferences. This means that what users see is 'filtered' by what they have read and 'liked' in the past. When we consume news via the press and other forms of the traditional media it is more likely that we will be exposed to content that we are not necessarily looking for, or that we agree with.[163] (Although, of course, as we saw in Chapter 2, like social media platforms, newspapers in particular are very often driven by the commercial and ideological agendas of their owners.[164]) Therefore, if we only use a particular newspaper to consume news because it accords with our own political or social views we are less likely to be exposed to more diverse and alternative content, albeit it is still more likely to occur than it is via a personalised news feed). To the contrary, the effect of the personalisation of feeds is that the diversity of news that users are exposed to is reduced significantly, and minority or alternative opinions to those held by the user are essentially filtered out of their feed altogether, thereby creating 'difficulties for the visibility of speakers with minority viewpoints'.[165] As Kate Klonick has stated, it is not a priority for social media platforms to ensure

---

[160] Koltay (n 7) 200.

[161] Ibid 199.

[162] Filter bubbles are discussed in more detail in Chapter 5 section 3.2. For a discussion on filter bubbles see Coe (n 51) 415–416; Koltay (n 7) 149–151.

[163] Koltay (n 7) 196.

[164] See Chapter 2 section 3.3.

[165] T. Gibbons, 'Providing a Platform for Speech: Possible Duties and Responsibilities' in A.T. Kenyon and A. Scott (eds), *Positive Free Speech: Rationales, Methods and Implications* (Hart Publishing, 2020) 11–23, 18; C.R. Sunstein, *#Republic Divided Democracy in the Age of Social Media* (Princeton University Press, 2017); Coe (n 51) 415–416.

adequate opportunities for all to participate in the public sphere.[166] Rather, they want to provide a 'comfortable' 'safe space' for as many users as possible, which, although not always compatible with being a robust defender of free speech[167] and contributing positively to the widening of the public sphere, is conducive to increasing user numbers, which ultimately makes them more attractive to advertisers.[168]

To the contrary, opponents of the filter bubble theory argue that our user habits disprove it. The basis of this contention is the large number of online news sources that are available to us, and the fact that no single platform is able to lock its users into an enclave, meaning that technology is, in fact, incapable of hindering democracy as we are able to obtain our news from diverse and independent sources.[169] This is supported by research commissioned by Facebook which found that its News Feed algorithm only suppresses sources that are unlikely to meet the preferences of its users to a minimal extent and, as a result, the service provides users with a significant amount of 'ideologically diverse' news.[170]

Perhaps unsurprisingly, Facebook's research, and its methodology, were subject to substantial criticism, with Facebook being accused of manipulating public opinion to escape its democratic responsibilities.[171] Regardless of the validity of the research, the arguments refuting the filter bubble theory can be attacked on other fronts. First, although in theory we are able to obtain our news from other independent sources, as we saw in the previous section and in section 3.1, in reality we are increasingly accessing these 'multiple sources' through news aggregation services provided by similar types of online platforms. In turn, these companies use comparable business models to achieve their commercial goals and are applying similar ideological principles to their algorithmic programming, or 'editing'. Consequently, they are arguably reinforcing, rather than countering, the filter bubble effect.[172] In section 3.1 we saw that the majority of us now use social media as our main source of

---

[166] K. Klonick, 'The New Governors: The People, Rules and Processes Governing Online Speech' (2018) 131 *Harvard Law Review* 1599, 1665.

[167] Koltay (n 7) 199.

[168] See generally A.E. Waldman, 'Manipulating Trust on Facebook' (2016) 29 *Loyola Consumer Law Review* 175.

[169] W.H. Dutton et al, *Social Shaping of the Politics of Internet Search and Networking: Moving Beyond Filter Bubbles, Echo Chambers and Fake News*, Quello Center Working Paper no. 2944191.

[170] E. Bakshy, S. Messing and A. Adamic, 'Exposure to Ideologically Diverse News and Opinion on Facebook', *Science*, 5 June 2015.

[171] For example, see C. Sandvig, 'The Facebook "Its Not Our Fault" Study', *Social Media Collective*, 7 May 2015.

[172] Koltay (n 7) 150.

news.[173] Thus, it is conceivable that a platform could grow to such a size that any possibility of obtaining diverse information from a variety of independent sources is eliminated.[174] As András Koltay suggests, in this case, although theoretically we may have access to other sources, the length of time we spend on platforms, combined with the detrimental effect that social media has had on the traditional media market,[175] means that our opportunities to engage with other sources will continue to decrease.[176] To an extent, this argument, and the filter bubble theory generally, are already borne out by Ofcom's findings in its 2020 *Online Nation Report* that among people who use social media for news, 41 per cent mostly get their news from social media posts, which includes posts from other users and links to online news stories posted by their contacts or by news outlets that they follow.[177] Indeed, according to Alice Marwick, 'virtually every story is augmented with someone's opinion' and, as a result, we scholars and journalists are only just 'beginning to understand the myriad impacts of social sharing'.[178]

It is clear from what has been discussed above and in the previous section that the personalisation of news feeds can limit the scope of, and distort, the public sphere by suppressing and filtering users' overall picture of news and information on public affairs. Consequently, the process can undermine the philosophical foundations upon which free speech is based[179] as users are unlikely to meet content that contradicts their own personal views and opinions unless they specifically look for them;[180] a situation that is evidenced by Ofcom's *Online Nation Report*.

5.3 Fake News, Junk News, Disinformation and Misinformation

In addition to how the internet and social media have encouraged sensationalised and lower-quality journalism,[181] and have contributed to appropriate

---

[173] Ofcom (n 3) [4.9].

[174] Koltay (n 7) 150.

[175] See section 4.

[176] Koltay (n 7) 150–151.

[177] Ofcom (n 25) 22. See also Ofcom (n 3) [4.9].

[178] A.E. Marwick, 'Why Do People Share Fake News? A Sociotechnical Model of Media Effects' (2018) *Georgetown Law Technology Review* 474.

[179] These are discussed in detail in Chapter 5.

[180] S. Eskens, N. Helberger and J. Moeller, 'Challenged by News Personalisation: Five Perspectives on the Right to Receive Information' (2017) 17(2) *Journal of Media Law* 259, 281.

[181] See sections 4.2 and 4.3.

source and fact checking being, in some instances, cast aside,[182] social media in particular is not always conducive to revealing 'truth',[183] as demonstrated by the role it has played in the dissemination of fake news, junk news,[184] disinformation and misinformation.[185] Although false news has always existed, even before the advent of media, the difference today is that social media provides the ideal technological architecture and environment for it to spread quickly to potentially millions of people,[186] as demonstrated by the amount of false content published during the COVID-19 pandemic.[187] Social media's ability to do this is amplified by the symbiotic relationship that now exists between citizen journalists and social media generally and the traditional media.[188]

---

[182] See section 4.2 and Chapter 2 section 3.2.2. See also L. Levi, 'Social Media and the Press' (2012) 90 *North Carolina Law Review* 1531, 1555–1572.

[183] This issue is discussed further in relation to false news in the context of libertarianism and John Stuart Mill's argument from truth in Chapter 5, section 3.1; P. Coe, 'Redefining "Media" Using a "Media-as-a-constitutional-component" Concept: An Evaluation of the Need for the European Court of Human Rights to Alter Its Understanding of "Media" Within a New Media Landscape' (2017) 37(1) *Legal Studies* 25, 42–44. It has been argued that the internet and social media have, at the very least, weakened a general societal consensus on a commonly accepted truth, as every social group, if not each person, has it or their own 'truth' on the internet. See K. Viner, 'How technology disrupted the truth', *The Guardian*, 12 July 2016.

[184] For the difference between fake and junk news see n 96.

[185] Disinformation has been defined by Philip N. Howard as 'purposefully crafted and strategically placed information that deceives someone into believing a lie or taking action that serves someone else's political interest'. Misinformation is 'contested information that reflects political disagreement and deviation from expert consensus, scientific knowledge, or lived experience'. See Howard (n 96) 14–15.

[186] P. Bernal, 'Fakebook: Why Facebook Makes the Fake News Problem Inevitable' (2018) 69(4) *Northern Ireland Legal Quarterly* 513; L. Levi, 'Real "Fake News" and Fake "Fake News"' (2018) 16 *First Amendment Law Review* 232; A.E. Marwick, 'Why Do People Share Fake News? A Sociotechnical Model of Media Effects' (2018) *Georgetown Law Technology Review* 474. The Competition & Markets Authority has stated that greater competition for Facebook and Google would 'see a decline in the prevalence of so called "fake news"'. See Competition & Markets Authority, 'Online platforms and digital advertising: Market study final report', 1 July 2020, 320. In its 'Online Harms White Paper: Full government response to the consultation' (n 68) the UK government confirmed that once the Online Safety Bill is enacted, for the first time, online misinformation and disinformation that 'could cause significant harm to an individual' will come under the remit of a government regulator (Ofcom) and fall within scope of the duty of care (the response confirms that where 'disinformation is unlikely to cause this type of harm it will not fall in scope of regulation'): [2.80]–[2.88]. Clause 98 of the Online Safety Bill requires Ofcom to establish a committee to provide it with advice on the prevention and handling of misinformation and disinformation. See below for further discussion on this.

[187] Coe (n 97) 119–122.

[188] See sections 1 and 3.1.

Information published on social media platforms is often used as a source of news by the traditional media.[189] Thus, in the same way that citizen journalists may regurgitate false or misleading information obtained from traditional media outlets or other bloggers, the traditional media may do the same in respect of information obtained from social media.[190] The fact that 'trusted' mainstream media have published it serves to justify and support the information, creating a self-fulfilling cycle.[191]

The way in which news is presented on social media also inadvertently helps to spread false news. For instance, Facebook's News Feed presents all information in the same way, regardless of whether it is a piece of investigative journalism relating to something of important public interest or whether it is celebrity gossip, or simply false information.[192] This means that high-quality journalistic content often gets lots amongst a mass of lower-quality or even false content.[193] According to research conducted by the Oxford Internet Institute, during the 2016 US presidential election 'there was a one-to-one ratio of junk news to professional news shared by voters over Twitter', meaning that 'for each link to a story produced by a professional news organisation, there was another link to content that was extremist, sensationalist or conspiratorial or to other forms of junk news'.[194] Likewise, *Cairncross* found that 'fake news … is particularly hard to spot on social media, where news content is often presented alongside content that has no relationship to news at all'[195] and that consequently 'online consumption makes it harder for public-interest news to reach audiences, but easier for fake news to do so'.[196] The ACCC has also recognised the issue of journalistic content getting lost amongst false news on online platforms. In addition to imposing minimum standards relating to how Google and Facebook algorithmically aggregate and present news, and how they use user data obtained from their news services, the ACCC's 'News media and digital platforms mandatory bargaining code' requires Facebook and Google to 'appropriately [recognise] original news content' distributed via their services.[197] Similarly, as explained in section 3.2, in its response to the Online Harms White Paper consultation the UK government has said that to

---

[189] Frankel (n 38).

[190] Coe (n 51) 417.

[191] Coe (n 97) 119–122.

[192] See n 29 for how much content is currently shared on social media platforms.

[193] Andrews (n 48) 64.

[194] Howard (n 96) 12. For further discussion on false news in the context of libertarianism and truth discovery, and in relation to elections and the Cambridge Analytica scandal, see Chapter 5 section 3.1.

[195] Cairncross (n 3) 33.

[196] Ibid.

[197] See nn 62, 125, 131, 145 and 146; ACCC (n 147) 3.

protect media freedom, once the Online Safety Bill is enacted it 'will include robust protections for journalistic content shared on in-scope services' (such as Facebook and other social media platforms).[198] When the government's response to the White Paper was published, how it intended journalistic content to be separated from non-journalistic content, and how that would be determined, and who would be responsible for making that determination was, at that stage, an unanswered question.[199] However, the 'duties to protect journalistic content' set out at clause 14 of the Online Safety Bill is clear that it is the Category 1 platforms themselves that will be required to 'operate a service using systems and processes' to identify content that is journalistic. For the reasons discussed in sections 3.2 and 5.1, allowing the platforms to take on these responsibilities could seriously impact upon the scope on the democratic public sphere.

A further free speech concern that has emerged from the government's publication of its response to the consultation is that once enacted the Online Safety Bill will place online false news under the remit of Ofcom.[200] Additionally, the legislation will give the regulator the power to fine companies up to £18 million, or 10 per cent of annual global turnover, whichever is higher, if they are failing in their duty of care.[201] The fact that false news that *could* cause significant harm is now within the scope of the duty, the potentially huge fines that could be levied on platforms failing to discharge that duty, and the fact that the core free speech duties pursuant to clauses 12, 13 and 14 of the Bill only require platforms to 'have regard to' or 'take into account' free speech rights or the protection of democratic or journalistic content means that platforms may simply pay lip service to these 'softer' duties when a conflict arises with the legislation's harder and manifold 'safety duties'. This is likely to lead to platforms adopting an over-cautious approach to monitoring content by removing

---

[198] 'Online Harms White Paper: Full government response to the consultation' (n 68) [23]. See n 70.

[199] Ibid. According to the response, the government engaged with a range of stakeholders to develop its proposals, which were eventually included in the Bill.

[200] Ibid.

> Disinformation and misinformation that could cause significant harm to an individual will be within scope of the duty of care. Some types of disinformation and misinformation are likely to be proposed in secondary legislation as categories of priority harm that companies must address in their terms and conditions. In addition to the requirements under the duty of care, the legislation will introduce further provisions to address the evolving threat of disinformation and misinformation. [34].

Clause 98 of the Online Safety Bill requires Ofcom to establish a committee to provide it with advice on the prevention and handling of misinformation and disinformation.

[201] Ibid [38] and clause 85(4) of the Online Safety Bill.

anything that *may* be false news and that would therefore bring them within the scope of the duty and regulatory sanctions. Such an approach is likely to lead to legitimate content being removed because it is incorrectly thought to be false. More cynically, it may give platforms an opportunity, or excuse, to remove content that does not conform with their ideological values on the basis that it *could* be false.[202] Of course, this free speech concern and the argument that I have made here does not just apply to false information; it is applicable to *any* content that falls within the scope of the legislation.

Our transition to consuming news online, often through social media and other news aggregators, has created the perfect environment for the generation and spread of false news.[203] The impact that this type of content has on the media, public sphere and democracy generally is summed up by Philip Howard:

> While the internet has certainly opened new avenues for civic participation in political processes – inspiring hopes of democratic reinvigoration ... divisive social media [false news] campaigns have heightened ethnic tension, revived nationalistic tensions, intensified political conflict, and even resulted in political crisis – while simultaneously weakening public trust in journalism, democratic institutions and electoral outcomes.[204]

6   DIGITALLY DEMOCRATISING THE PUBLIC SPHERE?

In the previous two sections we have seen how the internet and social media have *negatively* affected the public sphere by undermining the viability of the press and by distorting it in other interrelated ways. The purpose of this final section is to set out their *positive* impact on the democratisation of the public sphere, specifically through their facilitation of citizen journalism.

6.1   The 'Modern Public Sphere'

Although not everybody using the internet and social media does so to communicate with each other, or to generate, publish or consume news, they have unquestionably caused a tectonic shift in the media ecology by altering our perceptions of the limits of communication, and reception of information. It is no longer the case that the transmission and reception of information is con-

---

[202] See section 5.1.
[203] See generally Howard (n 96).
[204] Ibid 18.

strained by boundaries such as location, time, space or culture,[205] or dictated by a media organisation's ownership, political bias or commercial partners. The internet and social media provide the means for individuals and journalists to overcome institutional, financial and technological barriers to communication, and to news production and consumption[206] as, in theory at least, they allow anybody with a computer or mobile device and a WiFi signal to communicate with potentially millions of people instantaneously, from anywhere in the world, at any time of the day.[207] This has shifted the media paradigm as the ability to generate news content and to communicate it to mass audiences is no longer monopolised by the traditional media.[208] Accordingly, in echoing Justice Stevens' prophetic judgment in *Reno v American Civil Liberties Union*[209] that online chatrooms would enable anyone to become a 'town crier with a voice that resonates further than it would from a soap box',[210] Justice Kennedy, in *Packingham v North Carolina*,[211] said the internet is the 'modern public square',[212] as 'one of the most important places to exchange views is cyberspace, particularly social media'.[213] The importance of this digital

---

[205] See generally F. Webster, *Theories of the Information Society* (4th edn., Routledge, 2014) 20; I. Barron and R. Curnow, *The Future with Microelectronics: Forecasting the Effects of Information Technology* (Pinter, 1979); G. Mulgan, *Communication and Control: Networks and the New Economies of Communication* (Polity, 1991); S. Coleman and J. Blumler, *The Internet and Democratic Citizenship – Theory, Practice and Policy* (Cambridge University Press, 2009) 27–28.

[206] Koltay (n 7) 74.

[207] See generally B. Wellman, 'Physical Space and Cyberspace: The Rise of Personalized Networking' (2001) 25(2) *International Journal of Urban and Regional Research* 227–251; P. Coe, 'The Social Media Paradox: An Intersection with Freedom of Expression and the Criminal Law' (2015) 24(1) *Information & Communications Technology Law* 16, 21–22.

[208] The United Nations Human Rights Committee has stated that the internet and social media have created 'a global network for exchanging ideas and opinions that does not necessarily rely on the traditional mass media intermediaries'. Human Rights Committee, General Comment 34: Freedoms of opinion and expression, CCPR/C/GC/34 (GC 34) 12 September 2011, [15]; see also, M. O'Flaherty, 'Freedom of Expression: Article 19 of the ICCPR and Human Rights Committee's General Comment No 34' (2012) 12 *Human Rights Law Review* 627.

[209] (1997) 521 US 844.

[210] Ibid 870.

[211] 582 U.S. 2017.

[212] Ibid 1737.

[213] The Court cited its decision in *Reno v American Civil Liberties Union* 521 U.S. 844, 870 (1997) in which it found that cyberspace offers a 'relatively unlimited, low-cost capacity for communication of all kinds'. *Reno* is discussed further in relation to anonymous and pseudonymous speech in Chapter 7.

The internet, social media and citizen journalism 87

democratisation process has been emphasised by the Council of Europe's Committee of Ministers:

> Citizens' communication and interaction in online environments and their participation in activities that involve matters of public interest can bring positive, real-life, social change. When freedom of expression and the right to receive and impart information and freedom of assembly are not upheld online, their protection offline is likely to be undermined and democracy and the rule of law can also be compromised.[214]

6.2 To What Extent Does Citizen Journalism Contribute to the Digital Public Sphere?

As discussed in Chapter 1, and below, undoubtedly citizen journalism has contributed to the robustness of the democratic public sphere by, to an extent at least, increasing our capacity to participate in public discourse, either as speakers or recipients of diverse content.[215] In doing so, it complements and, at times, replaces the traditional media as the public's watchdog,[216] and makes them more accountable,[217] by publishing the type of content that members of the mainstream media operating within a corporate structure may be reluctant to provide. And, as previously discussed, citizen journalists also act as a valuable, and often more reliable, source for the mainstream media.[218]

The internet and social media have acted as a stimulus for the movement, with citizen journalists today tending to publish through social media platforms. This is because they provide the ideal environment for citizen journalism to flourish by facilitating three factors that have enabled citizen journalism to make an important contribution to the robustness of the public sphere. However, because of the challenges created for the public sphere by the internet and social media, as we shall see, these factors are not without limitations that prevent citizen journalists from playing what could be an even greater role in the public sphere's democratisation. As will be discussed below, although it is not a panacea, some of these limitations can be overcome, or at

---

[214] Council of Europe's Committee of Ministers, 'Declaration by the Committee of Ministers on the protection of freedom of expression and information and freedom of assembly and association with regard to Internet domain names and name strings' [3] (Adopted by the Committee of Ministers on 21 September 2011).

[215] Baker (n 8) 110.

[216] Weaver (n 90) 187.

[217] Baker (n 8) 111; D. Gillmore, *We the Media: Grassroots Journalism by the People, For the People* (O'Reilly Media, 2004) 61–64.

[218] See section 3.1. Although, to the contrary see the discussions in sections 5.3 and 6.2.1.

least alleviated, by the application of the media-as-a-constitutional-component concept and the framework that it provides. Thus, the purpose here is not to introduce the concept, as this happens in Chapter 5; rather it is to provide sign-posting to later chapters that consider how adopting it could remedy some of the limitations, thereby widening the scope of the public sphere.

6.2.1 Technological and financial barriers

The internet and social media remove some of the financial and technological barriers to the news-gathering process, and content generation and dissemination. For instance, gathering information can be done using online research and interviews can be conducted remotely using services such as Zoom and Microsoft Teams, amongst others. Blog and website hosting services such as WordPress enable journalists to build and operate blogs inexpensively[219] and social media provides the platforms for instant and free mass dissemination. This results in reduced production and distribution costs, thereby removing, or at the very least lowering, a significant barrier to entry into the media market. In turn, this widens the public sphere by creating more opportunities for a wider variety of commercial, non-commercial and voluntary non-commodified actors, such as citizen journalists, to create and offer a greater diversity of content to the public.[220]

Despite the liberating effects of technology on journalism, there are issues associated with its use that can devalue digital journalistic activity. First, the transition that journalists have made from a physical 'beat' – that is physically gathering information for stories by, for example, speaking to contacts and interviewing witnesses in person – to digital 'beats', in which they rely on online sources to provide information for stories, can make audiences more sceptical as to the quality and accuracy of the journalism,[221] particularly as people become more aware of the proliferation of false news and how it is often inadvertently spread by journalists.[222] Secondly, technology such as Facebook Live has enabled anybody to capture content as it happens. As discussed above, platforms such as Facebook present all information in the same way regardless of its quality and value to public discourse.[223] The effect

---

[219] WordPress allows users to build a site for free. The company recommends the 'Premium' plan for freelancers, which costs £7 per month. See https://wordpress.com/.

[220] Baker (n 8) 101–102.

[221] For example, see David Simon's Testimony to the US Senate Committee on Commerce, Science, and Transportation Subcommittee on Communications, Technology, and the Internet Hearing on the Future of Journalism, *Real Clear Politics*, 9 May 2009.

[222] See Chapter 2 section 3.3.2 and section 5.3.

[223] See section 5.3.

of this service is to add further content to an already crowded space, thereby, in some instances, making it harder for users to distinguish between information that is merely captured and actual journalistic activity that has benefited from the contextualisation that a journalist can provide from their experience.[224] Thirdly, this technology is largely controlled by the new breed of digital gatekeepers discussed in the previous section, meaning that the problems associated with how they operate are likely to affect any journalist relying on technology to both gather and disseminate content. This creates a filtering cycle, in that the information they rely on may come from a filtered source and, in turn, the content they produce may also, ultimately, be filtered. This cycle is particularly concerning for public discourse and the scope of the public sphere when considering the symbiotic relationship between social media, citizen journalists and the mainstream media discussed above[225] as the information that is being regurgitated is subject to increasing filtration.

6.2.2 The structure and 'norms' of the institutional media

Social media and the internet have enabled journalists to operate outside of the institutional media, its structure and some of its 'norms'. This means that a citizen journalist can engage in journalistic activity without journalistic education and training and without being employed by a member of the institutional media,[226] thereby 'opening up' journalism to a wider variety of actors. However, this can raise concerns over quality and professionalism, particularly because citizen journalism tends to circumvent the editorial process,[227] and because it exists, like all journalism, within a voluntary regulatory environment that has not been designed with citizen journalists in mind, meaning that they have tended not to engage with it.[228] Indeed, although there are many excellent blogs publishing high-quality content, there is also low-quality and irresponsible citizen journalism.[229] Consequently, it also attracts credibility issues in that it may prevent citizen journalists who are not recognised as

---

[224] See n 147 for the ACCC's response to this issue.

[225] See sections 5.1 and 5.3.

[226] Coe (n 183) 40; Y. Kim and W. Lowrey, 'Who are Citizen Journalists in the Social Media Environment?' *Digital Journalism*, 3.2, 298–314, 299.

[227] D. Simmons, *The emergence of Citizen Journalism* (self-published, 2014) ch. 1.

[228] Lord Justice Leveson, *An Inquiry into the Culture, Practices and Ethics of the Press: Report*, HC 780, November 2012, 171, [4.20]; Coe (n 51) 430–431; L. Taylor, 'Balancing the Right to a Private Life and Freedom of Expression: Is Pre-publication Notification the Way Forward?' (2017) 9(1) *Journal of Media Law* 72, 89. A regulatory scheme that is better suited to the needs of citizen journalists and would therefore encourage them to become members of such a scheme is introduced in the following section and advanced in Chapter 9.

[229] D. Simmons, *The Emergence of Citizen Journalism* (self-published, 2014) ch. 1.

media from gaining access to, for example, press conferences, court documents or legal proceedings and other events that are open to the 'media' but are otherwise closed to the public.

Although journalists publish anonymously in traditional media outlets,[230] as we will see in Chapter 7, being able to operate outside of the institutional media presents *more* opportunities for journalists to publish anonymously and pseudonymously. The ability to publish in this way can contribute to the widening of the public sphere by allowing actors to participate in the exchange of important information and ideas who would perhaps not do so if they were unable to publish anonymously or under a pseudonym.[231] To the contrary, more opportunities to publish anonymously and pseudonymously can encourage more dissemination of harmful speech, including false news,[232] which can undermine the credibility of anonymous and pseudonymous journalists and the trust we have in them.

6.2.3   Liberating Journalists from the Dominant Proprietor and Corporate Ownership Models and the Concentration Problem

Finally, the internet and social media can, to an extent, liberate journalists, particularly citizen journalists, from some of the constraints and pressures imposed on the press by the dominant proprietor and corporate ownership models that were considered in Chapter 2. For example, journalists operating outside of an institutional structure are far less likely to be subject to an owner's social, political or business agenda, or the commercial pressures generated by working for a newspaper operating within the corporate model that is having to attract and appease advertisers. This freedom presents 'watchdog' advantages to citizen journalists over the institutional press, which benefits the public sphere[233] as they can provide the investigative, minority and alternative journalism that traditional journalists operating within a corporate structure are increasingly being prevented from delivering.[234] This means they are more likely to be able to offer a greater diversity of perspectives on the issues of the day.

As explained in section 6.2.1, however, the problems associated with how gatekeepers such as Facebook and Google operate undoubtedly translate to

---

[230] For example, it is the policy of *The Economist* to publish its articles anonymously. See Chapter 7; P. Coe, 'Anonymity and Pseudonymity: Free Speech's Problem Children' (2018) 22(2) *Media & Arts Law Review* 173, 190.

[231] For example, see the discussion in Chapter 7 on the anonymous blog *Night Jack*, which was the 2009 recipient of the Orwell Prize for citizen journalism.

[232] See the discussion in Chapter 7.

[233] Weaver (n 90) 187.

[234] Gillmore (n 217); Baker (n 8) 111, 120.

The internet, social media and citizen journalism

the activities of citizen journalists, which means that they are not entirely free of corporate control, albeit it is less tangible and in an 'indirect' context as opposed to it coming directly from a journalist's employer. Although there are now a huge number of citizen journalists providing a wide variety of content, a combination of the credibility and trust issues discussed in sections 6.2.1 and 6.2.2 and the market forces generated by the dominance of the big online platforms has created a concentration problem. In 2007 Baker's research found that 'even though there are apparently millions of self-publishing bloggers, concentration of audience attention is extreme' and that the 'audience for blogs is not only concentrated, it seems to be much more concentrated ... than is the audience for newspapers'.[235] More recent research from both James Curran and Matthew Hindman (conducted independently of each other) provides support for Baker's findings and suggests that this situation has not improved, at least not dramatically. They found that blogs do not usually attract large audiences,[236] and the most powerful and popular websites tend to be the online versions of the dominant offline news outlets that have exploited their economic power to dominate the online markets.[237] Thus, despite the ubiquity of citizen journalists we are still going to the same sources for news, as borne out by the statistics in section 3.1.

6.3 How Can the Media-as-a-constitutional-component Concept Remedy Some of These Limitations?

The concept is introduced in Chapter 5 and developed in Chapter 6. Its basic premise is that adherence to certain norms of public discourse (in other words the *type* of speech conveyed by the actor) and standards of professional behaviour (for example, acting ethically and in good faith, and publishing content that is based on appropriate research to verify the provenance of it and its sources), rather than the education, training or employment of the actor, should define who is a 'journalist'. In turn, this functional rather than institutional approach to defining media determines who should benefit from the enhanced right to media freedom and be subject to its concomitant duties and responsibilities. Thus, the concept's norms of discourse and standards of behaviour create a threshold.[238] Actors operating within this are classed as 'media' and are therefore entitled to the benefits that come with being defined

---

[235] Baker (n 8) 107–110.

[236] Curran (n 84) 23–25; M. Hindman, *The Myth of Digital Democracy* (Princeton University Press, 2009).

[237] Curran (n 84) 23; A.T. Kenyon, 'Assuming Free Speech' (2014) 77 *Modern Law Review* 379, 403.

[238] See Chapters 5 and 6.

as such, whilst those operating outside of it are not afforded the same status, and the protection that comes with it, albeit, of course, they are still subject to the general right to freedom of expression pursuant to Article 10 of the European Convention on Human Rights (ECHR).[239] In addition to providing a conceptual framework that (i) improves the credibility of anonymous and pseudonymous speech through its harmonisation of speaker and audience interests;[240] (ii) helps to maintain fair trials, while allowing citizen journalists to access court documents and legal proceedings; and (iii) better promotes and protects media freedom in the context of the law of defamation,[241] these norms and standards also provide the conceptual rationale that underpins the regulatory scheme advanced in Chapter 9. Membership of the scheme comes with incentives (and sanctions) that encourage conformity with the values that underpin it. These include, amongst others, the awarding of a kitemark to demonstrate a commitment by the member to responsible journalism and, consequently, access to a wide range of 'arenas' that are typically open to the news media, but not the public.[242]

The concept widens the public sphere by providing a framework for more actors to be recognised as media and therefore to benefit from the enhanced right to media freedom. However, as this carries with it responsibilities, the concept's underlying values that must be adhered to for the actor to be recognised as media, and the regulatory scheme that they underpin, provide an objective way for an audience to assess a citizen journalist and their content, regardless of whether they are or are not publishing anonymously or under a pseudonym. For instance, if they engage with the regulatory scheme, the audience will know that these actors are, in principle at least, committed to responsible journalism. Thus, as acknowledged in section 6.2, although the concept is unable to remedy all the limitations attached to each of the factors discussed (for instance, it cannot prevent gatekeepers from filtering news content, or remove ideological biases, or stop the distortive effect of filter bubbles, nor can it force citizen journalists to join the regulatory scheme), what it does do is provide a philosophical and normative framework which can at the very least alleviate the limitations relating to credibility and trust, thereby reducing the concentration of blogs that are used, and improving media plurality more generally.

---

[239] See Chapters 4 and 5.
[240] See Chapter 7.
[241] See Chapter 8.
[242] See Chapter 9.

7   CONCLUSION

Although it is clear that some of the early predictions for the transformative effect of the internet and social media on the democratisation of the public sphere have turned out to be pipe dreams rather than prophecies, they have undoubtedly caused huge changes to the media ecology. As a result of our transition from print to online news consumption, and the commercial pressures that this has generated, much of the traditional institutional press is in a perilous position and is unable, or unwilling, to contribute to the public sphere in a way that conforms with its public watchdog role. The way in which social media platforms operate add to this problem, by *distorting* the public sphere in other interrelated ways that can inadvertently impact upon the ability of all types of journalists to positively contribute to the public sphere.

Far from just negatively impacting upon the scope of the public sphere, the internet and social media have also brought many positive changes, not least their facilitation of citizen journalism. Citizen journalists contribute to public discourse and the democratisation of the public sphere by providing a diversity of, very often, high-quality content, thereby stepping into the watchdog shoes of the traditional media, and by being a reliable source of information for the mainstream media. As Dan Gillmor has said: 'The rise of the citizen journalist will help us listen. The ability of anyone to make the news will give new voice to people who've felt voiceless – and whose words we need to hear.'[243] However, their ability to make an even greater contribution to the public sphere is often limited by their status, and their credibility and the trust that is placed in them by audiences, which has resulted in increased concentration. These are limitations that can, at the very least, be remedied by the media-as-a-constitutional-component concept.

---

[243]   Gillmor (n 217) xviii.

PART II

Theoretical considerations

4. Unpacking media freedom as a distinct legal concept

1   INTRODUCTION

In Chapter 3 we saw how the internet and social media have altered the media ecology, and how citizen journalists in particular are making positive contributions to the democratisation of the public sphere. Consequently, in a world where citizen journalists can fulfil, and very often are fulfilling, a vital constitutional function by reporting on matters of public interest, being able to identify who is and who is not media is critical to the effective operation of the enhanced right to media freedom. Chapter 5 will introduce the key to address this problem: a functional definition of the media, founded upon a media-as-a-constitutional-component concept that effectively delineates media from non-media actors. Before that however, this chapter will lay the foundations for the chapters that follow in this Part, and in Part III. Section 2 will distinguish media freedom from freedom of expression, and will establish that the former provides enhanced protection, over and above the right to freedom of expression, for actors operating as part of the media. In doing this, it compares the jurisprudence of the ECtHR with US scholarship and jurisprudence from the US Supreme Court. As discussed in section 2, and developed in section 5.1, the dominant view in the US is based upon the press-as-technology model, which rejects the notion that the media has any constitutional privileges in excess of other speakers. This comparison with the position of the Strasbourg Court forms the foundation for section 5.1, which discredits the model as a method for distinguishing media from non-media actors in the current media environment. Section 3 will analyse the concept of media freedom. In doing so it will, first, explain its role and why the right is conceptually important to media actors. Secondly, it sets out what the right means in reality to its beneficiaries in respect of the protection it affords media speech and the media institutionally. This is categorised as defensive and positive rights. Section 4 provides the rationale for why there is a need to distinguish media from non-media entities. This leads into section 5, which argues that the growth of citizen journalism means that the ability to reach mass audiences is no longer reserved to the traditional media. This blurring of

96   *Media freedom in the age of citizen journalism*

the lines between our perceptions of the traditional institutional media, citizen journalists and casual social media users has created doctrinal uncertainty as to how the courts should determine the beneficiaries of media freedom. Thus, it identifies the shortfalls of the traditional methods adopted by the courts and commentators for distinguishing between media and non-media actors (including the press-as-technology model), and therefore who/what is subject to media freedom.

2   MEDIA FREEDOM AS A DISTINCT RIGHT TO FREEDOM OF EXPRESSION

Freedom of the media is mentioned specifically in a variety of international treaties and domestic laws. For example, pursuant to Article 11(2) of the Charter of the Fundamental Rights of the European Union (CFREU),[1] 'freedom and pluralism of the media shall be respected'.[2] Similarly, in the US, the First Amendment states that '[c]ongress shall make no law ... abridging the freedom of speech, or of the press ...'.[3] Within the context of the ECHR, freedom of expression is protected by Article 10(1), and qualified by Article 10(2):

> (1)   Everyone has the right to freedom of expression. This right shall include freedom to hold opinions and to receive and impart information and ideas without interference by public authority and regardless of frontiers. This Article shall not prevent States from requiring the licensing of broadcasting, television or cinema enterprises.
>
> (2)   The exercise of these freedoms, since it carries with it duties and responsibilities, may be subject to such formalities, conditions, restrictions or penalties

---

[1]   The Charter was initially solemnly proclaimed at the Nice European Council on 7 December 2000. At that time, it did not have any binding legal effect. However, on 1 December 2009, with the entry into force of the Treaty of Lisbon, the Charter became legally binding on the European Union institutions and on national governments: http://ec.europa.eu/justice/fundamental-rights/charter/index_en.htm.

[2]   See also Article 5(1)2 of the German Basic Law, which provides a separate provision for the specific protection of media expression, thus creating a clear distinction from free expression guarantees for private individuals ('[f]reedom of the press and freedom of reporting by means of broadcasts and films shall be guaranteed'); Article 21(2) of the Italian Constitution; Article 25(1) of the Belgian Constitution; the media clauses in Article 17 of the Swiss Constitution; the Swedish Constitution Freedom of the Press Act; and the Law of July 29 1881 on the Freedom of Press (French Press Freedom Law). See generally J. Oster, 'Theory and Doctrine of 'Media Freedom' as a Legal Concept' (2013) 5(1) *Journal of Media Law* 57–78, 59; E. Barendt, *Freedom of Speech* (2nd edn., Oxford University Press, 2005) 417–419.

[3]   However, despite a specific free press clause, the US position is very different, and is discussed below.

Unpacking media freedom as a distinct legal concept   97

as are prescribed by law and are necessary in a democratic society, in the interests of national security, territorial integrity or public safety, for the prevention of disorder or crime, for the protection of health or morals, for the protection of the reputation or rights of others, for preventing the disclosure of information received in confidence, or for maintaining the authority and impartiality of the judiciary.

Article 10(1) does not specifically provide for protection of media freedom[4] in distinction to that of private individuals and non-media institutions. Rather, in interpreting Article 10, the ECtHR has attached great importance to the role of the media[5] and, in doing so, as illustrated by the cases discussed below,[6] has afforded it preferential treatment. Thus, the media's contribution to democracy and democratic self-governance,[7] and its 'role of public watchdog',[8] have been clearly established by the jurisprudence of the Court. Indeed, it recognises a duty on the media to convey information and ideas on political issues and public interest,[9] and the right of the public to receive this information.[10]

The special position of the media in relation to freedom of expression explains why the jurisprudence of the ECtHR interprets Article 10(1) to contain privileged protection of the media, even in the absence of express provisions to that effect. Indeed, according to Eric Barendt, media freedom is 'an institutional right' and a 'constitutional value which should influence the whole of the law' because 'the media foster free speech, in particular

---

[4]   This also applies to Article 19 of the United Nations International Covenant on Civil and Political Rights and Article 13 of the American Convention on Human Rights, both of which are discussed in more detail in section 3.

[5]   For example, see *Bladet Tromsø and Stensaas v Norway* (2000) 29 EHRR 125, [59]; *Bergens Tidende v Norway* (2001) 31 EHRR 16, [48]; *Busuioc v Moldova* (2006) 42 EHRR 14, [64]–[65]; *Jersild v Denmark* (1995) 19 EHRR 1; *Janowski v Poland (No 1)* (2000) 29 EHRR 705, [32].

[6]   *Busuioc v Moldova* (2006) 42 EHRR 14, [64]–[65]; *Wojtas-Kaleta v Poland* [2009] App. no. 20436/02; *Vejdeland and others v Sweden* [2012] ECHR 242.

[7]   For example, see *Perna v Italy* (2004) 39 EHRR 28.

[8]   *The Observer and The Guardian v United Kingdom* (1991) 14 EHRR 153, [59]; *Goodwin v United Kingdom* (1996) 22 EHRR 123, [39]; *Thorgeir Thorgeirson v Iceland* (1992) 14 EHRR 843, [63]; *Bladet Tromsø and Stensaas v Norway* (2000) 29 EHRR 125, [62].

[9]   *Thorgeir Thorgeirson v Iceland* (1992) 14 EHRR 843, [63]; *Lingens v Austria* (1986) 8 EHRR 103, [26]; *Oberschlick v Austria (No 1)* (1991) 19 EHRR 389, [58]; *Castells v Spain* (1992) 14 EHRR 445, [43]; *Jersild v Denmark* (1995) 19 EHRR 1, [31].

[10]   *Sunday Times v United Kingdom* (1979) 2 EHRR 245, [65]; *Fressoz and Roire v France* (2001) 31 EHRR 2, [51]; *Bergens Tidende v Norway* (2001) 31 EHRR 16, [52].

98   *Media freedom in the age of citizen journalism*

by providing fora for vigorous and uninhibited debate'.[11] Media freedom is, therefore, 'special' because a journalist or media company is 'governed by a different set of factors concerning the scope and intensity of protection when preparing, editing or issuing a publication, compared to freedom of expression afforded to private individuals or non-media entities'.[12] Thus, the fact that a statement can be classed as media expression, as opposed to expression by a private individual or non-media institution, adds to the burden of justifying its restrictions.[13] The following three cases serve to illustrate the special treatment of media freedom.

Busuioc v Moldova[14] concerned a civil servant who had been ordered to pay damages by the domestic court for publishing an article that alleged favouritism amongst civil servants. The respondent cited the ECtHR's judgment in *Janowski v Poland (No. 1)*,[15] which stated: 'civil servants must enjoy public confidence in conditions free of undue perturbation if they are to be successful in performing their tasks and it may therefore prove necessary to protect them from offensive and abusive verbal attacks when on duty.'[16] However, the Strasbourg Court distinguished the present case from *Janowski* on the basis that in that case it was held that the applicant, 'although a journalist by profession, [had] clearly acted as a private individual on this occasion'[17] and thus did not engage media freedom, whereas, to the contrary, Busuioc's article was written in his capacity as a journalist, bringing it within the ambit of the right. Consequently, the Court held that the Moldovan authorities were subject to a more restrictive margin of appreciation when deciding whether there was a 'pressing social need' to interfere with Busuioc's right to free speech.[18]

The applicant in *Wojtas-Kaleta v Poland*[19] was a journalist employed by a public television company. She complained that the quality of public television programmes was undermined by competition from private broadcasters and that support for classical music was insufficient. As a result, her employer disciplined her. The ECtHR, 'having regard to the role played by journalists in society and to their responsibilities to contribute to and encourage public debate',[20] determined that the obligation of discretion and constraint under

---

[11]   E. Barendt, 'Press and Broadcasting Freedom: Does Anyone Have Any Rights to Free Speech?' (1991) 44 *Current Legal Problems* 63, 66–67.

[12]   Oster (n 2) 59.

[13]   Ibid.

[14]   [2004] App. no. 61513/00.

[15]   [1999] App. no. 25716/94.

[16]   Ibid [33].

[17]   Ibid [32].

[18]   [2004] App. no. 61513/00, [64] and [65].

[19]   [2009] App. no. 20436/02.

[20]   Ibid [46].

general employment law 'cannot be said to apply with equal force to journalists, given that it is in the nature of their functions to impart information and ideas'.[21]

In *Vejdeland and others v Sweden*[22] the applicants, who were not associated with the media, had been convicted for distributing homophobic leaflets in a secondary school. The ECtHR unanimously held that there was no violation of Article 10, while in a concurring opinion, Judge Zupančič observed that '[i]f exactly the same words and phrases were to be used in public newspapers … they would probably not be considered a matter for criminal prosecution and condemnation'.[23] Thus, the special protection afforded to media expression permits the use of wide discretion as to the methods and techniques adopted to report on matters and how that material is subsequently presented.[24] It allows the media to have recourse to exaggeration and even provocation,[25] including the use of strong terminology or polemic formulations.[26] Additionally, as discussed in more detail at section 3.2.2, the ECtHR has held that this protection extends beyond the dissemination of the journalist's or media organisation's own opinions, to encapsulate those expressed by third parties in the context of, for example, interviews.[27]

The ambit of media freedom is not just limited to stronger protection for media speech; instead, it extends to rights that are not, in any way, available pursuant to freedom of expression guarantees. Consequently, as stated above,[28] and discussed in greater detail in section 3.3, media freedom and freedom of expression differ in relation to the intensity of the protection and in respect of the scope of the protected action. This position equates to institutional protection of the media that, sequentially, guarantees rights that are not exclusively concerned with expression, but also relate to the media vis-à-vis its newsgathering or editorial activities, or even to the existence of an independent media.[29]

---

[21]   Ibid.

[22]   [2012] ECHR 242.

[23]   [2012] ECHR 242, 20, [12].

[24]   *Jersild v Denmark* (1995) 19 EHRR 1, [31]; *Bladet Tromsø and Stensaas v Norway* (2000) 29 EHRR 125, [63]; *Bergens Tidende v Norway* (2001) 31 EHRR 16, [57].

[25]   *Prager and Oberschlick v Austria* (1995) 21 EHRR 1, [38]; *Thoma v Luxembourg* (2003) 36 EHRR 21, [45]–[46]; R. Clayton QC and H. Tomlinson QC, *Privacy and Freedom of Expression* (2nd edn., Oxford University Press, 2010) 271, [15.254].

[26]   *Thorgeir Thorgeirson v Iceland* (1992) 14 EHRR 843, [67]; *Oberschlick v Austria (No 2)* (1998) 25 EHRR 357, [33]; Oster (n 2) 59.

[27]   *Jersild v Denmark* (1995) 19 EHRR 1.

[28]   Oster (n 2) 59.

[29]   Ibid 60. See section 3.3.

This institutional protection afforded to media entities by the right to media freedom can be categorised as being both defensive, in that it protects the media against interference by the state, and positive, as it entitles the media to state protection.[30] This categorisation is animated by reference to a non-exhaustive list of ECtHR jurisprudence.[31] For instance, in relation to the defensive category, in *Halis Dogan and others v Turkey*, the Court held that media freedom includes the protection of the newspaper distribution infrastructure.[32] The case of *Gsell v Switzerland*[33] involved restrictions on road access to the World Economic Forum in Davos, consequently the Court recognised the existence of protection against state measures that could impinge upon the exercise of the journalist's profession. It has also been held that journalists cannot be made to give evidence concerning confidential information or sources, even if they have been obtained illegally.[34] They are also exempt from certain data protection and copyright provisions.[35] With regard to the positive category, states are required to protect the media through the safeguarding of media pluralism[36] and to protect journalists from acts of violence in the course of their work,[37] and from undue influence by financially powerful groups[38] or the government.[39]

In contrast to ECtHR jurisprudence, the position in the US is markedly different.[40] Commentators such as Justice Potter Stewart, Melvin Nimmer,

---

[30] Ibid. The institutional protection of the media, and these defensive and positive rights, are discussed in more detail in section 3.3.

[31] Ibid 60–61.

[32] *Halis Dogan and others v Turkey* [2006] App. no. 50693/99 (ECtHR 10 January 2006), [24].

[33] [2009] App. no. 12675/05, [49].

[34] *Goodwin v United Kingdom* (1996) 22 EHRR 123, [39]; *Radio Twist A.S. v Slovakia* [2006] ECHR 1129, [62]; *Sanoma Uitgevers BV v Netherlands* [2010] ECHR 1273, [50].

[35] For example, see Article 85 of the General Data Protection Regulation and paragraph 26, Part 5 of Schedule 2 to the Data Protection Act 2018. See Chapter 6 section 3.1.3 for a discussion of the 'journalistic exemption'. See also Article 9 Data Protection Directive 95/46/EC, OJ L281/31; Article 5(3)(c) Copyright Directive 2001/29/EC, OJ L167/19.

[36] *Informationsverein Lentia and others v Austria* [1993] ECHR 57, [32]–[34]; *TV Vest & Rogaland Pensjonistparti v Norway* [2008] ECHR 1687, [78].

[37] *Ozgur Gundem v Turkey* [2000] ECHR 104, [38ff].

[38] Article 21(4)(2) EC Merger Regulation 139/2004, OJ L24/1; Part 5 Chapter 2 Communications Act 2003 ch. 21.

[39] *Manole v Moldova* [2009] ECHR 1292, [109]; *Centro Europa 7 Srl and Di Stefano v Italy* App. no. 38433/09 (ECtHR 7 June 2012), [133].

[40] The US view is worthy of consideration at this juncture because of its wealth of press freedom scholarship, and because it provides useful parallels with the ECtHR position that animates the debate on how the media is defined and how the courts can

Randall Bezanson, Floyd Abrams, Vincent Blasi and Sonja West,[41] and dissenting Supreme Court judgments,[42] have argued that the specific free press clause 'or of the press' in the First Amendment to the US Constitution creates a similar distinction to that provided by the CFREU and the jurisprudence of the ECtHR. Yet, despite the force of this claim, it has been opposed by commentators such as Eugene Volokh,[43] and resisted by the Supreme Court.[44] Consequently, the dominant view in the US is based on the press-as-technology model. This model, which is discussed in greater detail at section 5,[45] has roots in English common law,[46] and is founded on the premise that media freedom should not be subject to privileges or duties over and above freedom of expression.[47] According to Volokh, freedom of the press is technological. It

---

determine who or what should benefit from media freedom. This is discussed in more detail in section 5.

[41] P. Stewart, 'Or of the Press' (1975) 26 *Hastings Law Journal* 631, 633; M.B. Nimmer, 'Is Freedom of the Press a Redundancy: What Does it Add to Freedom of Speech?' (1974–1975) 26 *Hastings Law Journal* 639; R.P. Bezanson, 'The New Free Press Guarantee' (1977) 63 *Virginia Law Review* 731, 733; F. Abrams, 'The Press Is Different: Reflections on Justice Stewart and the Autonomous Press' (1979) 7 *Hofstra Law Review* 563, 585; V. Blasi, 'The Checking Value in First Amendment Theory' (1977) *American Bar Foundation Research Journal* 521; S.R. West, 'Awakening the Press Clause' (2011) 58 *UCLA Law Review* 1025, 1032. See also C.E. Baker, *Human Liberty and Freedom of Speech* (Oxford University Press, 1989) chs. 10–11; R.P. Bezanson, 'Whither Freedom of the Press?' (2012) 97 *Iowa Law Review* 1259; T.B. Dyk, 'Newsgathering, Press Access, and the First Amendment' (1992) 44 *Stanford Law Review* 927, 931–932; P. Horwitz, 'Universities as First Amendment Institutions: Some Easy Answers and Hard Questions' (2007) 54 *UCLA Law Review*, 1497, 1505.

[42] See the dissenting judgments of Stevens J in *Citizens United v FEC* 130 S Ct 876, 951 n 57 (2010); Powell J in *Saxbe v Wash Post Company* 417 US 843, 863 (1974); and Douglas J in *Branzburg v Hayes* 408 US 665, 721 (1972).

[43] E. Volokh, 'Freedom for the Press as an Industry, or the Press as a Technology? From the Framing to Today' (2012) 160 *University of Pennsylvania Law Review* 459. See n 51.

[44] For example, see the majority decision in *Citizens United v FEC* 130 S Ct, 905 (2010); see also Volokh (n 43) 506–510 for a summary of other Supreme Court cases that have held the same.

[45] It is argued here that the press-as-technology model is no longer an appropriate method for distinguishing media from non-media entities.

[46] *R v Shipley (Dean of Saint Asaph's Case)* (1784) 21 How. St. Tr. 847 (KB); *R v Rowan* (1794) 22 How. St. Tr. 1033 (KB); *R v Burdett* (1820) 106 Eng. Rep. 873 (KB) 887; 4 B. & Ald. 95, 132.

[47] For example, see D.L. Lange, 'The Speech and Press Clauses' (1975) 23 *UCLA Law Review* 77; W.W. van Alstyne, 'The Hazards to the Press of Claiming a "Preferred Position"' (1977) 28 *Hastings Law Journal* 761, 768–769; A. Lewis, 'A Preferred Position for Journalism' (1978–9) 7 *Hofstra Law Review* 595; C.E. Baker, 'Press Performance, Human Rights, and Private Power as a Threat' (2011) 5 *Law & Ethics of Human Rights* 219, 230; Volokh (n 43) 538–539.

102 *Media freedom in the age of citizen journalism*

is, therefore, available to all forms of communication classed as technologies, which covers everything.[48] In Volokh's assessment, freedom of the press does not just protect the press industry but secures the right of everyone to use communications technology.[49] Therefore, the ambit of the model extends not only to the institutional press and other forms of traditional media and citizen journalists, but also, for example, to casual users of social media.[50]

This originalist interpretation is prevalent in US jurisprudence and scholarship, both historically and currently.[51] Despite the Supreme Court recognising that the press operates 'as a powerful antidote to any abuses of power by government officials',[52] it continues to reject the argument that the institutional press has any constitutional privilege in excess of other speakers.[53] Thus, the majority in *Citizens United v FEC*,[54] echoing previous judgments of Brennan J,[55] agreed that the First Amendment protects 'speech'[56] as opposed to the

---

[48] Bezanson, 'Whither Freedom of the Press?' (n 41).

[49] Volokh (n 43) 462–463.

[50] The press-as-technology model has been given other labels, including 'the equivalence model', which is based on the premise that courts, in a number of jurisdictions, seem to recognise that free speech claims of the media are indistinguishable from speakers generally (see H. Fenwick and G. Phillipson, *Media Freedom under the Human Rights Act* (Oxford University Press, 2006) 20–25) and the 'neutrality doctrine', which stems from the notion that the state is under an obligation to be neutral, in relation to the mass media and speakers generally, in granting free speech rights (see Lewis (n 47) 599–605) compare with M.J. Rooney, 'Freedom of the Press: An Emerging Privilege' (1983) 67 *Marquette Law Review* 34, 52–56).

[51] *Republica v Oswald* 1 Dall. 319, 325 (Pa. 1788); *Commonwealth v Freeman*, HERALD OF FREEDOM (Boston) Mar. 18, 1791, at 5 (Mass. 1791); *In re Fries*. 9 F. Cas. 826, 839 (Justice Iredell, Circuit Judge, C.C.D. Pa. 1799) (no. 5126); *Runkle v Meyer* 3 Yeates 518, 519 (Pa. 1803). For commentary, see Volokh (n 43); Lange (n 47) 88–99; Lewis (n 47) 600; A. Lewis, 'The Right to Scrutinize Government: Toward a First Amendment Theory of Accountability' (1980) 34 *University of Miami Law Review* 793, 806; R.D. Sack, 'Reflections on the Wrong Question: Special Constitutional Privilege for the Institutional Press' (1979) 7 *Hofstra Law Review* 629, 633; D.A. Anderson, 'The Origins of the Press Clause' (1982–3) 30 *UCLA Law Review* 455.

[52] *Mills v Alabama* 384 US 214, 219 (1966); see also *Estes v Texas* 381 US 532, 539 (1965).

[53] *Citizens United v FEC* 130 S Ct 876, 905 (2010); *Associated Press v United States* 326 US 1, 7 (1945); *Branzburg v Hayes* 408 US 665, 704 (1972); *Pell v Procunier* 417 US 817, 834 (1974); *Saxbe v Washington Post Company* 417 US 843, 848–849 (1974); *In re Grand Jury Subpoena, Miller* 397 F 3d 964 (DC Cir 2005) *cert denied* 125 S Ct 2977 (2005).

[54] 130 S Ct 876 (2010).

[55] For example, see *Dun & Bradstreet, Inc. v Greenmoss Builders, Inc.* 472 US 749, 781 (1985).

[56] *Citizens United v FEC* 130 S Ct 876, 905 (2010) (Scalia J concurring).

source of that expression, whether that emanates from a professional journalist or a casual Twitter user. However, the press-as-technology model is not immune from criticism and opposing views, from both US Supreme Court judges and legal scholars.[57] This is discussed in more detail in section 5, where it is argued that it lacks merit in the modern media environment.[58]

This section has established, within an ECHR context at least, the distinction between the freedom of expression right afforded to private individuals compared with that of non-media institutions, pursuant to media freedom: if the expression emanates from a media entity it will be subject to the privileged protection set out above; to the contrary, if the expression comes from a non-media entity, it will, nonetheless, be subject to general freedom of expression protection. Furthermore, only journalists and media organisations can take advantage of the freedom bestowed upon the media as an institution, for example with regard to newsgathering activities.[59]

3 UNPACKING MEDIA FREEDOM

In the previous section I argued that, within the context of ECtHR jurisprudence at least, media freedom is a concept distinct from that of freedom of expression. This means that a media actor, whether that be a person or an organisation, is subject not only to the right to freedom of expression, but also to enhanced protection under the right to media freedom when they issue a publication, as compared to non-media actors who benefit exclusively from the right to freedom of expression. The purpose of this section is to analyse the contents of media freedom. It will begin by explaining why it is important. This will be followed by an assessment of the contents of media freedom for media entities. In particular, it will consider how the protection afforded to media actors by the right is bifurcated, in that it first protects media speech and secondly provides defensive and positive institutional protection of the

---

[57] For example, see generally *Bartnicki v Vopper* 532 US 514 (2001); *Minneapolis Star & Tribune Company v Minneapolis Commissioner of Revenue* 460 US 575, 592–593 (1983); *Gertz v Robert Welch Inc* 418 US 323 (1974); see the dissenting judgments in *Citizens United v FEC* 130 S Ct 876 (2010) (in particular Stevens J at 951 n. 57); Powell J's dissenting judgment in *Saxbe v Washington Post Company* 417 US 843, 863 (1974); Douglas J's dissenting judgment in *Branzburg v Hayes* 408 US 665, 721 (1972); Stewart (n 41) 634; Dyk (n 41) 931–932; Horwitz (n 41) 1505; West (n 41) 1027–1029. See also Bezanson's rejoinder to Volokh's article: Bezanson, 'Whither Freedom of the Press?' (n 41).

[58] In addition to the press-as-technology model, section 5 also considers the merits of the mass audience approach and the 'professionalised' publisher approach for determining the beneficiaries of media freedom.

[59] Oster (n 2) 61–62.

104 *Media freedom in the age of citizen journalism*

media. Thus, pursuant to speech protection, it will consider: what the freedom to hold opinions (section 3.2.1) and impart information and ideas (section 3.2.2) means; and the extent of editorial freedom (section 3.2.2.1). In respect of the institutional protection of the media, it will discuss three defensive rights against state action, namely media independence (section 3.3.1), protection of media research and investigation (section 3.3.2) and protection of media sources (section 3.3.3); and the media's positive rights entitling it to state action in various circumstances (section 3.3.4). The concomitant duties and responsibilities placed on media actors by virtue of the privileges bestowed upon them pursuant to the right to media freedom are touched upon in Chapter 5[60] and discussed in detail in Chapter 6.

3.1 The Importance and the Role of Media Freedom

Media freedom is inextricably linked to the notion that the media's primary function is to act as a 'public watchdog'[61] in that it operates as the general public's 'eyes and ears' by investigating and reporting abuses of power.[62] Thus, the importance attached to media freedom is not only justified by the individual liberty of the publisher, but also because the media plays a critical role in facilitating public discourse within democratic societies.[63] Accordingly, Jan Oster states that '[i]deal public discourse means that all relevant questions, issues and contributions are brought up and processed in debates on the basis of the best available information and arguments'.[64] This is not controversial. However, Oster goes on to argue: 'The mass media is regularly, and on a grand scale, concerned with contributions to such public debates. The expression of opinion and the dissemination of information by the institutional mass media

---

[60]   See section 4.2.2.

[61]   *Observer and Guardian v United Kingdom* (1992) 14 EHRR 153, [59].

[62]   *Attorney-General v Guardian Newspapers Ltd (No. 2)* [1990] 1 AC 109, 183 per Sir John Donaldson MR; see also Barendt (n 2) 418; D. Weiss, 'Journalism and Theories of the Press' in S. Littlejohn and K. Foss (eds), *Encyclopedia of Communication Theory. Volume 2* (Sage, 2009) 574–579, 577.

[63]   P. Garry, 'The First Amendment and Freedom of the Press: A Revised Approach to the Marketplace of Ideas Concept' (1989) 72 *Marquette Law Review* 187, 199. This view has been articulated by ECtHR jurisprudence emanating from a number of cases: *Axel Springer AG v Germany (No. 1)* [2012] App. no. 39954/08, [79]; *Von Hannover v Germany (No. 2)* [2012] App. nos. 40660/08 and 60641/08, [102]; *Sunday Times v United Kingdom (No. 1)* [1979] App. no. 6538/74, [65]; *Bladet Tromsø and Stensaas v Norway* [1999] App. no. 21980/93, [62]; *Times Newspapers Ltd v United Kingdom (Nos. 1 and 2)* [2009] App. nos. 3002/03 and 23676/03, [40].

[64]   J. Oster, *Media Freedom as a Fundamental Right* (Cambridge University Press, 2015) 29.

Unpacking media freedom as a distinct legal concept 105

are, in their sheer quantity and influence, distinct from speech of private individuals.'[65]

The claim I make throughout this book is that although the institutional press and mass media generally can be concerned with 'contributions to such public debates', as established in Chapter 2, this is not always the case. Indeed, it was argued in that chapter that the traditional institutional press's focus (and the focus of the traditional media generally) has shifted from its role as the public watchdog to exploiting commercial opportunities.[66] Pursuant to the media-as-a-constitutional-component concept and its definition of media, both of which are introduced in the following chapter, the training and employment of the actor is irrelevant. Rather, it is the dissemination of speech of constitutional value, which in turn enables democratic self-governance[67] and adherence to standards of professional behaviour deriving from the social responsibility theory, that are critical to distinguishing media from non-media actors and, therefore, the beneficiaries of media freedom. The concept renders the right to media freedom applicable to any actor fulfilling this role, whether that be a 'traditional professional' journalist or citizen journalist. Thus, by adopting a functional approach to defining media, the concept dictates that media freedom is no longer reserved to the institutional mass media.

So, what role does media freedom play in enabling media actors to facilitate public discourse by fulfilling this constitutional function? As observed by Martin Rooney, in order for the media to achieve this it must be guaranteed 'effective means to gather and disseminate news'.[68] In theory at least, the media requires privileged protection, or minimal restriction, to encourage the publication and dissemination of more information,[69] which in turn means that as many views and ideas as possible are represented.[70]

---

[65] Ibid.

[66] See Chapter 2 section 3.3.2.

[67] This is also discussed in detail in the following chapter along with the other philosophical foundations for free speech.

[68] Rooney (n 50) 58.

[69] J.S. Nestler, 'The Underprivileged Profession: The Case for Supreme Court Recognition of the Journalist's Privilege' (2005) 154 *University of Pennsylvania Law Review* 201, 211; Oster (n 64) 31.

[70] From the US Supreme Court see *Dennis v United States* (1951) 341 US 494, 584 (1951); see also J.S. Alonzo, 'Restoring the Ideal Marketplace: How Recognizing Bloggers as Journalists Can Save the Press' (2006) 9 *Legislation and Public Policy* 751, 762. Although this statement is, in essence, correct, it is my contention that media freedom should not come without qualification in respect of both the rationale and values that underpin it, and the regulation that enforces its concomitant obligations and responsibilities. Thus, Chapter 5 considers in detail the appropriateness of libertarian theory as a normative paradigm for free speech and, in particular, its philosophical foundations, including the argument from truth and marketplace of ideas.

In essence, the ability of societies to effectively democratically self-govern is largely dependent on media actors facilitating the process by virtue of their freedom to operate in the ways discussed in sections 3.2 and 3.3. This view is articulated by jurisprudence from a number of jurisdictions. For instance, according to the ECtHR the right to media freedom 'affords the public one of the best means of discovering and forming an opinion of the ideas and attitudes of political leaders. It is incumbent on the [media] to impart information and ideas on political issues and other subjects of public interest.'[71] The Inter-American Court of Human Rights (IACHR), which adjudicates on the American Convention on Human Rights (ACHR), says that the media acts as a catalyst for the 'social dimension' of free speech in a democratic society, which makes the media's ability to gather diverse information and opinions fundamental to the operation of democracy.[72] For this reason, in the IACHR's view, the media, through its publications and broadcasts, provides 'one of the most important manifestations of freedom of expression and information'.[73] Therefore, it is essential, says the IACHR, that the media 'should enjoy the necessary protection and independence to exercise their functions comprehensively, because it is they who keep society informed, and this is an indispensable requirement to enable society to enjoy full freedom'.[74] In respect of the International Covenant for Civil and Political Rights (ICCPR) the United Nations Human Rights Committee (HRC) has also examined the role played by a free media in the democratic process. In *Bodrožić v Serbia and Montenegro*[75] the Committee acknowledged that 'in circumstances of public debate in a democratic society, especially in the media, concerning figures in the political domain, the value placed by the Covenant upon uninhibited expression is particularly high'.[76] This is because, through the media, citizens gain wider access to information and have the opportunity to disseminate information and opinions about 'the activities of elected bodies and their members'.[77]

---

[71] *Centro Europa 7 Srl and Di Stefano v Italy* [2012] App. no. 38433/09, [131]; *Lingens v Austria* [1986] App. no. 9815/82, [41]–[42]; *Sürek v Turkey (No. 1)* [1999] App. no. 26682/95, [59]; *Thoma v Luxembourg* [2001] App. no. 38432/97, [45].

[72] *Fontevecchia and D'Amico v Argentina* [2011] Case 12.524, [44]; *Ivcher-Bronstein v Peru* [2001] Case 11.762, [149]; *Herrera-Ulloa v Costa Rica* [2004] Case 12.367, [117].

[73] Advisory Opinion OC-5/85, [71].

[74] *Ivcher-Bronstein v Peru* [2001] Case 11.762, [150]; *Herrera-Ulloa v Costa Rica* [2004] Case 12.367, [119].

[75] [2005] Communication no. 1180/2003.

[76] Ibid [7.2].

[77] *Gauthier v Canada* [1999] Communication no. 633/95, [13.4].

Unpacking media freedom as a distinct legal concept 107

Thus, rather than being an inherent right, pursuant to, for instance, ECtHR jurisprudence, media freedom is, in fact, an instrumental one.[78] Consequently, as Oster explains, media freedom protects the media 'for fulfilling a beneficial function for society in general, that is, informing the public about matters of general concern ... media freedom is more than merely freedom of expression for journalists: affording particular protection to the media is based on a consequentialist and functional understanding of media activity.'[79] As stated above, and as will become apparent in the following sections, the protection provided by media freedom is bifurcated. Not only does it protect media speech, as in publications or broadcasts, but it also affords the media defensive and positive institutional protection from state interference. Section 3.2 will deal with how media freedom protects media speech, followed by section 3.3, which considers the scope of the institutional protection afforded by the right to media entities.

3.2   Media Freedom's Protection of Media 'Speech'

Media freedom includes, and can be sub-categorised[80] into, the freedom to (i) hold opinions and (ii) receive and impart information and ideas without interference by public authorities and regardless of frontiers. This right (and its sub-categories) is enshrined within Article 10(1) ECHR, along with other international Conventions and legal instruments, including the ICCPR[81] and the ACHR.[82]

At this juncture it is worth noting that Articles 19(1) and 13(1) of the ICCPR and ACHR respectively protect all forms of expression, and their means of conveyance. Pursuant to ECtHR jurisprudence Article 10(1) ECHR protects the substance of ideas and information, the form in which they are conveyed and the method of dissemination,[83] which can encompass any medium, such as books, newspapers, television, radio and social media.[84] The enhanced right to media freedom takes this protection a step further as it also includes

---

[78]   Barendt (n 2) 422; Oster (n 64) 33. However, compare the US position discussed in section 5.1 in respect of the press-as-technology model.

[79]   Oster (n 64) 33.

[80]   Ibid 69.

[81]   See Article 19(1) and (2).

[82]   See Article 13(1). Rather than 'hold opinion' this Article protects the right to 'freedom of thought'.

[83]   For example, see *Autronic AG v Switzerland* [1990] App. no. 12726/87, [47]; *Jersild v Denmark* [1994] App. no. 15890/89, [31]; *De Haes and Gijsels v Belgium* [1997] App. no. 19983/92, [48]; *Murphy v Ireland* [2003] App. no. 44179/98, [61]; *Radio France and others v France* [2004] App. no. 53984/00, [39].

[84]   Oster (n 64) 77.

108   *Media freedom in the age of citizen journalism*

the right to decide upon the method and technique of reporting, and the way in which the material is presented.[85] Therefore, the right to media freedom consists of a positive freedom: the right to gather and to publish information in a particular way. However, it also includes a negative freedom: not to have to publish certain information. This would include, for instance, the freedom not to have to publish articles that benefit the owner of the media outlet, or before information provided by sources has been properly verified. Thus, this negative aspect of the right manifests in editorial freedom as to what to publish.[86] The following sections will set out what the sub-categories mean for actors operating as media.

3.2.1   The freedom to hold opinions

As a constituent element of the right to freedom of expression the freedom to hold opinions without interference acts as a precondition to the right of individuals to freely express themselves.[87] In respect of media freedom, HRC jurisprudence relating to the ICCPR tells us that this means that a media actor may freely have an opinion that they may change, or not have an opinion at all. Regardless, this must not be subject to any interference or punishment.[88] The various international Conventions and instruments within which freedom of expression is enshrined, including Article 10(1) ECHR, Article 19(1) ICCPR and Article 13(1) ACHR, protect all types of opinions, including those of a political, scientific, historic, moral or religious nature.[89] However, there are some subtle differences between them. Article 19(1) ICCPR provides an absolute right to hold opinions (as does Article 9(1) ECHR in respect of freedom of thought), whereas Article 10(2) ECHR and Article 13(2) ACHR qualify the right within the respective Conventions. Notwithstanding this, in line with Article 9(1) ECHR and Article 19(1) ICCPR, unlike free speech, which acts as an external manifestation, or forum externum, of one's opinions and thoughts, the freedom to hold an opinion and the freedom of thought are part of an individual's forum internum and, consequently, should be unrestricted.

---

[85]   For example, see *Jersild v Denmark* [1994] App. no. 15890/89, [31]; *De Haes and Gijsels v Belguim* [1997] App. no. 19983/92, [48]; *Bergens Tidende and others v Norway* [2000] App. no. 26132/95, [57]; *Radio France and others v France* [2004] App. no. 53984/00, [39].

[86]   This is discussed in more detail at section 3.2.2.1.

[87]   Oster (n 64) 70.

[88]   For example, see *Mpaka-Nsusu v Zaire* [1986] Communication no. 157/1983, [10]; *Primo Jose Essono Mika Miha v Equatorial Guinea* [1994] Communication no. 414/1990, [6.8]; *Faurisson v France* [1996] Communication no. 550/93; *Kang v Republic of Korea* [2003] Communication no. 878/1999, [7.2]; General Comment no. 34, [9].

[89]   General Comment no. 34, [9].

Unpacking media freedom as a distinct legal concept 109

Thus, measures that coercively manipulate opinions should be unjustifiable in all circumstances.[90]

3.2.2 The freedom to impart information and ideas

The importance of the media's role in imparting information and ideas has been consistently reiterated in ECtHR jurisprudence, according to which '[f]reedom of the press ... affords the public one of the best means of discovering and forming an opinion of the ideas and attitudes of political leaders and on matters of general interest'.[91] So, what does the right to impart information and ideas actually mean and include for the media?

The ECtHR's famous passage from its judgment in *Handyside v United Kingdom*[92] serves as a starting point. It tells us that the right to freedom of expression, and by extension media freedom, is applicable not only to information or ideas 'that are favourably received or regarded as inoffensive or as a matter of indifference, but also to those that offend, shock or disturb the State or any sector of the population. Such are the demands of that pluralism, tolerance and broadmindedness without which there is no "democratic society".'[93] Similarly, the US Supreme Court in *Cohen v California* stated that 'one man's vulgarity is another's lyric'.[94] The critical question for lawyers, therefore, is whether restriction of particular expression is justified in the specific circumstances, bearing in mind any conflicting rights and interests that are engaged.[95]

The freedom to impart information and ideas is not simply confined to the publishing media actor. It also applies to statements made by, for instance, interviewees and other third parties. According to the ECtHR in *Selistö v Finland*[96] and *Axel Springer AG v Germany (No. 2)*[97] this aspect of the right to media freedom is critical to the media's ability to perform its function as

---

[90] Oster (n 64) 70–71.

[91] *Lingens v Austria* [1986] App. no. 9815/82, [42]. This has been reiterated in a number of cases, including *Oberschlick v Austria (No. 1)* [1991] App. no. 11662/85, [58]; *Thoma v Luxembourg* [2001] App. no. 38432/97, [45]; *Scharsach and News Verlagsgesellchaft mbH v Austria* [2003] App. no. 39394/98, [30]; *Cumpănă and Mazăre v Romania* [2004] App. no. 33348/96, [93].

[92] [1976] App. no. 5493/72.

[93] Ibid [49]; see also *Sunday Times v United Kingdom (No. 1)* [1979] App. no. 6538/74, [65]; *Lingens v Austria* [1986] App. no. 9815/82, [41]; *Axel Springer AG v Germany (No. 1)* [2012] App. no. 39954/08, [78]; *Thorgeir Thorgeirson v Iceland* [1992] App. no. 13778/88, [63].

[94] 403 US 15, 25 (1971).

[95] Oster (n 64) 73.

[96] [2004] App. no. 56767/00.

[97] [2014] App. no. 48311/10.

110   *Media freedom in the age of citizen journalism*

the public watchdog.[98] Therefore, and in line with the Strasbourg Court's judgment in *Handyside*, media actors are not required to distance themselves from statements made by interviewees that may be provocative or offensive to others, or damage their reputation.[99] Consequently, media actors should only be punished for disseminating information emanating from their sources in very limited circumstances, such as when their publication is providing a platform for inciting violence and hatred in situations of conflict and tension.[100] According to both the ECtHR and the IACHR this is because punishing media actors for publishing information from third parties would negatively impact upon the media's ability to facilitate public discourse on matters of public concern.[101] It follows that this is only true when the media are facilitating public discourse as there is a clear distinction between reporting on violence or hate speech, which falls within the ambit of media freedom, as compared to advocating it, which does not.

Anonymous and pseudonymous speech is dealt with in detail in Chapter 7. This chapter provides detailed analysis of the treatment of such speech by, amongst others, UK and US courts and by the ECtHR in the context of conflicting audience and speaker interests. It is predominantly concerned with how the polarised jurisprudence from these jurisdictions impacts upon the anonymous or pseudonymous author and the respective publications' audience.[102] Therefore, for the purposes of analysing the contents of media freedom, the remainder of this section will consider how anonymous and pseudonymous speech has been treated by the ECtHR in respect of information emanating

---

[98]   *Selistö v Finland* [2004] App. no. 56767/00, [59]; *Axel Springer AG v Germany (No. 2)* [2014] App. no. 48311/10, [69].

[99]   *Radio France and others v France* [2004] App. no. 53984/00, [37]; *July and SARL Liberation v France* [2008] App. no. 20893/03, [71]; *Orban and others v France* [2009] App. no. 20985/05, [52]; *Pedersen and Baadsgaard v Denmark* [2004] App. no. 49017/99, [77].

[100]   *Sürek v Turkey (No. 1)* [1999] App. no. 26682/95, [63]; *Sürek v Turkey (No. 2)* [1999] App. no. 24122/94, [36].

[101]   ECtHR: *Jersild v Denmark* [1994] App. no. 15890/89, [35]; *July and SARL Liberation v France* [2008] App. no. 20893/03, [69]. IACHR: *Herrera-Ulloa v Costa Rica* [2004] Case 12.367, [134].

[102]   For detailed treatment of anonymous and pseudonymous speech generally in a number of contexts, see S. Levmore, 'The Internet's Anonymity Problem' in S. Levmore and M. Nussbaum (eds), *The Offensive Internet* (Harvard University Press, 2010); J. Bartlett, *The Dark Net Inside the Digital Underworld* (Random House, 2014) ch. 2; E. Barendt, *Anonymous Speech* (Hart Publishing, 2016); J. Oster, *European and International Media Law* (Cambridge University Press, 2017) 46–50; R. Arnold and M. Rajan, 'Do Authors and Performers Have a Legal Right to Pseudonymity' (2017) 9(2) *Journal of Media Law* 189; P. Coe, 'Anonymity and Pseudonymity: Free Speech's Problem Children' (2018) 22(2) *Media & Arts Law Review* 173.

from a third party. As touched upon in Chapter 3,[103] and as is discussed in detail in Chapter 7, anonymous and pseudonymous publications are prevalent online and among citizen journalists, who regularly write and publish anonymously or using a pseudonym. Thus, as citizen journalists often act as a source of news for the press and other traditional media entities,[104] the Strasbourg Court's recognition in *Albert-Engelmann-Gesellschaft mbH v Austria*[105] that editors have the right to publish information emanating from anonymous and, by extension, pseudonymous sources, is relevant to both citizen journalists and the traditional media.[106] In cases involving the publication of information coming from anonymous and pseudonymous sources, assessing the veracity of the publication has been central to the reasoning of the ECtHR, as illustrated by the following cases. *Print Zeitungsverlag v Austria*[107] concerned a newspaper that had published an article quoting a letter that had been sent to members of a tourism association supervisory board. The letter included defamatory imputations, from which the newspaper distanced itself. However, the Court held that by publishing the anonymous letter, the newspaper had communicated it to a far larger audience than the restricted group of board members. As a result, in the Court's view, the dissemination of the letter exceeded the limits of permissible reporting.[108] In *Lavric v Romania*[109] a newspaper published the defamatory content of a complaint made by a defendant against a public prosecutor. The newspaper presented this material as the objective truth, as opposed to the statements of a third party, and did not check the accuracy of its sources, nor give the individual concerned the opportunity to respond to the accusations made against her.[110] The Court held that the newspaper lacked the professional care required by journalists[111] and that, as a result, it had 'exceeded the acceptable limits of comment in relation to a debate of general interest'.[112] In the Court's view, the newspaper's right to freedom of expression did not outweigh the applicant's right to reputation. Consequently, it found that there had been a violation of Article 8 ECHR.[113] The judgment in *Lavric* was, on the facts, surely correct. However, the decision in *Print Zeitungsverlag* is troubling. If

---

[103] See Chapter 3 section 6.2.2.
[104] See Chapter 2 section 3.3.2 and Chapter 3 section 3.1.
[105] [2006] App. no. 46389/99, [32].
[106] See the detailed discussion in Chapter 7 relating to *Author of a Blog v Times Newspapers Ltd* [2009] EMLR 22.
[107] [2013] App. no. 46389/99, [32].
[108] Ibid [40]–[41].
[109] [2014] App. no. 22231/05.
[110] Ibid [47].
[111] Ibid [48].
[112] Ibid [49].
[113] Ibid.

the media actor, in this case the newspaper, gave the victim an opportunity to comment prior to publication and did not claim that the allegations made in the anonymous material were true, then they are demonstrating responsible reporting pursuant to the right to media freedom: they are fulfilling their concomitant obligations and responsibilities, as set out in Chapter 6.[114] This means that, so long as the content of the anonymous letter relates to an issue of public concern, the newspaper in this case should have been able to publish the letter despite the fact that it may have been defamatory.[115] In these circumstances, a decision to the contrary inhibits the media's role as the public watchdog and conflicts with the right to media freedom.

Both the ECtHR and the European Commission on Human Rights have handed down judgments relating to media actors' treatment of interviewees. Pursuant to the right to media freedom, it has been held by the ECtHR that media actors should not be subject to a general obligation to obtain permission from an interviewee before publishing an interview. According to the Court, this is because requiring members of the media to obtain such authorisation would inhibit their work and negatively impact on the quality of public discourse in the following ways: (i) media actors may be deterred from asking difficult and provocative questions for fear of the interviewees preventing publication by refusing to grant their permission; or (ii) interviewees would choose which members of the media to talk to based on their reputation as being cooperative.[116] Furthermore, in *Haider v Austria*[117] the Commission held that Article 10 ECHR does not entitle an interviewee to be interviewed in a specific way by the media[118] as it is 'in the interest of freedom of political debate that the interviewing journalist may also express critical and provocative points of view and not merely give neutral cues for the statements of the interviewed person, since the latter can reply immediately'.[119] Although in *Haider* the case, and the Commission's judgment, related to a politician and political debate, it is consistent with ECtHR jurisprudence that is of general application. For instance, in *Filatenko v Russia*[120] the Court stated: 'The punishment of a journalist for having worded his questions in a specific manner would seriously hamper the contribution of the press to discussion of matters of public interest

---

[114] Sections 3.2 and 3.3.

[115] Oster (n 64) 75.

[116] *Wizerkaniuk v Poland* [2011] App. no. 18990/05, [82].

[117] [1995] App. no. 25060/94.

[118] Ibid 7.

[119] Ibid 8.

[120] [2007] App. no. 73219/01.

Unpacking media freedom as a distinct legal concept 113

and should not be envisaged unless there are particularly strong reasons for doing so.'[121]

3.2.2.1   *Editorial freedom: a normative perspective*

As explained above media freedom consists of the negative right of not having to impart certain information and ideas:[122] a facet of the right that manifests in editorial freedom. In Chapter 2 we saw how editorial freedom can be problematic from an epistemological perspective in that the proprietor of, for instance, a newspaper, and/or its commercial partners, can influence editorial decisions.[123] The purpose of this section is to consider this freedom from a normative legal perspective.

Editorial freedom has been consistently recognised as a fundamental element of the right to freedom of expression, and the enhanced right to media freedom, pursuant to Article 10 ECHR.[124] It has also been the subject of jurisprudence from other jurisdictions, particularly the US. In the leading case of *Miami Herald v Tornillo*[125] the Supreme Court unanimously held that a Florida statute that provided a mandatory right of reply to election candidates whose character was attacked by a newspaper was invalid. The Supreme Court's decision was based on, inter alia, the fact that the statute conflicted with the function of editors to determine the contents of the newspaper and the treatment of public issues as, pursuant to the statute, they would be forced to publish a reply regardless of whether or not they considered it appropriate.[126] Similarly, in Germany media freedom enables editors to choose letters for publication and allow anonymous[127] contributions by authors,[128] and includes the freedom to determine their respective publications' general outlook and views on particular political and social issues.[129] It has been held by the ECtHR, and in the UK, that editorial judgement allows the press to determine the technique of reporting adopted and the form in which the ideas and information are con-

---

[121]   Ibid [41].

[122]   See section 3.2.

[123]   See section 3.3.2.

[124]   For example, see *Melnychuk v Ukraine* [2005] App. no. 28743/03, 6; *Manole and Others v Moldova* App. no [2009] 13936/02, [98]; *Centro Europa 7 S.R.L. and Di Stefano v Italy* [2012] App. no. 38433/09, [133].

[125]   418 US 241 (1974).

[126]   Ibid 258 per Burger CJ. In *Associated Press v National Labor Relations Board* 301 US 103 (1937) 133 Roberts J held that newspapers can discharge any editorial employee who fails to comply with editorial policies.

[127]   See section 3.1.2. Anonymity and pseudonymity are also discussed in more detail in Chapter 7.

[128]   95 BVerfGE 28 (1996).

[129]   52 BVerfGE 283, 301 (1979); 97 BVerfGE 125 (1998).

114 *Media freedom in the age of citizen journalism*

veyed.[130] Consequently, Randall Bezanson has described editorial discretion as the 'essence of press freedom' as, in his view, it is the equivalent of free will, or liberty, which is protected for individuals by the free speech clause of the First Amendment.[131] In the US, the right to editorial freedom has also been extended to both private and public broadcasters, pursuant to which they can determine programme schedules, reject political advertisements,[132] determine the format and content of televised debates,[133] and are free to editorialise, and to take a distinctive view on controversial public issues.[134]

3.3 Beyond Speech Rights: Media Freedom's Institutional Protection of Media Actors

The previous section has set out how the right to media freedom protects media speech. However, media freedom goes beyond this. It also protects media actors from state interference not directly related to specific publications in that it protects them as institutions performing their role as the public watchdog and the Fourth Estate.[135] Within this institutional context media freedom differs from the right to freedom of expression, not only in respect of the intensity of the protection it provides, as is the case with media speech, but also in terms of the scope of protected action.[136] Thus, pursuant to this institutional protection of the media, rights that are not directly speech related, but are instead connected to the media's newsgathering, editorial and distribution process, and to the media's independence, are guaranteed.[137]

---

[130] From the ECtHR see *Jersild v Denmark* [1994] App. no. 15890/89, [31]; *News Verlags GmbH & Co KG v Austria* (2000) 31 EHRR 246, [39]. From the UK see *Flood v Times Newspapers Limited* [2012] UKSC 11 per Lord Mance, [132], [170] and Lord Dyson, [194], [199]; [2010] EWCA Civ 804 per Moore-Bick LJ, [100]; *Re Guardian News and Media Ltd* [2010] AC 697 per Lord Rodger, [63]; *In re British Broadcasting Corporation* [2010] 1 AC 145 per Lord Hope of Craighead, [25]; *Jameel and others v Wall Street Journal Europe Sprl* [2006] UKHL 44 per Lord Hoffman, [51]; *Campbell v Mirror Group Newspapers Limited* [2004] 2 AC 457 per Lord Hoffman, [59].

[131] R.P. Bezanson, 'Institutional Speech' (1995) 80 *Iowa Law Review* 735, 806–815; R.P. Bezanson, 'The Developing Law of Editorial Judgment' (1999) 78 *Nebraska Law Review* 754. See also Barendt (n 2) 425.

[132] *Columbia Broadcasting System v Democratic National Committee* 412 US 94 (1973).

[133] *R (Liberal Democrats and another) v ITV Broadcasting Ltd* [2019] EWHC 3282 (Admin) per David LJ and Warby LJ, [110]–[111].

[134] *FCC v League of Women Voters of California* 468 US 384 (1984).

[135] Oster (n 102) 52–53.

[136] Ibid.

[137] Ibid.

Unpacking media freedom as a distinct legal concept   115

This institutional protection of the media can be divided into defensive and positive rights.[138] Under defensive rights, the following sections will deal with how the right to media freedom protects media: (i) independence; (ii) research and investigation; and (iii) sources. In respect of positive rights, we shall consider what the media is entitled to for it to effectively utilise media freedom.

3.3.1 Defensive right 1: media independence

In *Manole and others v Moldova*[139] the ECtHR held that if a powerful economic or political group obtained a position of dominance over the media and, as a result, influenced and/or limited their editorial freedom, this would undermine the media's fundamental democratic role.[140] Media freedom therefore protects media actors from undue governmental influence and monopolies. The need for this protection derives from the fact that within a democracy the citizens that the respective government serves mandate state authority. In turn, as the media has the power to influence public opinion and ideology, its independence from the state[141] and commercial influence is critical to the effective functioning of democracy.[142]

3.3.2 Defensive right 2: protection of media research and investigation

Beneficiaries of the right to media freedom are protected against unjustified interferences with activities related to all forms of newsgathering.[143] This is demonstrated by the fact that the Council of Europe has stated, and the ECtHR has consistently held, that media freedom includes the right of media actors to seek information, pursuant to which they are at liberty to determine whether they need to employ investigative journalism to obtain the information.[144] Thus, in *Társaság a Szabadságjogokért v Hungary*[145] the Court stated that 'the law cannot allow arbitrary restrictions which may become a form of indirect censorship should the authorities create obstacles to the gathering of infor-

---

[138] Oster (n 64) 84–101.

[139] [2009] App. no. 13936/02.

[140] Ibid [98]. See also *Centro Europa 7 Srl and Di Stefano v Italy* [2012] App. no. 38433/09, [133].

[141] See generally Fenwick and Phillipson (n 50) 39–41.

[142] See Chapter 2 for further discussion on media ownership and independence.

[143] This includes undercover work. See *Nordisk Film & TV A/S v Denmark* [2005] App. no. 40485/02; *Haldimann and others v Switzerland* [2015] App. no. 21830/09.

[144] Council of Europe, Declaration by the Committee of Ministers on the protection and promotion of investigative journalism (26 September 2001). ECtHR: *Cumpănă and Mazăre v Romania* [2004] App. no. 33348/96, [96]; *Dammann v Switzerland* [2006] App. no. 77551/01, [52]; *Társaság a Szabadságjogokért v Hungary* [2009] App. no. 37374/05, [27]; *Bremner v Turkey* [2015] App. no. 37428/06, [76].

[145] [2009] App. no. 37374/05, [27].

mation[, which] is an essential and preparatory step in journalism and ... an inherent, protected part of press freedom'.[146]

The protection against unjustified interferences with media's newsgathering practice has a very wide ambit. For instance, as illustrated by the case of *Gsell v Switzerland*,[147] measures that are equally applicable to the media and general public have been held to contravene the right if the media actor is disproportionately inhibited from exercising their profession.[148] Further, it has been recognised by both the US Supreme Court and the ECtHR that freedom of the media allows media actors to publish information obtained unlawfully, so long as the public interest in receiving it is greater than the state's or an individual's interest in confidentiality.[149] However, media freedom does not extend to illegal activity or violation of public safety rules that apply to everyone.[150]

3.3.3   Defensive right 3: protection of media sources

In the seminal case of *Goodwin v United Kingdom*[151] the ECtHR stated that '[p]rotection of journalistic sources is one of the basic conditions for press freedom. Without such protection, sources may be deterred from assisting the press in informing the public on matters of public interest.'[152] Undoubtedly an informed media, and effective journalism, is dependent upon the use of sources, who tend to be insiders working in or associated with the subject matter of the publication, to provide the most effective information.[153] As

---

[146] Ibid [27]. It is important to note that Társaság a Szabadságjogokért is a non-governmental organisation. According to the ECtHR, [27]:

> The function of the press includes the creation of forums for public debate. However, the realisation of this function is not limited to the media or professional journalists. In the present case, the preparation of the forum of public debate was conducted by a non-governmental organisation. The purpose of the applicant's activities can therefore be said to have been an essential element of informed public debate. The Court has repeatedly recognised civil society's important contribution to the discussion of public affairs ... The applicant is an association involved in human rights litigation with various objectives, including the protection of freedom of information. It may therefore be characterised, like the press, as a social 'watchdog' ... In these circumstances, the Court is satisfied that its activities warrant similar Convention protection to that afforded to the press.

[147] [2009] App. no. 12675/05. Discussed at section 2.
[148] Ibid [49].
[149] US Supreme Court: *New York Times Co. v United States* 403 US 713 (1971); *Bartnicki v Vopper* 532 US 514 (2001); ECtHR: *Radio Twist a.s. v Slovakia* [2006] App. no. 62202/00, [62]; *Nagla v Latvia* [2013] App. no. 73469/10, [97].
[150] Oster (n 102) 53.
[151] [1996] App. no. 17488/90.
[152] Ibid [39]. See also *Ashworth Hospital Authority v MGN Ltd* [2002] 4 All ER 193.
[153] Fenwick and Phillipson (n 50) 311.

Lord Denning observed in *Attorney-General v Mulholland and Foster*,[154] '[the journalist] can expose wrong-doing and neglect of duty which would otherwise go unremedied ... the mouths of his informants will be closed to him if it is known that their identity will be disclosed ...',[155] which would in turn undermine the media's role as the public watchdog. Thus, the protection of media sources is a fundamental aspect of media freedom and is recognised as such by a variety of European legal instruments,[156] jurisprudence[157] and legal scholarship.[158] Within an ECHR context, this is illustrated by the fact that the Strasbourg Court has consistently held that journalistic rights pursuant to media freedom are interfered with by virtue of the very existence of an order to disclose a source's identity, regardless of whether or not the order is actually enforced.[159] However, despite the high level of importance attached to the

---

[154] [1963] 2 QB 477.

[155] Ibid 489.

[156] United Nations Commission on Human Rights, Report of the Special Rapporteur on the Promotion and Protection of the Right to Freedom of Opinion and Expression, Mr Abid Hussain, submitted pursuant to Commission Resolution 1997/27, E/CN.4/1998/40/Add.1, [17] and [22]; Human Rights Resolution 2005/38: The Right to Freedom of Opinion and Expression, E/CN.4/RES/2005/38; Council of Europe, Committee of Ministers, Recommendation No. R(2000) 7 on the Right of Journalists not to Disclose their Sources of Information; Parliamentary Assembly, Recommendation 1950 (2011): The Protection of Journalistic Sources.

[157] For example, see *Goodwin v United Kingdom* [1996] App. no. 17488/90, [39]; *Roemen and Schmit v Luxembourg* [2003] App. no. 51772/99, [57]; *Cumpănă and Mazăre v Romania* [2004] App. no. 33348/96, [106]; *Radio Twist a.s. v Slovakia* [2006] App. no. 62202/00, [62]; *Voskuil v Netherlands* [2007] App. no. 64752/01, [65]; *Tillack v Belgium* [2007] App. no. 20477/05, [53]; *Financial Times Ltd and others v United Kingdom* [2009] App. no. 821/03, [59]; *Sanoma Uitgevers BV v Netherlands* [2010] App. no. 38224/03, [50]; *Nagla v Latvia* [2013] App. no. 73469/10.

[158] For example, see D. Carney, 'Theoretical Underpinnings of the Protection of Journalists' Confidential Sources: Why an Absolute Privilege Cannot be Justified' (2009) 1 *Journal of Media Law* 97; E. Barendt, 'Bad News for Bloggers' (2009) 2 *Journal of Media Law* 141, 146; S. Helle, 'The News-gathering/Publication Dichotomy and Government Expression' (1982) *Duke Law Journal* 1, 27–28; C.C. Monk, 'Evidentiary Privilege for Journalists' Sources: Theory and Statutory Protection' (1986) 51 *Missouri Law Review* 1, 14–15; E. Chemerinsky, 'Protect the Press: A First Amendment Standard for Safeguarding Aggressive Newsgathering' (2000) 33 *University of Richmond Law Review* 1143; Nestler (n 69); E. Ugland, 'Demarcating the Right to Gather News: A Sequential Interpretation of the First Amendment' (2008) 3 *Duke Journal of Constitutional Law and Public Policy* 118; D. Abramowicz, 'Calculating the Public Interest in Protecting Journalists' Confidential Sources' (2009) 108 *Columbia Law Review* 101.

[159] *Financial Times Ltd and others v United Kingdom* [2009] App. no 821/03, [56]; *Sanoma Uitgevers BV v Netherlands* [2010] App. no. 38224/03, [50]; *Roemen and Schmit v Luxembourg* [2003] App. no. 51772/99, [57]; *Telegraaf Media Nederland*

118   *Media freedom in the age of citizen journalism*

protection of media sources, it is not absolute.[160] This is illustrated by *Roeman and Schmit v Luxembourg*[161] and *Financial Times Ltd and others v United Kingdom*[162] in which the ECtHR found that the following factors will determine whether or not a legitimate interest in disclosure outweighs the right not to disclose information pertaining to the identity of the source: (i) the nature of the interest in the disclosure; (ii) in particular, the public interest in preventing and punishing criminal offences; (iii) the authenticity of the information; (iv) the conduct and good faith of the source; and (v) the availability of alternative, less intrusive means of obtaining the information sought.[163]

Furthermore, if the sole or predominant purpose of the search of media premises and the seizure of journalistic material is to identify media sources then the search and seizure are in direct conflict with the right to media freedom as they have 'an intolerable chilling effect on journalistic work and may also deter informants from providing information that they are only willing to provide confidentially'.[164] Indeed, the Strasbourg Court has held that the mere threat to search media premises causes a 'chilling effect' and is, prima facie, irreconcilable with media freedom.[165] Of particular significance to citizen journalists, who may well operate from home, is the fact that, in addition to their right to media freedom being interfered with by searches and seizures of their journalistic material, such activity also constitutes a breach of the right to respect of one's home as an aspect of personal privacy pursuant to Article 8 ECHR[166] and the entitlement to the enjoyment of property under Article 1 ECHR.[167]

In contrast, in the US, although the value of source protection is recognised, it is not regarded as an aspect of the media free speech right. In *Branzburg v Hayes*[168] the Supreme Court held that the First Amendment does not confer

---

Landelijke Media BV and others v Netherlands [2012] App. no. 39315/06, [127]. See also the House of Lords case of *British Steel Corporation v Granada Television Ltd* [1981] 1 All ER 417.

[160] *Goodwin v United Kingdom* [1996] App. no. 17488/90, [39]. For example, for the UK see section 10 Contempt of Court Act 1981.

[161] [2003] App. no. 51772/99.

[162] [2009] App. no. 821/03.

[163] *Roeman and Schmit* [2003] App. no. 51772/99, [58]; *Financial Times* [2009] App. no. 821/03, [67].

[164] Oster (n 102) 54.

[165] *Sanoma Uitgevers BV v Netherlands* [2010] App. no. 38224/03, [71].

[166] This applies even if the search and seizure were conducted on business premises as 'home'. See *Niemietz v Germany* [1992] App. no. 13710/88, [30]; *Saint-Paul Luxembourg SA v Luxembourg* [2013] App. no. 26419/10, [37].

[167] See also Article 21 ACHR.

[168] 408 US 665 (1972). See also *Cohen v Cowles Media Co* 510 US 663, 669 (1991); *Judith Miller, Petitioner v US and M Cooper and Time inc, Petitioners v US*, Supreme Court (2005) No. 04-1508.

protection for media sources. However, statutes providing 'shield' laws for journalistic rights were enacted by some states prior to the *Branzburg* decision, and more have been enacted since by a number of states and by Congress.[169] Thus, unlike the UK and the ECtHR, in which the protection of journalistic sources is regarded as synonymous with media speech, the US treats the protection of sources as a 'background' right.[170] Similarly, Australia does not constitutionally protect journalistic sources. However, as with the US, some Australian state legislatures have enacted shield laws to protect the confidentiality of sources.[171] In contrast, Canada takes the same stance as the US and Australia but does not have shield laws to protect journalists. If a media actor fails to comply with a court order to disclose the identity of a source, they could be faced with legal charges, including the threat of imprisonment.[172] Thus, in respect of these jurisdictions, Helen Fenwick and Gavin Phillipson observe that

> in contrast to the ECHR stance, there is significant doubt as to the harmony of interests between free speech and source protection. Source protection in these [jurisdictions] appears to be seen as a journalistic privilege, not viewed as worthy of the high levels of protection accorded to speech, despite the link between the two.[173]

3.3.4 Positive rights

One of the features that distinguishes media freedom from freedom of expression is the fact that, in addition to defensive rights against the state, the right also includes positive entitlements to state action. These entitlements provide the preconditions that enable the media to effectively utilise media freedom to fulfil its role as the public watchdog, and to inform the public on matters of public interest.[174] According to case law, legal instruments and scholarship from a number of jurisdictions, these entitlements include: (i) the right to enable a publisher to distribute their publications by any appropriate means;[175]

---

[169] For a detailed discussion of US shield laws, see generally Ugland (n 158).

[170] Fenwick and Phillipson (n 50) 314.

[171] See W. Bacon and C. Nash, 'Confidential Sources and the Public Right to Know' (1999) 21(2) *Australian Journalism Review* 1.

[172] Fenwick and Phillipson (n 50) 314.

[173] Ibid.

[174] Oster (n 64) 93–94. Consequently, they form part of the non-statutory incentives available under the new regulatory framework advanced in Chapter 9 section 6.5.

[175] ECtHR: *VgT Verein gegen Tierfabriken v Switzerland (No. 1)* [2001] App. no. 24699/94, [48]; IACHR: *Palamara-Iribarne v Chile* [2005] Case 11.571, [73].

(ii) privileged access to government information,[176] press conferences[177] and court proceedings;[178] and (iii) the obligation of the state to protect media actors in the performance of their work, in particular from violence.[179] In respect of positive entitlements, the protection granted by the ECtHR is more robust than that provided by US Supreme Court jurisprudence. This is demonstrated by the Court's judgment in *Schweizerische Radio-und Fernsehgesellschaft SRG v Switzerland*[180] in which it held that the Swiss authorities' refusal to permit the media to film inside a prison and to conduct an interview with an inmate was disproportionate.[181] In contrast, in *Pell v Procunier*[182] and *Saxbe v Washington Post*[183] the Supreme Court held that the First Amendment does not provide the media with rights to special access or immunities. Consequently, the Supreme Court rejected the claims of newspapers to enter prisons and conduct interviews with inmates. This contrasting jurisprudence is indicative of the approach of the ECtHR, which is instrumental and objective and provides privileged protection of the media, compared to the 'press-as-technology' model adopted by the US Supreme Court, which does not afford any constitutional protection of the media. This model is discussed in more detail in section 5, where it is argued that it is no longer a suitable approach for delineating media from non-media actors.

This section has not only established the importance of media freedom as a concept, but also what it 'contains' and means for members of the media in reality. Section 4 will briefly set out why we need to be able to effectively distinguish media from non-media actors. This will then be followed in section 5 by analysis of the traditional methods for distinguishing media from non-media actors, and therefore the beneficiaries of media freedom.

---

[176] For example, from the US see section (4)(A)(ii)(II) of the US Freedom of Information Act.

[177] Human Rights Committee: *Gauthier v Canada* [1999] Communication no. 633/95, [13.4]. See also D.A. Anderson, 'Freedom of the Press' (2002) 80 *Texas Law Review* 429, 432.

[178] See Chapter 8 for analysis of the offence of contempt of court and the open justice principle.

[179] ECtHR: *Özgür Gündem v Turkey* [2000] App. no. 23144/93, [38ff].

[180] [2012] App. no. 34124/06.

[181] Ibid [65].

[182] 417 US 817 (1974).

[183] 417 US 843 (1974).

Unpacking media freedom as a distinct legal concept   121

4   THE NEED TO DISTINGUISH MEDIA FROM NON-MEDIA ACTORS

The previous chapter explained how the internet and social media stimulated the emergence and development of citizen journalism, and how this has contributed to the robustness of the public sphere. This has, according to Ian Cram, created new 'opportunities for deliberation in conditions of approximate political equality among citizens'.[184] However, although citizen journalists now play a vital role in imparting and receiving news, their contribution to matters of public interest cannot be overrated, just as traditional institutional journalism should not be underestimated.[185] This is because the internet and social media facilitate the instantaneous, and often spontaneous, expression of opinions and venting and sharing of emotions, thoughts and feelings. Consequently, as discussed in that chapter, social media platforms and the internet generally are saturated with poorly researched, biased and meaningless material emanating from the institutional media, citizen journalists and non-media actors alike.[186] For instance, in his *Inquiry*, Leveson LJ refers to *Popbitch*,[187] which, in his opinion, is 'clear in its ambition to entertain and understands itself to "poke fun" and comment on the "lighter" side of celebrity culture'.[188] Furthermore, we also saw in Chapter 3 that because social media enables users to personalise, and therefore be selective as to the information they receive, combined with the human psychological trait that seeks out material that endorses, rather than is critical of, our existing beliefs, the range of information that users are exposed to is decreasing.[189] Consequently, there is reduced potential for a richer and more balanced dialogue, which in turn limits the scope of the public sphere.[190]

Despite the best intentions of some citizen journalists, they may still lack the education, qualifications and experience to distinguish themselves from pro-

---

[184] I. Cram, *Citizen Journalists: Newer Media, Republican Moments and the Constitution* (Edward Elgar Publishing, 2015) 5. See Chapter 3 section 6.

[185] Oster (n 2) 63.

[186] See Chapter 3 sections 4, 5 and 6.

[187] *Popbitch* is a blog that publishes celebrity gossip stories. See www.popbitch .com.

[188] Lord Justice Leveson, *An Inquiry into the Culture, Practices and Ethics of the Press: Report*, HC 780, November 2012, 168, [4.3].

[189] C.R. Sunstein, *Republican.com 2.0* (Princeton University Press, 2009). See also Cram (n 184) 5–6. See Chapter 3 section 5.2 and Chapter 5 section 3.2 for a discussion on user preferences, the creation of trends and filter bubbles.

[190] See Chapter 3 section 5. This issue with social media's facilitation of citizen journalism is discussed further in the following chapter in respect of the marketplace of ideas theory at section 3.2.

fessional journalists. Indeed, bloggers post information despite being uncertain as to its provenance and without verifying it for reliability, and instead rely on readers to judge its accuracy.[191] To the contrary, a blog by a professional journalist may include spontaneous comments and conversation, while being supported by professional experience and resources.[192] In conclusion, there exists a symbiosis between citizen journalism and the traditional media that has been articulated by a number of commentators. Essentially, this relationship is mutually beneficial because professional journalists and traditional media entities research and cover the findings of citizen journalism, which in turn adds credence to the citizen journalists' work and facilitates the wider dissemination of their research.[193]

In a world where anyone can disseminate information to potentially huge audiences via blogs and other social media platforms, there is a need to distinguish media from non-media actors, not only for the purposes of determining the beneficiaries of the rights and responsibilities attributed to media freedom, but also to identify those who could be subject to a regulatory regime.[194] Thus, the following section will look at the traditional approaches used to determine who benefits from media freedom, and why these are not appropriate for the modern media era.

---

[191] Alonzo (n 70) 755.

[192] Jacob Rowbottom argues for a high- and low-level distinction for speech that is based on the context within which the expression is made, as opposed to a value-based distinction deriving from the content of the expression. See J. Rowbottom, 'To Rant, Vent and Converse: Protecting Low Level Digital Speech' (2012) 71(2) *Cambridge Law Journal* 355, 371. See also P. Coe, 'Redefining "Media" Using a "Media-as-a-constitutional-component" Concept: An Evaluation of the Need for the European Court of Human Rights to Alter Its Understanding of "Media" Within a New Media Landscape' (2017) 37(1) *Legal Studies* 25, 36. It is argued in the following chapter that these concerns are paradigms of the rejoinders raised in relation to Justice Oliver Wendell Holmes' marketplace of ideas and, although John Stuart Mill's argument from truth is not concerned with these issues, the criticisms levelled at the theory. See Chapter 5 sections 3.1 and 3.2.

[193] Oster (n 2) 64; C. Calvert and M. Torres, 'Putting the Shock Value in First Amendment Jurisprudence: When Freedom for the Citizen-Journalist Watchdog Trumps the Right of Informational Privacy on the Internet' (2011) *Vanderbilt Journal of Entertainment and Technology Law* 323, 345; J. Curran and J. Seaton, *Power Without Responsibility – Press, Broadcasting and the Internet in Britain* (7th edn., Routledge, 2010) 286.

[194] See Chapter 9.

5 THE TRADITIONAL APPROACHES FOR DETERMINING THE BENEFICIARIES OF MEDIA FREEDOM

Traditionally courts and commentators from different jurisdictions have used the press-as-technology model, the mass audience approach, and the professionalised publisher approach to determine whom and what should benefit from the existence of a distinct right to media freedom.[195] However, the growth of citizen journalism, and the ability of citizen journalists to reach mass audiences, has created doctrinal uncertainty as to how the courts should determine the beneficiaries of media freedom. Arguably, in the context of the modern media, of which citizen journalism is now a central component, these factors can no longer be relied upon to distinguish between media and non-media actors. As a result, this section will argue that although these three approaches may once have been effective, they now lack merit and are, potentially, redundant.

5.1 Press-as-technology Model

As previously explained the dominant view in the US, based upon the press-as-technology model, is that the media should not be subject to any privileges or special duties,[196] a position that is juxtaposed with the instrumental approach of the ECtHR, which grants privileged protection to the media. Accordingly, pursuant to the model's rationale, there is no need to distinguish the media at all and, as a result, this model does not provide the means to do so. This is because, so the press-as-technology movement argues, the framers of the Constitution understood the words 'or of the press' to secure the right of every person to use communications technology as opposed to laying down a right exclusively available to members of the publishing industry.[197] As a result, in the view of the Supreme Court, the First Amendment protects speech not speakers, regardless of whether the source of the expression is a professional journalist or media organisation, or whether it is a casual social media user.[198] In the case of *Branzburg v Hayes*,[199] White J, giving the opinion of the majority, resisted attempting to conceptualise the media and define what it consists of. In White J's judgment, this is because 'freedom of the press is

---

[195] See generally Oster (n 2) 64–68.
[196] See sections 2 and 3.3.4, and see generally Volokh (n 43).
[197] Ibid 463.
[198] *Citizens United v FEC* 130 S Ct 876, 905 (2010). See also Sack (n 51) 633.
[199] 408 US 665, 704 (1972).

a fundamental personal right' which is not confined to the mass media but, instead, attaches to 'every sort of publication which affords a vehicle of information and opinion'.[200] There appears a concern that in attempting to define the media, there is a risk of creating either an over-inclusive or over-exclusive interpretation of journalism.[201] The former could, potentially, be misused,[202] while the latter could give rise to allegations of discrimination.[203] This is because non-journalists who may contribute to matters of public importance, such as business leaders, scientists and artists, would not fall within the province of the additional protection afforded to the media.[204] However, protecting the media with specific provisions or clauses that provide extra privileges and duties does not mean those who are not defined as media would be deprived of their rights. For instance, within the context of ECtHR jurisprudence, artistic[205] and commercial expression[206] are subject to a relatively high level of protection. Similarly, Article 13 CFREU protects freedom of science and freedom of the arts. Thus, there is no reason to suggest that, within these legal frameworks at least, privileged protection of the media would operate against business leaders, artists or scientists.[207]

There are wider-reaching reasons why the press-as-technology model is subject to criticism. First, and more broadly, there is a strong judicial and academic counter-movement in the US that not only correlates more closely with ECtHR jurisprudence, but also undermines the model within the modern media era. The specific media protection clauses enshrined within legal instruments, such as Article 11(2) CFREU and the First Amendment, in addition to those provisions safeguarding freedom of expression,[208] strongly suggest that, for example, the European Union and the framers of the US Constitution intended to distinguish the two, in that they could apply to different entities and mean something different. Taking the First Amendment as an example, as discussed in section 2, commentators and justices of the Supreme Court have argued that these provisions must mean something more otherwise they would be redun-

---

[200] Ibid.

[201] Oster (n 2) 65.

[202] C.E. Baker, 'The Independent Significance of the Press Clause under Existing Law' (2007) 35 *Hofstra Law Review* 955, 1013–1016.

[203] V.D. Amar, 'From Watergate to Ken Starr: Potter Stewart's "Or of the Press" A Quarter Century Later' (1999) 50 *Hastings Law Journal* 711, 714–715.

[204] Ibid; Oster (n 2) 65.

[205] *Müller v Switzerland* (1991) 13 EHRR 212; *Otto Preminger v Austria* (1995) 19 EHRR 34; *IA v Turkey* (2007) EHRR 30.

[206] *Markt Intern v Germany* (1989) 12 EHRR 161, [33].

[207] Oster (n 2) 65–66.

[208] See section 2.

dant.[209] For Justice Stewart the First Amendment free press clause operates as a structural guarantee to enable the press to fulfil its constitutional functions of acting as the Fourth Estate; to provide additional checks and balances on the government.[210] Accordingly, the twin speech and press rights are 'no constitutional accident, but an acknowledgment of the critical role played by the press …'.[211] Further, according to West, in addition to the Fourth Estate function, the press fulfils another primary role beyond the values served by the general right to freedom of expression: dissemination of information of public interest.[212]

Secondly, in the current media era, clearly the institutional press is not the only means to provide a check and balance on government or convey matters of public interest. Other forms of media can, and do, fulfil this role effectively.[213] Consequently, these views of the press clause are not exclusively institutional.[214] The functions of the press identified by the likes of Justice and West as being conducive to its constitutional role, are served by the traditional institutional media and non-institutional citizen journalists.[215] Arguably, therefore, when constitutions, statutes and normative theory require protection of the media in addition to freedom of expression, it is incumbent on the courts to delineate between the two, as demonstrated by ECtHR jurisprudence, despite the fact that such a challenging line-drawing exercise will generate controversial judgments.[216] Accepting that media speech is different to individual speech and, as argued in this book, accepting that who or what is media should be defined functionally, meaning it can include non-traditional and non-institutional actors,[217] is vitally important within the context of the modern media, in which we can be constantly bombarded by a cacophony of information from different forms of media. It is the fulfilment of the unique

---

[209] See nn 41 and 42. See also K. Pasich, 'The Right to the Press to Gather Information under the First Amendment' (1978) 12 *Loyola University of Los Angeles Law Review* 357, 385; F. Schauer, 'Towards an Institutional First Amendment' (2005) 89 *Minnesota Law Review* 1256, 1263–1264; Ugland (n 158) 136.

[210] As opposed to a more 'organic' guarantee that derives from case law. Stewart (n 41) 634. As stated in section 2, this is a view supported by Nimmer, Abrams and Bezanson (n 41).

[211] *Houchins v KQED Inc.* 438 US 1, 17 (1978).

[212] West (n 41) 1069–1070.

[213] See Chapter 1 sections 1 and 2 and Chapter 3 section 6.

[214] Bezanson, 'Whither Freedom of the Press?' (n 41) 1267.

[215] See Chapter 2. According to Oster, media freedom identifies the rights holder. It is concerned with freedom of the press and of the media, and therefore does not convey a right on to a vehicle of publication. In other words, it is 'not the freedom to publish anything with certain media': Oster (n 2) 66.

[216] Schauer (n 209) 1260. See also Baker (n 202) 1016; West (n 41) 1048.

[217] The media-as-a-constitutional-component concept is discussed in greater detail in the following chapter. In particular see sections 4 and 5.

functions identified by Justice Stewart and the proponents of his claim that serves to distinguish the media-as-a-constitutional-component from mere media entertainment, as the activities of the latter are not subject to the same legal protection,[218] at least within an ECHR and CFREU context. Thus, although at first glance the 'protecting speech not speakers' First Amendment rationale that the press-as-technology model supports may appear to correlate with the functional approach for defining media advanced by the media-a s-constitutional-component concept, the very fact that the concept uses this definition to distinguish media from non-media actors for the purposes of determining the beneficiaries of media freedom, albeit functionally rather than institutionally, means that it is teleologically incompatible with the model.

5.2 Mass Audience Approach

According to the HRC, '[j]ournalism is a function shared by a wide range of actors, including professional full-time reporters and analysts, as well as bloggers and others who engage in forms of self-publication in print, on the internet or elsewhere…'.[219] On this analysis, anyone with the ability to disseminate information to a mass audience could be considered to be media and therefore be subject to the same privileges.[220] Historically this approach could have enabled a distinction to be made between media and non-media actors as professional journalists, and the newspapers, publishers and broadcasters they worked for, tended to be the only entities with the ability to reach mass audiences. However, the facilitation of citizen journalism by the internet and social media means that this ability is no longer reserved to these organisations and their journalists or broadcasters. Instead, anybody with access to the internet can, in theory at least, convey information to millions of people through the creation of a blog, posting a YouTube video or by using platforms such as Twitter, Facebook or Instagram. If you consider the reach of sporting celebrities such as Cristiano Ronaldo, Andy Murray and Lewis Hamilton through their social media accounts, based on the HRC's formulation, they would be considered 'journalists'.[221]

---

[218]   Anderson (n 177) 442.

[219]   United Nations Human Rights Committee, General Comment No 34: Freedoms of opinion and expression (CCPR/C/GC/34) 12 September 2011, [44].

[220]   Oster (n 2) 66–67.

[221]   By way of example, in March 2021 Cristiano Ronaldo had 91.7 million followers on Twitter alone. Also, on Twitter, Roger Federer had 12.7 million, Lewis Hamilton had 6.2 million, Andy Murray had 3.5 million and Rory McIlroy had 3.1 million followers.

Unpacking media freedom as a distinct legal concept 127

This situation is paradigmatic of the over-inclusive interpretation of media expression explained above[222] as it captures virtually every internet publication, including tweets by celebrity footballers. Furthermore, as discussed in section 4, clearly the appearance and quality of information available on the internet, whether that be through blogs, websites or social media, varies drastically. Despite these apparent inconsistencies, the mass audience approach would classify a casual tweet from Cristiano Ronaldo as being legally indistinguishable from a citizen journalist using their blog to report from a war zone. It would be incorrect to classify all publications capable of reaching mass audiences as media: the internet, as a vehicle through which information can be conveyed, must not be confused with the media as a legal concept, just as the medium 'paper' does not, necessarily, constitute the press.[223] Consequently, it is imperative to identify diligent journalists operating within the media-as-a-constitutional-component, regardless of the form that takes, and distinguish these from media entertainment and other information.

5.3 'Professionalised' Publisher Approach

The Committee of Ministers of the Council of Europe and the jurisprudence of the ECtHR regularly refer to 'media professionals'.[224] Thus, in cases such as *Perrin v United Kingdom*[225] and *Willem v France*[226] the ECtHR did not grant protection to private and non-professional internet publications. This view is mirrored in the US in that, for example, under New York shield law, only 'professional journalists' working for 'gain or livelihood'[227] are entitled to benefit from special journalistic dispensations.[228] These positions lend support to an approach whereby a publisher must be connected with, and remunerated

---

[222] See nn 201 and 202.

[223] Oster (n 2) 67.

[224] For example, see Appendix to Recommendation No R (2000) of the Committee of Minsters of the Council of Europe to Member States on the right of journalists not to disclose their sources of information: 'For the purposes of this Recommendation ... the term "journalist" means any natural or legal person who is regularly or professionally engaged in the collection and dissemination of information to the public via any means of mass communication'; *Surek and Ozdemir v Turkey* App. nos. 23927/94 and 24277/94 (ECtHR 8 July 1999), [63]; *Wizerkaniuk v Poland* App. no. 18990/05 (ECtHR 5 July 2011), [68]; *Kaperzynski v Poland* App. no. 43206/07 (ECtHR 3 April 2012), [70].

[225] App. no. 5446/03 (ECtHR 18 October 2005).

[226] App. no. 10883/05 (ECtHR 16 July 2009).

[227] N.Y. Civ. Rights Law 79-h (a)(6) (2007).

[228] For detailed discussion of US shield laws, see generally Ugland (n 158).

by, a traditional media company and/or have undertaken formal journalistic education and training to benefit from privileges attributed to media freedom.

In contrast to the mass audience approach, this approach animates concerns of over-exclusivity[229] for reasons that are relevant within the context of citizen journalism. First, who amounts to a professional journalist cannot be defined by membership of a professional body, as unlike lawyers and doctors, journalists are not required to be members of such organisations. Secondly, just because a person has not undergone formal journalistic education or training does not mean they cannot be diligent and professional reporters. Equally, requiring that a person be employed by a professional media organisation eliminates anyone not subject to regular remuneration. This would include many citizen journalists, despite the fact their work may contribute to matters of public interest.[230] However, it is important to note at this juncture that the argument I have made here in relation to this approach does not preclude media actors from being required to adhere to standards of professional behaviour. Indeed, this is a requirement of the media-as-a-constitutional-component concept, and is something I consider in the following chapter[231] and develop further in Chapter 6.

The 'professionalised' publisher approach is unconvincing when considering that blogs published by citizen journalists can be the only source of news coverage from, for example, war zones, as was the case during the Arab Spring uprising.[232] In contrast, educated and professionally trained journalists, employed by media organisations, do not always write or broadcast material that is in the public interest.[233] Instead, this work may be subject to conflicting interests, such as commercialism or political bias.[234] Thus, establishing a presumption that a tabloid journalist reporting on a 'kiss-and-tell' story should be subject to greater legal protection, under the auspices of media freedom, than a private citizen journalist diligently blogging from an area embroiled in conflict, merely because the former is remunerated by a media organisation

---

[229] See section 5.2.

[230] Ugland (n 158) 136–137; Coe (n 192) 40.

[231] See section 4.

[232] See Chapter 1 section 2 and see generally D. McGoldrick, 'The Limits of Freedom of Expression on Facebook and Social Networking Sites: A UK Perspective' (2013) 13 *Human Rights Law Review* 125; N. Miladi, 'Social Media and Social Change' (2016) 25(1) *Digest of the Middle East* 36. This issue is also discussed in Chapter 5 section 6.1.

[233] See generally R. Barnes, *Outrageous Invasions: Celebrities' Private Lives, Media and the Law* (Oxford University Press, 2010). The notion of public interest is considered in detail in Chapter 6 section 3.

[234] See Chapter 2 section 3.

and is professionally trained and educated, is unmeritorious and illogical.[235] The former could be classed as mere media entertainment, while the latter is paradigmatic of the media-as-a-constitutional-component.[236]

6   CONCLUSION

This chapter has distinguished media freedom from freedom of expression and has established that the former provides enhanced protection, over and above the right to freedom of expression, for actors operating as part of the media. It has also set out why media freedom is conceptually important for media actors and what it means in reality for its beneficiaries, in respect of both speech and institutional protection. Finally, it has identified the shortfalls of the traditional methods adopted by courts and commentators for distinguishing between media and non-media actors, and therefore who/what is subject to media freedom: they simply do not fit in the modern media arena, of which citizen journalism is now very much a part.

In the following chapter I will introduce the media-as-a-constitutional-component concept and its functional definition of the media. In Chapter 6 I explain what this new normative framework will mean for media freedom. Specifically, I set out the standards of professional behaviour and norms of discourse, or concomitant duties and responsibilities, imposed by the concept, which are applied to the specific legal challenges considered in Part III.

---

[235] Coe (n 192) 41; Oster (n 2) 68.
[236] This issue is discussed in more detail in the following chapter.

5. The media-as-a-constitutional-component concept: a new theoretical foundation for media freedom

1   INTRODUCTION

This chapter, at section 5, will introduce the conceptual 'key' to address the problem that was identified in the previous chapter, namely how those entities operating as media should be distinguished from those that are not for the purposes of media freedom. This key is a functional rather than institutional definition of media, deriving from the media-as-a-constitutional-component concept. As explained in Chapter 1,[1] this conceptualisation is based on the premise that the performance of a constitutional function, such as positively contributing to the public sphere by reporting on a matter of public concern, and adherence to certain standards of 'professional' behaviour, should define the beneficiaries of media freedom, rather than the fact that the actor is already contributing to public opinion, or their education, training or employment. However, before discussing the concept, and how it can be applied to deal with a variety of legal challenges, this chapter will address the normative problem identified in Chapter 1:[2] one of the dominant philosophical theories that underpins free speech and media freedom is John Stuart Mill's argument from truth, a distinct interpretation or form of which is the marketplace of ideas theory.[3]

---

[1]   See Chapter 1 section 3.

[2]   Ibid.

[3]   This theory was formulated by Justice Oliver Wendell Holmes in *Abrams v United States* 250 US 616 (1919) 616, 630–631. As discussed in section 3, in *R v Secretary of State for the Home Department, ex parte Simms* [2000] 2 AC 115, 126 Lord Steyn treated Mill's argument from truth and Justice Holmes' marketplace of ideas as interchangeable. This view is supported by a number of commentators, including Andrew Nicol QC, Gavin Millar QC and Andrew Sharland QC (see A. Nicol QC, G. Millar QC and A. Sharland, *Media Law and Human Rights* (2nd edn., Oxford University Press, 2009) 2–3, [1.05]) and Frederick Schauer (see F. Schauer, *Free Speech: A Philosophical Enquiry* (Cambridge University Press, 1982) 15–16) who treat

The media-as-a-constitutional-component concept

I make the claim in this chapter that because the argument from truth and the marketplace of ideas are based on historical means of communication, they are ill-suited for twenty-first-century speech and the modern media, of which the internet, social media and citizen journalists are no longer outliers but central components. Therefore, although, as will be established below, libertarianism has historically underpinned the notion of the Fourth Estate, has a 'hold' on First Amendment jurisprudence and is arguably the dominant normative paradigm for online speech, in conflict with the scholarly observations referred to in the following section, it is not, in fact, the appropriate normative framework for such speech or the media-as-a-constitutional-component concept.

Thus, in section 2 it is argued that libertarianism is the de facto normative paradigm. This claim forms the foundation for section 3, which, based on analysis of the argument from truth and the marketplace of ideas, contends that libertarianism should be rejected as a normative framework for online speech and the media-as-a-constitutional-component concept. It considers the medium through which citizen journalists tend to communicate, namely the internet and social media. In doing this it explains the problems and challenges associated with citizen journalists operating online in a libertarian framework. This leads on to section 4, in which I advance the proposition that social responsibility theory should be embraced as the dominant normative paradigm. I argue here that it is better suited to underpin the modern media because it: (i) provides an effective compromise between libertarianism and paternalism; (ii) supports the argument from democratic self-governance, which is an ideal philosophical foundation for the media-as-a-constitutional-component concept; and (iii) enables a new functional definition of the media, which is introduced in section 5. In making this argument in section 4 I discuss the relationship between the media-as-a-constitutional-component concept and other participatory theories of free speech, including Robert Post's participatory theory of democracy and how this theory differs from the concept in relation to how they secure equal access to the public sphere. Finally, section 6 considers how the new normative framework advanced throughout this chapter, in offering an alternative means of interpreting free speech that recognises twenty-first-century methods of communication, could better deal with some of the legal challenges that arise from the media operating within the current libertarian paradigm. In doing so,

---

the marketplace of ideas as simply an extension of the argument from truth. However, in line with commentators such as Paul Wragg (P. Wragg, 'Mill's Dead Dogma: The Value of Truth to Free Speech Jurisprudence' (2013) April, *Public Law* 363, 368–369), Vincent Blasi (V. Blasi, 'Reading Holmes through the Lens of Schauer' (1997) 72(5) *Notre Dame Law Review* 1343, 1355) and Eric Barendt (E. Barendt, *Freedom of Speech* (2nd edn., Oxford University Press, 2005) 11–13), this book treats the theory as a distinct interpretation, or form, of the argument from truth.

132   *Media freedom in the age of citizen journalism*

I set out the challenges that will be examined in Part III of this book, namely: what this conceptualisation of the media means for media freedom; balancing speaker and audience interests in respect of anonymous and pseudonymous social media speech; ensuring the integrity of trials and the open justice principle and achieving a balance between reputational rights and free speech; and regulating citizen journalists.

2   LIBERTARIANISM

2.1   Introducing Libertarianism: The De Facto Normative Paradigm for Free Speech?

From an Anglo-American perspective this theory[4] has served as an exegesis to the arguments advanced by John Locke, John Milton, John Erskine, John Stuart Mill,[5] Thomas Jefferson and Justice Oliver Wendell Holmes,[6] and has tended to support the traditional notion of the press as the Fourth Estate.[7] In the US, the theory was made an explicit and foundational tenet of democracy, as it is enshrined within the First Amendment,[8] pursuant to which 'Congress shall make no law ... abridging the freedom of speech, or of the press'.[9] Central to the influence of libertarianism on free speech has been Milton's self-righting process,[10] Mill's argument from truth and, in particular, Justice Holmes' marketplace of ideas theory[11] that was laid down in *Abrams v United States*.[12] As explained below, this theory encapsulates the self-righting process as it is

---

[4]   See section 2.2 for an explanation as to what the theory means.

[5]   P. Wragg, *A Free and Regulated Press. Defending Coercive Independent Press Regulation* (Hart Publishing, 2020) ix.

[6]   These theorists are discussed at section 2.

[7]   D. Weiss, 'Journalism and Theories of the Press' in S. Littlejohn and K. Foss (eds), *Encyclopedia of Communication Theory Volume 2* (Sage, 2009) 576.

[8]   Ibid; P. Plaisance, 'The Mass Media as Discursive Network: Building on the Implications of Libertarian and Communitarian Claims for New Media Ethics Theory' (2005) 15(3) *Communication Theory* 292, 295.

[9]   Consequently, US Supreme Court decisions have consistently defended media freedom from government intervention and regulation based on libertarian ideology. For example, see *New York Times v Sullivan* 376 US 254 (1964); *New York Times v United States* 403 US 713 (1971). See generally P. Stewart, 'Or of the Press' (1975) 26 *Hastings Law Journal* 631.

[10]   This is discussed at section 2.2.

[11]   See S. Baran and D. Davis, *Mass Communication Theory: Foundations, Ferment and Future* (7th edn., Wadsworth Publishing, 2014) 68; Weiss (n 7) 577; F. Siebert, T. Peterson and W. Schramm, *Four Theories of the Press* (University of Illinois Press, 1956) 44–45.

[12]   250 US 616 (1919).

The media-as-a-constitutional-component concept 133

based on the premise that 'truth', or the 'best' ideas, will win out as they will naturally emerge from the competition of ideas in the marketplace.[13] Thus, as Eric Barendt observes:

> It is almost impossible to exaggerate the central hold of the 'market-place of ideas' metaphor on US jurisprudence and general thinking about the First Amendment freedom of speech. From it stems the belief that the best corrective for the expression of pernicious opinion is not regulation, let alone suppression, but more speech. Truth, it is said, will emerge from the competition of ideas in the market-place ... This is the central tradition of US free speech jurisprudence ... it is now taken quite literally as the appropriate framework for First Amendment jurisprudence.[14]

In the context of online speech the internet (and it is suggested, by extension, social media) has provided the perfect environment for libertarianism, and specifically the marketplace of ideas theory, to flourish as it 'provides a space for information exchange and individual decision-making free of bureaucracy, administrative power and other restrictions of "real" space'.[15] It has therefore been recognised by commentators that libertarianism has become the de facto communication theory for online speech within Western democracies.[16] This is because 'cyberspace is founded on the primacy of individual liberty'[17] and, as a result, there now exists a 'normative assumption that all nation-states should adopt a libertarian orientation toward their oversight of new media'.[18]

2.2   What Is Meant by 'Libertarianism'?

In his essay *The Libertarian Theory*, found in *Four Theories of the Press*, Fred Siebert uses the term 'libertarianism' to describe an alternative model of press freedom to social responsibility theory.[19] The ambiguity of this conception, can, however, be problematic, for two reasons: first, because, as stated above, much of this conception is an exegesis of Locke et al,[20] it is easy to conclude

---

[13]   *Abrams v United States* 250 US 616 (1919) 616, 630–631; see also *Gitlow v New York* 268 US 652 (1925) 673 per Justice Holmes.

[14]   E. Barendt, 'The First Amendment and the Media' in I. Loveland (ed), *Importing the First Amendment: Freedom of Speech and Expression in Britain, Europe and the USA* (Hart Publishing, 1998) 43. See also F. Schauer, 'The Political Incidence of the Free Speech Principle' (1993) 64 *University of Colorado Law Review* 935, 949–952.

[15]   L. Dahlberg, 'Cyber-libertarianism 2.0: A Discourse Theory/Critical Political Economy Examination' (2010) 6(3) *Cultural Politics* 331, 332–333.

[16]   Ibid; Weiss (n 7) 579.

[17]   M. Kapor, 'Where is the Digital Highway Really Going?' (1993) 1(3) *Wired* 53.

[18]   Weiss (n 7) 579.

[19]   Siebert et al (n 11) 2.

[20]   Wragg (n 5).

that by libertarianism Siebert actually meant classic liberalism;[21] secondly, the term can also refer to 'socialist libertarianism', which means 'the abolition of capitalism and the withering of the state to night-watchman status', which 'leads in the direction of anarchism, Marxism, and revolutionary socialism'.[22] Thus, to prevent any misunderstanding it is important for me to be clear in my meaning of libertarianism. When I discuss the term 'libertarianism' in this book I do not mean classic liberalism, nor do I mean the concept of socialist libertarianism. Rather, I am referring to an interpretation of libertarianism that recognises the expression market, rather than the state, as the only means of achieving the ends of media freedom, and which aims to further laissez-faire thinking and expression.[23]

The origins of this interpretation of the theory can be traced back to sixteenth-century Europe[24] and, in particular, John Milton's *Areopagitica*, which was published in 1644.[25] Although not a comprehensive statement of the principles of freedom of expression and of the press it provided strong libertarian arguments against authoritarian controls of free speech and the press and for intellectual freedom.[26] Milton's tract laid down the self-righting process, which underpins libertarianism,[27] and as stated above, is enshrined within the marketplace of ideas theory. The process dictates that everyone should be free to express themselves and, ultimately:

> The true and sound will survive; the false and unsound will be vanquished. Government should keep out of the battle and not weigh the odds in [favour] of one side or the other. And even though the false may gain a temporary victory, that which is true, by drawing to its [defence] additional forces, will through the self-righting process ultimately survive.[28]

---

[21] Ibid.

[22] Ibid.

[23] This is a view I share with Paul Wragg. Ibid.

[24] J.H. Altschull, *From Milton to McLuhan The Ideas Behind American Journalism* (Pearson, 1990) chs. 4–9.

[25] J. Milton, *Areopagitica* (Clarendon Press Series, Leopold Classic Library, 2016).

[26] Authoritarians justified this control, and the authoritarian theory's requirement to acquiesce to those in power, on the basis that it was necessary to protect and preserve a divinely ordained social order. In most countries this control rested in the hands of the monarch, who would grant royal charters or licences to media practitioners. If the charters or licences were violated, then they could be revoked, and those responsible could be jailed. Consequently, censorship was indicative of authoritarianism, as was the arbitrary and erratic ways in which control was exercised. See Siebert et al (n 11) ch. 1; Baran and Davis (n 11) 63.

[27] Siebert et al (n 11) 51.

[28] Ibid 45.

Early libertarians such as Milton and John Erskine[29] argued that if individuals could be freed from restrictions on communication, people would 'naturally' follow the dictates of their conscience, seek truth, engage in public debate and, consequently, create a better life for themselves and others.[30]

In applying this brand of libertarianism to the modern media, John Merrill suggests that from a pure libertarian perspective the media should be characterised by 'uncontrolled, full, unregulated laissez-faire journalism – with a clear separation of State and [media]'.[31] Indeed, in Merrill's view, freedom should be the underlying moral principle of any press theory: '[t]here is a basic faith, shown by libertarian advocates, that a free press – working in a laissez-faire, unfettered situation – will naturally result in a pluralism of information and viewpoints necessary in a democratic society.'[32] This resonates with two statements made by Siebert: first, he observes that libertarians have opposed government support 'since it led to domination', and rather they trust the 'capitalist system of private enterprise to find a way';[33] Secondly, he says that the self-righting process determines that

> the public at large be subjected to a barrage of information and opinion, some of it possibly true, some of it possibly false, and some of it containing elements of both. Ultimately the public could be trusted to digest the whole, to discard that not in the public interest and to accept that which served the needs of the individual and of the society of which he is a part.[34]

In the context of online speech this correlates closely with the view of cyber-libertarians, who argue that 'the harm in regulating online speech is greater than the harm caused by the online speech'[35] and who 'favour an archaic, unregulated internet free from state control, fearing that regulation will stifle internet development and associated freedoms'.[36] Thus, libertari-

---

[29]   Some 50 years after Milton published *Areopagitica* Erskine advanced the libertarian principles of freedom of speech and of the press in defence of publishers accused of violating the law. See T. Howell, *A Complete Collection of State Trials London: 1704, Volume 22* (T.C. Howard, 1817) 414.

[30]   Baran and Davis (n 11) 63.

[31]   J.C. Merrill, *The Imperative of Freedom: A Philosophy of Journalistic Autonomy* (Freedom House, 1990) 11.

[32]   Ibid 35.

[33]   Siebert et al (n 11) 52.

[34]   Ibid 51.

[35]   I. Nemes, 'Regulating Hate Speech in Cyberspace: Issues of Desirability and Efficacy' (2002) 11(3) *Information & Communication Technology Law* 193.

[36]   Ibid 199. See also B. Leiter, 'Clearing Cyber-Cesspools: Google and Free Speech' in S. Levmore and M. Nussbaum (eds), *The Offensive Internet* (Harvard University Press, 2010) 156; J. Bartlett, *The Dark Net* (Random House, 2014) 8–9.

anism, as it is referred to in this book, dictates that free speech is an intrinsic natural right that individuals are born with, and it does not propagate duties and responsibilities that attach to the right to freedom of expression and, by extension, media freedom. It rests on the moral principle of autonomous agency,[37] and as a result assumes that free individuals will express their ideas and opinions, and that other free individuals will listen.[38] In contrast to the social responsibility model of the media, which, as is discussed below at section 4, identifies with a collectivist theory of society, libertarianism sprang from individualistic theory.[39] As Michael Freeden explains, libertarianism stresses individualism and assumes the superior rationality of the individual. Consequently, 'liberty alone, in its purest form, is the message that should be extracted from the liberal tradition and employed to guide social and political ... life',[40] hence the libertarian notion of the self-righting process.

Despite the efforts of the likes of Milton and Erskine, it was not until the eighteenth century that authoritarian press control by the Crown and Church began to decline, and state monopolies in publishing were eventually abolished. By the end of the century the authoritarian regime had been entirely replaced by libertarian principles protecting freedom of speech and the press from state and Church intervention.[41] Later proponents of libertarian theory, such as Thomas Jefferson[42] and, in particular, Mill and Justice Holmes, were equally as influential in this shift away from authoritarianism as Milton had been in the theory's emergence. Indeed, it is because of Mill's argument from truth, and the introduction by Justice Holmes of the marketplace of ideas theory, that libertarian free speech ideology continued to flourish in the nineteenth and into the twentieth centuries.[43] In the twentieth century the Royal Commission on the Press[44] in the UK, and the Commission on Freedom of

---

[37] This contrasts with the social responsibility theory, discussed at section 4, which has a communitarian focus. Plaisance (n 8) 298, 300–301.

[38] Siebert et al (n 11) 96–97.

[39] Ibid 53, 82; Plaisance (n 8) 300.

[40] M. Freeden, *Liberalism: A Very Short Introduction* (Oxford University Press, 2015) 35–36.

[41] Siebert et al (n 11) 44.

[42] Thomas Jefferson, during his presidency, consistently emphasised the theory in his defence of freedom of the press. For example, see A. Lipscomb (ed), *The Writings of Thomas Jefferson* (Memorial Edition, Thomas Jefferson Memorial Association, 1904, Vol. 11) 32–34.

[43] Siebert et al (n 11) 44–45.

[44] The Royal Commission on the Press, 1947–1949, *Report* (Cmnd. 7700) was formed at the instigation of the National Union of Journalists. It was established 'with the object of furthering the free expression of opinion through the Press and the greatest possible accuracy in the presentation of news, to inquire into the control, management and censorship of the newspaper and periodical Press and the news agencies, including

the Press (otherwise known as the Hutchins Commission)[45] and the work of William Ernest Hocking[46] in the US, were catalysts for the emergence of the social responsibility theory.[47] Yet, despite the theory being underpinned by a dogmatic devotion to voluntary self-regulation of the press,[48] the 'doctrine has always been relegated to the fringes of journalism education and the newsroom'.[49] For the reasons discussed above, this marginalisation of the social responsibility doctrine is certainly the case in respect of online speech.[50] Thus, largely due to the influence of the argument from truth and, in particular, the marketplace of ideas, which are analysed in the following section, libertarianism remains a dominant communication theory, not just in respect of US free speech jurisprudence,[51] but also in relation to the underlying principles of the Fourth Estate and, significantly, in the context of online speech and citizen journalism.[52]

---

the financial structure and the monopolistic tendencies in control, and to make recommendations thereon'.

[45] The Commission on Freedom of the Press, *A Free and Responsible Press* (University of Chicago Press, 1947). The Commission was set up in 1942 and reported in 1947. Its aim was 'to examine areas and circumstances under which the press of the United States is succeeding or failing; to discover where freedom of expression is or is not limited, whether by government censorship pressure from readers or advertisers or the unwisdom of its proprietors or the timidity of its management'. According to Denis McQuail, it was created in 'response to widespread criticism of the American newspaper press, especially because of its sensationalism and commercialism, but also its political imbalance and monopoly tendencies'. See D. McQuail, *McQuail's Mass Communication Theory* (5th edn., Sage, 2005) 170–171.

[46] Although the emergence of the theory is attributed to the Hutchins Commission, the chief architect of the theory was, in fact, one member of the Commission, William Ernest Hocking, rather than the Commission itself. See W.E. Hocking, *Freedom of the Press: A Framework of Principle* (University of Chicago Press, 1947).

[47] McQuail (n 45); J. McIntyre, 'Repositioning a Landmark: The Hutchins Commission and Freedom of the Press' (1987) 4 *Critical Studies in Mass Communication* 95; Siebert et al (n 11) ch. 3.

[48] See sections 4.1, 6.2 and 6.3.

[49] C. Christians, J. Ferré and P. Fackler, *Good News: Social Ethics and the Press* (Oxford University Press, 1993) 38.

[50] P. Coe, '(Re)embracing Social Responsibility Theory as a Basis for Media Speech: Shifting the Normative Paradigm for a Modern Media' (2018) 69(4) *Northern Ireland Legal Quarterly* 403, 406–407.

[51] Barendt (n 14) 43.

[52] Dahlberg (n 15) 332–333.

3 REJECTING LIBERTARIANISM AS A FLAWED NORMATIVE FRAMEWORK: PROBLEMS WITH THE ARGUMENT FROM TRUTH AND THE MARKETPLACE OF IDEAS

Justifications for the protection of freedom of expression and media freedom are predominantly underpinned by four philosophical theories. These are (i) the argument from truth; (ii) the marketplace of ideas; (iii) the argument from self-fulfilment; and (iv) the argument from democratic self-governance.[53] This philosophical foundation is apparent, to varying degrees, within contemporary domestic jurisprudence and that of the ECtHR.[54] For instance, the House of Lords recognised the existence of all of these rationales in *R v Secretary of State for the Home Department, ex parte Simms*,[55] where Lord Steyn stated the often repeated passage[56] that freedom of expression 'serves a number of broad objectives' and is intrinsically valuable because

> [f]irst, it promotes the self-fulfilment of individuals in society. Secondly, in the famous words of Mr Justice Holmes (echoing John Stuart Mill), 'the best test of truth is the power of the thought to get itself accepted in the competition of the market.' ... Thirdly, freedom of speech is the lifeblood of democracy. The free flow of information and ideas informs political debate ...[57]

---

[53] There are other free speech theories, such as Jürgen Habermas' concept of discourse and the public sphere and Robert Post's theory of participatory democracy. These theories, and their relationship with the media-as-a-constitutional-component concept, are discussed in section 4.2.1.

[54] According to Helen Fenwick and Gavin Phillipson, in *Handyside v United Kingdom* (1976) 1 EHRR 737 the ECtHR referred, at least implicitly, to these theories, when it stated, at [49]: 'Freedom of expression constitutes one of the essential foundations of such a society, one of the basic conditions for its progress and for the development of every man.' However, Fenwick and Phillipson go on to observe that although freedom of expression can be defended on all of these rationales, only the argument from democratic self-governance has been prominently employed by the ECtHR: see H. Fenwick and G. Phillipson, *Media Freedom under the Human Rights Act* (Oxford University Press, 2006) 39, 707–710; P. Wragg, 'A Freedom to Criticise? Evaluating the Public Interest in Celebrity Gossip after *Mosley* and *Terry*' (2010) 2(2) *Journal of Media Law* 295, 318.

[55] [2000] 2 AC 115.

[56] Lord Steyn's judgment has been referred to numerous times within domestic jurisprudence. For example, see *R (on the application of Lord Carlisle of Berriew QC and others) v Secretary of State for the Home Department* [2014] UKSC 60 per Lord Kerr, [164].

[57] [2000] 2 AC 115, 126.

The media-as-a-constitutional-component concept 139

Leading commentators, including Ronald Dworkin, Frederick Schauer, Joseph Raz, Eric Barendt, Thomas Scanlon and Kent Greenawalt, and more recent commentators, such as Paul Wragg, John Charney, and Helen Fenwick and Gavin Phillipson,[58] have already provided rich and extensive coverage of these arguments in a variety of contexts, which this book does not intend to repeat.[59] Instead, this section seeks to do the following: it will analyse how the argument from truth and the marketplace of ideas operates in the context of online speech and citizen journalism and, in doing so, it will demonstrate why these philosophical arguments are ill-suited to support the modern media. This analysis will defend the proposition set out in section 1 that, despite its dominance over free speech jurisprudence, libertarianism does not provide an appropriate normative framework for media speech and the media-as-a-constitutional-component concept. This leads into the discussion at section 4, which sets out why the social responsibility model of the media is better suited to this task. Ultimately, it will be argued that it provides a suitable basis for the argument from democratic self-governance, which is an ideal philosophical foundation for media speech and the media-as-a-constitutional-component concept.

3.1   The Argument from Truth

The argument from truth is located in Mill's nineteenth-century text *On Liberty* and, predominantly, his essay 'Of the Liberty of Thought and Discussion'.[60] Unfortunately for Mill, *On Liberty* is often misconceived as an argument that truth is most likely to emerge from totally uninhibited freedom of thought and expression, or that 'unimpeded debate eradicates error in popular debate';[61] an

---

[58]   For example, see R. Dworkin, *Do We Have a Right to Pornography?* in *A Matter of Principle* (Harvard University Press, 1985); R. Dworkin, *Freedom's Law* (Oxford University Press, 1996); Schauer (n 3); J. Raz, 'Free Expression and Personal Identification' (1991) 11 *Oxford Journal of Legal Studies* 303; Barendt (n 3); T. Scanlon, 'A Theory of Freedom of Expression' (1972) 1(2) *Philosophy & Public Affairs* 204; K. Greenawalt, 'Free Speech Justifications' (1989) 89 *Columbia Law Review* 119; Wragg (n 5) 138–145; Wragg (n 3); J. Charney, *The Illusion of the Free Press* (Hart Publishing, 2018); Fenwick and Phillipson (n 54).

[59]   See also L. Alexander, *Is there a Right to Freedom of Expression?* (Cambridge University Press, 2005); T. Campbell and W. Sadurski, *Freedom of Communication* (Dartmouth, 1994); J.M. Balkin, 'Digital Speech and Democratic Culture: A Theory of Freedom of Expression for the Information Society' (2004) 79 *New York University Law Review* 1.

[60]   J.S. Mill, *On Liberty, Essays on Politics and Society* in J.M. Robson (ed), *Collected Works of John Stuart Mill*, vol. XVIII (University of Toronto Press, 1977) ch. 2, 228–259.

[61]   Wragg (n 5) 138. For example, see L.C. Bollinger, *The Tolerant Society* (Oxford University Press, 1986) 74; B. Williams, *Truth and Truthfulness* (Princeton

140 *Media freedom in the age of citizen journalism*

enduring interpretation that Wragg describes as 'frustrating as well as bewildering'[62] when one considers that Mill himself is clear in *On Liberty* that such claims are nonsense.[63] What, then, is Mill's claim?

In his view, thought and discussion protects individual liberty from its predominant threat,[64] which is not 'political oppression', but 'social tyranny':[65] a 'tyrannical majority'[66] that does not allow for autonomous thought, expression or opposition, but instead requires absolute accord with its own ideas and opinions.[67]

As will be seen below, in relation to the four facets of Mill's argument, it is subject to a conflict between the discoverability of truth and the constant need for disagreement about that truth.[68] Mill argues that truth does not always and immediately triumph, but rather that it will continually be subject to rediscovery, and will eventually emerge victorious, despite suppression.[69]

According to Schauer, for Mill, the issue is not certain truth; instead, his primary concern is 'epistemic advance'.[70] Indeed, Mill regards truth, at times, as merely a by-product of open discussion.[71] Thus, of paramount importance to Mill is not the discovery of truth, but the process of discussion and debate.[72] Mill argues that the foundations and reasoning upon which opinions are based must be continually tested and, as result, the acceptance of alternative views by others, and ultimately the reliable discovery of truth, must derive from effective persuasion rather than coercion.[73]

Additionally, Mill says that why we should not use truth to determine what is acceptable and unacceptable speech, and therefore, by extension, why we should not regulate based on truth, has four facets. First, the state would expose its own fallibility if it suppressed opinion on account of that opinion's perceived falsity as, in fact, it may be true.[74] Secondly, even if the suppressed

---

University Press, 2002) 212; Schauer (n 3) 25; O. O'Neill, 'Practices of Toleration' in J. Lichtenberg (ed), *Democracy and the Mass Media* (Cambridge University Press, 1990) 158; Fenwick and Phillipson (n 54) 14.

[62] Wragg) 139.
[63] Mill (n 60) 238–239.
[64] Ibid 229.
[65] Ibid 220.
[66] Ibid 219.
[67] Ibid 219–220; Wragg (n 3) 365.
[68] Wragg) 365; the importance of truth is discussed in more detail below.
[69] Ibid 365
[70] Schauer (n 3) 25.
[71] J. Gray, *Mill on Liberty: A Defence* (2nd edn., Routledge, 1996) 110.
[72] Schauer (n 3) 20; This is discussed in relation to problems with the justifications below.
[73] Mill (n 60) 217–223.
[74] Ibid 258; see generally Barendt (n 3) 8.

opinion is objectively false, it has some value as it may (and in Mill's opinion very commonly does) contain an element of truth.[75] Thirdly, since the dominant opinion on any given subject is rarely, or never, the whole truth, what remains will only appear as a result of the collision of adverse opinions.[76] Finally, notwithstanding the third facet, even if the received opinion is not only true, but the entire truth, unless it is rigorously discussed and debated it will not carry the same weight, as the rationale behind it may not be fully and accurately comprehended.[77] Consequently, unless opinions can be frequently and freely challenged, by forcing those holding them to defend their views, the very meaning and essence of that true belief may, itself, be weakened, become ineffective, or even lost:[78] In Mill's words, the true belief 'will be held as a dead dogma, not a living truth'.[79]

As Wragg says, Mill values open discussion and debate instrumentally and intrinsically,[80] 'as a condition of that rationality and belief which he conceives of as a characteristic feature of a free man'.[81] Mill argues that there should be 'freedom of opinion and sentiment on all subjects, practical or speculative, scientific, moral or theological'.[82] Accordingly, the very existence of disagreement is critical to the health of society[83] and the type or quality of expression is irrelevant as the 'usefulness of an opinion is itself a matter of opinion' and to make an assessment of quality is an 'assumption of infallibility'.[84] It therefore appears that Mill envisaged the argument to apply to the expression of opinion and debate. However, it can also be used in support of freedom of information claims as 'the possession of pertinent information about a subject will nearly always be a prerequisite to the formation of a well-worked-out opinion on the matter'.[85]

Despite Schauer's argument that the desirability of truth within society is almost universally accepted,[86] and the fact that this view seems to correlate

---

[75] Mill (n 60) 229.

[76] Ibid 252, 258.

[77] Ibid 258.

[78] Ibid 258; see also Wragg (n 5) 139–140; Wragg (n 3) 365.

[79] Mill) 243.

[80] Wragg (n 3) 365; see also H. Fenwick, *Civil Liberties and Human Rights* (4th edn., Routledge Cavendish, 2007) 302.

[81] Gray (n 71) 107.

[82] Mill (n 60) 226.

[83] Wragg (n 3) 365.

[84] Mill (n 60) 233–234; see also K.C. O'Rourke, *John Stuart Mill and Freedom of Expression: The Genesis of a Theory* (Routledge, 2001) 108.

[85] Fenwick and Phillipson (n 54) 15.

[86] Schauer (n 3) 17; see also J. Feinberg, *Social Philosophy* (Prentice-Hall, 1973) 26.

142   *Media freedom in the age of citizen journalism*

with Jacob LJ's obiter statement in *L'Oreal SA v Bellure NV*[87] that pursuant to various international laws[88] 'the right to tell – and to hear – the truth has high international recognition',[89] the assumption derived from the argument that freedom of expression leads to truth, can be attacked on a number of fronts. First, there is not necessarily a causal link between freedom of expression and the discovery of truth.[90] This is particularly pertinent with regard to online speech, where anybody can express opinions or views, or disseminate information. Consequently, the internet is saturated with information emanating from the traditional media, citizen journalists and non-media actors that is inaccurate, misleading or untrue. This issue is animated by the phenomenon of false news explored in Chapter 3.[91] Not only has this phenomenon become synonymous with events such as the COVID-19 pandemic[92] and the Cambridge Analytica scandal, it has also led to social media platforms being asked to deal with the proliferation of false news on their sites,[93] particularly in the context of elections. For example, in the wake of the 2016 US election, Facebook, in particular, was the subject of strong criticism,[94] which resulted in the platform announcing a partnership with a third-party fact-checking organisation to deal with the challenge of false news.[95] This issue with false news, and Facebook's

---

[87]   [2010] EWCA Civ 535.

[88]   Article 19 Universal Declaration of Human Rights; Article 19(2) ICCPR; Article 10(1) ECHR; Article 11(1) Charter of the Fundamental Rights of the European Union: [2010] EWCA Civ 535, [10].

[89]   [2010] EWCA Civ 535, [10].

[90]   Schauer (n 3) 15.

[91]   See Chapter 3 section 5.3.

[92]   See the discussion on false news and COVID-19 in Chapter 2 section 3.3.2, and see P. Coe, 'The Good, The Bad and The Ugly of Social Media During the Coronavirus Pandemic' (2020) 25(3) *Communications Law* 119.

[93]   E. Klaris and A. Bedat, 'With the Threat of Fake News, Will Social Media Platforms Become [like] Media Companies and Forsake Legal Protections?' *Inforrm*, 21 December 2016.

[94]   H. Allcott and M. Gertzkow, 'Social Media and Fake News in the 2016 Election' (2017) 31(2) *The Journal of Economic Perspectives* 211; O. Solon, '2016: the year Facebook became the bad guy', *The Guardian*, 12 December 2016. See Chapter 3 section 5.3 for a discussion on Twitter's role in disseminating junk news in the 2016 US election.

[95]   'Addressing Hoaxes and Fake News', https://newsroom.fb.com/news/2016/12/news-feed-fyi-addressing-hoaxes-and-fake-news/, 15 December 2016. Online platforms are not just working with fact checking organisations in relation to elections. In November 2020 it was announced that *Full Fact* will coordinate the collaboration of *YouTube, Facebook* and *Twitter*, along with governments and research bodies, to combat the spread of misinformation about potential COVID-19 vaccines: 'YouTube, Facebook and Twitter align to fight Covid vaccine conspiracies', *BBC*, 20 November 2020. These collaborations are only likely to increase in light of the UK government's

response, betrays a deeper problem for social networking platforms: these measures (partnering with a fact-checking organisation) clearly run counter to libertarian ideology yet, at the same time, Facebook is trying to maintain a grip on liberal values, demonstrated by its reiteration of its commitment to 'giving people a voice' and that it 'cannot become an arbiter of truth'.[96] Thus, social media platforms such as Facebook are struggling to come to terms with a conflict between the reality of online speech and the libertarian values upon which they, as organisations, were originally founded. In other words, libertarianism is not compatible with what they have become. In the same vein, the fact that Cambridge Analytica harvested over 50 million user profiles without Facebook's permission and manufactured sex scandals and false news to influence voters in elections around the world[97] is even more damning of libertarian ideology. The relative ease with which the firm breached Facebook's data security enabled it to essentially hijack democracy, demonstrating that the philosophical rationales underpinning libertarianism, in the form of the argument from truth and the marketplace of ideas, are fundamentally flawed and unrealistic, particularly in the context of online speech.

Secondly, notwithstanding Jacob LJ's statement, there is no right to truth per se[98] and, contrary to Schauer's contention, arguably the dissemination of truth is not always a good thing. In some situations, the protection of other, countervailing, values should take precedence. Ironically, this is illustrated by the international instruments referred to by Jacob LJ in *L'Oreal*. Taking the ECHR as an example, Article 10(2) enables expression, and therefore both truths and untruths, to be legitimately withheld on grounds of, inter alia, health or morals, national security, public safety, protecting the reputation and honour of private individuals, the prevention of disorder or crime, and breach of confidence. Equally, this can be applied to trade secrets, medical information, data protection, confidentiality agreements or official secrecy. Within the context of social media, the revenge porn phenomenon illustrates this dichotomy. Under the law of England and Wales, this offence, which exists by virtue of

---

response to the Online Harms White Paper consultation and the introduction of the Online Safety Bill. Upon the enactment of the Bill online misinformation and disinformation will come under the remit of Ofcom, the online harms regulator. See clause 98 of the Online Harms Bill and 'Online Harms White Paper: Full government response to the consultation', 15 December 2020, [2.80]–[2.88]. See Chapter 2 section 3.3.2 and the discussion at Chapter 3 section 5.3.

[96] 'Addressing Hoaxes and Fake News' (n 95).

[97] P. Bernal, *The Internet, Warts and All. Free Speech, Privacy and Truth* (Cambridge University Press, 2018) 16, 91, 243; P.N. Howard, *Lie Machines* (Yale University Press, 2020) 64, 161; P. Greenfield, 'The Cambridge Analytica files: the story so far', *The Guardian*, 26 March 2018.

[98] Wragg (n 3) 372.

section 33 of the Criminal Justice and Courts Act 2015, was essentially created to combat individuals sharing, via text messages and social media, sexually explicit content of an ex-partner without that person's permission.[99] Although the explicit pictures, videos and accompanying text may well be 'true', the dissemination of this content could clearly harm the victim's health and morals, their reputation and honour, and be a misuse of private information.[100] Thus, as Barendt argues, '[i]t is not inconsistent to defend a ban on the publication of propositions on the ground that their propagation would seriously damage society, while conceding that they might be true'.[101]

Finally, a further argument that undermines the argument from truth as a rationale to defend free speech claims relates to its lack of application in ECtHR case law. Strasbourg jurisprudence is most closely aligned with the argument from democratic self-governance, which the European Court has made clear is at the core of Article 10 ECHR.[102] Of course, the UK's courts are able to develop the concept of free speech domestically so as to provide for a right that encapsulates the broader arguments for freedom of expression found in the argument from truth, the marketplace of ideas and the argument from self-fulfilment.[103] Indeed, as illustrated by the judgments of Lord Steyn and Jacob LJ in *R v Secretary of State for the Home Department, ex parte Simms*[104] and *L'Oreal*[105] respectively, the argument from truth has been employed domestically.[106] However, in conflict with these judgments the House of Lords consistently interpreted the obligation imposed on judges to take Strasbourg jurisprudence into account in domestic proceedings, pursuant to section 2 Human Rights Act 1998, strictly, meaning that the domestic development of

---

[99] Section 96(6)(c) states that section 33 applies to England and Wales only. For further analysis, see P. Coe, 'The Social Media Paradox: An Intersection with Freedom of Expression and the Criminal Law' (2015) 24(1) *Information & Communications Technology Law* 16, 27–29.

[100] Prior to the Criminal Justice and Courts Act 2015 coming into force, a number of criminal offences and civil causes of action were applied to revenge porn. See ibid.

[101] Barendt (n 3) 8, 133; Coe (n 50) 410.

[102] *Lingens v Austria* (1986) 8 EHRR 407; *Jersild v Denmark* (1995) 19 EHRR 1; L. Wildhaber, 'The Right to Offend, Shock or Disturb? Aspects of Freedom of Expression under the European Convention on Human Rights' (2001) 36 *Irish Jurist* 17; Wragg (n 54) 314.

[103] Wragg (n 54) 314.

[104] [2000] 2 AC 115, 126.

[105] [2010] EWCA Civ 535, [10].

[106] See also *R (on the application of Animal Defenders International) v Secretary of State for Culture, Media and Sport* [2008] UKHL 15. However, as stated by Wragg, arguably the argument from democratic self-governance could also have been applied to protect free speech in each of these cases: Wragg (n 54) 318.

The concept of free speech in this way is hard to justify.[107] For instance, in *R (on the application of Ullah) v Special Adjudicator*[108] Lord Bingham stated that the 'duty of the national courts is to keep pace with the Strasbourg jurisprudence as it evolves over time: no more, but certainly no less'.[109] Consequently, domestic jurisprudence should 'mirror' the jurisprudence of the ECtHR.[110] According to Lord Bingham in *Ullah*, failure to follow 'clear and constant' Strasbourg jurisprudence would be unlawful under section 6(1) of the Human Rights Act 1998[111] unless there were 'special circumstances'[112] that justify departure from that approach.[113] Despite Lord Bingham's judgment in *Ullah* being the subject of both judicial and academic criticism,[114] the mirror principle remains in place. Thus, unless it can be persuasively argued that such 'special circumstances' exist, then the philosophical argument that must be applied to domestic case law, in line with Strasbourg jurisprudence, is the argument from democratic self-governance, as opposed to the inherently libertarian argument from truth and the marketplace of ideas.

3.2   The Marketplace of Ideas

Although the marketplace of ideas is a distinct theory, it is generally regarded as deriving from Mill's argument from truth.[115] It emanates from Justice

---

[107]   Wragg (n 54) 314.

[108]   [2004] 2 AC 323.

[109]   Ibid 350.

[110]   *R (on the application of Quark Fishing Ltd) v Secretary of State for Foreign and Commonwealth Affairs* [2006] 1 AC 529, [34] per Lord Nicholls. See also J. Lewis, 'The European Ceiling on Human Rights' [2007] *Public Law* 720; Wragg, 'A Freedom to Criticise?' (n 54) 314.

[111]   Section 6(1) states: 'It is unlawful for a public authority to act in a way which is incompatible with a Convention right'; Pursuant to section 6(3) the definition of 'public authority' includes the courts.

[112]   It is unclear what amounts to 'special circumstances'. See Wragg (n 54) 314.

[113]   Ibid.

[114]   In *R (on the application of Children's Rights Alliance for England) v Secretary of State for Justice* [2013] EWCA Civ 34, [62]–[64] Laws LJ stated:
    I hope the *Ullah* principle may be revisited. There is a great deal to be gained from the development of a municipal jurisprudence of the Convention Rights, which the Strasbourg court should respect out of its own doctrine of the margin of appreciation, and which would be perfectly consistent with our duty to take account of (not to follow) the Strasbourg cases.
For academic criticism, see R. Masterman, 'Taking the Strasbourg Jurisprudence into Account: Developing a "Municipal" Law of Human Rights under the Human Rights Act' (2005) 54 *International and Comparative Law Quarterly* 907; Lewis (n 110).

[115]   See n 3.

146 *Media freedom in the age of citizen journalism*

Holmes' judgment in *Abrams v United States*,[116] in which it was asserted that 'the best test of truth is the power of the thought to get itself accepted in the competition of the market'.[117] Subsequently, Holmes J's judgment garnered support from other influential judges, including Justice Brandeis in *Whitney v California*;[118] Justice Hand in *United States v Dennis*[119] and *International Brotherhood of Electrical Workers v NLRB*;[120] and Justice Frankfurter in *Dennis v United States*,[121] who observed that 'the history of civilization is in considerable measure the displacement of error which once held sway as official truth by beliefs which in turn have yielded other truths. Therefore, the liberty of man to search for truth ought not be fettered, no matter what orthodoxies he may challenge.'[122] Echoing Milton's self-righting process, the theory dictates that an open and unregulated market, which allows for ideas to be traded through the free expression of all opinions, is most likely to lead to the truth and, consequently, increased knowledge.[123] Hence, the examination of an opinion within the 'marketplace' subjects it to a test that is more reliable than individual or governmental appraisal.[124]

Herein lies an initial problem with the theory: it is, essentially, a variation of a fundamental principle of capitalism – namely the notion of a self-regulating consumer marketplace. Consequently, it is open to both economic and democratic interpretations.[125] Although this section, and this book, are predominantly concerned with the democratic interpretation as this has generated more scholarship and jurisprudence relating to the operation of the theory in respect of free speech, the economic interpretation is worthy of brief consideration as it does present problems applicable to citizen journalism, and media speech more widely.

The eighteenth-century economist Adam Smith formulated the principle of the 'invisible hand', or laissez-faire doctrine, guiding free consumer markets.

---

[116] 250 US 616 (1919).

[117] Ibid 630–631. See also *Gitlow v New York* 268 US 652 (1925) 673 per Justice Holmes.

[118] 274 US 357 (1927) 375–378.

[119] 181 F2d 201 (2d Cir 1950); *Dennis v United States* 341 US 494, 584 (1951).

[120] 181 F2d 34 (2d Cir 1950).

[121] 341 US 494 (1951) 546–553.

[122] See also Frankfurter J's judgment in *Kovacs v Cooper* 336 US 77, 95–97 (1949).

[123] See generally J. Oster, 'Theory and Doctrine of "Media Freedom" as a Legal Concept' (2013) 5(1) *Journal of Media Law* 57–78, 70; J. Alonzo, 'Restoring the Ideal Marketplace: How Recognizing Bloggers as Journalists Can Save the Press' (2006) 9 *NYU Journal of Legislation and Public Policy* 751, 762.

[124] Schauer (n 3) 16; see also Alonzo (n 123) 762.

[125] P. Napoli, 'The Marketplace of Ideas Metaphor in Communications Regulation' (1999) 49 *Journal of Communication* 151, 151–152.

The media-as-a-constitutional-component concept   147

Pursuant to this principle, there is no need for government regulation of markets as an open and unregulated marketplace should regulate itself; if one manufacturer charges too much for a product, or produces an inferior product, competitors will either charge less, or produce a higher-quality product, to attract buyers. Thus, government interference is not required to protect consumers or to force manufacturers to meet consumer needs.[126] According to the marketplace of ideas theory, Smith's principle should be applied to the media; that is, if ideas are 'traded' freely within society, the correct or best ideas will eventually prevail.[127]

However, there are considerable difficulties in applying this logic to the modern media and in particular citizen journalists operating online and through social media. Media content is far less tangible than other consumer products.[128] As a result, and in contrast to the consumer marketplace, the perceived meaning of individual media messages can vary depending on the respective recipient. Taking this a step further, the medium through which the information is communicated can influence not only the communication's perceived meaning, but also the impact that it has on its intended and potentially non-intended audience. This point is illustrated by jurisprudence emanating from both the ECtHR and the US Supreme Court relating to the regulation of different forms of media.[129] In *Jersild v Denmark*[130] the European Court stated that 'the potential impact of the medium concerned is an important factor and it is commonly acknowledged that the audiovisual media have often a much more immediate and powerful effect than the print media ... conveying through images meanings which the print media are not able to impart'.[131]

The US Supreme Court has also acknowledged the significance of a medium in respect of the influence it can have on recipients of information. In *Burstyn v Wilson*,[132] which concerned cinema regulation, the Court noted how a medium 'present(s) its own particular problems'.[133] Similarly, in *Metromedia v City of San Diego*,[134] a case relating to billboard regulation, the Court stated that each method of communication is a 'law unto itself' and, consequently, the law

---

[126] A. Skinner (ed), *Adam Smith, The Wealth of Nations* (Penguin, 1982). See also Weiss (n 7) 577; Baran and Davis (n 11) 67.

[127] Baran and Davis (n 11) 67.

[128] Ibid.

[129] See generally D. Mac Síthigh, *Medium Law* (Routledge, 2018) 24–28; M. Feintuck and M. Varney, *Media Regulation, Public Interest and the Law* (2nd edn., Edinburgh University Press, 2006) 81.

[130] (1995) 19 EHRR 1.

[131] Ibid [31].

[132] 343 US 495 (1952).

[133] Ibid 503.

[134] 453 US 490 (1981).

148   *Media freedom in the age of citizen journalism*

must respond to differences between media, in terms of their 'natures, values, abuses and dangers'.[135] In *FCC v Pacifica Foundation*,[136] which related to television broadcasting regulation, the Court recognised television's immediacy and accessibility and its peculiarly pervasive and intrusive potential.[137] In a similar vein, albeit in respect of the internet rather than television, in *Reno v American Civil Liberties Union*[138] the Court was of the opinion that 'the Internet is not as invasive as radio or television'.[139] In coming to this decision, the Court relied upon the finding of the District Court that

> [c]ommunications over the Internet do not invade an individual's home or appear on one's computer screen unbidden. Users seldom encounter content by accident ... [a]lmost all sexually explicit images are preceded by warnings as to the content ... odds are slim that a user would come across a sexually explicit sight by accident'.[140]

This judgment is indicative of the pace at which online and social media communication has developed, as the findings upon which the decision is based are arguably at odds with current online expression.[141] Internet communications, in particular those transmitted via social media, can be invasive. To an extent this may be 'allowed' by the user of the platform by virtue of registering with the platform and joining particular communities. However, users are still subject to 'unbidden' messages regularly appearing on their mobile telephone, tablet and laptop screens.[142] Further, the availability of overt and covert sexually explicit content has been proliferated by social media and is synonymous with platforms such as WhatsApp, Snapchat[143] and YouTube.[144]

---

[135] Ibid 501.

[136] 438 US 726 (1978).

[137] Ibid 727.

[138] 521 US 844 (1997).

[139] Ibid 869.

[140] *American Civil Liberties Union v Reno* 929 F Supp 824 (ED Pa, 1996) (finding 88).

[141] This judgment is discussed again in Chapter 7 section 3.1 in the context of anonymous and pseudonymous speech.

[142] For detailed analysis of how the economic constructs of social media have influenced this issue, see J. Dijck, *The Culture of Connectivity* (Oxford University Press, 2013) 163–176; see also Coe (n 50) 413.

[143] As demonstrated by the 'revenge porn' phenomenon. See Coe (n 99) 28–29; Leiter (n 36) 155.

[144] For example, see A. Griffin, 'Porn videos secretly hidden on YouTube as pirates bypass Google's sexual content controls', *The Independent*, 16 January 2017; L.-M. Eleftheriou-Smith, 'Explicit porn videos disguised with Irish subtitles were live on YouTube for months before being removed', *The Independent*, 12 February 2015.

Although these cases pre-date the advent of citizen journalism and ubiquitous online speech, the concerns articulated by the ECtHR and the Supreme Court are almost prophetic as they are equally applicable, if not more pertinent, to online communication. As discussed in Chapter 3, the internet and social media have enabled journalists to operate outside of the structure and norms of the institutional media, which allows citizen journalists to circumvent the normal editorial and production processes.[145] This can enable excellent citizen journalism[146] but, through the speech it encourages and conveys, it can also breed its own 'abuses and dangers'.[147] Because social media is arguably more immediate, pervasive and accessible to individuals than even television broadcasting, its messages have a potentially greater impact than any other medium.

Turning now to the democratic interpretation of the theory, it has been suggested that discovering truth is dependent upon unregulated competition in the actual, as opposed to the ideal, marketplace.[148] To the contrary, it has been said that the marketplace of ideas is grounded in relativism in that the ideas that emanate from the competitive market are the truth, leaving nothing more to be said.[149] Oster relies heavily upon this rationale to distinguish media from non-media actors.[150] In his view, because of the media's power and ability to communicate via multiple channels, the theory requires that the media should be subject to protection and only minimal restriction. This is because this 'privilege' for journalists encourages the dissemination of more information, which in turn generates more valuable and truthful information.[151] However, arguably this reasoning is flawed as it is the very reasons used by Oster to support his approach that render the theory unsuitable to that which it has been applied. Indeed, according to Barendt, whatever interpretation is adopted, the theory 'rests on shaky grounds',[152] which 'appear particularly infirm in the context of mass media communications'[153] for reasons that are pertinent to online speech

---

[145] See Chapter 3 sections 6.2.2 and 6.2.3.

[146] Coe (n 50) 413–414.

[147] Ibid. See the discussion in Chapter 3 section 6.2.2.

[148] B. Williams, *Truth and Truthfulness* (Princeton University Press, 2002) 214–215; see also Barendt (n 3) 12.

[149] Barendt (n 3) 12.

[150] Oster (n 123) 70–71; J.S. Nestler, 'The Underprivileged Profession: The Case for Supreme Court Recognition of the Journalist's Privilege' (2005) 154 *University of Pennsylvania Law Review* 201, 211. Contrary to Oster's reliance on the marketplace of ideas theory to distinguish media from non-media actors, it is advanced in section 4 that, in fact, the argument from democratic self-governance is a more suitable philosophical foundation for this task.

[151] Oster (n 123) 70–71; Nestler (n 150) 211.

[152] Barendt (n 3) 12; see also Barendt (n 14) 43–46.

[153] Barendt (n 14).

150   *Media freedom in the age of citizen journalism*

and citizen journalism, but also apply equally to the traditional institutional media using social media and citizen journalists as a source of news.

First, if the assertion that one statement is stronger than another (whether these statements are communicated via a tweet, or a post on Facebook or YouTube, or whether they are printed in a newspaper) cannot be intellectually supported and defended, the notion of truth loses its integrity,[154] as history demonstrates: falsehood frequently triumphs over truth, to the detriment of society.[155] Secondly, in line with Jürgen Habermas' concept of discourse and the public sphere, which aims at reaching a rationally motivated consensus and is based on the assumption of the prevalence of reason,[156] the theory assumes that recipients of the communication consider what they read or view within the context of the marketplace rationally; deciding whether to accept or reject it, based on whether it will improve their lifestyle, and society generally.[157] This assumption accords with Lord Kerr's view in *Stocker v Stocker*,[158] in which his Lordship referred to a 'new class of reader: the social media user', who understands that an online platform 'is a casual medium in the nature of conversation' rather than carefully chosen expression'.[159] For the reasons set out below, however, this assumption upon which the theory is based, and incidentally Lord Kerr's judgment, are unrealistic within the modern media marketplace.[160] As a consequence, this basis of rationality makes a fallacy of the marketplace of ideas theory.

The first observation to be made about rationality is that citizen journalism, and the internet and social media generally, proliferate a huge amount of infor-

---

[154] Barendt (n 3) 12.

[155] R. Abel, *Speech and Respect* (Stevens & Sons Limited, 1994) 48; D. Milo, *Defamation and Freedom of Speech* (Oxford University Press, 2008) 57.

[156] J. Habermas, *The Structural Transformation of the Public Sphere* (Polity Press, 1962); *The Theory of Communicative Action, vol. 1: Reason and the Rationalization of Society* (Beacon Press, 1984) 25, 39, 99; *The Theory of Communicative Action, vol. 2: Lifeworld and System: A Critique of Functionalist Reason* (Beacon Press, 1987) 120, 319; *Between Facts and Norms: Contributions to a Discourse Theory of Law and Democracy* (William Rehg trans., Polity Press, 1996); J. Oster, *Media Freedom as a Fundamental Right* (Cambridge University Press, 2015) 29–31. We return to the Habermasian concept of discourse and the public sphere in section 4.2.1, where its relationship with the argument from democratic self-governance is discussed.

[157] J. Weinberg, 'Broadcasting and Speech' (1993) 81 *California Law Review* 1103; S. Ingber, 'The Marketplace of Ideas: a Legitimizing Myth' [1984] *Duke Law Journal* 1; J. Skorupski, *John Stuart Mill* (Routledge, 1991) 371–372.

[158] [2019] UKSC 17.

[159] Ibid [41] and [43].

[160] F. Schauer, 'Free Speech in a World of Private Power' in T. Campbell and W. Sadurski (eds), *Freedom of Communication* (Dartmouth, 1994) 6; Barendt (n 3) 12. See also A. Kenyon, 'Assuming Free Speech' (2014) 77(3) *Modern Law Review* 379, 382.

mation that is poorly researched or simply untrue, yet has the potential to, and very often does, emerge as the dominant 'view', regardless of the detrimental impact this may have on society.[161] In turn, the traditional media using citizen journalists and social media as a source of news may regurgitate this information, which, as discussed in Chapter 2, can gain credibility with the public and other publishers by the very fact that a 'trusted' member of the institutional media has published it.[162] Arguably, this issue is amplified by the ubiquity of anonymity and pseudonymity on the internet and social media, making it hard, if not impossible, for readers to accurately and rationally assess the veracity of the speaker.[163] Thus, in reality, in a marketplace that contains true and untrue or misleading information in at least equal proportions, some of which may be published anonymously or under a pseudonym, it may be impossible for recipients of the communication to make a rational assessment of what they have read, viewed or listened to.[164]

This point leads on to a second observation based on cognitive psychology research that, although it pre-dates the advent of social media, is relevant to online speech. In order to deal with the endless flow of information we are subjected to on a daily basis we try to fit each new piece of information into a set of pre-existing cognitive structures, or schemas, that provide 'simplified mental models' of the world.[165] Processing new ideas and information in this way creates problems when people encounter information that cannot be processed in this manner, as they reject information that conflicts with their schemas.[166] According to commentators such as Mark Peffley et al, Doris Graber and William McGuire, in these circumstances people are predisposed to deny the validity of the new information and, instead, reinterpret it so that it conforms to the schema within which they want the information to fit, or,

---

[161] P. Coe, 'Redefining "Media" Using a "Media-as-a-constitutional-component" Concept: An Evaluation of the Need for the European Court of Human Rights to Alter Its Understanding of "Media" Within a New Media Landscape' (2017) 37(1) *Legal Studies* 25, 45. This criticism reflects that levelled at Mill's argument from truth at section 3.1 in relation to false news and there not necessarily being a causal link between free speech and the discovery of truth. See also the discussion relating to the reporting of the COVID-19 pandemic in Chapter 2 section 3.3.2, and how social media has distorted the public sphere at section 5 of Chapter 3.

[162] Chapter 2 section 3.3.2.

[163] Anonymous and pseudonymous speech is dealt with in detail in Chapter 7.

[164] See the discussion in Chapter 3 section 5.3.

[165] D.A. Graber, *Processing The News: How People Tame The Information Tide* (2nd edn., Guildford Publications, 1988) 31.

[166] Weinberg (n 157) 1159.

152 *Media freedom in the age of citizen journalism*

alternatively, they process it as an isolated exception.[167] Therefore, because people interpret ambiguous reality to accord with their schemas they become self-reinforcing and, in turn, more powerful as they are repeatedly 'tested' but never disconfirmed.[168] This is indicative of arguments suggesting that the mass media are better at reinforcing existing attitudes and beliefs than changing them[169] as we largely ignore information that we deem to be irrelevant to our existing schemas.[170] As Jonathan Weinberg states, once people 'make up their mind' and 'reach closure' on an issue, they tend to reject new information, regardless of whether it supports or conflicts with their views.[171] Conversely, people seek out and resonate with information that is compatible with their schemas and will, in turn, 'support' this information.[172] In Stanley Ingber's view, it is impossible to create a collective marketplace of unfettered discourse and discovery if we are constrained by our adherence to long-established mental patterns.[173] This results in the 'packaging' of an argument determining how well it is received, as opposed to it being assessed on the merits of its 'contents'.[174] Consequently, because our schemas influence what ideas and information we are willing to accept, 'people's social location ... control[s] the manner in which they perceive and understand the world'.[175] This research has been described as having 'distressing implications for the marketplace theory'.[176] Indeed, it reinforces the point that the marketplace of ideas' basis of rationality makes a fallacy of the theory in that, to the extent that our schemas constrain how we react to new ideas and information, the way we think is not 'characterised by reason'.[177] This observation is significant to social media,

---

[167] Graber (n 165) 174–177; W.J. McGuire, 'Attitudes and Attitude Change' in G. Lindzey and E. Aronson (eds), *Handbook of Social Psychology* (3rd edn., Lawrence Elbaum Association, 1986) 275–276; M. Peffley, S. Feldman and L. Sigelman, 'Economic Conditions and Party Competence: Processes of Belief Revision' (1987) 49 *Journal of Politics* 100, 101.

[168] M.A. Fajer, 'Can Two Real Men Eat Quiche Together? Storytelling, Gender-Role Stereotypes and Legal Protection for Lesbians and Gay Men' (1992) 46 *University of Miami Law Review* 511, 525.

[169] L. Jaffe, 'The Editorial Responsibility of the Broadcaster: Reflections on Fairness and Access' (1972) 85 *Harvard Law Review* 768, 769–770; Weinberg (n 157) 1160.

[170] Graber (n 165) 186.

[171] Weinberg (n 157) 1160.

[172] S. Fiske and S. Taylor, *Social Cognition* (2nd edn., Sage, 1991) 218–220.

[173] Ingber (n 157) 34–36.

[174] C.E. Baker, 'Scope of the First Amendment Freedom of Speech' (1978) 25 *UCLA Law Review* 964, 976–977; Graber (n 165) 261.

[175] Baker (n 174) 967.

[176] Weinberg (n 157) 1162.

[177] Ibid.

The *media-as-a-constitutional-component* concept   153

which, due to the sheer amount of information it generates and the invasive way in which it can potentially disseminate it, arguably only serves to amplify how we process information using pre-exiting schemas and, in doing so, makes the issue with rationality more acute. The false news phenomenon and its association with social media 'filter bubbles' touched upon in Chapter 3 animate this.[178] Filter bubbles are created by algorithms that filter our online experiences, effectively placing us in echo chambers of our own beliefs,[179] which means we are more likely to interact with content which conforms with our pre-existing views[180] and which, as a result, is likely to contribute to greater polarisation. Therefore, the more we interact with particular 'types' of information on social media, whether that be generated by the press, citizen journalists or casual social media users, or whether it is true or false, the more of that particular 'type' of information we will be exposed to by virtue of the filter bubble. Thus, within the context of online speech at least, as Weinberg declares, '[t]o the extent that our most basic views and values are relatively immune to rational argument, the marketplace metaphor seems pointless'.[181]

The third and final reason why the theory is flawed relates ·to truth discovery. The theory assumes that the marketplace contains expression that solely represents the views of the proponents of, for instance, publications or broadcasts, as opposed to being conveyed on the basis of restrictions such as editorial control, ownership, political bias or a need or desire to increase commercial revenue through advertising and/or sales.[182] To an extent this may be true within the context of online speech, where there are, in theory at least, fewer restrictions. However, as discussed in Chapter 3, citizen journalists are by no means totally uninhibited by, and are not immune to, at least some of the pressures felt by the institutional media that limit the scope of the public sphere.[183] For the reasons set out in Chapters 2 and 3, the theory's premise in this respect is acutely problematic and unrealistic in respect of the traditional institutional media, and in particular the press, for two reasons. First, many

---

[178] Chapter 3 section 5.2.

[179] See generally D. Spohr, 'Fake News and Ideological Polarization: Filter Bubbles and Selective Exposure on Social Media' (2017) 34(3) *Business Information Review* 150; E. Pariser, *The Filter Bubble: What the Internet is Hiding from You* (Penguin, 2011).

[180] N. Stroud, 'Media Use and Political Predispositions: Revisiting the Concept of Selective Exposure' (2008) 30 *Political Behaviour* 341.

[181] Weinberg (n 157) 1162.

[182] See Chapter 2 section 3.3.2 and Chapter 3 sections 4 and 5.

[183] See Chapter 3 sections 5 and 6.

154 *Media freedom in the age of citizen journalism*

outlets are driven by these restrictions, to the detriment of investigative journalism,[184] as observed by Thomas Gibbons:

> The liberal theory of the media appears to be influential, yet there is a countervailing view, supported by much evidence, that the media have a tendency to distort our understanding of the world ... The media devote a relatively small part of their content to public affairs, including official wrong-doing, preferring to emphasise entertainment more generally. They also devote little time to wider sources of power including economic power. Furthermore, news may be managed to serve the media's interests, whether they be the proprietor's or the company's more broadly.[185]

Thus, as Andrew Kenyon states, there is a 'disjunction between ideas of political equality and economic communication markets'.[186] These markets are inconsistent with democratic requirements as, unlike citizen journalism, the orientations of commercial media have primarily been to advertisers and to audiences as consumers.[187] Consequently, research points towards there being a 'narrowness of political views within major media'.[188] As Baker acknowledges, the market-based media cannot be expected to serve audiences as well as citizens.[189]

Secondly, as has been previously discussed, traditional institutional media outlets use citizen journalists, and social media generally, as a source of news. Therefore, in the same way that citizen journalists may recycle false or misleading information obtained from the press or other bloggers, the traditional

---

[184] See Chapter 2 sections 1 and 3.3.2 and Chapter 3 section 4.

[185] T. Gibbons, '"Fair Play to All Sides of the Truth": Controlling Media Distortions' (2009) 62(1) *Current Legal Problems* 286, 289. See also J. Curran, 'Mediations of Democracy' in J. Curran and M. Gurevitch (eds), *Mass Media and Society* (4th edn., Hodder Arnold, 2005) 129.

[186] Kenyon (n 160) 386.

[187] Ibid; Gibbons (n 185) 290.

[188] Kenyon (n 160) 387; T. Gibbons, 'Freedom of the Press: Ownership and Editorial Values' [1992] *Public Law* 279, 286–287; E. Bechtold, 'Has the United States' Response to the COVID-19 Pandemic Exposed the Marketplace of Ideas as a Failed Experiment?' (2020) 25(3) *Communications Law* 150–160. See also the study by Toril Aalberg and James Curran et al which investigated the content of print and broadcast news and ordinary people's knowledge and understanding of matters of political and more general public interest: T. Aalberg and J. Curran (eds), *How Media Inform Democracy: A Comparative Approach* (Routledge, 2012); B.H. Bagdakian, *The Media Monopoly* (6th edn., Beacon Press, 2000) xxvii–xxxi; R.W. Chesney, *Rich Media, Poor Democracy* (University of Illinois Press, 1999); N. Chomsky, *Media Control: The Spectacular Achievements of Propaganda* (2nd edn., Seven Stories Press, 2002); see Chapter 2 section 3.1.

[189] See generally C.E. Baker, *Media, Markets and Democracy* (Cambridge University Press, 2002).

media may do the same in respect of information obtained from citizen journalists and social media.

Ultimately, libertarianism is flawed as a normative paradigm as it is based on the unproven assertion that the product of the media marketplace, which is only one out of an infinite number of potential outcomes, gains a de facto privileged status as the 'truth'.[190] As Richard Schwarzlose states, this creates the 'dilemma of libertarianism': in the marketplace of ideas 'is it truth that survives, or is whatever survives the truth?'[191] Based on the arguments advanced in this section, libertarianism, as a normative paradigm founded upon philosophical doctrine such as the argument from truth and the marketplace of ideas, is unable to provide a suitably robust rejoinder to this 'dilemma'.[192] This demonstrates that libertarian ideology is an inadequate normative framework for the modern media and the media-as-a-constitutional-component concept. The following section argues that the social responsibility model, underpinned by democratic justifications of free speech, provides a more suitable basis for such a framework.

4 SOCIAL RESPONSIBILITY THEORY

In this section it will be argued that the social responsibility theory, underpinned by the argument from democratic self-governance, creates a more appropriate normative and philosophical framework for the modern media than libertarianism as it endorses an approach to media expression based on behavioural standards and norms of discourse and can, as a result, improve access to the public sphere. The theory dictates that media freedom is distinct from personal freedom of expression, a view that correlates with the jurisprudence of the ECtHR.[193] This distinction means that certain demands can be placed on media actors in performance of their duties over and above what would apply to individuals. As Leveson LJ acknowledges in his *Inquiry*, unlike individual expression freedom of the press (and by extension the wider media)

---

[190] G. Wuliger, 'The Moral Universe of Libertarian Press Theory' (1991) 8 *Critical Studies in Media Communication* 152, 156; Plaisance (n 8) 297.

[191] R.A. Schwarzlose, 'The Marketplace of Ideas: A Measure of Free Expression' (1989) 118 *Journalism Monographs* 1, 8.

[192] Indeed, Paul Wragg suggests that in the context of press regulation, as a normative paradigm, libertarianism is 'derelict'. This is a contention that I wholeheartedly agree with. See Wragg (n 5) 255.

[193] See Chapter 4 section 2. This also correlates with the evidence given by Baroness Onora O'Neill to the Leveson Inquiry. Baroness O'Neill has long held the view that media freedom is normatively distinct from personal freedom of expression: Lord Justice Leveson, *An Inquiry into the Culture, Practices and Ethics of the Press: Report*, HC 780, November 2012, 55, [3.7]. See nn 260 and 261.

156 *Media freedom in the age of citizen journalism*

is valued only instrumentally, as opposed to intrinsically, when it performs democratic functions with a view to developing commercially as a sector, such as informing the democratic process, and acting as a check and balance on political, corporate or individual power.[194]

Based on a combination of jurisprudence and scholarship, and by recourse to the argument from democratic self-governance, this section formulates a functional media-as-a-constitutional-component concept approach to distinguishing media from non-media actors. In line with the values underpinning the social responsibility theory, it will suggest that the media should be defined functionally rather than institutionally, in that the performance of a constitutional function, and adherence to certain behavioural standards, should determine the beneficiaries of media freedom, as opposed to the individual being defined as media simply based upon their employment or training, or because they have previously contributed to discourse. Ultimately, it seeks to establish the principle that media freedom, and its privileges, attach to the concept and could therefore apply to anyone serving a constitutional function: that is, operating within the parameters of the social responsibility paradigm by adhering to the standards of professional behaviour and the norms of discourse set out below.

4.1 The Media-as-a-constitutional-component Concept, Social Responsibility Theory, and Standards of Professional Behaviour

Like libertarianism, the social responsibility theory is an Anglo-American concept. As stated in section 2.2, the catalyst for the emergence of the theory was the work of William Hocking,[195] and two reports commissioned on either side of the Atlantic in the 1940s: The Royal Commission on the Press[196] in the UK and the Hutchins Commission report[197] in the US. The Hutchins Commission report, which drew heavily on the work of Hocking, who was one of its members,[198] was particularly influential in establishing this new communication paradigm and in finding a balance between libertarianism and paternalism. Accordingly, in Baker's view it 'provides the most influential modern account of the goals of journalistic performance' and is virtually treated as the 'official Western view'.[199] In simple terms the report laid down

---

[194]   Leveson (n 193) 55, [4.1]–[4.5].
[195]   Hocking (n 46).
[196]   Royal Commission (n 44).
[197]   Hutchins Commission (n 45).
[198]   See n 46.
[199]   Baker (n 189) 154. Baker has also described it as 'the most important, semi-official, policy orientated study of the mass media in US history': C.E. Baker,

five requirements of media performance: first, to provide a truthful, comprehensive and intelligent account of the day's events in a context which gives them meaning, and to clearly distinguish fact from opinion; secondly, to be a forum for the exchange of comment and criticism by operating as common carriers of public discussion, even if this means disseminating views contrary to their own; thirdly, to project a representative picture of the constituent groups in society; fourthly, to be responsible for the presentation and clarification of the goals and values of society; and fifthly, to provide full access to the day's intelligence.[200]

The Royal Commission and Hutchins Commission reports, and the eventual establishment of the theory, were born out of diminishing faith in libertarianism's optimistic notion that the self-righting process carried 'built-in correctives' for the media.[201] Echoing the concerns advanced by the CPEP discussed in Chapter 2,[202] Theodore Peterson, in his essay *The Social Responsibility Theory*, distils the themes of criticism of the media's behaviour and its effect on the public sphere at the time as follows: (i) it used its power for its own ends, with owners propagating their own opinions to their political and economic advantage at the expense of opposing views; (ii) it had been subservient to big business, with advertisers controlling editorial policies and content; (iii) it resisted social change; (iv) it was more willing to publish superficial and sensational stories than to publish 'significant' stories; (v) it had endangered public morals; (vi) it invaded the privacy of individuals without just cause; (vii) it was controlled by an elite socio-economic class, meaning that access to the industry was difficult, which consequently endangered the free and open marketplace of ideas.[203] This disillusionment gave rise to an extreme anti-libertarian movement grounded in paternalism, which resulted in increased pressure on the UK and US governments to regulate the media. As Peterson states (from a US perspective): '[a] rather considerable fraction of articulate Americans began to demand certain standards of performance from the press. They threatened to enact legislation ... if the press did not meet ... those standards.'[204] Within the Hutchins Commission itself there was a clear divide between those who held strong libertarian views and those who favoured some form of press regulation due to, in their view, the fragility of the marketplace of ideas theory making the media vulnerable to subversion

---

Media Concentration and Democracy: Why Ownership Matters (Cambridge University Press, 2007) 2.

[200] Baker (n 189) 20–30.
[201] Siebert et al (n 11) 77.
[202] See Chapter 2 sections 2 and 3.
[203] Siebert et al (n 11) 78–79.
[204] Ibid 77.

by anti-democratic forces.[205] These proponents of regulation were guided by a philosophy of public communication developed by social researchers at the University of Chicago during the 1940s.[206] In opposing the notion of the marketplace of ideas the Chicago School argued that an unregulated press served the interests of large or socially dominant groups. To their minds, the protection of free speech was not the same as the provision of free speech.[207] Therefore, they wanted government regulation to play an 'interventionary role' in order 'to provide enabling structures for a healthy public sphere'.[208]

Ultimately, because the Commission feared that the imposition of compulsory regulation could act as a catalyst for official control of the press,[209] it was clear in its report that the press should regulate itself.[210] However, in caveating this recommendation it left open the possibility for government intervention in the activity of the press, albeit '[w]ithout intruding on press activities ... government may act to improve the conditions under which they take place so that the public interest is better served'.[211] And, in doing so, it recognised that '[n]ew legal remedies and preventions' as 'aids to checking the more patent abuses of the press'[212] may be required. However, it was explicit that any such laws or preventions should be permissive rather than restrictive, in that they should not be 'subtractions from freedom', but rather a 'means of increasing freedom, through removing impediments to the practice and repute of the honest press'.[213] Consequently, the Commission found an acceptable compromise between libertarian ideology and paternalism in the form of the social responsibility theory, which was founded on faith placed in the press by the Commission's members, who emphasised that the press needed to refocus its efforts on serving the public, which would 'obviate governmental action

---

[205]   Baran and Davis (n 11) 73.

[206]   Ibid. See also V. Pickard, *America's Battle for Media Democracy: The Triumph of Corporate Libertarianism and the Future of Media Reform* (Cambridge University Press, 2015) 154.

[207]   Baran and Davis (n 11) 73.

[208]   V. Pickard, 'Whether the Giants Should Be Slain or Persuaded to Be Good: Revisiting the Hutchins Commission and the Role of Media in a Democratic Society' (2010) 27 *Critical Studies in Media Communication* 391, 394.

[209]   See generally D. Davis, 'News and Politics' in D. Swanson and D. Nimmo (eds), *New Directions in Political Communication* (Sage, 1990); J. McIntyre, 'Repositioning a Landmark: The Hutchins Commission and Freedom of the Press' (1987) 4 *Critical Studies in Mass Communication* 95.

[210]   Hutchins Commission (n 45) 126.

[211]   Ibid 127. In making this recommendation the Commission drew on the work of Hocking (n 46).

[212]   Ibid.

[213]   Ibid 127–128.

to enforce [its public responsibility]' through regulation.[214] As James Curran states:

> [The Commission] endorsed professional responsibility ... [as] a way of reconciling market flaws with the traditional conception of the democratic role of the media. [The Commission's report] asserted journalists' commitment to higher goals – neutrality, detachment, a commitment to truth. It involved the adoption of certain procedures for verifying facts, drawing on different sources, presenting rival interpretations. In this way, the pluralism of opinion and information, once secured through the clash of adversaries in the free market, could be recreated through the 'internal pluralism' of monopolistic media. Market pressures to sensationalize and trivialize the presentation of news could be offset by a commitment to inform.[215]

In the UK this faith placed in the press to 'do the right thing', and a resistance to anything other than voluntary self-regulation, has run consistently through government policy, from 1949 when the Royal Commission on the Press presented its findings, up to the present day, in the recommendations made by Leveson LJ at the conclusion of his *Inquiry*. The result of the first government inquiry was the creation of the Press Council, whose primary function 'should be to safeguard the freedom of the Press; to encourage the growth of the sense of public responsibility and public service amongst all engaged in the profession of journalism ...; and to further the efficiency of the profession and the well being of those who practice [*sic*] in it.'[216] If we fast forward to 2012, the same sentiments come through in Leveson LJ's ideal outcome for the press: 'what is required is independent self-regulation. By far the best solution to press standards would be a body, established and organised by the industry, which would provide genuinely independent and effective regulation of its

---

[214] Hutchins Commission (n 45) 91. See also Baran and Davis (n 11) 72.

[215] J. Curran, 'Mass Media and Democracy: A Reappraisal' in J. Curran and M. Gurevitch (eds), *Mass Media and Society* (Edward Arnold, 1991) 98. In section 6.2 I argue that this blind faith placed in the press to 'do the right thing' by the Commission and social responsibility theorists that followed, which led to a dogmatic resistance to anything other than blunt and self-serving voluntary self-regulation of the press, is a deficiency of the theory; it represents nothing more than an idealistic *hope* that has been consistently undermined by the behaviour of the press. As I suggest in that section, and as I set out in detail in Chapter 9, the media-as-a-constitutional-component concept seeks to rectify this by advancing a regulatory scheme that, although it operates within a voluntary and approved self-regulatory model, differs significantly from the current regime in that it provides statutory and non-statutory incentives and has statutory powers to impose sanctions on publishers, which not only go well beyond section 34 and the currently inactive section 40 of the Crime and Courts Act 2013, but would apply to citizen journalists.

[216] Royal Commission (n 44) ch. XI, [683]–[684].

160 *Media freedom in the age of citizen journalism*

members and would be durable.'[217] As Wragg observes, this 'sanguinity' has not just been found in either of the public inquiries.[218] For instance, in 2012 Lord Chief Justice Igor Judge endorsed the idea that self-regulation is the 'only' way to ensure independence from government.[219]

In summary, the theory is based on the following rationale: unlike libertarianism, which does not propagate duties and responsibilities that attach to the right to freedom of expression and media freedom, under social responsibility doctrine, this freedom carries concomitant responsibilities and obligations to society, employers and the market.[220] If the media does not at least attempt to meet these responsibilities and obligations then as a consequence it cannot benefit from the right to media freedom.[221] The theory rests on the moral principle of justice,[222] hence the right to free speech and media freedom must be balanced against the private rights of others and vital social interests: as beneficiaries of the right to media freedom the media are obligated to continually strive to preserve democracy[223] by fulfilling essential constitutional normative functions of mass communication that extend beyond the mere provision of a robust marketplace of ideas,[224] including: (i) 'servicing the political system' by providing information, discussion and debate on public affairs; (ii) 'enlightening the public' so as to make it capable of democratic self-governance by disseminating information of public interest; and (iii) 'protecting the rights of the individual' by acting as the public watchdog.[225] In fulfilling these functions the media must ensure that it: sets and maintains high professional standards of truth and balance and conduct;[226] avoids the communication of material that may lead to or incite criminal activity; and refrains from offending minority or marginalised groups.[227] Finally, at the heart of the theory, is the requirement of the media to foster productive and creative 'Great Communities', in that it facilitates access to the public sphere by encouraging cultural pluralism and by being a voice for all people, not just elite or dominant groups.[228]

---

[217] Leveson (n 193) 1758, [4.1].

[218] Wragg (n 5) 66.

[219] Lord Judge, 13th Annual Justice Lecture, 'Press Regulation', 19 October 2011.

[220] Siebert et al (n 11) 74.

[221] Ibid 98. See Chapter 6 sections 3.2 and 3.3 for a detailed discussion on the media's obligations in respect of its conduct and acting in good faith.

[222] Plaisance (n 8) 300.

[223] Baran and Davis (n 11) 73.

[224] Siebert et al (n 11) 74; Plaisance (n 8) 300.

[225] (Siebert et al (n 11) 74.

[226] The media's obligations to conduct itself correctly and act in good faith are discussed in greater detail in the following chapter at sections 3.2 and 3.3 respectively.

[227] Weiss (n 7) 577.

[228] Baran and Davis (n 11) 73.

4.2 Social Responsibility Theory, the Argument from Democratic Self-governance, and Norms of Public Discourse

Although the argument from democratic self-governance has been applied by the US Supreme Court and the House of Lords to defend free speech claims,[229] it is most commonly associated with the jurisprudence of the ECtHR.[230] As explained above in relation to the argument from truth,[231] the ECtHR has consistently placed it at the core of its jurisprudence on Article 10[232] and, as a result, pursuant to the 'mirror principle', it should, in theory at least, underpin free speech domestically.[233] Regardless of how the argument has been treated jurisprudentially in the US, by the ECtHR, and by domestic courts, for reasons that are discussed below it is submitted that it is best suited to support modern media speech and the media-as-a-constitutional-component concept, and that as a result, the concept and its philosophical and normative foundations are consistent with Strasbourg jurisprudence. In line with the values underpinning social responsibility theory, as we shall see below, the argument is based on the premise that the predominant purpose of freedom of expression is to protect the right of citizens to understand political matters in order to facilitate and enable societal engagement with the political and democratic process.[234] Ultimately, an informed electorate is an ideal of democracy.[235] Thus, the argument complements the social responsibility paradigm by setting norms, or parameters, for the type of speech the media can convey within the confines of media freedom.

---

[229] For example, from the US Supreme Court see *Whitney v California* 274 US 357 (1927) per Brandeis J at 375–378; *Garrison v Louisiana* 379 US 64, 74–75 (1964); C. Estlund, 'Speech on Matters of Public Concern: The Perils of an Emerging First Amendment Category' (1990) 59(1) *George Washington Law Review* 1, 1; from the House of Lords, see *R v Secretary of State for the Home Department, ex parte Simms* [2000] 2 AC 115 per Lord Steyn at 126. See generally Barendt (n 3) 18.

[230] For example, see *Lingens v Austria* (1986) A 103, [42]; *Bladet Tromsø and Stensaas v Norway* (2000) 29 EHRR 125, [59]; *Bergens Tidende v Norway* (2001) 31 EHRR 16, [48].

[231] See section 3.1.

[232] *Lingens v Austria* (1986) 8 EHRR 407; *Jersild v Denmark* (1995) 19 EHRR 1. See also Wildhaber (n 102); Wragg (n 54) 314.

[233] See section 3.1 for detailed discussion of the 'mirror principle'.

[234] See generally Sir J. Laws, 'Meiklejohn, the First Amendment and Free Speech in English Law' in I. Loveland (ed), *Importing the First Amendment, Freedom of Speech and Expression in Britain, Europe and the USA* (Hart Publishing, 1998) 123–137; Nicol QC et al (n 3) 3, [1.06]; Barendt (n 3) 18.

[235] Therefore, 'there must be no constraints on the free flow of information and ideas': Oster (n 123) 69.

162 *Media freedom in the age of citizen journalism*

According to Robert Bork, speech regarding 'government behaviour, policy or personnel, whether ... executive, legislative, judicial or administrative'[236] was the original subject that was perceived as being protected by the right to freedom of expression.[237] However, the scope of this approach was seen as being overly restrictive[238] as focusing purely on political expression to the exclusion of other matters of public interest gave rise to an 'old-fashioned distinction between public and private power'.[239] Consequently, Alexander Meiklejohn, with whom this argument is primarily associated,[240] argued for the substitution of political expression with the wider and less restrictive notion of 'public discussion', relating to any matter of public interest, as opposed to expression linked purely to the casting of votes.[241] Meiklejohn stated that public discussion is speech which impacts 'directly or indirectly, upon the issues with which voters have to deal [i.e.] to matters of public interest'.[242] A result of this bifurcated interpretation of free speech is a two-tiered approach to freedom of expression:[243] expression that is not in the interest of the public is not protected and is therefore open to restriction to protect the general welfare of society.[244] In later writings, Meiklejohn clarified this wider view of 'public discussion' by stating that voting is merely the 'external expression of a wide and diverse number of activities by means of which citizens attempt to meet the responsibilities of making judgments'.[245] Accordingly, education, philosophy and science, literature and the arts, and public discussions on public issues

---

[236] R.H. Bork, 'Neutral Principles and Some First Amendment Problems' (1971) 47 *Indiana Law Journal* 1, 27–28.

[237] Oster (n 123) 69.

[238] Ibid; D. Milo, *Defamation and Freedom of Speech* (Oxford University Press, 2008) 63–64; M.R. Chesterman, *Freedom of Speech in Australian Law: A Delicate Plant* (Ashgate Publishing, 2000) 48; see also A. Kenyon, 'Defamation and Critique: Political Speech and *New York Times v Sullivan* in Australia and England' (2001) 25 *Melbourne University Law Review* 522, 539; R. Gilson and M. Leopold, 'Restoring the "Central Meaning of the First Amendment": Absolute Immunity for Political Libel' (1986) 90 *Dickinson Law Review* 559, 574.

[239] Chesterman (n 238) 48; Kenyon (n 238) 522; Gilson and Leopold (n 238) 574.

[240] Nicol QC et al (n 3) 3, [1.06].

[241] A. Meiklejohn, *Political Freedom: The Constitutional Powers of the People* (Oxford University Press, 1960) 42; A. Meiklejohn, 'The First Amendment is an Absolute' [1961] *Supreme Court Review* 245, 255–257; Milo (n 238) 63–64; Oster (n 123) 69.

[242] Meiklejohn, *Political Freedom* (n 241) 79.

[243] An advocate of this approach is Cass Sunstein. See generally C.R. Sunstein, *Democracy and the Problem of Free Speech* (The Free Press, 1993); C.R. Sunstein, *The Partial Constitution* (Harvard University Press, 1994).

[244] Milo (n 238) 62–63.

[245] Meiklejohn, 'The First Amendment is an Absolute' (n 241) 255.

The media-as-a-constitutional-component concept 163

are activities that will educate citizens for self-government.[246] This wider view of public discussion advanced by Meiklejohn reflects the fact that the ECtHR has resisted defining the democratic process value in free speech narrowly.[247] The wide ambit afforded to the argument from democratic self-governance by the Strasbourg Court is demonstrated by jurisprudence consistently finding the democratic process value to be at stake in commercial expression cases.[248]

Historically, due to its reach, it was incumbent upon the traditional institutional media to disseminate matters of public interest, and to act as the public watchdog and Fourth Estate; to provide a check and balance on government. Consequently, the ECtHR has consistently stated that media freedom provides one of the best means for the public to discover and form opinions about the ideas and attitudes of political leaders, and on other matters of general interest, and that the public has a right to receive this information.[249] However, as explored in Chapter 1, and in Chapter 3,[250] although this role can, and often is, met by the traditional institutional media, it is increasingly being fulfilled by citizen journalists. This argument helps to define the media by providing a clear delineation between media and non-media actors. Pursuant to its 'public discussion' scope, this rationale underpins the media-as-a-constitutional-component concept as it supports media freedom protection, beyond that afforded to private individuals pursuant to the right to freedom of expression, for *any* actor that adheres to the behavioural standards set out in the previous section and contributes regularly and widely to the dissemination of matters of public interest[251] and/or operates as a public watchdog. Rather than limiting the public sphere to those actors defined as media by virtue of operating within the traditional institutional paradigm, at the very heart of the media-as-a-constitutional-component concept, and its functional definition of media set out in section 5, is its enablement of actors *functioning* as media to be able to participate in public discourse as equals to

---

[246] Ibid 257, 263; for judicial application of this wider interpretation of the theory see *Reynolds v Times Newspapers Limited* [2001] 2 AC 127 (HL) per Lord Cooke at 220; *Jameel v Wall Street Journal Europe Sprl* [2007] 1 AC 359 (HL) per Baroness Hale at [158].

[247] Wragg (n 54) 318.

[248] For example, see *Krone Verlag GmbH & Co KG v Austria* (2006) 42 EHRR 28; see also ibid.

[249] *Lingens v Austria* App. no. 9815/82 (ECtHR 8 July 1986), [42]; *Oberschlick v Austria (No 1)* App. no. 1162/85 (ECtHR 23 May 1991), [58]; *Scharsach and News Verlagsgesellschaft v Austria* App. no. 39394/98 (ECtHR 13 November 2003), [30].

[250] See Chapter 3 section 6.

[251] The concept of public interest in the context of the component is discussed in more detail in the following chapter at section 3.1.

their institutional counterparts. Therefore, it increases the scope of the public sphere by recognising *more* actors as media.

4.2.1 The media-as-a-constitutional-component concept's relationship with other participatory theories of free speech

We have seen above that of fundamental importance to Meiklejohn's argument from democratic self-governance is the notion that speech must be public, that policy must be subject to open discussion, and that views considered dangerous by government should not be suppressed.[252] This aspect of the argument translates into the golden thread that runs through the media-as-a-constitutional-component concept. However, although it is acknowledged that the idea of providing a normative mechanism for securing citizen participation in the public sphere is not new, it will be argued here that it is unrefined and lacks coherence and is therefore ineffective for the new media paradigm described in Chapter 3.

This idea of citizens participating equally in public discourse was conceptualised by Habermas in his explanation of the public sphere found in his discourse theory of law and democracy.[253] This has since been adopted and expanded upon by Barendt in his interpretation of the argument from democratic self-governance, which he refers to as the 'argument from citizen participation in a democracy' (although not explicitly),[254] and, latterly, by Post in his participatory theory of democracy.[255] Barendt's and Post's theories will be turned to in a moment, but first the Habermasian concept of the public sphere will be considered. As touched upon in section 3.2, Habermas' vision of the public sphere was a place of rational discourse,[256] in which individuals speak to achieve the common goal of 'reaching agreement and coordinating action'.[257] According to Habermas, the 'ideal speech situation' for this to occur is one in which the public sphere allows every speaker to be at liberty to express and challenge views without interference.[258] In casting the public sphere in this way, Habermas assumed that those participating in it could set aside their

---

[252] S.B. Micova, 'The Collective Speech Rights of Minorities' in A. Kenyon and A. Scott (eds), *Positive Free Speech. Rationales, Methods and Implications* (Hart Publishing, 2020) 99–100.

[253] See n 156.

[254] Barendt (n 3) 18–21.

[255] R. Post, 'Participatory Democracy and Free Speech' (2011) 97 *Virginia Law Review* 477, 482–483.

[256] See n 156.

[257] Micova (n 252) 100.

[258] See n 156.

personal agendas and social status and contribute to discourse as equals.[259] In echoing Habermas, Baroness Onora O'Neill has argued that the public needs a press that provides 'adequate communication' to enable meaningful and productive engagement with the democratic process.[260] In her view, because society only needs those modes of communication that 'best enable and least obstruct' its shared goals for communication, then the press must not 'assume bogus authority nor mislead' and must respect divergent audience interests.[261]

The citizen participation aspect of Habermas' concept was borrowed by Barendt in his interpretation of Meiklejohn's argument. This version of the argument from democratic self-governance advances a conception of democracy that requires everyone to be allowed, and enabled, to participate in public discourse and debate,[262] pursuant to which 'the rights of minorities to contribute to political debate should be respected, partly because they may have better ideas than those of the elected majority'.[263] Although Barendt appears to be thinking predominantly of political minorities, his theory maintains that regardless of the majority in power, 'government should not be permitted to delimit the contours of public discourse' and that all people must be treated equally within that discourse.[264]

More recently, Post explicitly adopted the Habermasian thesis to develop his theory of participatory democracy, which is premised on democracy being achieved when those who are subject to law believe they are participants in its creation, and therefore that the law reflects their voices.[265] As a consequence, Post's primary concern is to strengthen a dimension of individual autonomy

---

[259] Micova (n 252) 100. Like Habermas, in his earlier account of democracy in *A Theory of Justice*, John Rawls emphasised the importance of civic-mindedness. In his view citizens are required to take their political education seriously so they can assess the competing claims made by electoral candidates. Although press freedom is less prominent in Rawls' disquisition, it still plays a significant role in ensuring citizens 'have the means to be informed about political issues'. See J. Rawls, *A Theory of Justice* (revised edn., Oxford University Press, 1999) 194, 198, 200.

[260] This view correlates with Baroness O'Neill's evidence given at the *Leveson Inquiry* (see n 193). See also O. O'Neill, *A Question of Trust* (Cambridge University Press, 2002).

[261] O. O'Neill 'Practices of Toleration' in J. Lichtenberg (ed), *Democracy and the Mass Media* (Cambridge University Press, 1990). This claim has been repeated in much the same way by Noam Chomsky and Edward Herman, and by Robert McChesney (see Chapter 2 sections 2 and 3.3.2 respectively). See also Chomsky (n 188); R.W. McChesney and J. Nichols, *Our Media, Not Theirs. The Democratic Struggle Against Corporate Media* (2nd edn., Seven Stories Press, 2002); Wragg (n 5) 26–27.

[262] Barendt (n 3) 18–21.

[263] Ibid 20.

[264] Ibid. See also Micova (n 252) 100.

[265] Post (n 255) 482.

that can be characterised as political autonomy – 'a sense of being, as active citizens, and potential authors of the law'.[266] It therefore follows that, like the media-as-a-constitutional-component concept, access to the public sphere is of critical importance to the operation of Post's concept, as without it the value of authorship is unrealisable: if citizens cannot participate in the public sphere then they are unable to believe that they are contributing to the formation of public opinion.[267] However, as discussed in Chapter 2, the traditional institutional press present structural and normative barriers that can limit access to the public sphere. As suggested in Chapter 3, it was hoped that the emergence of the internet and social media would overcome some of these barriers. Yet, as argued in that chapter, although they have undoubtedly created opportunities for the democratisation of the public sphere, not least in their facilitation of citizen journalism, they have also negatively impacted upon its scope by recreating some of the barriers associated with the traditional institutional media in an online context, and by creating new ones. It is because of this that Post's theory falls short as a basis for media speech.

Central to Post's thesis is equality *within* public discourse, as opposed to fair access to it: accordingly everyone who already has access to the public sphere should have *equal* autonomy, 'which reflects the political equality that all citizens enjoy within a democracy'.[268] This means that the state should treat with equal respect the ideas and opinions of those already engaged in the formation of public opinions, but it cannot introduce mechanisms to ensure fair participation in it.[269] The scope of free speech protection afforded by Post's theory is therefore reduced to those already contributing to public opinion, meaning that it tends to reproduce the inequality that benefits dominant speakers, to the detriment of weaker ones. Consequently, his theory is structurally limited to, predominantly, the institutional media and the dominant online platforms as it excludes groups or individuals who cannot gain, or who have difficulties gaining, access to the public sphere,[270] which for the reasons discussed in Chapter 3 could be citizen journalists or any number of alternative or minority voices. Although Post acknowledges the existence of exceptions, they are limited to his recognition that '[d]emocracy requires only that inequities that undermine democratic legitimation be ameliorated'.[271] Thus, as Charney suggests, this solution is a 'circular trap, as the elements of democratic legit-

---

[266] Charney (n 58) 74.

[267] Ibid 76.

[268] Post (n 255) 484.

[269] This argument was also advanced by Post in R. Post, 'Democracy and Equality' (2005) 1 *Law, Culture and the Humanities* 142, 148.

[270] Charney (n 58) 76.

[271] Post (n 269) 153.

The media-as-a-constitutional-component concept 167

imation recognised by Post ... are reduced to government accountability to and equal autonomy for those who are *already* engaged in public discourse'.[272]

This is the point at which Post's conception of participation in the public sphere and that cast by the media-as-a-constitutional-component concept diverge. Unlike the theory of participatory democracy, which arguably does little more than maintain the public sphere status quo, the media-as-a-constitutional-component concept is not concerned with the actor having institutional 'status' by virtue of their education, training or employment, or because they already are contributing, or have previously contributed, to public discourse. Rather, it expands the public sphere by normatively securing access to it as media for *any* actor that adheres to its standards of professional behaviour and norms of discourse, which are equally applicable to all citizens.

4.2.2 An overview of the parameters imposed by the media-as-a-constitutional-component concept on media freedom[273]

In Chapter 4 it was suggested that media freedom grants protection to those operating as media beyond that afforded to non-media actors by freedom of expression. However, as discussed in more detail in the following chapter, pursuant to the media-as-a-constitutional-component concept, media actors that are subject to these privileges, beyond private individuals, are also subject to duties and responsibilities in excess of those expected of non-media entities. The reach of both the traditional institutional media and citizen journalists does not just enable those institutions and citizen journalists to fulfil their constitutional functions. This power can be abused in equal measure. Due to their reach the potential impact of abuse of power is far greater than any impact emanating from private individuals. The institutional media and citizen journalists are not just capable of invading the private lives of individuals, or damaging reputations, they can also shape and mislead public opinion.[274] As established in section 3, 'abuse' of this kind by the media is more likely if it is operating within a libertarian paradigm. To the contrary, section 6 sets out how the concept is better able to combat some of these potential abuses.

Therefore, social responsibility ideology, together with the argument from democratic self-governance, endorses an approach to media expression based on behavioural standards and norms of discourse.[275] First, public discussion

---

[272] Charney (n 58) 77 (emphasis in original).
[273] Although introduced here, these parameters are discussed in greater detail in the following chapter.
[274] See section 3.1.
[275] Oster (n 123) 71–72.

168 *Media freedom in the age of citizen journalism*

should be protected. However, if the expression is not of public interest, it should not be afforded the same level of protection compared to that which is of public concern. This includes speech primarily concerned with commercial or financial matters,[276] speech relating to private or intimate matters,[277] and hate speech.[278] Further, as argued in the following chapter, the theory and the argument from democratic self-governance rationale, and its public discussion ambit, dictates that the media's privileged protection, pursuant to it being a constitutional component, is subject to it acting ethically and in good faith, and publishing or broadcasting material that is based on reasonable research to verify the provenance of it and its sources.[279] Incidentally, the only legal instruments that qualify the right to free speech or expression with express reference to these extra duties and responsibilities are Article 10(2) ECHR and Article 19(3) ICCPR. These qualification clauses apply to both media and non-media entities; however, according to Oster, their main purpose is to provide member states with a tool to combat abuses of power by the media.[280]

Consequently, and in conclusion, the privilege afforded to the media, deriving from the ambit of the social responsibility theory and the argument

---

[276] Barendt (n 3) 392–416; from a US Supreme Court perspective see *Central Hudson Gas & Electric Corp v Public Service Commission* 447 US 557 (1980); *Dun & Bradstreet Inc v Greenmoss Builders Inc* 472 US 749, 762 (1985). For ECtHR jurisprudence see *Markt Intern Verlag and Klaus Beerman v Germany* App. no. 10572/83 (ECtHR 20 November 1989), [33].

[277] Barendt (n 3) 230; Fenwick and Phillipson (n 54) 661; P. Keller, *European and International Media Law: Liberal Democracy, Trade and the New Media* (Oxford University Press, 2011) 307; *Von Hannover v Germany (No. 1)* App. no. 59320/00 (ECtHR 24 June 2004), [65]; *MGN Ltd v United Kingdom* App. no. 39401/04 (ECtHR 18 January 2011), [143]; *Mosley v United Kingdom* App. no. 48009/08 (ECtHR 10 May 2011), [14].

[278] Article 20(2) ICCPR states: 'Any advocacy of national, racial or religious hatred that constitutes incitement to discrimination, hostility or violence shall be prohibited by law.' For example, see *Ross v Canada* App. no. 736/97 (UN Human Rights Committee, 18 October 2000), [11.5]. For ECtHR jurisprudence, see *Lehideux and Isorni v France* App. no. 55/1997/839/1045 (ECtHR 23 September 1998), [47]; *Norwood v United Kingdom* App. no. 23131/03 (ECtHR 16 November 2004).

[279] The media's conduct and the media acting in good faith in respect of the media-as-a-constitutional-component concept are discussed in more detail in the following chapter at sections 3.2 and 3.3 respectively.

[280] Oster (n 123) 72–73; these duties and responsibilities are particularly significant when applied as factors of the qualified privilege defence, as defined by Lord Nicholls in *Reynolds v Times Newspapers* [2001] 2 AC 127, 205 (see also *Jameel v Wall Street Journal Europe Sprl* [2007] 1 AC 359, 383 per Lord Hoffmann; *Flood v Times Newspapers Ltd* [2012] UKSC 11, [30] per Lord Phillips) and now enshrined, to an extent at least, within the Defamation Act 2013, section 4 defence of honest opinion (although see the discussion in Chapter 8 section 3.2.2).

The media-as-a-constitutional-component concept in *Slater v Blomfield* determined

from democratic self-governance, is based upon a utilitarian, consequential-ist and functional understanding of media freedom that has the potential to expand the scope of the public sphere by recognising more actors as media. The media-as-a-constitutional-component concept means that media actors are protected when they adhere to the standards of professional behaviour and norms of discourse set out above. However, this protection carries with it the obligation to fulfil these functions. If it fails to do this, it relinquishes its protection and may be subject to regulatory sanctions and/or criminal or civil liability.

5 A FUNCTIONAL DEFINITION OF 'THE MEDIA' BASED ON SOCIAL RESPONSIBILITY THEORY VALUES

The High Court of New Zealand's decision in *Slater v Blomfield*[281] determined that a blogger could be considered a journalist for the purposes of section 68 of the New Zealand Evidence Act 2006 provided, inter alia:

(i) the medium used by the journalist disseminates the information to the public or a section of the public; (ii) what is disseminated is news and observations on news; and (iii) the person claiming to be a journalist is a person who, in the normal course of that person's work, might be given information by informants in the expectation that it will be published in a news medium.[282]

Consequently, in dealing with these points, Asher J's judgment provides a number of guiding principles that can be applied to a new functional definition of media. First, an actor can begin publishing as non-media, and later become media once a certain level of work and content is achieved.[283] Secondly, an actor that regularly disseminates news to a significant body of the public can be a journalist.[284] Thirdly, just because an actor is a blogger does not mean they cannot be considered media.[285] Indeed, 'a blogger who regularly

---

[281] [2014] NZHC 2221.

[282] Ibid [34].

[283] Ibid [36].

[284] Ibid [54].

[285] This accords with the treatment of citizen journalists by the Court of Justice of the European Union in the context of data protection jurisprudence, which, as explained in more detail in section 3 of Chapter 9, has afforded citizen journalists the same status, and the ability to take advantage of the same exemptions, as the traditional media: see Case C-73/07 *Tietosuojavaltuutettu v Satakunnan Markkinapörssi Oy, Satamedia Oy* (*Satamedia*); Case C-345/17 *Sergejs Buivids v Datu valsts inspekcija*.

170 *Media freedom in the age of citizen journalism*

disseminates news to a significant body of the public can be a journalist'.[286] Fourthly, an actor that publishes a single news item would not qualify as media. Regular commitment to publishing new or recent information of public interest is required for a blog, for instance, to be considered news media. However, the quantity of stories does not have to be equivalent to an institutional media organisation.[287] Finally, to determine whether an actor's work within the context of the medium makes them media, the following factors are relevant: (i) whether the receiving and disseminating of news through a news medium is regular; (ii) whether it involved significant time on a frequent basis; (iii) whether there was revenue derived from the medium;[288] and (iv) whether it involved the application of journalistic skill.[289]

Based on the media-as-a-constitutional-component concept of media freedom advanced above, it is suggested that a functional and egalitarian, as opposed to institutional, approach should be adopted to define the media. In line with the social responsibility theory, and the argument from democratic self-governance, this principle and its definition will focus on the functions that are performed by the media actors, as opposed to their inherent characteristics.[290] Therefore, media freedom does not have to be a purely institutional privilege; it can apply to any actor that conforms to the definition. As a consequence of the requirement that these functions are fulfilled in order to satisfy the concept, it will also give consideration to the obligations of the media. By applying the guidelines laid down in *Slater*, and scholarship and jurisprudence from both the US and Europe,[291] examined in preceding sections, the following definition of media is proposed: (1) a natural and legal person (2) engaged in the process of gathering information of public concern, interest and significance (3) with the intention, and for the purpose of, disseminating this information to a section of the public (4) while complying with objective standards governing the research, newsgathering and editorial process. These

---

[286] *Slater v Blomfield* [2014] NZHC 2221.

[287] Ibid [54], [65].

[288] For reasons previously discussed, this criterion is clearly irreconcilable with the media-as-a-constitutional-component concept. Consequently, it does not form part of the definition advanced below.

[289] *Slater v Blomfield* [2014] NZHC 2221, [74].

[290] As discussed in Chapter 4, this is the case with the traditional methods of distinguishing media from non-media actors. See T. Gibbons, 'Conceptions of the Press and the Functions of Regulation' (2016) 22(5) *Convergence: The International Journal of Research into New Media Technologies* 484, 487.

[291] For instance, compare Oster and Erik Ugland for definitions from a European and US perspective respectively: Oster (n 123) 74; E. Ugland, 'Demarcating the Right to Gather News: A Sequential Interpretation of the First Amendment' (2008) 3 *Duke Journal of Constitutional Law and Public Policy* 118, 138.

The media-as-a-constitutional-component concept 171

standards would include, for instance, the time spent researching stories and ensuring the provenance and reliability of information.

As the media's privileged protection is based upon the media-as-a-constitutional-component concept, one of the fundamental requirements for determining that an actor is media is its contribution to matters of public interest.[292] Oster's argument that for this requirement to be fulfilled it must occur periodically[293] is, arguably, over-exclusive. Actors can fulfil the definition above, and therefore operate as media, on one-off occasions or on an ad hoc basis.[294] This is particularly the case within a citizen journalism context, in which contributions to the public interest to the public sphere may be made sporadically via a variety of platforms.

6   CONCLUSION

As identified in section 2, despite the emergence of social responsibility theory, its historical and ongoing marginalisation[295] has become more acute as a result of libertarianism's position as the de facto normative paradigm for online expression. Consequently, some of the problems distilled by Peterson[296] that the Royal Commission and the Hutchins Commission were set up to consider, and attempted to resolve, in respect of the press through the creation of the theory, are being repeated, albeit within a modified media context. This section will explain how embracing social responsibility theory and the media-as-a-constitutional-component concept could go some way at least to solving these problems, thereby providing a more robust and realistic normative framework for modern media speech (many of these issues will be unpacked in more detail in the chapters that form Part III of this book). However, in doing so, it sketches how the concept seeks to resolve the shortcomings of social responsibility theory in relation to its resistance to anything other than the blunt and self-serving system of voluntary self-regulation, which is underpinned by an almost blind trust in the press 'doing the right thing',[297] and which is currently in place in the UK.

---

[292]   Section 3.1 of the following chapter explores the concept of public interest in detail and, in doing so, explains the parameters imposed upon it by the media-as-a-constitutional-component concept.

[293]   Oster (n 123) 74.

[294]   *Editions Plon v France* App. no. 58148/00 (ECtHR 18 May 2004), [43]; *Lindon, Otchakovsky-Laurens and July v France* App. nos. 21279/02 and 36448/02 (ECtHR 22 October 2007), [47].

[295]   C. Christians, J. Ferré and P. Fackler, *Good News: Social Ethics and the Press* (Oxford University Press, 1993) 38.

[296]   Siebert et al (n 11) 78–79. See section 4.1.

[297]   See n 215.

6.1 The Public Sphere, Resistance to Social Change, and the Polarisation of Communities

As argued in Chapter 3, the internet and social media provide the architecture for greater access to the public sphere. By facilitating online speech and citizen journalism, in theory at least, they enable social change through their enablement of cultural pluralism and the fostering of the 'Great Communities' envisaged by the Hutchins Commission. This is particularly evident in the Arab World and the Middle East,[298] where citizen journalism and social media 'have been hailed as tools for the empowerment of marginalized communities such as women and the youth, [and have] also brought new opportunities that have resulted in the breaking of the communication monopoly by those in power'.[299] For example, the Arab Spring that began in Tunisia in December 2010 and ended in the revolution of 14 January 2011, and has since been followed in Egypt, Libya and Syria, illustrates citizen journalism's role in galvanising activists and facilitating social change.[300] However, online speech, including that emanating from the institutional media, citizen journalists and non-media actors, does not always stimulate social change; to the contrary, it can encourage social inertia. As identified at section 3.2 and in Chapter 3,[301] filter bubbles and user preferences can actively undermine the marketplace of ideas by entrenching people's views. Rather than exposing us to new and opposing ideas and perspectives, these filter bubbles can create echo chambers, giving rise to what has been referred to as 'my news, my world'.[302] Thus, instead of being a catalyst for social change by encouraging cultural plurality and the galvanisation of 'Great Communities', filter bubbles and echo chambers can polarise communities, in particular already marginalised groups.

It is recognised that embracing the social responsibility theory will not prevent filter bubbles as arguably they are an inherent characteristic of online speech, regardless of the underpinning normative paradigm. However, Stanley Baran and Dennis Davis have observed, social responsibility theory will continue to be revitalised by new and emerging technologies, such as social media and its facilitation of citizen journalism.[303] The effect of this could be

---

[298] See generally D. McGoldrick, 'The Limits of Freedom of Expression on Facebook and Social Networking Sites: A UK Perspective' (2013) 13(1) *Human Rights Law Review* 125, 130; Coe (n 99) 30.

[299] N. Miladi, 'Social Media and Social Change' (2016) 25(1) *Digest of the Middle East* 36, 36.

[300] Ibid 37.

[301] See chapter 3 section 5.2.

[302] Baran and Davis (n 11) 81.

[303] Ibid 79.

The media-as-a-constitutional-component concept   173

threefold. First, promotion of the underlying values of social responsibility theory through the media-as-a-constitutional-component concept, particularly its focus on cultural pluralism and media responsibility, *may* discourage the continued widespread implementation of filter bubbles which would actively reduce the amount of echo chambers we are inadvertently captured by. Secondly, as social media and citizen journalism has the potential to give new strength to the social responsibility model, by virtue of its rationale, this rejuvenation of the theory *may* encourage more speech adhering to the theory's values. Thus, although not solving the filter bubble issue, it *may* encourage the dissemination of, and make available, more speech that complies with the standards of professional behaviour and norms of discourse set out in section 3 of Chapter 6. (You will notice that I have placed emphasis on the word *may* in respect of these points. My reasoning for this is explained in the following section.) Thirdly, and finally, the social responsibility theory dictates that the government must actively promote the freedom of its citizens,[304] which can be achieved, in part, by guaranteeing adequate media performance.[305] Arguably, this includes the obligation to support diverse speech environments (in other words, 'Great Communities' that encourage cultural pluralism). More broadly, unlike libertarianism, the theory supports the notion of 'positive' free speech; as observed by a number of scholars,[306] and the Grand Chamber of the ECtHR in *Centro Europa 7 Srl v Italy*,[307] the concept places positive obligations on the state to ensure media plurality (in addition to its negative duty of non-interference). This is equally important in respect of the internet and social media as it is for the traditional institutional media because, as discussed in Chapter 3,[308] the internet and social media, and by extension citizen journalism, are not exempt from 'corporate dominance, market concentration, controlling gatekeepers, employee exploitation, manipulative rights manage-

---

[304] Barendt (n 3) 36, 105–107.

[305] Siebert et al (n 11) 95; Hocking (n 46) 182–193; see also *Özgür Gündem v Turkey* (2001) 31 EHRR 1082, [43].

[306] A. Kenyon and A. Scott (eds), *Positive Free Speech. Rationales, Methods and Implications* (Hart Publishing, 2020); Kenyon (n 160) 391–402; T. Emerson, *The System of Freedom of Expression* (Vintage, 1970) 4; J.M. Balkin, 'Some Realism About Pluralism: Legal Realist Approaches to the First Amendment' [1990] *Duke Law Journal* 375, 401; A. Hutchinson, 'Talking the Good Life: From Free Speech to Democratic Dialogue' (1989) 1 *Yale Journal of Law and Liberation* 17, 25; T. Gibbons, 'Free Speech, Communication and the State' in M. Amos, J. Harrison and L. Woods (eds), *Freedom of Expression and the Media* (Martinus Nijhoff, 2012) 42.

[307] [2012] ECHR 974, [134]; see also *Manole v Moldova* [2010] ECHR 1112, [107].

[308] See Chapter 3 sections 5.1 and 6.2.3.

174 *Media freedom in the age of citizen journalism*

ment, economic exclusion through "tethered appliances" and encroachment upon the information commons'.[309]

6.2 The Problem with Rationality: Dealing with Media Distortion, Sensationalised Stories, False News, Entrenched Views and Anonymous and Pseudonymous Speech

In contrast to libertarianism, social responsibility theory does not accept the proposition that we are innately driven to search for truth and use it as a guide, and it is, at best, sceptical of people's ability to think rationally, particularly in the context of the marketplace. It views us as being lethargic, prone to passively accepting what we see, hear and read, and reluctant to apply reason when it does not satisfy our immediate needs and desires. Consequently, as Peterson states, the theory perceives us as being 'easy prey for demagogues, advertising pitchmen, and others who would manipulate [us] for their selfish ends'.[310] Thus, unlike libertarian ideology, the social responsibility theory acknowledges the inherent flaws in our nature. In applying this to a modern context, and the discussions in section 3, it recognises that we are vulnerable to sensationalised stories, false news and its regurgitation, entrenchment of views by virtue of preconceived schemas, the fact that we are often unable to assess the veracity of anonymous and pseudonymous speakers and that we are largely unaware of the machinations of online platforms, and, as a result of all of this, our inability to rationally assess the marketplace. Consequently, it is realistic, as opposed to being idealistic.

Significantly, it is this pragmatism that makes it a suitable normative framework for the modern media and the media-as-a-constitutional-component concept. By being a concept that offers a mechanism for distinguishing who or what is media from who or what is not media, it provides a way of identifying those actors that should benefit from media freedom and should be subject to its concomitant obligations and responsibilities. Thus, it makes it clearer who or what should be operating in ways which conform to the underlying values of the paradigm and, for instance, be subject to regulation,[311] regardless of whether that actor is a member of the institutional media, is a citizen journalist and/or is disseminating information anonymously or pseudonymously.

Although not a panacea, arguably the concept's requirement that to be classed as media and benefit from the enhanced right to media freedom the

---

[309] J. Curran, N. Fenton and D. Freedman, *Misunderstanding the Internet* (Routledge, 2012) 180.

[310] Siebert et al (n 11) 100.

[311] This is discussed further below and in Chapter 9.

actor must fulfil a constitutional function and, in doing so, conform to the underlying principles of the social responsibility theory, lends itself to certain behaviours. In turn, exercising these behaviours helps to protect us against some of the flaws and vulnerabilities in human nature outlined above. For instance it (i) *may* mean that more care is taken over source checking to reduce the regurgitation of false or misleading information; (ii) *may* discourage the publication of sensationalised stories and encourage the dissemination of valuable information; as a result it (iii) means that the audience can have more faith in material published anonymously and pseudonymously without having to compromise the identity of the speaker, and ultimately discourage such speech to the detriment of freedom of expression.[312] Essentially, the social responsibility theory and the media-as-a-constitutional-component concept provide us with a more suitable platform from which to assess the marketplace rationally.

You will notice that I have placed emphasis on the word *may* in respect of these points, and the points I made in the previous section. This is because, it is my *hope* that embracing social responsibility theory and the concept will, on its own, be enough to promote and encourage compliance with the concept's behaviours and norms. This is not a new hope. Indeed, as explained in section 4.1, it represents the genesis of the theory from the findings of the Hutchins Commission, and reflects similar arguments that have been advanced since the Commission's report by the likes of Claude-Jean Bertrand, Marc Franklin and William Hocking,[313] and by Leveson LJ in his *Inquiry*.[314] However, I am under no illusion that in light of the past, and continued, behaviour of the press, realising these hopes is perhaps not impossible, but certainly improbable.[315] This is a view I share with Paul Wragg, who has eloquently said that

> the twenty-first century press shows no remorse for not only decades of public distrust but also, moreover, the shame, in the strongest sense, arising from the litany of unethical – and illegal – practices that Leveson uncovered in his inquiry. Quite obviously, reliance solely upon self-directed, ethical decision-making is a poor means of improving press standards.[316]

This brings us to the question of regulation, and a deficiency in social responsibility theory; namely how, in the UK, this idealistic faith in the press has led to

---

[312]   Anonymous and pseudonymous speech is discussed further in Chapter 7.

[313]   C.-J. Bertrand, *Media Ethics and Accountability Systems* (Transaction Publishers, 2000) 46; M.A. Franklin, 'A Constitutional Problem in Privacy Protection, Legal Inhibitions on Reporting of Fact' (1963) 16 *Stanford Law Review* 107, 146; Hocking (n 46) 187.

[314]   Leveson (n 193) 1758, [4.1].

[315]   See n 215.

[316]   Wragg (n 5) 65.

176   *Media freedom in the age of citizen journalism*

a devotion by successive governments to a scheme of voluntary self-regulation that is not fit for purpose.[317]

6.3   Balancing the Interests of the State and Individuals with the Media: Is It Time to Reimagine Regulation?

Chapter 8 argues that the offence of contempt of court and the law of defamation, and the principles upon which they are founded, can be at odds with media freedom, which can create an imbalance between the state or claimants and the media. However, as set out in that chapter, the adoption of the media-as-a-constitutional-component concept, and the standards of professional behaviour and norms of discourse that it imposes on media actors, provides a mechanism to at least alleviate this imbalance.

Notwithstanding this, both the traditional institutional press and wider media and citizen journalists can damage reputations,[318] invade personal privacy[319] and spread false news, and can detrimentally affect the integrity of the trial process. The media-as-a-constitutional-component concept offers two layers of protection against this. First, publications that damage reputation and/ or invade privacy without justification will fall short of its norms of discourse as they would not be in the public interest.[320] As a result they would not, in that instance, be classed as media publications under the new definition and would therefore not be subject to media freedom.

The second layer of protection, which is the concern of Chapter 9, is regulation. However, as I have touched upon in this chapter, and as we will see

---

[317]   Ibid 64–71. As explained in section 4.1, this devotion is evident from the findings of the first Royal Commission on the Press, to the present-day recommendations made by Leveson LJ in his *Inquiry*.

[318]   *Smith v ADVFN plc* [2008] EWHC 1797; *McAlpine v Bercow* [2013] EWHC 1342 (QB); *Monroe v Hopkins* [2017] EWHC 433 (QB).

[319]   E. Barendt, 'Privacy and Freedom of Speech' in A. Kenyon and M. Richardson (eds), *New Dimensions in Privacy Law: International and Comparative Perspectives* (Cambridge University Press, 2006); R. Wacks, *Privacy and Media Freedom* (Oxford University Press, 2013); B. Markesinis, *Protecting Privacy* (Oxford University Press, 1999); R. Barnes, *Outrageous Invasions: Celebrities' Private Lives, Media and the Law* (Oxford University Press, 2010); Sir M. Warby and N. Moreham (eds), *The Law of Privacy and the Media* (Oxford University Press, 2016) ch. 3; P. Wragg, 'Protecting Private Information of Public Interest: *Campbell's* Great Promise Unfulfilled' (2015) 7 *Journal of Media Law* 225; R. Barnes and P. Wragg, 'Social Media, Sporting Figures and the Regulation of Morality' in D. Mangan and L. Gillies (eds), *The Legal Challenges of Social Media* (Edward Elgar Publishing, 2017) 155–176.

[320]   The notion of public interest, and the parameters imposed upon it by the media-as-a-constitutional-component concept, are discussed in greater detail in the following chapter at section 3.1.

in Chapter 9, as things currently stand in the UK, this layer of protection is problematic. Unlike libertarianism, the social responsibility theory allows for regulation, albeit within a voluntary and self-regulatory model that lacks robustness and is self-serving. This is the point at which social responsibility theory and the concept diverge, at least to an extent. As will be advanced in Chapter 9, the concept provides the scaffolding, or blueprint, for a modified voluntary self-regulatory scheme, which although drawing upon social responsibility values, differs significantly from the current regulatory regime, and which could, if implemented, effectively regulate citizen journalists and the institutional press.[321] Ultimately, it will be argued that, if adopted, the scheme's combination of statutory and non-statutory incentives, and statutory powers to impose sanctions on publishers that go well beyond sections 34 and 40 of the Crime and Courts Act 2013,[322] could remedy the deficiencies created by the social responsibility theory's trust in the press and its consequential adherence to voluntary self-regulation.

Furthermore, as set out above, the concept enables the effective delineation of media from non-media actors and, therefore, the identification of those entities that can benefit from the right to media freedom and should be subject to its concomitant obligations and responsibilities. In doing this it helps regulators to identify who or what is eligible to join a regulatory system. Taking this a step further, as discussed in Chapter 9, the concept's ability to clarify who and what is media may encourage more citizen journalists to voluntarily join the regulatory scheme that it advances. This is because (i) they will be able to identify themselves as 'media' when perhaps previously they did not realise they were in fact operating as media; and (ii) the concept would classify citizen journalists adhering to its standards of professional behaviour and norms of discourse as media, which would, in turn, confer upon them the right to media freedom and enable them to take advantage of the incentives available to members of the regulatory scheme. In summary, the concept's underlying values provide a normative framework from which to 'hang' a regulatory regime suitable for citizen journalists and the institutional press.

---

[321] For reasons explained in that chapter, a mandatory regime is ill-suited to citizen journalists.

[322] Section 40 is not currently in force. Both provisions are discussed in Chapter 9 section 2.

6. What the media-as-a-constitutional-component concept means for media freedom

1   INTRODUCTION

In this chapter the parameters that are imposed by the media-as-a-constitutional-component concept on media freedom will be set out at section 2. This leads into a discussion at section 3 as to the standards of professional behaviour and norms of norms of discourse imposed on the media by the concept, which answers, in the affirmative, one of the four broad questions that I posed in Chapter 1: if we accept the existence of certain 'duties and responsibilities' in the case of institutional journalists, should the same or similar 'burdens' apply to citizen journalists? Specifically, the section explores the notion of public interest, media conduct and the media's requirement to act in good faith pursuant to the concept. In respect of public interest, it makes the claim that the concept, and the social responsibility theory and argument from democratic self-governance rationales underpinning it, align it clearly with the jurisprudence of the ECtHR: a position that is diametrically opposed to a divergent line of English and Welsh case law supporting a 'role model' principle. As a result, it advances three factors to be taken into account to provide guidance on what is in the public interest in line with the norms and values inherent within the concept.

2   THE MEDIA-AS-A-CONSTITUTIONA L-COMPONENT CONCEPT'S PARAMETERS FOR MEDIA FREEDOM

History tells us that the power associated with the privileged position that the press, and the media generally, enjoys is very often abused, for reasons such as financial gain, political leverage or ideological advancement;[1] the impact of this abuse of position is greater than if it came from a private individual as it

---

[1]   See the discussions in Chapters 2 and 3.

The media-as-a-constitutional-component concept and media freedom 179

can affect the private lives of individuals, damage reputations, and detrimentally affect the fairness of trials and undermine the principle of open justice.[2] Furthermore, it has the ability to shape, distort and mislead public opinion.[3]

Online speech adds a further dynamic to this ability, and the impact of media malfeasance. Commentators such as James Curran and Jean Seaton and Clay Calvert and Mirelis Torres have acknowledged that the traditional institutional media, operating online, remains a gatekeeper to the awareness of the broader public and the 'public agenda'. In their view, by conducting research and editing and publishing using online resources the institutional media can influence the level of attention paid by the public to certain publications, even amongst the proliferation of other available information on the internet.[4] As discussed in Chapter 3, the role played in news generation and distribution by online platforms such as Google and Facebook has only contributed to this. For example, as I discussed in that chapter, Facebook's new Facebook News function is likely to prioritise content from its partner publishers, which will drive readers away from other non-partner publishers.[5] Taking this a step further, the symbiotic relationship that now exists between citizen journalists and the institutional press and wider media identified in earlier chapters[6] means that citizen journalists increasingly act as a source of news for traditional media outlets. In turn, this adds credence to the respective citizen journalist's work as

---

[2]   Indeed, in his *Inquiry*, Leveson LJ acknowledged that press malfeasance, in both the context of its newsgathering and publication activities, causes 'real harm ... to real people'. Lord Justice Leveson, *An Inquiry into the Culture, Practices and Ethics of the Press: Report*, HC 780, November 2012, 50, [2.2]. See also P. Wragg, *A Free and Regulated Press. Defending Coercive Independent Press Regulation* (Hart Publishing, 2020) 60–61. These issues were dealt with briefly in Chapter 5 section 6.3. They are considered in greater depth in Chapter 8 section 3.

[3]   P. Coe, 'Redefining "Media" Using a "Media-as-a-constitutional-component" Concept: An Evaluation of the Need for the European Court of Human Rights to Alter Its Understanding of "Media" Within a New Media Landscape' (2017) 37(1) *Legal Studies* 25, 49; T. Gibbons, '"Fair Play to All Sides of the Truth": Controlling Media Distortions' (2009) 62(1) *Current Legal Problems* 286, 289; T. Gibbons, 'Freedom of the Press: Ownership and Editorial Values' [1992] *Public Law* 279, 286–287; see also J. Curran, 'Mediations of Democracy' in J. Curran and M. Gurevitch (eds), *Mass Media and Society* (4th edn., Hodder Arnold, 2005) 129.

[4]   J. Curran and J. Seaton, *Power without Responsibility – Press, Broadcasting and the Internet in Britain* (7th edn., Routledge, 2009) 286; C. Calvert and M. Torres, 'Putting the Shock Value in First Amendment Jurisprudence: When Freedom for the Citizen-Journalist Watchdog Trumps the Right of Informational Privacy on the Internet' (2011) 23 *Vanderbilt Journal of Entertainment and Technology Law* 323, 345. See also J. Oster, *Media Freedom as a Fundamental Right* (Cambridge University Press, 2015) 34.

[5]   See Chapter 3 section 5.1.

[6]   In particular, see Chapter 3 section 5.3.

180   *Media freedom in the age of citizen journalism*

well as raising their profile further.[7] As alluded to in the concluding sections of the previous chapter, arguably this symbiosis only serves to amplify the collective media's ability to exert even greater influence over the weight attached to certain publications and pieces of information and, ultimately, wider public opinion. Thus, according to the ECtHR in *Novaya Gazeta and Borodyanskiy v Russia*,[8] '[i]n a world in which the individual is confronted with vast quantities of information circulated via traditional and electronic media and involving an ever-growing number of players, monitoring compliance with journalistic ethics takes on added importance'.[9]

2.1   The Media-as-a-constitutional-component Concept and Robert Post's 'Norms of Civility'

In his book, *Media Freedom as a Fundamental Right*, Jan Oster makes the argument that journalistic ethics, as boundaries to media freedom, should be defined by Robert Post's 'norms of civility',[10] categorised as individual rights of others (such as privacy and reputation)[11] and social norms required for public discourse.[12] However, as Post himself states, such norms cannot be subject to 'pure fidelity' as, inter alia, 'the norms that define public speech, like all social norms, are the product of a specific community, and because different communities may have different norms, a pure fidelity to a "moral tact" would hegemonically establish the dominance of the perspectives of a particular community'.[13] The media-as-a-constitutional-component concept does not just subsume Post's individual and social norms of civility, but also offers a normative mechanism for dealing with this fidelity issue. Pursuant to the concept, media freedom's parameters must be determined, and are justified, by the norms set out at section 4.2 of Chapter 5, which define, and make possible, speech that fulfils a constitutional function. At the concept's very core is the requirement of the media to prioritise cultural pluralism, by being a voice for all people, not just elite or dominant groups. Thus, by virtue of it being underpinned by social responsibility theory and the argument from dem-

---

[7]   Ibid.

[8]   [2013] App. no. 14087/08.

[9]   Ibid [42].

[10]   R. Post, 'The Constitutional Concept of Public Discourse: Outrageous Opinion, Democratic Deliberation, and *Hustler Magazine v Falwell*' (1990) 103 *Harvard Law Review* 601; R. Post, 'Racist Speech, Democracy, and the First Amendment' (1991) 32 *William and Mary Law Review* 267, 286; R. Post, 'Reconciling Theory and Doctrine in First Amendment Jurisprudence' (2000) 88 *California Law Review* 2353, 2365.

[11]   Ibid.

[12]   Oster (n 4) 33–36.

[13]   Post, 'The Constitutional Concept of Public Discourse' (n 10) 681.

The media-as-a-constitutional-component concept and media freedom

ocratic self-governance, the concept, which determines that media freedom is applicable to any actor who is disseminating speech of constitutional value, provides a more appropriate mechanism for setting the limits to media freedom than the 'rules of civility'.

The limits placed on media freedom by the concept, and by the rules of civility, create what Post has described as the 'paradox of public discourse'.[14] On the one hand is the libertarian argument, discredited in the previous chapter, that conceptually media freedom necessitates being free of regulatory requirements. On the other hand, in line with the media-as-a-constitutional-component concept and its normative foundations, is the social responsibility argument that the enjoyment of media freedom, from both a publisher and audience perspective, is contingent upon the fulfilment of certain standards of professional behaviour and norms of discourse, or concomitant duties and responsibilities.[15] However, as Oster states, so long as the media is properly conceptualised, the apparent conflict between these principles is largely superficial as the media's privileges in, and its duties and responsibilities for, the public discourse complement one another.[16] This is because, if the media and individuals were subject to the same freedoms and enjoyed identical duties and responsibilities, the privileges attached to media freedom would be rendered obsolete. As a result, these privileges bestowed upon the media pursuant to the right to media freedom justify the greater demands placed on the media by virtue of the right's concomitant duties and responsibilities.

The concept and its social responsibility rationale provide a foundation upon which free speech and media freedom can be based. As established in the previous chapter, this foundation sets the parameters and limitations for media freedom operating within this new conceptual normative framework, which can be placed into two categories, namely protecting (i) vital social interests and (ii) the private rights of other individuals. In respect of the former, it is important to note that not all contraventions of vital social interests render media publications illegal. In *Handyside v United Kingdom*[17] the ECtHR laid down the often cited principle that free speech and media freedom are not only applicable to information and ideas 'that are favourably received or regarded as inoffensive or as a matter of indifference, but also to those that offend, shock or disturb the State or any sector of the population'.[18] However, as opposed to

---

[14]   Ibid.
[15]   See Chapter 5 sections 4.1 and 4.2, and section 3 of this chapter.
[16]   Oster (n 4) 34.
[17]   [1976] App. no. 5493/72.
[18]   Ibid [49]; see also *Sunday Times v United Kingdom (No. 1)* [1979] App. no. 6538/74, [65]; *Lingens v Austria* [1986] App. no. 9815/82, [41]; *Axel Springer AG v Germany (No. 1)* [2012] App. no. 39954/08, [78]; *Thorgeir Thorgeirson v Iceland*

contributing positively to the public sphere, the press can undermine it, and therefore do not conform to the norms previously referred to, if their publication, inter alia, unjustifiably invades personal privacy or damages an individual's reputation, causes violence or incites hatred, leads to unwarranted panic, damages national security interests, prejudices a fair trial, or offends religious beliefs or moral standards of a particular community.[19] The rights of others as a limitation on free speech and media freedom is underpinned by philosophical arguments advanced by Immanuel Kant and John Rawls. For instance, Kant articulated his understanding of law as the 'sum of the conditions under which the choice of one [person] can be united with the choice of another [person] in accordance with a universal law of freedom'.[20] Consequently, Kant justifies limiting individuals' right to freedom of action on the basis that it is required to reconcile it with everyone else's freedom. Similarly, according to Rawls' first principle of justice, 'each person is to have an equal right to the most extensive basic liberty compatible with a similar liberty for others'.[21] Indeed, inherent within international human rights law is a general duty placed on individuals not to violate the rights of others whilst exercising their own liberties. The limitations placed on free speech and media freedom pursuant to individuals' rights are now widely recognised as qualifications to free speech in international Conventions (and their jurisprudence), such as Article 10(2) ECHR and Article 19(3) ICCPR.

3   THE STANDARDS ATTACHED TO MEDIA DISCOURSE AND CONDUCT BY THE MEDIA-AS-A-CONSTITUTIONAL-COMPONENT CONCEPT

The previous section has suggested that the right to media freedom must be balanced against conflicting rights and interests. The media-as-a-constitutional-component concept dictates that the protection afforded to the press and media generally by media freedom does not exist for a purpose that is exclusively and intrinsically beneficial to the media. Rather,

---

[1992] App. no. 13778/88, [63]. This principle has also been accepted by the IACHR since *Herrera-Ulloa v Costa Rica* [2004] Case 12.367, [113]. From the US Supreme Court see *Cohen v California* 403 US 15, 25 (1971). See also T. Scanlon, 'Freedom of Expression and Categories of Expression' (1979) 40 *University of Pittsburgh Law Review* 519.

[19]   Oster (n 4) 36.

[20]   I. Kant, *The Metaphysics of Morals* (edited by L. Denis and translated by M. Gregor, revised edn., Cambridge University Press, 2017) 24, 27–28.

[21]   J. Rawls, *A Theory of Justice* (Harvard University Press, 1971) 60.

pursuant to the concept, and the norms underpinning its social responsibility rationale, the intensity of the protection afforded to the media by virtue of media freedom is dependent upon the respective publication's constitutional value to society. Thus, factors to be taken into account when determining this include: (i) the extent to which the media actor, through the publication, is contributing to the public sphere by, for example, fulfilling the role of public watchdog by reporting on a matter of public interest; (ii) the actor's conduct pre-publication; and (iii) whether the actor acted in good faith. Although the concept provides the theoretical justification for the application of these standards on media discourse and conduct, legal support for their imposition derives from the concomitant 'duties and responsibilities' clauses found in Articles 10(2) ECHR and 19(3) ICCPR. Unlike any other Convention or Covenant rights, these Articles expressly provide that the exercise of freedom of expression 'carries with it duties and responsibilities'.[22] Although this qualification applies equally to media and non-media actors, the chief purpose of the qualification is to provide Member States with a mechanism for preventing the modern mass media from abusing its power.[23] This means that the operation of media freedom in any given situation, and the extent to which the protection it affords is applied, is dependent upon whether the media actor has carried out its concomitant 'duties and responsibilities' in the particular circumstances. In situations where the media actor has not carried out these obligations, the extent of the protection afforded by media freedom is significantly lowered and, as a result, interference with media freedom is, usually, justified.[24] Therefore, according to Rainer Grote and Nicola Wenzel, the 'duties and responsibilities' clause is, doctrinally, an aspect of the balancing exercise conducted by judges when they apply the principle of proportionality.[25] The following sections will consider how the standards of professional behaviour set out above operate for the purposes of the concept.

---

[22] To the contrary, Article 14 ACHR provides limitations to free speech. Although the IACHR does not expressly qualify free speech, its jurisprudence has consistently emphasised the responsibilities that attach to media actors in the exercise of their function. For example, see *Herrera-Ulloa v Costa Rica* [2004] Case 12.367, [117]; *Fontevecchia and D'Amico v Argentina* [2011] Case 12.524, [44].

[23] M. Bossuyt, *Guide to the 'Travaux Préparatoires' of the International Covenant on Civil and Political Rights* (Martinus Nijhoff Publishers, 1987) 386.

[24] Oster (n 4) 141.

[25] Ibid citing R. Grote and N. Wenzel (2013) 'Meinungsfreiheit' in T. Marauhn and R. Grote (eds), *EMRK/GG Konkordanzkommentar zum europäischen und deutschen Grundrechtsschutz* (2nd edn., Mohr Siebeck) ch. 18, [72].

184

3.1   A Matter of Public Interest?

As the media-as-constitutional-component concept subsumes within its ambit the notion of public discussion[26] one of the fundamental requirements for determining that an actor is operating as part of the media is its contribution to matters of public interest. In such a case, the constitutional value attached to the dissemination of information that fulfils this requirement supports the media actor's claim for enhanced protection. To the contrary, publications that are not in the public interest enjoy less protection and may even constitute an abuse of media freedom if they relate exclusively to private or intimate matters.[27] As discussed below, this position reflects ECtHR jurisprudence and certain domestic case law.[28] It is also evident in US jurisprudence, albeit, as explained in the next paragraph, this is subject to opposing views. It was suggested in the previous chapter that Oster's argument that for this requirement to be fulfilled it must occur periodically is over-exclusive.[29] Actors can fulfil the workable definition of media and operate as a constitutional component on one-off occasions or on an ad hoc basis.[30]

Scholarship and jurisprudence from the US, the UK and the ECtHR suggest that this requirement could be met with differences of opinion.[31] From a US scholarship perspective, it may be opposed on a doctrinal basis, as content discrimination is not permitted under the First Amendment.[32] As Eugene

---

[26]   See Chapter 5 section 4.2; A. Meiklejohn, *Political Freedom: The Constitutional Powers of the People* (Oxford University Press, 1960) 42; A. Meiklejohn, 'The First Amendment is an Absolute' [1961] *Supreme Court Review* 245, 255–257; D. Milo, *Defamation and Freedom of Speech* (Oxford University Press, 2008) 63–64. The link between public interest and the argument from democratic self-governance is borne out by jurisprudence from, for instance, the US Supreme Court, the ECtHR and the UK courts (discussed in detail below).

[27]   Oster (n 4) 37.

[28]   See the discussion later in this section relating to 'celebrity gossip'.

[29]   See Chapter 5 section 5. J. Oster, 'Theory and Doctrine of "Media Freedom" as a Legal Concept' (2013) 5(1) *Journal of Media Law* 57, 74.

[30]   *Editions Plon v France* App. no. 58148/00 (ECtHR 18 May 2004), [43]; *Lindon, Otchakovsky-Laurens and July v France* App. no. 21279/02 and 36448/02 (ECtHR 22 October 2007), [47]; Coe (n 3) 51.

[31]   Ibid.

[32]   L.L. Berger, 'Shielding the Unmedia: Using the Process of Journalism to Protect the Journalist's Privilege in an Infinite Universe of Publication' (2003) 39 *Houston Law Review* 1371, 1411; C.E. Baker, 'The Independent Significance of the Press Clause under Existing Law' (2007) 35 *Hofstra Law Review* 955, 1013–1016; J. Rubenfeld, 'The First Amendment's Purpose' (2001) 53 *Stanford Law Review* 767, 787–788; E. Volokh. 'The Trouble with "Public Discourse" as a Limitation on Free Speech Rights' (2011) 97 *Virginia Law Review* 567, 594.

Volokh suggests, it is a fundamental First Amendment principle that it is 'generally not the government's job to decide what subjects speakers and listeners should concern themselves with'.[33] This 'negative' freedom of expression rationale has also been referred to by, in particular, Frederick Schauer, as the 'suspicion' or 'distrust' of government theory.[34] To the contrary, however, according to Cass Sunstein, 'it would be difficult to imagine a sensible system of free expression that did not distinguish among categories of speech in accordance with their importance to the underlying purposes of the free speech guarantee'.[35] This view correlates with Cynthia Estlund's contention that '[t]he central importance of speech on public issues, or "matters of public concern" is long-established First Amendment dogma'.[36] The 'dogma' referred to by Estlund is illustrated by *Garrison v Louisiana*[37] in which the Supreme Court highlighted the inextricable link between the argument from democratic self-governance and public interest: 'speech concerning public affairs is more than self-expression; it is the essence of self-government'.[38] Similarly, in *First National Bank v Bellotti*[39] the Supreme Court placed public interest speech 'at the heart of the First Amendment's protection'[40] and in *Carey v Brown*[41] matters of public interest were recognised as sitting on the 'highest rung of the hierarchy of First Amendment values'.[42] Indeed, the US Supreme Court, the Supreme Court of Canada and the Court of Appeal, House of Lords and Supreme Court in the UK have made consistent reference to the public interest requirement. The courts have expressed this in a number of ways, including:

---

[33] E. Volokh, 'Freedom of Speech and Information Privacy: The Troubling Implications of a Right to Stop People From Speaking About You' (2000) 52 *Stanford Law Review* 1049, 1089.

[34] F. Schauer, *Free Speech: A Philosophical Enquiry* (Cambridge University Press, 1982) 81, 148, 162–163. See also E. Barendt, *Freedom of Speech* (2nd edn., Oxford University Press, 2005) 21–23. In his 'Two Concepts of Liberty', Isaiah Berlin referred to the notions of negative and positive freedom. According to Berlin, negative liberty relates to the absence of, for example, barriers, constraints and interference, whereas positive liberty requires the presence of something, such as control, self-mastery, self-determination or self-realisation: I. Berlin, 'Two Concepts of Liberty' in *Four Essays on Liberty* (Oxford University Press, 1969).

[35] C.R. Sunstein, 'Pornography and the First Amendment' (1986) 35 *Duke Law Journal* 589, 605.

[36] C.Y. Estlund, 'Speech on Matters of Public Concern: The Perils of an Emerging First Amendment Category' (1990) 59(1) *George Washington Law Review* 1, 1.

[37] 379 US 64 (1964).

[38] Ibid 74–75.

[39] 435 US 765 (1978).

[40] Ibid 776.

[41] 447 US 455 (1980).

[42] Ibid 467.

186   *Media freedom in the age of citizen journalism*

'public interest' or 'public concern';[43] 'of political, social or other concern to the community';[44] 'influences social relations and politics on a grand scale'; or is part of a 'debate about public affairs'; makes a 'contribution to the public debate'; stimulating 'political and social changes';[45] more than 'mere curiosity or prurient interest' with the public having a 'genuine stake in knowing about the matter published'.[46]

The myriad of ways in which 'public interest' has been explained by the courts demonstrates the concept's inherently vague nature. It has even been suggested that efforts to define it are 'doomed to fail'.[47] This view certainly correlates with, for instance, the position of the Information Commissioner's Office (ICO), which states in its *Data Protection and Journalism: A Guide for the Media* that what is in the public interest will differ on a case-by-case basis. Consequently, the guide refers to industry codes of practice, such as the BBC's Editorial Guidelines,[48] to 'help organisations think about what is in the public interest',[49] a position that echoes Justice Stewart's often cited phrase from

---

[43]   For example, from the US Supreme Court, see *Gertz v Robert Welch Inc* 418 US 323, 246 (1974); *Dun & Bradstreet Inc v Greenmoss Builders* 472 US 749, 761 (1985); *Hustler Magazine v Falwell* 485 US 46, 50 (1988); *Bartnicki v Vopper* 532 US 514, 528, 533–534 (2001). From the House of Lords/Supreme Court, see *London Artists v Littler* [1969] 2 QB 375, 391 (CA) (per Lord Denning); *Reynolds v Times Newspapers Ltd* [2001] 2 AC 127, 205 (per Lord Nicholls); *Jameel v Wall Street Journal Europe Sprl* [2007] 1 AC 359, 376 (per Lord Bingham); *Flood v Times Newspapers Ltd* [2012] UKSC 11, [24] (per Lord Phillips).

[44]   *Connick v Myers* 461 US 138, 146 (1983).

[45]   From the US, see *Roth v United States* 354 US 476, 484 (1957); *New York Times v Sullivan* 376 US 254, 269 (1964); *Hustler Magazine v Falwell* 485 US 46, 53 (1988). From the UK, see *Lion Laboratories Ltd v Evans* [1984] 1 WLR 526, 530; *Francome v Mirror Group Newspapers Ltd* [1984] 1 WLR 892, 897; *Reynolds v Times Newspapers Ltd* [2001] 2 AC 127, 205 (per Lord Nicholls).

[46]   For example, see the Canadian Supreme Court case of *Grant v Torstar Corporation* 2009 SCC 61, [105]. Of course, any speaker's freedom can be restrained according to, for example, defamation law or privacy laws, and, equally, 'public interest' can provide protection for them regardless of their status.

[47]   Oster (n 4) 39.

[48]   See section 7: http://www.bbc.co.uk/editorialguidelines/guidelines.

[49]   Information Commissioner's Office, *Data Protection and Journalism: A Guide for the Media*, 32–34. The ICO's guidance is consistent with section 32(3) of the now-repealed Data Protection Act 1998, which, for the purposes of determining whether the belief of a data controller that the publication would be in the public interest was or is a reasonable belief pursuant to section 32(1)(b), refers to any code of practice designated by the Secretary of State. In the Data Protection (Designated Codes of Practice) (No 2) Order 2000 the Secretary of State has designated a number of codes, including the BBC's Editorial Guidelines. Section 32 of the Data Protection Act 1998 provides a journalistic, literary and artistic exemption for most statutory provisions relating to the processing of personal data if the data is being processed only for one of

Jacobellis v Ohio[50] of 'I know it when I see it' in respect of his refusal to define hard-core pornography. A way of not determining what is in the public interest is to leave this decision to the public or media. If either were responsible for deciding what private information is relevant or irrelevant then, arguably, public interest would be conceptually confused with what is of 'interest to the public'. As Oster is surely correct in stating, public desire for information, such as private or intimate details of people in the public sphere, does not, per se, justify its supply. The damage that would be inflicted by the media intruding into, and reporting on, such matters outweighs the 'interest in the satiation of public appetite for such entertainment'.[51]

3.1.1 Public interest and celebrity gossip

This free speech and public interest/privacy dichotomy is acutely apparent within the context of celebrity gossip. The jurisprudence generated from this type of speech from the UK courts and ECtHR illuminates conflicting interpretations of public interest that are of significance to the argument from democratic self-governance and, by extension, the media-as-a-constitutional-component concept, and its social responsibility foundations. The discussions relating to the philosophical foundations of freedom of expression in the previous chapter[52] established that at the heart of Strasbourg jurisprudence relating to free speech claims is the argument from democratic self-governance[53] that incorporates the notion of 'public discussion' relating to matters of public interest.[54] As a result, the argument has influenced the Court's interpretation of the notion of public interest. This is evident in the public interest test laid down in *Von Hannover v Germany (No 1)*[55] that where the sole purpose of the expression is 'to satisfy the curiosity of a particular readership regarding the details of the applicant's private life', the publication 'cannot be deemed to contribute to any debate of general interest to society despite the applicant

---

these special purposes. Section 32 has been imported into the General Data Protection Regulation and the Data Protection Act 2018 by virtue of Article 85 and paragraph 26, Part 5 of Schedule 2 respectively. This provision is discussed in more detail below.

50   378 US 184 (1964).

51   Oster (n 4) 38.

52   See the discussions at Chapter 5 sections 3.1 to 4.2.

53   *Lingens v Austria* (1986) 8 EHRR 407; *Jersild v Denmark* (1995) 19 EHRR 1; L. Wildhaber, 'The Right to Offend, Shock or Disturb? Aspects of Freedom of Expression under the European Convention on Human Rights' (2001) 36 *Irish Jurist* 17; P. Wragg, 'A Freedom to Criticise? Evaluating the Public Interest in Celebrity Gossip after *Mosley* and *Terry* (2010) 2(2) *Journal of Media Law* 295, 314.

54   Meiklejohn, *Political Freedom* (n 26) 42; Meiklejohn, 'The First Amendment is an Absolute' (n 26) 255–257; Milo (n 26) 63–64.

55   [2004] App. no. 59320/00.

being known to the public' and 'in these conditions freedom of expression calls for a narrower interpretation'.[56] Thus, as Paul Wragg states: 'It is abundantly clear from the Strasbourg case law that the democratic process value is at the core of Article 10, and it is this value that articulates the meaning of "general interest" in the *Von Hannover* test'.[57] As discussed in the previous chapter, the 'mirror principle' dictates that domestic case law must 'mirror' Strasbourg jurisprudence. Failure to do this would be unlawful under section 2(1) of the Human Rights Act 1998.[58]

Three high-profile decisions from the UK clearly mirror the *Von Hannover* test. In *Campbell v Mirror Group Newspapers Ltd*[59] Lord Hope was of the view that revelations about Naomi Campbell's private life did not engage political or democratic values.[60] Similarly, Baroness Hale found that many forms of expression are vital to democracy and democratic societies and are, therefore, deserving of protection. However, in this case, it was difficult to justify the expression involved on these grounds. Accordingly, Her Ladyship stated: '[T]he political and social life of the community and the intellectual, artistic or personal development of individuals are not obviously assisted by poring over the intimate details of a fashion model's private life.'[61] Two years later, in *Jameel v Wall Street Journal Europe Sprl (No. 3)*,[62] Baroness Hale defined 'public interest' as something 'very different from … information which interests the public – the most vapid tittle-tattle about the activities of footballers' wives and girlfriends interests large sections of the public but no one could claim any real public interest in our being told about it'.[63] As Wragg says, Eady J's judgment in *Mosley v News Group Newspapers*[64] corresponds with this line of jurisprudence.[65] In finding that the only permissible

---

[56] Ibid [65]–[66]. For subsequent application of the test, see, for example, *Mosley v UK* App. no. 48009/08 (ECtHR 10 May 2011), [114]; *Hachette Filipacchi Associes v France* App. no. 12268/03 (ECtHR 23 July 2009), [40]; *Eerikainen and others v Finland* App. no. 3514/02 (ECtHR 10 February 2009), [62]; *Standard Verlags GmbH v Austria (No 2)* App. no. 21277/05 (ECtHR 4 June 2009), [52]; *MGN Ltd v UK* [2011] App. no. 39401/04, [143]; *Von Hannover (No 2) v Germany* [2012] App. nos. 40660/08 and 60641/08; *Axel Springer AG v Germany* [2012] App. no. 39954/08.

[57] Wragg (n 53) 314.

[58] See Chapter 5 section 3.1.

[59] [2004] 2 All ER 995.

[60] Ibid [117].

[61] Ibid [148]–[149].

[62] [2006] UKHL 44.

[63] Ibid 147.

[64] [2008] EWHC 1777 (QB).

[65] See generally Wragg (n 53). Wragg provides comprehensive and persuasive coverage of the privacy/public interest dichotomy in the context of celebrity gossip. The article offers up analysis of the treatment of the link between morality and public

The media-as-a-constitutional-component concept and media freedom 189

interference with Article 8 ECHR raising 'a countervailing public interest ... strong enough to outweigh it'[66] would be a necessary and proportionate intrusion for the purpose of exposing illegal activity or to prevent the public from being misled or because the information would make a contribution to a debate of general interest,[67] Eady J effectively applied the *Von Hannover* test. Consequently, in employing the test, in his view, the stories or accompanying images did not make any recognisable contribution to the public interest, and certainly not enough to defeat a privacy claim.[68]

To the contrary, however, in recent years a divergent line of domestic case law based on a 'role model' principle has emerged, which, in contravention of section 2(1) of the Human Rights Act 1998, does not mirror the Strasbourg Court's jurisprudence. This more generous approach to the contribution of celebrity gossip to the public interest[69] not only endorses the publication of speech by the press that is not of constitutional value, but may also conflict with individual privacy rights. The role model principle was established by Lord Woolf LCJ in *A v B plc*,[70] where it was held that revelations of adultery by Premiership footballer Gary Flitcroft were in the public interest on the basis that professional footballers 'are role models to young people and undesirable behaviour on their part can set an unfortunate example'.[71] In his judgment Lord Woolf LCJ went on to state that 'the courts must not ignore the fact that if newspapers do not publish information which the public are interested in, there will be fewer newspapers published, which will not be in the public interest'.[72]

The judgment, and the principle itself, became the subject of academic and judicial disapproval. Helen Fenwick and Gavin Phillipson, for example,

---

interest by Eady J and Tugendhat J in this context in *Mosley v UK* App. no. 48009/08 (ECtHR 10 May 2011) and *Terry (previously LNS) v Persons Unknown* [2010] EWHC 119 (QB) respectively.

[66] *Mosley v UK* App. no. 48009/08 (ECtHR 10 May 2011), [131].
[67] Ibid.
[68] Ibid [134].
[69] Wragg (n 53) 299.
[70] [2002] 3 WLR 542.
[71] Ibid [45].
[72] [2002] 3 WLR 542, 552. In giving a talk on the privacy/free speech dichotomy, Lord Neuberger MR seemed to support Lord Woolf's judgment:

> We, or most of us, like to think that we live in an open society. Which is a society committed to liberal, democratic principles and the rule of law. An open society has a number of essential features: political institutions accountable through free and fair elections, an independent and impartial judiciary upholding the law, and a free press ... [A] free press is often not merely truth-seeking and challenging, but strident, biased and shallow; again, however, without a free press we are damned to servitude.

Privacy & Freedom of Expression: A Delicate Balance, 28 April 2010.

observed that 'a cruder definition of public interest is hardly imaginable',[73] and in *McKennit v Ash*[74] Buxton LJ stated that '[t]he width of the rights given to the media by *A v B* cannot be reconciled with Von Hannover'.[75] Yet, notwithstanding such significant criticism, and despite *A v B plc* coming before *Von Hannover* and *Jameel*, and the principle seemingly being in direct conflict with Baroness Hale's judgment in *Jameel*,[76] it gained traction in a line of cases involving footballers that came *after* these decisions. For instance, in *Ferdinand v Mirror Group Newspapers Limited*[77] Rio Ferdinand failed to prevent details of his affair with a long-time 'friend' from being published. Nicol J determined there was a public interest in publication as Ferdinand had portrayed himself as a mature, stable 'family-man'. On Nicol J's assessment, Ferdinand, as a former England captain, was a role model, a ubiquitous position not simply confined to the football pitch.[78] More recently *McClaren v News Group Newspapers*[79] involved an application by Steve McClaren for an interim non-disclosure order to prevent News Group Newspapers from publishing information regarding an extra-marital 'sexual encounter' which had taken place a few days previously. Lindblom J held in favour of the Defendant and, as a consequence, the story was published.[80] The judge determined that there was a public interest in publishing the story as McClaren, as a former England manager, was a 'prominent public figure' from whom the 'public could reasonably expect a higher standard of conduct'.[81] In coming to their decisions, both Nicol J and Lindblom J, in *Ferdinand* and *McClaren* respectively, placed emphasis on Lord Woolf LCJ's *A v B plc* role model principle.[82]

---

[73] H. Fenwick and G. Phillipson, *Media Freedom under the Human Rights Act* (Oxford University Press, 2006) 799.

[74] [2008] QB 73.

[75] Ibid [62].

[76] See n 63 and surrounding text.

[77] [2011] EWHC 2454.

[78] Ibid [84]–[87].

[79] [2012] EWHC 2466 (QB).

[80] R. Dale, 'McClaren's affair with Sven's ex', *The Sun*, 19 August 2012.

[81] [2012] EWHC 2466 (QB), [34].

[82] *Ferdinand v Mirror Group Newspapers Limited* [2011] EWHC 2454, [87]; *McLaren v News Group Newspapers* [2012] EWHC 2466 (QB), [18]. The principle has also been applied by Ouseley J in *Theakston v Mirror Group Newspapers Ltd* [2002] EWHC 137. According to Wragg, Tugendhat J's judgment in *Terry (previously LNS) v Persons Unknown* [2010] EWHC 119 (QB) 'hint[s] at a resurgence – and, it is submitted, broadening – of the role model analysis prevalent in Lord Woolf's decision in *A v B plc* and likewise apparent in *Theakston v MGN Ltd*'. For an excellent discussion on *Terry*, and how Tugendhat J's 'freedom to criticise' analysis differs, albeit subtlety, from the role model principle, see Wragg (n 53) 315.

The media-as-a-constitutional-component concept and media freedom   191

Almost without exception, celebrity gossip cases such as these relate to publications of mere entertainment. They very rarely make any positive contribution to the public sphere. In accordance with authority such as *Von Hannover*, *Campbell* and *Jameel*, in the instance that a journalist or newspaper engages with this type of journalistic activity, they are not fulfilling their democratic functions,[83] nor are they conforming to the requirements of the media-as-a-constitutional-component concept and its definition of media proposed in the previous chapter.[84] Thus, the concept, and the way in which it defines media, can exclude from media privileges actors that have traditionally been considered part of the media and have enjoyed the protection offered by media freedom,[85] despite their primary purpose being to treat the private lives of those in the public eye as a highly lucrative commodity by exposing aspects of people's private lives or engaging in entertainment and sensationalism.

3.1.2   Public interest and the creation of artificial supply and demand

If we were to ignore Baroness Hale's definition of public interest in *Jameel*[86] and follow the premise of Lord Woolf's judgment in *A v B plc* that 'if newspapers do not publish information which the public are interested in, there will be fewer newspapers published, which will not be in the public interest',[87] as the cases discussed above have done, then we are essentially leaving to the public or the media the decision as to what is or is not in the public interest, which could conceivably lead to the 'tyranny of the majority' and the 'tyranny of the prevailing opinion and feeling' that John Adams and John Stuart Mill warned of.[88] Indeed, this raises a question relating to the relationship between cause and effect and supply and demand. Although, as we saw in Chapters 2 and 3, the institutional media has historically played, and continues to play, a valuable role in maintaining the health and prosperity of the public sphere, it has, at times, purposefully and proactively encouraged the public's appetite for information relating to the private lives of certain people to create what amounts to

---

[83]   This is a view echoed by Wragg, who has said that 'it is arguable that by reporting celebrity gossip the media are strikingly distracted from performing ... vital [democratic] functions', Wragg (n 53) 316.

[84]   See Chapter 5 section 5.

[85]   See Chapter 4 section 3.

[86]   See text at n 63.

[87]   See n 72.

[88]   J. Mill, *On Liberty* in J.M. Robson (ed), *Collected Works of John Stuart Mill* (University of Toronto Press, 1977) 219–220; J. Adams, 'A Defence of the Constitutions of the Government of the United States of America' in C. Adams (ed), *The Works of John Adams, Second President of the United States: with a Life of the Author, Notes and Illustrations, by his Grandson Charles Francis Adams*, vol. 6 (Little, Brown and Co., 1851) 63.

192 *Media freedom in the age of citizen journalism*

artificial demand, as opposed to the public creating the demand initially and the media reacting to satisfy it.[89] Thus, despite it not being within the media's remit to create a 'pseudo-public sphere'[90] by making public what is private, certain members of the press and wider media have conferred, and continue to confer, a public status on private information by kindling the public's desire for 'sensational and ... lurid news, intended to titillate and entertain, [that is] aimed at satisfying the curiosity of a particular readership regarding aspects of a person's strictly private life'.[91]

Accordingly, in Post's view, any attempt to establish a definition of public interest by simply applying quantitative criteria would risk being either over-inclusive, in that it considers trivial matters that interest factions of the public, or under-inclusive if it excludes matters that most people have not heard of, even they affect them, such as state secrets.[92] The number of people interested in a particular subject should not be the determinative factor for deciding what is in the public interest. Rather, it should serve as just one of many indicators. Evidently, due to its vagueness, creating an exhaustive definition of public interest is probably impossible, particularly because it is a dynamic and ever-changing concept: what is in the public interest today may not be tomorrow, and vice versa. To the contrary, because of the independence of the judiciary, and its greater accountability, leaving judges to determine what is or is not in the public interest, at least in the context of case law, is preferable as it is less likely to lead to the tyranny described by Adams and Mill.

3.1.3   A need for guidance on what public interest is?

Rather than attempting to deliver an inevitably abstract definition, echoing the position of the ICO, it is preferable to provide guidance for both lawyers and media actors as to what public interest is, which, in turn, creates greater legal certainty. A proposal for such guidance is set out in section 3.2.4. However, at this juncture, it is worthy of note that the need for robust guidance on what is in the public interest has become particularly significant in respect of the operation of the section 32 Data Protection Act 1998 exemption for 'journalistic,

---

[89]   Oster (n 4) 38–39.

[90]   J. Habermas, *The Structural Transformation of the Public Sphere* (1962) (translation by T. Burger, Polity Press, 1992) 162.

[91]   *Mosley v United Kingdom* App. no. 48009/08 (ECtHR 10 May 2011), [114]; *Von Hannover v Germany (No 1)* App. no. 59320/00 (ECtHR 24 June 2004), [65]; *Hachette Filipacchi Associes v France* App. no. 12268/03 (ECtHR 23 July 2009), [40]; *Eerikainen and others v Finland* App. no. 3514/02 (ECtHR 10 February 2009), [62]; *Standard Verlags GmbH v Austria (No 2)* App. no. 21277/05 (ECtHR 4 June 2009), [52]; *MGN Ltd v United Kingdom* App. no. 39401/04 (ECtHR 18 January 2011), [143].

[92]   Post, 'The Constitutional Concept of Public Discourse' (n 10) 673.

The media-as-a-constitutional-component concept and media freedom 193

literary or artistic' purposes. Although it has now been repealed, the provision was imported into the General Data Protection Regulation (GDPR) by virtue of Article 85 and the Data Protection Act 2018 (DPA 2018) by paragraph 26, Part 5 of Schedule 2.[93] Pursuant to the exemption, if the data controller can demonstrate that (i) the data is processed only for one of the special purposes; (ii) with a view to publication of some material;[94] (iii) it reasonably believes that the publication is in the public interest;[95] and (iv) it reasonably believes that compliance with the respective DPA 2018/GDPR provision(s) would be incompatible with the special purpose,[96] then it provides an exemption from most statutory provisions under the DPA 2018/GDPR which apply to the processing of personal data. According to the ICO the purpose of the exemption is to 'safeguard freedom of expression'.[97] Traditional institutional media organisations have consistently used it[98] to protect their freedom of expression, a trend that has extended to citizen journalists, as illustrated by *The Law Society and others v Kordowski*.[99] In recognising that private individuals can engage in journalistic activity that could use the exemption, Tugendhat J stated:

> Journalism that is protected by section 32 involves communication of information or ideas to the public at large in the public interest. Today anyone with access to the internet can engage in journalism at no cost. If what the Defendant communicated to the public at large had the necessary public interest, he could invoke the [section 32] protection for journalism and Article 10.[100]

Thus, citizen journalists can not only be subject to causes of action under data protection law, like the institutional media, they can also avail themselves of its protection, so long as they demonstrate they have met the conditions set out above. The protection afforded by the exemption has become more important for media actors in light of the Defamation Act 2013. Arguably the introduction of the test under section 1(1) that claimants must demonstrate 'serious harm', which for claimants trading for profit means 'serious financial loss', has made defamation a less attractive cause of action for claimants wanting

---

[93]   The GDPR and DPA 2018 have added 'academic purposes' to the list.

[94]   Section 32(1)(a)/para. 26(2)(a).

[95]   Section 32(1)(b)/para. 26(2)(b).

[96]   Section 32(1)(c)/para. 26(3).

[97]   Information Commissioner's Office (n 49) 28.

[98]   For recent examples see *ZXC v Bloomberg LP* [2017] EWHC 328 (QB); *Stunt v Associated Newspapers Ltd* [2017] EWHC 695 (QB) (at the time of writing an appeal is outstanding).

[99]   [2014] EMLR 2. *Kordowski* relates to the application of section 32 of the 1998 Act.

[100]   Ibid [99].

to vindicate their reputation.[101] Consequently, there has been an increase in claimants using the DPA 1998 and 2018 to defend their reputation.[102] In turn, as illustrated by *Stunt v Associated Newspapers Ltd*[103] and *ZXC v Bloomberg LP*,[104] media organisations have relied on the exemption to defend these claims. Like the privacy/free speech dichotomy previously discussed, what is and is not in the public interest is critically important within the context of the data protection/free speech debate, and to the operation of the exemption. In line with the arguments set out above in respect of celebrity gossip, Hugh Tomlinson QC has stated that 'entertainment journalism' would not be protected by section 32 and, by extension, its DPA 2018 successor, as it would fail the public interest condition.[105]

3.1.4 Guiding factors

To provide pragmatic and robust guidance three factors need to be considered[106] pursuant to the norms and behaviours underpinning the media-as-constitutional-component concept. The first factor relates to the form of the question that is asked when considering public interest. As opposed to asking the binary question of whether something is or is not in the public interest, the extent to which the subject matter is in the public interest should, instead, be established. This is because the subject matter, and the speech that pertains to it, can be at the same time inherently of both public and private concern. For example, the alleged marital difficulties of a member of the UK government's Cabinet, on the one hand, clearly relate to the individual's private life, and are therefore a matter of private concern. On the other hand, there may exist a legitimate public interest in the story if the difficulties detrimentally impact upon the individual's ability to fulfil the responsibilities

---

[101] See generally P. Coe, 'An Analysis of Three Distinct Approaches to Using Defamation to Protect Corporate Reputation from Australia, England and Wales, and Canada' (2021) 41 *Legal Studies* 111; P. Coe, 'The Defamation Act 2013: We Need to Talk About Corporate Reputation' (2015) 4 *Journal of Business Law* 313.

[102] M. Patrick and A. Mendonca, 'Using Data Protection Law to Defend Your Reputation: What About the New Data Protection Bill?' *Inforrm*, 5 September 2017.

[103] [2017] EWHC 695 (QB).

[104] [2017] EWHC 328 (QB). Two years after this initial failed application by the claimant for an interim injunction Nicklin J granted a permanent injunction after a full trial ([2019] EWHC 970 (QB)). However, at this stage the section 32 argument was not raised by *Bloomberg*.

[105] H. Tomlinson QC, 'The "Journalism Exemption" in the Data Protection Act: Part 2, Some Practicalities', *Inforrm*, 29 March 2017.

[106] Oster (n 4) 39–44.

The media-as-a-constitutional-component concept and media freedom 195

of their role.[107] Accordingly, the questions to be asked are: to what extent is the subject matter of public interest? And, therefore, to what extent can the media report upon its details? This is because the more a publication relates to a matter of public interest, the greater protection it will be afforded during the balancing exercise that will be undertaken by lawyers and judges when weighing up the conflicting private and public interests. The 'status', or role, of the individual concerned would also impact upon this decision. For instance, if a celebrity was being treated for alcohol addiction this is, quite clearly, a private matter relating to their health and well-being. However, there may, in such a case, also exist a degree of public interest, as the celebrity's addiction, and the way in which they are dealing with it, may negatively or positively affect the public's attitude towards alcohol. If the story related to a Cabinet Minister, for instance, it would attract a greater degree of public interest, not only because it would raise the same issues as those relating to the celebrity, but it may also impact upon the Minister's ability to exercise their office, which could affect democracy itself.

The second factor is case law. Jurisprudence from the ECtHR has regularly referred to 'matters of general public interest' and 'matters of public concern' within a variety of different circumstances, and thus offers an abundance of examples that may serve as indicators for future cases. The concept has been applied to, amongst many other things,[108] national and local-level political speech and reporting;[109] criticism of public administration and justice;[110] abuse of police power;[111] criticisms of businesses and those operating businesses;[112] the search for historical truth, including scholarly historical debates regard-

---

[107] This is analogous to the case of *Trimingham v Associated Newspapers Limited* [2012] EWHC 1296 (QB) in which Tugendhat J held that the publications complained of were in the public interest as they exposed Christopher Huhne MP's 'improper conduct in deceiving his wife and the electorate in circumstances which would affect his public responsibilities as a Minister' [109]. Similarly, in *AAA v Associated Newspapers Ltd* [2013] EWCA Civ 554 the Court of Appeal held that the public had an interest in knowing that Boris Johnson's extra-marital affair resulted in the conception of a child, in so far as, according to the court, it showed his 'reckless behaviour' (at [43]).

[108] For a more comprehensive list, see Oster (n 29) 75; Oster (n 4) 41–42.

[109] *Bowman v United Kingdom* App. no. 141/1996/760/961 (ECtHR 19 February 1998), [42]; *Jerusalem v Austria* App. no. 26958/95 (ECtHR 27 February 2001), [41]; *Filatenko v Russia* App. no. 73219/01 (ECtHR 6 December 2007), [40].

[110] *De Haes and Gijsels v Belguim* App. no. 19983/92 (ECtHR 24 February 1997), [37]; *Pedersen and Baadsgaard v Denmark* App. no. 49017/99 (ECtHR 17 December 2004), [71]; *Perna v Italy* App. no. 48898/99 (ECtHR 6 May 2003), [39].

[111] *Thorgeir Thorgeirson v Iceland* App. no. 13778/88 (ECtHR 25 June 1992).

[112] *Fressoz and Roire v France* App. no. 29183/95 (ECtHR 21 January 1999), [50]; *Steel and Morris v United Kingdom* App. no. 68416/01 (ECtHR 15 February

ing particular events and their interpretation;[113] violations of law, especially criminal and terrorist activity[114] and their prevention, investigation and prosecution;[115] publications on various matters of public interest, such as animal protection,[116] issues relating to tobacco advertising in sport,[117] the programming policy of public media[118] and failed cosmetic surgery provided at a private clinic by a particular surgeon.[119]

The final factor to consider when attempting to establish the degree to which a publication is of public interest is the extent to which it is a purely private matter. As stated above, the two concepts can overlap. Therefore, the critical questions are, first, to what degree is the subject of public interest and, secondly, to what extent is it of private interest? Like public interest, private interest does not attract a definitive definition. Rather, Convention provisions and jurisprudence relating to the concept of privacy provide indications as to what private interest may mean. Pursuant to Article 8 ECHR and Article 17 ICCPR privacy incorporates the following: family, home and correspondence; an individual's name[120] or picture,[121] physical intimacy (such as nakedness, illness or

---

2005), [89]; J. Oster, 'The Criticism of Trading Corporations and their Right to Sue for Defamation' (2011) 2 *Journal of European Tort Law* 255.

[113] *Monnat v Switzerland* [2006] App. no. 73604/01, [59]; *Radio France and others v France* [2004] App. no. 64915/01, [69]; *Perinçek v Switzerland* [2013] App. no. 27510/08, [103].

[114] *Leroy v France* [2009] App. no. 36109/03, [41]; *Brunet Lecomte et Lyon Mag v France* [2010] App. no. 17265/05, [41].

[115] *White v Sweden* [2006] App. no. 42435/02, [29]; *Egeland and Hanseid v Norway* [2009] App. no. 34438/04, [58]; *Salumäki v Finland* [2014] App. no. 23605/09, [54].

[116] *VgT Verein gegen Tierfabriken v Switzerland (No. 1)* [2001] App. no. 24699/94, [70]; *PETA Deutschland v Germany* [2012] App. no. 43481/09, [47]; *Animal Defenders International v United Kingdom* [2013] App. no. 48876/08, [102].

[117] *Société de Conception de Press et d'Edition et Ponson v France* [2009] App. no. 26935/05, [55].

[118] *Wojtas-Kaleta v Poland* [2009] App. no. 20436/02, [46].

[119] *Bergens Tidende and others v Norway* [2000] App. no. 26132/95, [51].

[120] ECtHR: *Burghartz v Switzerland* [1994] App. no. 16213/90, [24]; *Standard Verlags GmbH v Austria (No. 3)* [2012] App. no. 34702/07, [36]. See also Article 24(2) ICCPR and Article 18 ACHR.

[121] ECtHR: *Schüssel v Austria* [2002] App. no. 42409/98; *Von Hannover v Germany (No. 1)* [2004] App. no. 59320/00, [50ff]; *Eerikäinen and others v Finland* [2009] App. no. 3514/02, [61].

injury[122]), sexuality and sexual life and orientation,[123] the personality of each individual in their relations with other individuals[124] and personal data.[125]

Conceptually, privacy rights run counter to the notion of a general right to know all information about everybody.[126] However, privacy is a relative term, which is, first and foremost, defined by the individual to whom the privacy right attaches. For instance, some people voluntarily weaken their expectation of privacy, or perhaps give up their privacy right entirely (in specific circumstances) by publishing aspects (or all) of their private life on social media with no privacy setting,[127] whereas others protect their private 'sphere' and, as a result, are entitled to a stronger expectation of privacy.[128] However, as Oster states, this private 'sphere' is not a purely spatial notion.[129] Clearly legitimate privacy interests exist in public spaces, yet, as stated above, subject matter relating to an individual's private domain may also be of public interest depending on the circumstances. For instance, the use of violence and the commission of crimes are, at all times, matters of public interest per se, regardless of the view of the individuals concerned.[130]

3.2   Media Conduct

For a publication to be of value to the public sphere the media-as-a-constitutional-component concept requires that it derives from not only accurate, but also the best available information. As Post has stated, the integrity of public discourse, and I would suggest, by extension, discourse

---

[122] ECtHR: *X and Y v Netherlands* [1985] App. no. 8978/80, [22]; *Raninen v Finland* [1997] App. no. 152/1996/771/972, [63]; *Biriuk v Lithuania* [2008] App. no. 23373/03, [43].

[123] ECtHR. *Peck v United Kingdom* [2003] App. no. 44647/98, [57]; *Biriuk v Lithuania* [2008] App. no. 23373/03, [34]; *Ruusunen v Finland* [2014] App. no. 73579/10, [50].

[124] ECtHR: *Botta v Italy* [1998] App. no. 153/1996/772/973, [32]; *Von Hannover v Germany (No. 1)* [2004] App. no. 59320/00, [50].

[125] ECtHR: *S and Marper v United Kingdom* [2008] App. nos. 30562/04 and 30566/04, [41].

[126] For a fictional interpretation of this 'argument' see D. Eggers, *The Circle* (Penguin 2013).

[127] Jacob Rowbottom makes the observation that if, for instance, a person posts photographs of themselves on social media with no privacy setting then this is likely to weaken their expectation of privacy in relation to that information. But that does not necessarily mean that they are consenting to publication of the photo by the mass media to the world at large. J. Rowbottom, *Media Law* (Hart Publishing, 2018) 73.

[128] Oster (n 4) 43.

[129] Ibid.

[130] Ibid.

that is valuable to the public sphere, is contingent upon factual accuracy.[131] Historically, the institutional press and wider media's ability to reach large audiences meant that any false information it disseminated was likely to have a greater negative impact than incorrect or misleading information communicated by private individuals. The false news phenomenon and its association with filter bubbles discussed in the previous chapter and in Chapter 3[132] demonstrates that although it is still the case that false information communicated by the institutional media can detrimentally affect the health of the public sphere, this is no longer reserved to the printed press or broadcast media. Rather, the symbiotic relationship discussed in Chapter 3 that now exists between the traditional media and citizen journalists means that false information disseminated by citizen journalists or non-media actors can have an even greater impact as false information can be, and very often is, recycled by the institutional media. In turn, the fact that the institutional media has published it serves to justify, and add credence to, the false information.[133]

Consequently, as a rationale for media freedom, the media-as-a-constitutional-component concept, and its requirement for media actors to contribute positively to the public sphere, justifies media actors abiding by certain standards of conduct when gathering, editing and imparting information and ideas.[134] This requirement is particularly significant where the media discloses information that may negatively impact on an individual. The ECtHR has consistently held, in defamation claims for example, that the privileged protection afforded by media freedom is subject to the media acting with transparency[135] and on an accurate factual basis.[136] Of course, requiring a media actor to ensure that each factual statement they publish is correct would have a chilling effect on the media that would, in turn, negatively impact on public discourse and the dissemination of information of constitutional value. As a result, in certain situations, media actors may deviate from the requirement to verify the factual information they disseminate. Arguably, this issue is amplified in the fast-paced modern media landscape, where news

---

[131] Post, 'The Constitutional Concept of Public Discourse' (n 10) 659.
[132] See Chapter 5 sections 3.1 and 3.2 and Chapter 3 section 5.2.
[133] See Chapter 3 section 5.3.
[134] Oster (n 4) 44–45.
[135] In that at least the editor of the publication be immediately identifiable in order to facilitate effective protection against defamation and privacy violation. For example, see *Fatullayev v Azerbaijan* [2010] App. no. 40984/07. As discussed in the Chapter 7 section 3.1, this transparency requirement can cause issues for citizen journalists in respect of anonymous and pseudonymous expression.
[136] For example, see *Bladet Tromsø and Stansaas v Norway* [1999] App. no. 21980/93, [65]; *Fressoz and Roire v France* [1999] App. no. 29183/95, [54]; *Bergens Tidende and others v Norway* [2000] App. no. 26132/95, [53].

The media-as-a-constitutional-component concept and media freedom   199

is not only constantly accessible, but is expected to be disseminated immediately, thereby creating a 'race' amongst media actors to publish information as soon as possible.[137] However, their ability to do this is contingent upon the subject matter. If an individual's rights are engaged, then regardless of the situation, the media must take all reasonable steps to verify the accuracy of the information prior to publication.[138]

3.3   The Media Acting in Good Faith

The ECtHR has consistently held that media actors must act in good faith.[139] This is illustrated by the Court's decision in *Alithia Publishing Company Ltd and Constantinides v Cyprus*[140] in which it held that civil liability for a false, defamatory statement made in bad faith is always justifiable.[141] This begs the question, what does 'good faith' look like? According to Oster, the concept consists of two distinct components: (i) the veracity of the statement and (ii) the integrity of the motivation of the publisher,[142] both of which are indicative of the norms set out in Chapter 5 section 4.2 that facilitate speech that conforms with the media-as-a-constitutional-component concept and its social responsibility.

The 'veracity of the statement' component is relatively uncontroversial. Pursuant to Strasbourg jurisprudence it dictates that media actors must not intentionally distribute statements that are false and harmful, or act with a negligent disregard for the truth.[143] The ECtHR's case law indicates that the media must not publish statements based on improper motives or intentions, such as to stigmatise an individual or group, or to encourage violence and hatred.[144] Thus, the 'integrity of the motivation of the publisher' component is of even greater significance than the 'veracity of the statement' component, as it measures the value of the speech according to the speaker's intentions. Accordingly,

---

[137]   See Chapter 2 sections 2 and 3.3.2.
[138]   Oster (n 4) 45.
[139]   For example, see *Bladet Tromsø and Stansaas v Norway* [1999] App. no. 21980/93, [65]; *Fressoz and Roire v France* [1999] App. no. 29183/95, [54]; *Bergens Tidende and others v Norway* [2000] App. no. 26132/95, [53]; *Novaya Gazeta and Borodyankiy v Russia* [2013] App. no. 14087/08, [37].
[140]   [2008] App. no. 17550/03, [67].
[141]   See also *Pedersen and Baadsgaard v Denmark* [2004] App. no. 49017/99, [78].
[142]   Oster (n 4) 45–47.
[143]   *Alithia Publishing Company Ltd and Constantinides v Cyprus* [2008] App. no. 17550/03, [66]; *Gutiérrez Suárez v Spain* [2010] App. no. 16023/07, [38].
[144]   *Nilsen and Johnsen v Norway* [1999] App. no. 23118/93, [50]; *Selistö v Finland* [2004] App. no. 56767/00, [68]; *Lindon, Otchakovsky-Laurens and July v France* [2007] App. nos. 21279/02 and 36448/02, [57].

this consideration by the courts of the speaker's intentions in respect of factual statements means that they effectively determine whether the respective publication is morally acceptable or unacceptable. However, if the publication, and its factual statements subject to the dispute relate to a matter of public interest, the application of moral scrutiny should be rejected as it is not within the remit of the courts to impose their own moral standards on the media.[145] As advanced by Habermas and Oster, this position accords with the principles underpinning discourse theory: validity claims arising from descriptive sentences, which exist to ascertain facts, can be accepted or rejected from the standpoint of the truth of proposition; to the contrary, only evaluative sentences or value judgments can be accepted or rejected as a result of the speaker's express intentions or feelings.[146] Thus, in *Beckley Newspapers v Hanks Corporation*[147] the US Supreme Court held that where a false defamatory statement has been published 'from personal spite, ill will or desire to injure' it does not amount to malice pursuant to *New York Times v Sullivan*[148] so long as the speaker believed the statement to be true and was not reckless in respect of its truthfulness. Therefore, the Supreme Court applies the 'malice' standard 'only as an instrument pertaining to the factual veracity of the statement and so as a policy to minimize the chilling effect of the law of defamation on speech on public figures',[149] but not as a moral sincerity test.

Additionally, the ECtHR imposes a further 'duty and responsibility' on the media that correlates with the media-as-a-constitutional-component concept and social responsibility theory: to act according to the 'ethics of journalism' and the 'principles of responsible journalism'. This applies not only to the content of the publication, but also to the media actor's newsgathering activities and methods, and the manner in which the information is presented. These ethical standards are often found in media self-regulatory codes of conduct, such as the BBC's Editorial Guidelines, and are inherent within the new regulatory framework advanced in Chapter 9. Although not formal laws, they serve to animate the standards of care that media actors are subject to. Accordingly,

---

[145] Oster (n 4) 46.

[146] Ibid; J. Habermas, *The Theory of Communicative Action, vol. 1: Reason and the Rationalization of Society* (1981) (translation by T. McCarthy, Beacon Press, 1984) 39, 99; J. Habermas, *The Theory of Communicative Action, vol. 2: Lifeworld and System: A Critique of Functionalist Reason* (1981) (translation by T. McCarthy, Beacon Press, 1987) 120.

[147] 389 US 81, 82 (1967).

[148] 376 US 254 (1964).

[149] R. Post, 'Defaming Public Officials: On Doctrine and Legal History' [1987] *American Bar Foundation Research Journal* 539, 553; Oster (n 4) 47.

the Strasbourg Court has held that a violation of these ethics could tip the balance against media freedom in any given case.[150]

4   CONCLUSION

This chapter has established how the media-as-a-constitutional-component concept advanced in Chapter 5 affects the various elements critical to the application and operation of the right to media freedom. It has therefore complemented the previous chapter by providing a complete picture of the concept's impact on the freedom of the media, by exploring the parameters it sets, and the limits it imposes, to all media actors, regardless of the medium used to disseminate information. In doing so it has completed the normative framework which the remainder of this book will build upon. Specifically, it has set out the standards of professional behaviour and the norms of discourse that are imposed on media actors by the media-as-a-constitutional-component concept. Under this framework, for a media actor to benefit from the enhanced right to media freedom, it must abide by these standards and norms. In the chapters that follow we will explore how the concept, and its standards and norms, could offer a better solution to some of the legal challenges that arise from citizen journalism operating within the current libertarian paradigm.

---

[150] *Ricci v Italy* [2013] App. no. 30210/06, [57].

PART III

Legal challenges

7. Anonymous and pseudonymous speech

1 INTRODUCTION

This book has already alluded to how the internet and social media facilitates anonymous and pseudonymous expression, and how this has become synonymous with online speech and citizen journalism.[1] Because of the pervasiveness of online anonymity and pseudonymity, and because communicating in this way plays such an important role in the public sphere by encouraging and allowing certain actors, including citizen journalists, to contribute to public discourse, the purpose of this chapter is to examine this type of speech in more detail.

The chapter begins, at section 1.1, by briefly introducing the concepts of speaker and audience interests. It does this by setting out, in broad terms, the arguments that are analysed in detail throughout this chapter in favour of and against these conflicting interests. Section 2 sets out how anonymous and pseudonymous speech is treated in England and the US and by the ECtHR. It establishes that English jurisprudence has, traditionally, treated free speech, and by extension anonymous and pseudonymous expression, not as a right, but rather a liberty, in that it exists only where its exercise is not restricted by law. Recent case law suggests that this is a position predominantly based on audience interests, rather than those of the speaker.[2] It argues that this position

---

[1] See Chapter 3 section 6.2.2, Chapter 4 section 3.2.2 and Chapter 5 section 3.2. See generally P. Coe, 'Anonymity and Pseudonymity: Free Speech's Problem Children' (2018) 22(2) *Media & Arts Law Review* 173; S. Levmore, 'The Internet's Anonymity Problem' in S. Levmore and M. Nussbaum (eds), *The Offensive Internet* (Harvard University Press, 2010); J. Bartlett, *The Dark Net Inside the Digital Underworld* (Random House, 2014) ch. 2; E. Barendt, *Anonymous Speech* (Hart Publishing, 2016) ch. 6; R. Arnold and M.T. Sundara Rajan, 'Do Authors and Performers Have a Legal Right to Pseudonymity' (2017) 9(2) *Journal of Media Law* 189; see also the Director of Public Prosecution's comments relating to Crown Prosecution Service guidelines on prosecuting online crimes: 'Internet trolls targeted with new legal guidelines', *BBC*, 10 October 2016.

[2] *Author of a Blog v Times Newspapers Ltd* [2009] EMLR 22.

has evolved to an extent. Consequently, a right to free speech and therefore anonymous and pseudonymous expression, does, in fact, exist as part of the free speech guarantee. However, this right is not absolute and, as a result, is only subject to a limited level of protection. This view is then compared with the polarised position of the US (and to an extent, Germany) in which there exists a clearly recognised speaker interests-orientated right to anonymous and pseudonymous speech, which is subject to constitutional protection. What is apparent from the Strasbourg case law is that protection afforded for anonymous and pseudonymous expression falls short of an absolute right. Consequently, at present at least, it seems to sit, rather opaquely, somewhere between the two sides. This feeds into section 3, which examines the problems that are symptomatic of relying exclusively on either speaker or audience interests at the expense of the other. It argues that, particularly in the modern context of online speech and citizen journalism, this bifurcated approach, which has hitherto been applied in England, Europe and the US, can lead to a 'double-edged sword': on the one hand, pursuant to audience interests, people may be dissuaded from participating in the exchange of information and ideas, because their anonymity or pseudonymity is not protected; on the other hand, a constitutionally protected right to free speech based entirely on speaker interests could inadvertently protect unwanted and damaging speech. Ultimately, this chapter argues that neither interest should, in fact, trump the other. Rather, to support citizen journalism, which is now an integral part of the public sphere, and critical to public discourse, a balance needs to be struck between these interests. Thus, the chapter concludes at section 4 by exploring how the media-as-constitutional-component concept, as underpinned by social responsibility and the argument from democratic governance, can achieve this harmonisation.

1.1 Introducing the Concepts of Speaker and Audience Interests

As set out above, this chapter considers the contrasting positions of English, European and US jurisprudence in respect of reliance on speaker or audience interests. What these concepts mean in practice will depend on whether they are, in any given context, underpinned by free speech or privacy rationales. By way of introducing these concepts, the following paragraph sets out the broad arguments in favour of and against the competing interests. These arguments are applied and analysed in depth throughout the chapter.

The privacy rationale for anonymity and pseudonymity underpins the right to keep the speaker's identity secret.[3] From a freedom of expression and media freedom rationale perspective, particularly in the context of citizen journalism, protecting the speaker interests, by preserving their anonymity or pseudonymity, will encourage them, and others, to speak more freely, and therefore will facilitate public discourse; if they are permitted to communicate anonymously or pseudonymously they do not need to fear harassment or prosecution.[4] So far as audience interests are concerned, there are conflicting arguments. As set out in section 3, on the one hand, it can be said that the anonymity or pseudonymity of the speaker can benefit the audience in so far as it promotes free speech, as an anonymous or pseudonymous speaker is more inclined to impart information and ideas to the audience for the reasons explained above. On the other hand, the audience interest will usually favour transparency for the following reasons: (i) knowing the identity of the speaker enables the audience to evaluate the speaker's veracity; (ii) if the speaker's identity is known they are more likely to express themselves responsibly, and less likely to engage in harmful, offensive, irresponsible and damaging speech; (iii) remedial action and/or prosecution with respect to damaging, offensive and harmful speech is easier to facilitate if the identity of the speaker is known.[5] Section 4 advances the argument that the media-as-a-constitutional-component concept can bring harmony to these competing interests. By virtue of the standards of professional behaviour and norms of discourse it imposes, and the regulatory framework that it underpins,[6] its adoption could satisfy the audience interests in points (i) to (iii) while facilitating a speaker interest-orientated approach.

2   A POLARISATION OF LAW AND JURISPRUDENCE

Through recourse to both statute and case law relating, where possible, to online speech and citizen journalism, this section considers how the respective law has been applied to anonymous and pseudonymous speech. In doing so, it

---

[3]   See Human Rights Council, Report of the Special Rapporteur on the promotion and protection of the right to freedom of opinion and expression, David Kaye, 22 May 2015, A/HRC/29/32, [16]ff; J. Oster, *European and International Media Law* (Cambridge University Press, 2017) 47. The privacy rationale for anonymity and pseudonymity is considered in light of Eady J's judgment in *Author of a Blog v Times Newspapers Ltd* [2009] EMLR 22 at section 2.1.

[4]   Oster (n 3) 47; Arnold and Sundara Rajan (n 1) 198.

[5]   Arnold and Sundara Rajan (n 1) 198.

[6]   See Chapter 9.

206 *Media freedom in the age of citizen journalism*

looks at jurisdictions that have opposing views as to the extent to which such expression is protected.

2.1 The View from England and the European Court of Human Rights: A Qualified Right to Anonymous and Pseudonymous Speech

In his book *Anonymous Speech*, Eric Barendt provides a detailed history of anonymous and pseudonymous speech in England.[7] What is clear is that, despite this established tradition, and unlike the US, where a strong constitutional right to anonymous speech has emerged, in England an absolute right is not recognised.[8] This position derives from how freedom of expression has historically been treated under English law: as a bare or residual liberty rather than a right, existing only where the law does not restrict its exercise.[9] Thus, traditionally at least, the 'freedom lives ... in the gaps of the criminal and civil law'.[10] However, as illustrated by cases such as *Brutus v Cozens*[11] and *Redmond-Bate v DPP*,[12] a stronger principle of free speech has been applied by the courts to narrowly interpret legislation so that the respective statute's interference with freedom of expression is minimised. Equally, a common law right to free speech has been established by jurisprudence relating to, for instance, the creation and development of defences of fair comment and public interest

---

[7]   Barendt (n 1) ch. 2.

[8]   For the US and German positions, see section 2.1.1. This view on the positions of English and US law is supported by Arnold and Sundara Rajan (n 1) 197.

[9]   Barendt (n 1) 81, 89. Barendt provides examples of laws such as obscenity, libel and contempt of court, which have restricted the application of freedom of expression.

[10] Ibid 89.

[11] [1973] AC 854. The House of Lords held that the word 'insulting', pursuant to section 5 of the Public Order Act 1936, should not be interpreted to penalise the use of offensive language during an anti-apartheid demonstration at Wimbledon.

[12] [2000] HRLR 249; (1999) 7 BHRC 375; [1999] Crim LR 998. The case related to three women Christian fundamentalists who were preaching from the steps of Wakefield Cathedral. Fearing a breach of the peace amongst the crowd, a police officer asked the women to stop and subsequently arrested them for wilfully obstructing an officer in the execution of his duty contrary to section 89(2) of the Police Act 1996. The Court of Appeal held that the police had no right to stop citizens engaging in lawful conduct unless there were grounds to fear that it would, by interfering with the rights or liberties of others, provoke violence which in those circumstances might not be unreasonable. Accordingly, the preachers were entitled to say things which members of their audience may find irritating or controversial, but they did not threaten or provoke violence. As a result, the police officer was not acting in the execution of his duty when he told them to stop.

Anonymous and pseudonymous speech 207

privilege to libel actions.[13] The protection afforded to freedom of expression was strengthened further by the incorporation of the ECHR, including Article 10, into domestic law by the Human Rights Act 1998. As discussed in Chapter 5, pursuant to section 6(1), the courts must take account of the right when developing the common law.[14] Similarly, section 3 imposes an obligation on the judiciary to interpret legislation in conformity with Article 10. As a result, it is no longer correct to regard free speech as a mere residual liberty.[15]

How do these developments relate to online speech and, in particular, citizen journalism, in the context of anonymous and pseudonymous communication? As set out above, as is the case with the print and broadcast media, there is, under domestic law, a right, albeit not an absolute one, to communicate anonymously and pseudonymously online.[16] However, this type of communication is subject to the same legal restrictions that can be applied to the traditional media, such as public order laws, laws relating to hate speech, obscenity laws, the Protection from Harassment Act 1997[17] and, more specifically, section 127 of the Communications Act 2003,[18] section 1(1) of the Malicious Communications Act 1988 (as amended by section 32 of the Criminal Justice

---

[13] For example, see *Silkin v Beaverbrook Newspapers Ltd* [1958] 1 WLR 743; *Spiller v Joseph* [2011] 1 AC 852, [107]–[108]; *Reynolds v Times Newspapers Ltd* [2001] 2 AC 127; *Jameel v Wall Street Journal Europe* [2007] 1 AC 359.

[14] See Chapter 5 section 3.1.

[15] Barendt (n 1) 90.

[16] The existence of such a right is demonstrated by section 10 of the Contempt of Court Act 1981, which provides that a court cannot compel a person to disclose, nor is a person guilty of contempt of court for refusing to disclose, the source of information contained within a document for which that person is responsible, unless the court is satisfied that disclosure is necessary in the interests of justice or national security or for the prevention of disorder or crime. Pursuant to section 21, section 10 applies to England and Wales, Scotland and Northern Ireland.

[17] J. Rowbottom, 'To Rant, Vent and Converse: Protecting Low Level Digital Speech' (2012) 71 *Cambridge Law Journal* 355, 357–365.

[18] Section 127(1) makes it an offence to send through a 'public electronic communications network' a message which is 'grossly offensive or of an indecent, obscene, or menacing character'. For analysis of this provision see P. Coe, 'The Social Media Paradox: An Intersection with Freedom of Expression and the Criminal Law' (2015) 24(1) *Information & Communications Technology Law* 16, 31–35. See also *DPP v Woods* Unrep. October 2012 (MC); *Chambers v DPP* [2012] EWHC 2157. Under section 127(2) a 'person is guilty of an offence if, for the purpose of causing annoyance, inconvenience or needless anxiety to another he (a) sends by means of a public electronic communications network, a message that he knows to be false, (b) causes such a message to be sent; or (c) persistently makes use of a public electronic communications network'.

208   *Media freedom in the age of citizen journalism*

and Courts Act 2015)[19] and section 33[20] of the 2015 Act. In the context of civil liability and, in particular, the protection of reputation, section 5 of the Defamation Act 2013 provides website operators with a defence to defamation actions where an operator did not, itself, post the allegedly defamatory imputation on the website. The defence will operate so long as the claimant can identify the speaker who posted the imputation, or the operator takes steps to provide the claimant with the speaker's full name and address or, if the speaker prefers, to remove the statement from the website.[21] Consequently, the only way anonymous speakers will be able to keep their defamatory statements on websites is with the website operator's assistance. This is unlikely as the operator is then, by default, exposed to liability. Thus, these provisions, relating to both criminal and civil liability, appear to suggest that online anonymous communication is, to an extent, discouraged, and they clearly have the potential to limit freedom of anonymous and pseudonymous speech. Therefore, they could be subject to challenge. However, it is likely that this would be met with strong arguments to the contrary as the courts are unlikely to favour submissions that they should not be applied when they operate to protect against, for example, defamatory publications,[22] invasions of privacy and expression, which undermines the integrity of a trial.

The existence or otherwise of a right to anonymity was considered in *Author of a Blog v Times Newspapers Ltd*[23] as an element of personal privacy, as

---

[19] This amended the offence of sending a letter, electronic communication or article of any description which conveys a threat or abuse, pursuant to section 1(1) of the 1988 Act, to a triable either way offence. The amendment was made, partly, to tackle concerns over an increase in 'cyber-bullying'. In its *Modernising Communications Offences: A final report* Law Com. No. 399 HC 547, 20 July 2021, the Law Commission recommended replacing the section 1(1) 1988 Act and section 127(1) 2003 Act offences with a new triable-either way harm-based communications offence (24, [2.38]–[2.39]). The Commission has recommended replacing the section 127(2)(a) and (b) 2003 Act offences with a new summary offence that targets knowingly false harmful communications (78, [3.11], 94 [3.71]–[3.72]), and that the section 127(2)(c) offence is 'replaced with a summary offence to address hoax calls to the emergency services' (100, [3.94]).

[20] This provision has made 'revenge porn' a specific triable either way offence. It is defined as '[d]isclosing private sexual photographs and films with intent to cause distress' and covers the sharing of images, both online and offline. This means that images posted over the internet, as well as those distributed by text message, email or in hard copy, are captured.

[21] For detailed analysis of this provision, see H. Tomlinson QC and G. Vassall-Adams QC (eds), *Online Publication Claims: A Practical Guide* (Matrix Chambers, 2017); J. Price QC and F. McMahon (eds), *Blackstone's Guide to the Defamation Act 2013* (Oxford University Press, 2013) ch. 6.

[22] Barendt (n 1) 90.

[23] [2009] EMLR 22.

opposed to an aspect of the right to freedom of expression. The case concerned a blog, known as *Night Jack*. The author of the blog used it as a platform for discussing his work as a serving police officer. Within these discussions he was extremely critical of government ministers and police operations. Indeed, in his judgment, Eady J was of the opinion that much of what the claimant published could be characterised as 'political speech'.[24] *The Times* wanted to reveal the blogger's identity;[25] consequently he applied to the court for an interim injunction to prevent the newspaper from publishing any information that could lead to his identification as the person responsible for the blog. Hugh Tomlinson QC, on behalf of the claimant, argued in terms of his right to privacy. However, it is arguable that, additionally, some of the arguments were underpinned by the free speech rationale. Both the privacy and free speech arguments were predominantly based on the interests of the speaker. Tomlinson advanced the argument that the claimant, and other citizen journalists, would be 'horrified' if their anonymity could not be protected,[26] a proposition clearly based on the privacy rationale that anonymity (and, by extension, pseudonymity) allows speakers to keep certain information secret, including their identity.[27] He submitted, first, as a general proposition, that 'there is a public interest in preserving the anonymity of bloggers'.[28] This argument is founded on the free speech rationale and is based, foremost, on speaker interests, since preserving the anonymity of citizen journalists enables them to exercise their right to impart information and ideas, as guaranteed by Article 10(1) ECHR (and that, conversely, revealing their identity would restrict their right to do this).[29] Secondly, counsel suggested that there was no public interest in the disclosure of the claimant's identity as the publication of

---

[24]   Ibid [24].

[25]   Interestingly, this case dealt with rather unique circumstances: *The Times* journalist had identified the claimant by deduction, not, as was accepted by counsel for the claimant, by breach of confidence. Therefore, the matter related to whether an enforceable right to maintain anonymity existed in the situation where another person has been able to deduce the identity in question. Eady J recognised that bloggers generally may want to conceal their identity. However, in relying on *Mahmood v Galloway* [2006] EMLR 26, Eady J stated that it is a 'significantly further step to argue, if others are able to deduce their [the claimant's] identity, that they [*The Times*] should be restrained by law from revealing it'. Thus, potentially at least, the situation may be different if the identity of the speaker could not be deduced but, for example a newspaper, wanted to disclose it. Ibid [3], [9] and [10].

[26]   Ibid [4].

[27]   Kaye (n 3) [16]ff; Oster (n 3) 47.

[28]   *Author of a Blog v Times Newspapers Ltd* [2009] EMLR 22, [5].

[29]   Ibid [18]. Of course, there is the secondary argument that preserving the anonymity of bloggers protects the audience interest in receiving information of public interest as bloggers may be dissuaded from doing so should their identity be compromised.

210   *Media freedom in the age of citizen journalism*

such information would make no contribution to a debate of general interest.[30] In giving judgment for the defendant, Eady J did not expressly accept or reject any arguments based on the free speech rationale by the claimant. However, the judge rejected the claimant's application, and their privacy arguments, on the ground that 'blogging is essentially a public rather than a private activity',[31] consequently the claimant had no reasonable expectation of privacy.[32] He went on to state that even if this requirement had been met, the public interest in revealing that a police officer was expressing strong criticism of the police and political figures outweighed his right to privacy[33] and that revealing his identity enabled readers to assess his veracity.[34] Thus, the judgment seems, largely, to ignore any speaker-orientated arguments based on the free speech rationale advanced on behalf of the claimant and, rather, based on the interests of the audience, disagrees with counsel's second argument.

A discrete area of English law where the privacy rationale has successfully been applied to protect anonymity relates to *Norwich Pharmacal* orders.[35] For instance, in *Totalise plc v The Motley Fool Ltd*[36] the claimant had successfully applied for such an order for the disclosure by Motley Fool of the identity of a third party who had posted, pseudonymously, defamatory comments about the claimant on a bulletin board. In giving the judgment of the Court of Appeal, Aldous J said that in such cases 'the court must be careful not to make an order which unjustifiably invades the right of the individual to respect for his private life' and that there was 'nothing in Article 10' which supported the argument that 'it protects the named but not the anonymous' and that 'there are many situations in which ... the protection of a person's identity from disclosure may be legitimate'.[37] Consequently, as observed by Mr Justice Richard Arnold and Mira Sundara Rajan, in the context of pseudonymity specifically: 'Consistently with [*Totalise*] there have been cases ... in which *Norwich Pharmacal* orders for the disclosure of the identities of pseudonymous persons posting on cha-

---

[30]   Ibid [22].
[31]   Ibid [11], [29] and [33].
[32]   This is a threshold requirement for claimants pleading misuse of private information.
[33]   *Author of a Blog v Times Newspapers Ltd* [2009] EMLR 22, [21]–[23], [33].
[34]   Ibid [21]. See analysis and criticisms of this point at section 3.1.
[35]   *Norwich Pharmacal Co. v Customs and Excise Commissioners* [1974] AC 133: under the *Norwich Pharmacal* procedure the court can order an individual or entity who is not a party to the court proceedings but who is, innocently or not, mixed up in the wrongdoing, to assist a party to the proceedings by providing specified information or documents in respect of the proceedings.
[36]   [2001] EWCA Civ 1897; [2002] 1 WLR 1233.
[37]   Ibid [25].

trooms and websites have been refused on the ground that the wrongs alleged against them did not justify invading their private lives.'[38]

Notwithstanding the jurisprudence relating to *Norwich Pharmacal* orders, Eady J's judgment in *Author of a Blog* clearly suggests, and is indicative of the fact, that freedom of anonymous and pseudonymous speech enjoys very limited protection under modern domestic law. I return to this case in the sections that follow, and in section 3 I consider it with the US case of *Reno v American Civil Liberties Union*[39] as they animate the problems associated with relying exclusively on either audience or speaker interests respectively.

Under section 2(1) of the Human Rights Act 1998 UK courts must take into account decisions of the ECtHR, although they are not bound by any such rulings. As a result, anonymous and pseudonymous expression could be subject to stronger protection under UK law if there were a clear indication of the existence of a free speech anonymity right from the Strasbourg Court. However, the Court has, to date, not been required to consider the extent to which a limit imposed on anonymous speech would render any such limit incompatible with Article 10 ECHR. If such an issue were to be brought before the Court, it is likely that a state would robustly argue for restrictions to be placed on anonymous and pseudonymous expression, for example, on the basis that it needs to protect the right to respect for private life pursuant to Article 8 ECHR, including the right to reputation, which can require, as discussed above in relation to section 5 of the Defamation Act 2013, disclosure of the speaker's personal details. Additionally, far from providing clarity on the existence, or otherwise, of a right to freedom of anonymous speech conveyed online and via social media, ECtHR jurisprudence on the matter has been equivocal.

In *KU v Finland*[40] the Court held that any guarantee of privacy and freedom of expression rights for an individual placing an anonymous advertisement is not absolute and must accord precedence to other rights and interests, such as the prevention of crime and the protection of the rights of others. However, although the ECtHR's decision in *Delfi AS v Estonia*[41] seems to be based explicitly on audience interests in free speech,[42] the Court afforded online

---

[38] Arnold and Sundara Rajan (n 1) 202. The cases cited by Arnold and Sundara Rajan include *Sheffield Wednesday Football Club Ltd v Hargreaves* [2007] EWHC 2375 (QB) and *Clift v Clarke* [2011] EWHC 1164 (QB); [2013] Info TLR 13. See also M. Daly, 'Is There an Entitlement to Anonymity? A European and International Analysis' (2013) 35(4) *European Intellectual Property Review* 198.

[39] 521 US 844 (1997).

[40] App. no. 2872/02 (2009) 48 EHRR 52.

[41] App. no. 64569/09, Decision of the First Section Chamber of the Court, 10 October 2013 (2014) 58 EHRR 29, upheld by the Grand Chamber of the Court in a Decision of 16 June 2015, [2015] EMLR 26.

[42] Speaker and audience interests are discussed in section 3.

anonymous communication a greater level of importance. Delfi, an internet news portal service, had been required by the Estonian courts to compensate the victim of threatening and defamatory comments which had been posted on its service, even though it operated a 'notice-and-take-down' procedure when readers complained of these statements. The issue before the Court was whether or not there had been an infringement of the freedom of expression of the owner of Delfi. The Grand Chamber of the Court held that the Estonian Supreme Court's ruling was compatible with the ECHR, stating that '[i]t is mindful ... of the interest of internet users in not disclosing their identity'.[43] According to the Court, anonymity 'is capable of promoting the free flow of ideas and information in an important manner, including, notably, on the internet'.[44] Consequently, it rejected Delfi's argument that victims of defamatory statements must bring defamation proceedings against the authors of comments after their identity had been established.[45] Other Council of Europe institutions have emphasised the importance of online anonymous communication. For instance, in *Delfi* the Court considered a Declaration of the Council of Ministers on freedom of communication on the internet.[46] Principle 7 of the Declaration recognises that 'to ensure protection against online surveillance and to enhance the free expression of information and ideas, member states should respect the will of users of the internet not to disclose their identity'.[47] Additionally, an earlier Recommendation of the Committee of Ministers had suggested recognition of anonymity in the context of internet communications as an aspect of personal privacy protection.[48] Although these provisions, and the Strasbourg Court's decision in *Delfi*, do not go as far as establishing an absolute right to anonymous and pseudonymous speech, they do represent explicit recognition of the importance of anonymous and pseudonymous expression from the ECtHR[49] and Council of Europe institutions. As will be

---

[43] [2015] EMLR 26, [147].
[44] Ibid [147].
[45] Ibid [151].
[46] Ibid [44].
[47] Declaration of Council of Ministers adopted on 28 May 2003, Principle 7 (Anonymity).
[48] Council of Europe, Committee of Ministers, Recommendation No. R. (99) 5 *For the Protection of Privacy on the Internet*, 23 February 1999, Guidelines 3 and 4.
[49] See also *Høiness v Norway* [2019] App. no. 43624/14. In respect of *Delfi*, the Court acknowledged a right to remain anonymous as a speaker (but only if the platform or content provider provides this option for its users, so it cannot be considered a constitutionally protected right) but on the other hand, platforms and content providers can be held responsible for anonymous users' content. The issue, therefore, was whether this indirect responsibility was in line with Article 10 ECHR jurisprudence, which was answered by the Court in the affirmative. For further analysis of *Delfi* see A. Koltay,

Anonymous and pseudonymous speech 213

seen in the following section, the US position (and, to an extent, the position in Germany) is markedly different. In the US, a constitutional right to anonymous speech, both generally and online, has consistently been held to exist and has been protected.

2.2 The German and US Position: The *Spickmich Case* and *Mcintyre v Ohio Elections Commission* – An Absolute Right to Anonymous and Pseudonymous Speech?

Unlike the ECtHR's equivocal stance on anonymous and pseudonymous online expression, German jurisprudence provides an interesting comparator within a European context as it is clearer as to the courts' adopted position. This is illustrated by the *Spickmich* case,[50] which concerned a teacher who argued that her name, the details of her school and, specifically, anonymous assessments of her teaching by pupils should be removed from www .spickmich.de, a portal for community schools, which was accessible via registration, by providing the user's name, email address and school details. The issue before the German courts concerned conflicting rights. On the one hand, the teacher submitted that the storage and publication of the information contravened her right to informational self-determination – in that she should be able to determine what, if any, information should be made available to those with access to the portal. This privacy right is subject to robust protection under German law.[51] However, on the other hand, the argument was advanced that, based on the right to freedom of expression, students should be able to assess the teaching qualities of their teachers anonymously. The Federal Supreme Court,[52] in upholding the rulings of the lower court, dismissed the

---

'Internet Gatekeepers as Editors: The Case of Online Comments' in R.L. Weaver, J. Reichel and S.I. Friedland (eds), *Comparative Perspectives on Privacy in an Internet Era* (Carolina Academic Press, 2019).

[50] Decision of 23 June 2009, Neue Juristische Wochenschrift (NJW) 2009, 2888.

[51] The origins of the right to informational self-determination date back to 1983, when the German Federal Constitutional Court declared unconstitutional certain provisions of the Revised Census Act that had been adopted unanimously by the German Federal Parliament but were challenged by diverse associations before the Constitutional Court. BVerfGE 65, 1 – Volkzählung Urteil des Ersten Senats vom 15. Dezember 1983 auf die mündliche Verhandlung vom 18. and 19. Oktober 1983 – 1 BvR 209, 269, 362, 420, 440, 484/83 in den Verfahren über die Verfassungsbeschwerden; see generally A. Rouvroy and Y. Poullet, 'The Right to Informational Self-Determination and the Value of Self-Development: Reassessing the Importance of Privacy for Democracy' in S. Gutwirth, Y. Poullet, P. De Hert, C. de Terwangne and S. Nouwt (eds.) *Reinventing Data Protection?* (Springer, 2009).

[52] The Bundesgerichtshof.

214   *Media freedom in the age of citizen journalism*

teacher's complaint. The Court's decision was founded on three key points: first, anonymity is an inherent aspect of the use of the internet;[53] secondly, in any event, section 13 VI of the Telemedia Act 2007 protects anonymity and pseudonymity: pursuant to this provision service providers must, as far as is technically possible and reasonable, allow the anonymous or pseudonymous use of their services; and, finally, as a matter of principle, an obligation to identify an individual with the expression of a particular view would, both generally and in the specific context of this case, lead to self-censorship from fear of the negative consequences of identification.[54] The Court held that the imposition of such an obligation would be incompatible with Article 5.1 of the German Basic Law.[55] At this juncture it is worth considering that the Court's claim that 'anonymity is an inherent aspect of the use of internet' could be perceived as a naturalistic fallacy, and open to the rejoinder that just because anonymity is largely a part of cyber-culture does not force the conclusion that it ought to be that way.[56] Instead, the judgment is more subtle and nuanced as it does not impose a de facto 'cyber-right' to anonymity, but rather 'reveals the strong attachment' of German law to the freedom to use online communications anonymously,[57] in that it demonstrates that freedom of such speech takes precedence over the important countervailing right to informational self-determination as an element of personal privacy. Thus, the reasoning of the Court is clearly indicative of a speaker interest-orientated approach. It is less equivocal than the jurisprudence of the ECtHR and demonstrates stronger support for speaker interests than is present in England. For instance, although the context of the cases is different, in *Author of a Blog*, in Eady J's judgment, the speaker's identity was required to enable the audience to assess the value of his publications. In other words, the public interest dimension of the speaker's claim was impaired by anonymity.[58] In contrast, the citizen journalist's argument for anonymity was based on the fact that it allowed him (and other citizen journalists) to disseminate important information, as a whistleblower, without fear of reprisals from his employers or the state.[59] This argument is, fundamentally, the same as the Court's reasoning for dismissing the teacher's complaint

---

[53]   Indeed, this had been recognised in an earlier decision of the Court, which held that contributors to a discussion forum must accept the risk of personal attack from pseudonymous participants: Decision of 27 March 2007, NJW 2007, 2558.

[54]   Decision of 23 June 2009, Neue Juristische Wochenschrift (NJW) 2009, [38].

[55]   The Court also found that the portal facilitated the right of the students, parents and teachers to receive information, which is also protected by Article 5.1: ibid [40].

[56]   Coe (n 1) 182.

[57]   Barendt (n 1) 153.

[58]   *Author of a Blog v Times Newspapers Ltd* [2009] EMLR 22, [21]–[23].

[59]   Ibid [5].

in *Spickmich* as, in the Court's view, anonymity allowed the speaker (the children) to advance their honest view without fear of retribution. However, unlike the US position examined below, the *Spickmich* decision is not solely based on the interests of the speaker. Rather, the judgment also exhibits elements of an audience interest approach. This is on the basis that the free dissemination of information about the teacher enabled those with access to the portal to make an informed decision as to the performance of the teacher and the school.

In the US there has been even stronger jurisprudential support for freedom of anonymous and pseudonymous online expression, which is, therefore, diametrically opposed to the English position. The Supreme Court case of *McIntyre v Ohio Elections Commission*[60] concerned Margaret McIntyre, who had distributed leaflets at public meetings at an Ohio school. The leaflets expressed opposition to a proposed school tax levy. McIntyre had produced the leaflets at home on her own computer. In some of the leaflets she was identified as the author. However, others were addressed from 'Concerned Parents and Tax Payers'. She continued to distribute these leaflets despite being warned that they contravened §3599.09(A) of the Ohio Revised Code, pursuant to which authors were not permitted to write, print or disseminate campaigning literature without providing their name and address. Consequently, McIntyre was fined, a decision upheld by the Ohio State Supreme Court. As in *Author of a Blog*, the 'speech' in *McIntyre* was political in nature[61] as it engaged a State provision related specifically to 'campaign literature'. The fundamental basis of the State Supreme Court's judgment, founded on audience interests, is similar to Eady J's reasoning in *Author of a Blog*, in which it was held that the blogger's anonymity impaired the operation of the public interest as his identity was required to better enable the audience to determine his veracity.[62] According to the State Supreme Court, the burden placed on an author of campaign literature to identify themselves is 'more than counterbalanced' by the public interest in 'providing the audience to whom the message is directed with a mechanism by which they may better evaluate its validity' and enables the identification of authors publishing fraudulent and defamatory communications.[63] Eventually, the case was heard by the US Supreme Court.[64] Stevens

---

[60]   514 US 334 (1995).

[61]   *Author of a Blog v Times Newspapers Ltd* [2009] EMLR 22, [24].

[62]   Ibid [21]–[23].

[63]   618 NE 2d 152 (1993). The State Supreme Court relied on the case of *First National Bank of Boston v Bellotti* 435 US 765 (1978) in which it was held that not only are such interests sufficient to overcome the minor burden placed on individuals to disclose their identity in this context, but that these interests and pursuant regulations would survive constitutional scrutiny.

[64]   514 US 334 (1995).

J, giving the judgment of the Court, stated that 'an author's decision to remain anonymous ... is an aspect of the freedom of speech protected by the First Amendment'.[65] As a result of this seminal ruling, which has been followed in a number of subsequent cases,[66] enshrined within the First Amendment is an absolute free speech right to communicate anonymously or pseudonymously.[67]

Two strands emerge from Stevens J's judgment to justify the anonymity right.[68] The first is paradigmatic of the argument from democratic self-governance and, as is advanced at section 3, goes to a speaker's interest in anonymous expression. It advances the argument that '[a]nonymity is a shield from the tyranny of the majority'[69] and, according to Barendt, enables 'radicals and dissenters to express unpopular views free from the fear of retaliation or prosecution'.[70] This instrumental argument is clearly aligned to the free speech rationale arguments in *Author of a Blog*[71] and the speaker interest-orientated reasons given by the Federal Supreme Court in the *Spickmich* case. Similarly, in an earlier decision, the Supreme Court in *Talley v California*[72] recognised 'a tradition of anonymity in the advocacy of political causes';[73] accordingly, in the absence of anonymity, valuable political speech may not be published.[74] The second strand is rights based. According to Stevens J, 'the identity of the speaker is no different from other components of the document's content that the author is free to include or exclude'.[75] Thus, an author is free to determine the contents of their publication, and they are entitled to write anonymously or

---

[65] Ibid at 342. Ginsburg J and Thomas J gave separate concurring judgments. Thomas J gave an account of anonymous political writing in the US in the eighteenth century. From this examination he inferred that the Founding Fathers of the Constitution intended anonymous speech to be covered by the First Amendment: ibid 359–371.

[66] As Barendt observes, although the decision has been distinguished in cases relating to litigation concerning the disclosure of election expenditure, its 'fundamental correctness' has rarely been questioned within US jurisprudence. Barendt (n 1) 56 and ch. 7.

[67] For example, see *Hurley v Irish-American Gay, Lesbian and Bisexual Group of Boston* 515 US 557 (1995); *Buckley v American Constitutional Law Foundation* 525 US 182 (1999); *Watchtower Bible and Tract Society of New York v Stratton* 536 US 150 (2002); *American Civil Liberties Union of Nevada v Heller* 378 F3d 979 (2004).

[68] L. Lidsky and T. Cotter, 'Authorship, Audiences and Anonymous Speech' (2006) 82 *Notre Dame Law Review* 1537, 1542–1544.

[69] *McIntyre* 514 US 334 (1995) 357.

[70] Barendt (n 1) 58.

[71] [2009] EMLR 22, [4] and [18].

[72] 362 US 60 (1960).

[73] *McIntyre* 514 US 334 (1995) 343.

[74] Barendt (n 1) 58.

[75] *McIntyre* 514 US 334 (1995) 348.

Anonymous and pseudonymous speech 217

pseudonymously. As a rejoinder to the contention that an audience may have a real interest in knowing the identity of the author to assess their credibility and the strength of their views, Stevens J employed the argument that to compel an individual to disclose their name (or any other identifying details) is equivalent to requiring them to express a particular opinion.[76] This argument is considered in more detail in section 3.

The *McIntyre* decision has been followed in the context of online communications[77] and, therefore, by extension, would likely apply to citizen journalists publishing on social media and other online platforms. In *American Civil Liberties Union v Zell Miller*[78] a federal District Court held that a Georgia statute making it an offence to transmit messages over the internet using a false name was invalid as it contravened the First Amendment. In the same year, in *Reno v American Civil Liberties Union*,[79] the US Supreme Court, in determining that there was no basis for qualifying the protection afforded by the First Amendment guarantee of freedom of speech in the context of the internet, rejected the argument that the internet could be subject to similar special content regulation that had traditionally been applied to, and had constrained, broadcast media. In particular, the Court stated that although some of its earlier cases had recognised special justifications for regulation of the broadcast media, these are not, necessarily, applicable to other speakers.[80] It was of the opinion that the factors it had relied upon in relation to the broadcast media[81]

---

[76] Ibid 348–349. Consequently, the Supreme Court rejected the Ohio State's argument that the disclosure requirement was justified as it provided the audience with more information.

[77] However, the right to communicate anonymously on the internet is not absolute. For example, pursuant to federal statute it is an offence to use a telecommunications device, without the user disclosing their identity, with intent to abuse, threaten or harass any specific individual. See 47 US Code section 223(a)(1)(c); D.K. Citron, *Hate Crimes in Cyberspace* (Harvard University Press, 2014) 124–125. According to Barendt, this law would, almost certainly, survive constitutional challenge as true threats instilling a real fear of violence are not protected by the First Amendment: Barendt (n 1) 126; *Planned Parenthood of the Columbia/Williamette Inc. v American Coalition of Life Activists* 290 F3d 1058 (9th Cir, 2002).

[78] 977 F Supp 1228 (ND, GA 1997).

[79] 521 US 844 (1997).

[80] *Reno v American Civil Liberties Union* 521 US 844 (1997) 868. For instance, in *Red Lion Broadcasting Company v FCC* 395 US 367 (1969) 399–400 and *FCC v Pacifica Foundation* 438 US 726 (1978) the Court relied on the history of extensive government regulation of the broadcast media. Other factors included (i) the scarcity of available frequencies at its inception: *Turner Broadcasting Systems Inc. v FCC* 512 US 622 (1994) 637–638; and (ii) its 'invasive' nature: *Sable Communications of California Inc. v FCC* 492 US 115 (1989) 128.

[81] Ibid 868–869.

218   *Media freedom in the age of citizen journalism*

'are not present in cyberspace'.[82] Eady J's judgment in *Author of a Blog* was based exclusively on audience interests. To the contrary, this decision was based entirely on the interests of the speaker.[83] Thus, the right to communicate anonymously, both online and offline, has now been accepted as an integral part of the First Amendment.

This section has established that, at present, anonymous and pseudonymous online expression is faced with two opposing schools of thought. In England, freedom of expression provides a limited level of protection for such speech, whereas the US (and to a lesser extent Germany) clearly recognises a constitutional right for these types of communication. What is apparent from the Strasbourg case law is that protection afforded for anonymous and pseudonymous expression, at the moment at least, falls short of a clearly recognised right and, consequently, seems to sit, rather opaquely, somewhere between the two sides. However, based on the explicit importance placed upon anonymous and pseudonymous speech by the ECtHR in *Delfi* and by Council of Europe provisions, there seems to be potential for the establishment of such a right. These schools of thought are based on opposing interests: those of the speaker and the audience. The following section will consider these rights, and how they apply to online anonymous and pseudonymous speech.

3 SPEAKER VERSUS AUDIENCE INTERESTS: AN OBSOLETE DISTINCTION IN THE CONTEXT OF THE MODERN MEDIA?

The speaker versus audience interests dichotomy has consistently been the subject of arguments relating to free speech generally.[84] Within these arguments there has been a clear delineation between these 'competing' interests. The case law explored above demonstrates that, on the one hand, speaker interests in free speech (and privacy) have been used to support a right to anonymous expression, whereas, on the other hand, audience interests have tended

---

[82] Ibid.

[83] Both cases are considered again in section 3, which looks at the problems that are symptomatic of relying purely on one interest.

[84] For example, see T. Scanlon, 'A Theory of Freedom of Expression' (1972) 1 *Philosophy and Public Affairs* 204; R. Dworkin, 'Introduction' in *The Philosophy of Law* (Oxford University Press, 1977) 15; F. Schauer, *Free Speech: A Philosophical Inquiry* (Cambridge University Press, 1982) 105–106, 158–160; L. Alexander, *Is There a Right to Freedom of Expression?* (Cambridge University Press, 2005) 8–9; S. Kreimer, 'Sunlight, Secrets and Scarlet Letter: The Tension between Privacy and Disclosure in Constitutional Law' (1991) 140 *University of Pennsylvania Law Review* 1, 85–86; R. Post, 'The Constitutional Concept of Public Discourse' (1990) 103 *Harvard Law Review* 603, 639–640.

Anonymous and pseudonymous speech 219

to have been employed to argue for the author's identity to be known or, at the very most, for a limited level of protection for anonymous speech.[85] This section will advance the argument that the exclusive application of either interest as a basis for free speech, particularly within the context of anonymous and pseudonymous online expression, as has hitherto been the practice in England, the US and Europe, is problematic, for the following reasons: a US-type right to anonymous speech, based on speakers' interests, goes too far. It does not adequately protect other countervailing rights and, inadvertently, protects speakers who disseminate harmful and damaging speech. However, the English and ECtHR positions, which, at best, provide limited protection for anonymous and pseudonymous speech, based on audience interests, do not go far enough in protecting citizen journalists, who often rely on being able to communicate anonymously or pseudonymously.

3.1   The Problems Associated with Relying Exclusively on Audience or Speaker Interests

As we have seen, the Supreme Court's decision in *McIntyre* is based on the right of the speaker to determine the content of their speech. According to the Court, this speaker interest took precedence over the audience's right to information regarding the speaker's identity, in order for the reader to be able to properly assess the credibility of the author's publication. In its judgment the Supreme Court approved a New York court's decision in *New York v Duryea*[86] that, when it comes to anonymous sources, the public is able to determine the value of speech[87] as compared to communications from an identified speaker:

> Don't underestimate the common man. People are intelligent enough to evaluate the source of an anonymous writing. They can see it is anonymous. They know it is anonymous. They can evaluate its anonymity along with its message, as long as they are permitted, as they must be, to read the message. And then, once they have done so, it is for them to decide what is 'responsible', what is valuable, and what is truth.[88]

---

[85]   See the discussion on *Delfi AS v Estonia* [2015] EMLR 26 in section 2.1.

[86]   351 NYS 2d 978, 995 (1974); *McIntyre* 514 US 334 (1995) 348.

[87]   Indeed, Robert Post argues that speech should be assessed entirely divorced from the context in which it is made, including the origin of the communication: Post (n 84) 639–640.

[88]   This accords with Lord Kerr's view in *Stocker v Stocker* [2019] UKSC 17, [41] and [43], in which his Lordship referred to a 'new class of reader: the social media user', who understands that an online platform 'is a casual medium in the nature of conversation rather than carefully chosen expression'.

The decisions that followed, in cases such as *Hurley v Irish-American Gay, Lesbian and Bisexual Group of Boston*,[89] *Buckley v American Constitutional Law Foundation*,[90] *Watchtower Bible and Tract Society of New York v Stratton*,[91] *ACLU of Nevada v Heller*[92] and, in the context of online communication, *ACLU and Reno*,[93] were similarly based on speaker interests to support anonymous and pseudonymous expression. The interests of the speaker were also the dominant interests in the German Federal Supreme Court's ruling in *Spickmich*.

The Supreme Court's decision in *Reno* highlights some of the issues surrounding online and social media speech generally and, in particular, anonymous speech conveyed via these mediums. Thus, the efficacy of the judgment, based purely on speaker interests, if applied to a modern context, is questionable. Like *Author of a Blog*, it highlights problems symptomatic of applying one interest exclusively. As discussed in detail in Chapter 5,[94] the Court found that 'the Internet is not as invasive as radio or television'[95] by approving the District Court's finding that internet communications 'do not invade an individual's home or appear on one's computer screen unbidden'.[96] As I suggested in that chapter, this judgment demonstrates the speed at which online communication has developed, as it now seems incompatible with current online expression because, in the online world, we are regularly subjected to 'unbidden' messages. In the context of the discussion here, these 'unbidden' messages are, very often, anonymous or pseudonymous, meaning that there exists a lack of accountability, which can seriously impact upon an individual's ability to seek recourse,[97] for instance in relation to damage caused to their reputation by virtue of libel proceedings.[98]

Contrary to judgments based purely on speaker interests, Kreimer suggests that, in many situations, anonymous or pseudonymous expression is not appropriate as it is important for the audience to be able to identify the speaker. Knowing the origin of the speech enables the audience to attribute a value and assess the veracity of the speaker's previous communications as

---

[89] 515 US 557 (1995).
[90] 525 US 182 (1999).
[91] 536 US 150 (2002).
[92] 378 F3d 979 (2004).
[93] See section 2.1.1, and nn 78 and 79 respectively.
[94] See Chapter 5 section 3.2.
[95] Ibid.
[96] 929 F. Supp, 844 (finding 88).
[97] This is discussed in more detail below.
[98] B. Leiter, 'Cleaning Cyber-Cesspools: Google and Free Speech' in S. Levmore and M. Nussbaum (eds), *The Offensive Internet* (Harvard University Press, 2010) 155–173; Levmore (n 1) 50–67.

they will be publicly accessible. Therefore, this allows them to evaluate their prior experience.[99] This view is animated by Eady J's judgment in *Author of a Blog*,[100] in which he upheld *The Times'* argument that the public was entitled to know the identity of the author of the blog to assess the strength of his criticisms of the police force in which he was serving.[101] Accordingly, Frederick Schauer and Larry Alexander are of the opinion that free speech is predominantly concerned with audience interests. They believe that speakers enjoy only derivative rights, which are subject to protection only to ensure that the interests of the audience are safeguarded.[102] Some social media platforms have adopted this stance in respect of their anonymity and pseudonymity policies. Facebook, for example, at least 'officially', does not allow registration under a pseudonym.[103] The platform believes that users are more responsible in debate and social commentary when they use the site under their real name.[104] Similarly, between 2011 and 2014 Google+ required users to register under their 'common name' (the name by which they were known to family, friends and colleagues). It used an algorithm to detect likely pseudonyms and automatically suspend these accounts, even when these users were generally known by a pseudonym or nickname. Google said that it had introduced the policy to promote the safe use of the internet and to prevent the dissemination of anonymous spam. The views of Seth Kreimer, Schauer and Alexander, Eady J's judgment, and Facebook's policy correlate with Barendt's argument that the case for freedom of speech dictates that, when it comes to general political and economic discourse, the public should know something about the credentials of the speaker. Equally, an audience wants to know the identity of the speaker to enable it to evaluate the worth of the publication.[105]

---

[99] S. Kreimer, 'Sunlight, Secrets and Scarlet Letter: The Tension between Privacy and Disclosure in Constitutional Law' (1991) 140 *University of Pennsylvania Law Review* 1, 85–86.

[100] *Author of a Blog v Times Newspapers Ltd* [2009] EMLR 22. See section 2.1 for the facts of the case.

[101] Ibid [21].

[102] Schauer (n 84) 105–106; Alexander (n 84) 8–9.

[103] R. MacKinnon, *Consent of the Networked* (Basic Books, 2012) 150. Incidentally, Facebook's real name policy has been held to infringe German data protection law, specifically section 13, VI of the Telemedia Act 2007 and section 3a Data Protection Act 2003. The ruling was successfully challenged by Facebook in the state Administrative Court on the ground that the law only applied when the data controller was established in Germany or a non-EU state. The Court accepted that Facebook was established in Ireland, which did not prescribe in law the freedom to communicate anonymously: S. Schmitz, 'Facebook's Real Name Policy' (2013) 4 *Journal of Intellectual Property, Information Technology and Electronic Commerce Law* 190.

[104] Facebook Guidelines of March 2015 for the removal of hate content.

[105] Barendt (n 1) 66–67.

222 *Media freedom in the age of citizen journalism*

These views, the decision in *Author of a Blog*, and Facebook's policy are problematic, particularly in the context of anonymous and pseudonymous online expression, for the following reasons. First, they do not take into account the use of pseudonyms. If the audience is unaware that the speaker is communicating under a pseudonym they may not adjust the value they attribute to that respective communication.[106] Secondly, knowing the speaker's true identity does not, necessarily, add any value. Just because one can see the name of the speaker does not mean one can assess their credibility. This observation is particularly pertinent in respect of citizen journalism. These journalists, who may well be disseminating information of real value to the public sphere, may not have a 'background' to assess that is accessible to the public. In these circumstances, they may as well be acting under a pseudonym as their real identity does not provide any usable information for the audience to evaluate. Equally, the symbiotic relationship that I have argued exists between citizen journalists and the institutional media means that the institutional media often rely on citizen journalists as a source of news.[107] Consequently, speech is 'recycled' through the press and broadcast media that may come from speakers that are identified, but unknown, or from anonymous sources or from speakers operating under a pseudonym. Thirdly (and directly linked to the points above) Facebook's anonymity and pseudonymity policy relies on users to report fellow users using pseudonyms. In many instances it is likely that these users will have no idea that a pseudonym is being used. Notwithstanding this, from a practical perspective, it is almost impossible for online platforms, such as Facebook, to monitor and vet the millions of messages carried each week.[108] Furthermore, it also conflicts with the advice given to police officers to use a pseudonym on social media to protect their identity. Many police officers do use pseudonyms for this purpose on Facebook, among other social media platforms. For the same reason, the General Medical Council supports the right of doctors to express themselves online anonymously or pseudonymously.[109] Finally, the problems that could potentially flow from the decision in *Author of a Blog* are, as in *Reno*, in respect of speaker interests, symptomatic of applying audience interests exclusively. These judgments illustrate the need for a balance to be struck between both interests. There is currently an abundance of blogs, operated and published by citizen journalists, that are similar to *Night Jack*, which disseminate valuable information;[110] indeed, in 2009 *Night Jack* received the Orwell Prize for citizen journalism. Because the decision required

---

[106] Lidsky and Cotter (n 68) 1567.
[107] In particular, see Chapter 3 section 5.3.
[108] Levmore (n 1) 59.
[109] Barendt (n 1) 135.
[110] See Chapter 1 section 2.

Anonymous and pseudonymous speech 223

the author to identify himself it surely has the propensity to dissuade other citizen journalists from communicating in a similar way.

The decision in *Author of a Blog* illustrates a further challenge faced by citizen journalists.[111] Contrary to the media-as-a-constitutional-component concept, if these journalists are not considered 'media', they are not subject to the enhanced right to media freedom. As a result, they cannot avail themselves of a journalist's immunity from being required to disclose sources of information. If the author of *Night Jack* had taken his 'story' to *The Times*, rather than publishing it on his blog, the newspaper might have published it and then refused to identify its source because, as a recognised media entity, it would not have had to disclose its source pursuant to the right to media freedom. In doing so, it would have argued that the public interest in the story took precedence over any interest the police force had in identifying the whistleblower. The judgment, based exclusively on audience interests, seems to favour the institutional media in that, by virtue of the right to media freedom, it is immune from disclosing its sources, yet it is also able to identify a respected citizen journalist who independently publishes a story for which it could claim journalists' privilege.[112]

Taking this argument a step further, as well as bestowing certain privileges on the media, as discussed in the previous chapter, the right to media freedom, and the media-as-a-constitutional-component concept impose upon media actors concomitant duties and responsibilities, including transparency.[113] The journalistic media is subject to a right of reply.[114] Therefore, at least within a European context, the media has to make available certain information about the publisher or editor.[115] As Jan Oster states, '[w]hile anonymity is

---

[111] See generally P. Coe, 'Redefining "Media" Using a "Media-as-a-constitutional -component" Concept: An Evaluation of the Need for the European Court of Human Rights to Alter Its Understanding of "Media" Within a New Media Landscape' (2017) 37(1) *Legal Studies* 25.

[112] E. Barendt, 'Bad News for Bloggers' (2009) 2 *Journal of Media Law* 141, 146–147.

[113] See Chapter 6 section 3.2 and the ECtHR case of *Fatullayev v Azerbaijan* [2010] App. no. 40984/07.

[114] For example, see Article 28 Audiovisual Media Services Directive 2010/13/ EU, OJ L95; *Ediciones Tiempo S.A. v Spain* [1989] App. no. 13010/87; Resolution (74) 26 of the Committee of Ministers of the Council of Europe on the right of reply – Position of the individual in relation to the press; Recommendation Rec(2004) 16 of the Committee of Ministers to Member States on the right of reply in the new media environment (1974). For a general European overview, see A. Koltay, 'The Right of Reply in a European Comparative Perspective' (2013) 54(1) *Acta Juridica Hungarica* (*Hungarian Journal of Legal Studies*) 73.

[115] According to Oster, this presumably applies to all European countries: Oster (n 3) 49.

part of freedom of expression, responsible journalism requires that at least the editor of the publication be immediately identifiable in order to facilitate effective protection against defamation and privacy violation'.[116] This duty runs counter to a culture of anonymity and pseudonymity prevalent on the internet and amongst citizen journalists. Thus, notwithstanding the fact that a citizen journalist, such as *Night Jack*, is not considered media and therefore not subject to media freedom, even if they were, the fact that they are the 'source', 'author' and 'publisher' would mean that they would not be fulfilling their journalistic responsibilities pursuant to the right if they published anonymously or under a pseudonym. A journalist for *The Times*, on the other hand, could use their editor or the newspaper's publishing company to 'shield' their identity. Herein lies a significant challenge for citizen journalists: what is relevant to the concept of responsible journalism is that a person, whether that be the journalist or their editor, or an organisation, such as the publishing company, claims responsibility for a publication and can, as a result, be held liable. For example, it is the policy of *The Economist* to publish its articles anonymously.[117] However, it is clear that *The Economist Newspaper Ltd* is responsible for its articles and can, therefore, be held liable for them. Consequently, both *The Economist* and its journalists, in respect of this at least, comply with their journalistic responsibilities. To the contrary, the nature of citizen journalism, particularly the fact that many bloggers operate alone as both the author and the publisher, means they do not have the 'shield' of an identifiable editor or organisation that could be held liable. If they did, this would defeat the very purpose of their anonymity or pseudonym. However, by not providing the details of an identifiable person or organisation they are not conforming to the concept of responsible journalism. Indeed, Nicklin J's judgment in *Sooben v Badal*[118] adds weight to this argument as, pursuant to the decision, the *Reynolds* criteria[119] for responsible journalism should be applied

---

[116] Ibid.

[117] Historically, this was the case with all newspapers.

[118] [2017] EWHC 2638 (QB).

[119] The criteria for responsible journalism laid down by Lord Nicholls in *Reynolds v Times Newspapers Limited* [2001] 2 AC 127 (HL) 204–205 is explored in detail in Chapter 8 section 3.2.3. This section explains that the *Reynolds* defence was abolished in 2013 on the enactment of the Defamation Act 2013 and was replaced by section 4 of the Defamation Act 2013, which provides for a public interest defence. This section also deals with the Court of Appeal's judgment in *Economou v de Freitas* [2018] EWCA Civ 2591; [2019] EMLR 7, which determined, inter alia, that citizen journalists, bloggers and casual social media users alike may be able to avail themselves of the section 4 defence so long as they can show that they reasonably believed that publishing the defamatory statement was in the public interest, even if their conduct might fall

Anonymous and pseudonymous speech 225

to non-professional journalists.[120] Ultimately, this challenge faced by citizen journalists could undermine the value of such journalism and, paradoxically, damage audience interests as fewer people will engage with it, which will, in turn, hinder democratic participation and self-fulfilment.

Barendt suggests that the rights and interests of speakers, distinct from those of the audience, are 'emphasised' by the argument from self-fulfilment in that 'speech is an essential aspect of the right to self-development and fulfilment, or of individual autonomy, and so must be respected as an aspect of that autonomy'.[121] C. Edwin Baker takes this further. He argues that the right to freedom of expression should take precedence over countervailing rights because it facilitates autonomy – by allowing individuals to exercise self-expression or self-disclosure they control whether or not to reveal themselves to others, which therefore enables the respective individual to be treated as autonomous.[122] According to Barendt, this argument is problematic. He suggests that the argument from self-fulfilment is the 'least plausible rationale' for freedom of speech and that it would be 'odd' to base the right to free speech on the speaker's interest in self-development or fulfilment. Specifically, he asks, '[h]ow does the mask of anonymity claimed by someone who prefers to remain nameless or to publish under the disguise of a pseudonym advance that person's self-development as an individual?'[123] It is submitted that the position adopted by Barendt is flawed, in respect of anonymous and pseudonymous expression conveyed online, and by the traditional institutional media, for the reasons discussed below.

In *Reno* District Judge Dalzell stated that the internet is 'the most participatory form of mass speech yet developed'.[124] It provides a way of not only receiving information, but of transmitting views on any topic instantaneously. Consequently, it has facilitated a convergence of audience and producer.[125]

---

short of that expected of a trained and experienced journalist. Accordingly, the defence is not confined to media. Per Sharp LJ, [104]–[110].

[120]   *Sooben v Badal* [2017] EWHC 2638 (QB), [32]–[34].

[121]   Barendt (n 1) 62.

[122]   C.E. Baker, *Human Liberty and Freedom of Speech* (Oxford University Press, 1989) ch. 3; C.E. Baker, 'Autonomy and Hate Speech' in I. Hare and J. Weinstein (eds), *Extreme Speech and Democracy* (Oxford University Press, 2009) 142–146.

[123]   Barendt (n 1) 63.

[124]   *Reno v American Civil Liberties Union* 929 F Supp 824, 833 (ED Pa, 1996).

[125]   See Coe (n 18) 23; J.M. Balkin, 'The Future of Free Expression in a Digital Age' (2009) 34 *Pepperdine Law Review* 427, 440; J.M. Balkin, 'Digital Speech and Democratic Culture: A Theory of Freedom of Expression for the Information Society' (2004) 79 *New York University Law Review* 1; J. Rowbottom, 'To Rant, Vent and Converse: Protecting Low Level Digital Speech' (2012) 71 *Cambridge Law Journal* 355, 365.

Thus, anonymity and pseudonymity is a culturally inherent aspect of citizen journalism and online communication generally.[126] According to John Suler, the ability to communicate anonymously is a principal factor for online disinhibition effect, whereby people are less inhibited to say things online, which they would not say in a 'real life' encounter. It allows them to hide their identity and to operate under the assumption, at least, that their real identities cannot be linked to messages they send, and so they cannot be held responsible for the consequences of that expression.[127] In this context the 'mask' of anonymity or the 'disguise' of a pseudonym can advance a person's self-development as it gives them a voice in circumstances where, without anonymity or pseudonymity, they would not be able to express themselves. A pertinent example is academic speech. One only has to look at *Times Higher Education* to see regular instances of academics writing anonymously about controversial issues within their university, or higher education generally. Of even greater significance is academic speech in countries where academics fear persecution for expressing views.[128] In both of these examples, arguably academics are developing intellectually. In these type of situations where they could not, or would not want, to reveal their identity through fear of persecution or reprisals, by virtue of being able to express themselves anonymously or under a pseudonym, they are able to engage in dialogue with other academics and/or the process of research, writing and, ultimately, the peer review of their work (which tends to be conducted anonymously in any event).[129] Of course, the rejoinder to this

---

[126] M. Collins, 'The Ideology of Anonymity and Pseudonymity', *Huffington Post*, 2 August 2013.

[127] J. Suler, 'The Online Disinhibition Effect' (2004) 7 *CyberPsychology and Behaviour* 321, 322. It has been acknowledged that young people, in particular, are more likely to discuss their anxieties and attempt to form friendships online under a pseudonym rather than use their real name: S. Turkle, *Alone Together* (Basic Books, 2011) 189–198, 229–231.

[128] For example, see *Erdogan v Turkey* (346/04 and 39779/04) [2014] ECHR 530; A. Mendonca, 'European Court of Human Rights Upholds Academic Freedom: Mustafa Erdogan v Turkey' (2014) 25(8) *Entertainment Law Review* 304, 304–305; 'Turkey must stop persecuting its academics', *Times Higher Education*, 24 March 2016.

[129] In the humanities and social sciences, 'double blind' reviews remain standard practice (the author does not know the identity of the reviewer and vice versa) whereas within science and medical disciplines, 'single blind' reviews tend to be employed (the author does not know the identity of the reviewer, but the reviewer knows the author's name and institution): Report of Science and Technology Committee, *Peer Review in Scientific Publications*, HC 856 (2010–12), [15]–[16].

Anonymous and pseudonymous speech 227

argument is that such disinhibition, by virtue of anonymity and pseudonymity, can potentially act as a catalyst for irresponsible and unacceptable speech.[130]

It has been argued that John Stuart Mill's argument from truth, and the argument from democratic self-governance are, predominantly, associated with audience interests.[131] Indeed, in relation to the argument from democratic self-governance, and in the context of the regulation of speech at public meetings, Alexander Meiklejohn was of the opinion that it is important that 'not everyone shall get to speak, but that everything worth saying shall be said'.[132] However, in *McIntyre* the Supreme Court justified the existence of a right to anonymous and pseudonymous expression as a protection against the tyranny of the majority.[133] Consequently, an additional argument to support a right to anonymity based on speaker interests is that without such a right speakers would not participate at all in political discourse. According to scholars such as Ronald Dworkin, Robert Post and Martin Redish, such a right is incorporated within a speaker's right to contribute to public life.[134] The argument from democratic self-governance and the argument from self-fulfilment do not operate exclusively from each other as justifications for anonymous and pseudonymous speech. To the contrary, self-fulfilment is an integral and supportive aspect of an individual's ability to participate in democratic discourse. The argument from democratic self-governance, as supported by the argument from self-fulfilment, is particularly pertinent to online communication as it supports the primary rationale for a right to anonymous speech within these arenas; anonymous expression enables more people to engage in public discourse and, in so doing, contribute valuable information and ideas to society than would be the case if their speech were inhibited by a requirement to disclose their identity. Indeed, while he was the UN Rapporteur on the

---

[130] This is discussed below and is something that I consider in more detail in Coe (n 1) 195–199.

[131] See generally Barendt (n 1) 61; Sir J. Laws, 'Meiklejohn, the First Amendment and Free Speech in English Law' in I. Loveland (ed), *Importing the First Amendment, Freedom of Speech and Expression in Britain, Europe and the USA* (Hart Publishing, 1998) 123–137; A. Nicol QC, G. Millar QC and A. Sharland, *Media Law and Human Rights* (2nd edn., Oxford University Press, 2009) 3, [1.06]; E. Barendt, *Freedom of Speech* (2nd edn., Oxford University Press, 2005) 18; J. Oster, 'Theory and Doctrine of "Media Freedom" as a Legal Concept' (2013) 5(1) *Journal of Media Law* 57–78, 69.

[132] A. Meiklejohn, *Political Freedom: The Constitutional Powers of the People* (Oxford University Press, 1960) 64.

[133] 514 US 334 (1995) 357.

[134] See generally R. Dworkin in 'Foreword' to I. Hare and J. Weinstein (eds), *Extreme Speech and Democracy* (Oxford University Press, 2009); Post (n 84); M.H. Redish, 'The Value of Free Speech' (1982) 130 *University of Pennsylvania Law Review* 591.

228 *Media freedom in the age of citizen journalism*

promotion of freedom of expression, David Kaye robustly supported a right to communicate anonymously online. Kaye's support of anonymous communication on the internet is indicative of a combination of the arguments advanced above in that in authoritarian countries there will be universal reluctance to speak freely and contribute to public and political discourse, both online and offline, for fear of persecution.[135] As Barendt states, '[a]nonymity enables the circumvention of the myriad restrictions on the exercise of freedom of expression imposed by authoritarian governments'.[136] It can also facilitate democratic participation in liberal societies more tolerant of political dissent.[137] In fact, the example of academic speech in relation to self-fulfilment given above is equally applicable to this point. Anonymity is essential for individuals wishing to express views that may expose them to disciplinary action or dismissal by their employer or ostracism from colleagues.[138]

These are the very reasons why Eady J's judgment in *Author of a Blog*, based exclusively on audience interests, is so fundamentally flawed as, paradoxically, by potentially dissuading individuals from participating in citizen journalism, it damages audience interests as fewer people are exposed to information that may have a constitutional value. This can limit their engagement with democratic discourse and hinder their self-fulfilment. Equally, according to Edward Stein, protection of anonymous and pseudonymous speech, particularly in 'cyberspace', 'provides a context' for lesbians and gay men 'in which to speak freely, without identifying themselves, and without having to be physically present to communicate with others'.[139] This can be extended to vulnerable groups, such as asylum-seekers, immigrants and the mentally and physically disabled, amongst others, in that, for the same reasons, anonymity and pseudonymity enables them to exercise their freedom of speech and, therefore, not only develop intellectually, but also participate in, and contribute

---

[135] Kaye (n 3) [23], [31].

[136] Barendt (n 1) 129.

[137] Ibid. Oster refers to Justice Holmes' marketplace of ideas theory laid down in *Abrams v United States* 250 US 616 (1919) in which it was asserted that 'the best test of truth is the power of the thought to get itself accepted in the competition of the market' (630–631) in relation to this argument. He states that pursuant to the theory,

everyone should have a voice in public debate. If speech is either made anonymously or not all, then it is preferable that it is being made anonymously. This applies even more given that fear of harassment or sanctions often – but of course not necessarily – arises in cases in which the speaker wants to contribute to a controversial matter of general interest, such as political or religious affairs (Oster (n 3) 49).

[138] Ibid.

[139] E. Stein, 'Queers Anonymous: Lesbians, Gay Men, Free Speech and Cyberspace' (2003) 38 *Harvard Civil Rights – Civil Liberties Law Review* 159, 199–205.

Anonymous and pseudonymous speech 229

to, public discourse.[140] However, there is a robust rejoinder to this argument. Thomas Scanlon's individual autonomy concept, which is based on the right of the audience to receive information, to be exposed to every type of argument and to be free from governmental intrusion into the process of individual decision-making[141] is equally applicable as access to minority views, which may not be available without anonymous or pseudonymous communication, are an essential aspect of audience rights.

Thus, where citizen journalism and online communication are concerned, speakers have a particularly strong claim to the right to freedom of expression[142] and, by extension, the right to communicate anonymously or pseudonymously. As discussed in Chapter 2, this is because the audience and producer convergence contributed to the ascendance of citizen journalism.[143] Consequently, free speech is facilitated by the fact that these speakers are not subject to, for instance, political bias, censorship, the influence of media ownership and editorial control, at least to the same extent as they would be within the context of the institutional media,[144] where greater emphasis is usually placed on the interest of the audience, who, to assess the reliability of the journalist or broadcaster, are concerned with being apprised of that individual's identity.[145] Victoria Ekstrand argues that those who communicate online are more likely to tolerate anonymity,[146] either because it is generally accepted that anonymous and pseudonymous communication is 'normal' in these arenas[147] or because their expectations are lower as to the reliability of the information provided or the expertise of those responsible for disseminating the information. To the contrary, Danielle Citron suggests that certain aspects of the internet may make online communication potentially more damaging than information disseminated offline.[148] A consequence of the way in which online communication has become ingrained within our social and cultural fabric is that habits, conventions and social norms that were once informal manifestations of daily life are now infused within these methods of communication. What were casual and ephemeral actions and/or acts of expression, such as conversing with friends or colleagues or swapping/displaying pictures

---

[140]   Barendt (n 1) 64, 129.

[141]   Scanlon (n 84) 223; Schauer (n 84) 69.

[142]   Barendt (n 1) 130.

[143]   See section 1.

[144]   See Chapter 3 section 6.

[145]   Barendt (n 1) 61–65.

[146]   V.S. Ekstrand, 'The Many Masks of Anon: Anonymity as Cultural Practice and Reflections in Case Law' (2013) 18 *Journal of Technology Law and Policy* 1, 18.

[147]   Barendt (n 1) 130.

[148]   Citron (n 77) 4–12.

230   *Media freedom in the age of citizen journalism*

or exchanging thoughts that were once kept private or maybe shared with a select few, have now become formalised and permanent. These actions and expressions are, in the click of a mouse or the flick of a finger, publicised for the world to see. Thus, unlike broadcasts or newsprint, which are perceived to be more transitory in nature and are 'tomorrow's fish and chips paper',[149] online communication lends itself to permanency;[150] it enters the 'public domain, with the potential for long-lasting and far reaching-consequences'.[151] Search engines, such as Google, provide users with links to harmful communications. These can remain accessible to the public, sometimes for very long periods of time, and certainly longer than with the traditional media, after they were initially published.[152] This can have negative and long-lasting effects on individuals' lives.

The fact that information disseminated online can, potentially, remain available permanently and is easily accessible by anybody gives rise to three issues, which are amplified by anonymous and pseudonymous expression, particularly in the context of citizen journalism. These issues form the foundation for a strong audience interest-based argument against a speaker interest-orientated right to anonymous and pseudonymous speech. Thus, they provide support for the restriction of anonymous and pseudonymous speech in an online context.

As stated above, many citizen journalists choose to publish their material anonymously, or operate under a pseudonym, often for entirely legitimate reasons.[153] In fact, in a social media context, in contrast to platforms such as Facebook that have adopted real name policies,[154] some sites have implemented policies that enable their users to communicate anonymously or under a pseudonym.[155] As set out in section 1.1, this conflicts with the audience interest preference for transparency, which gives rise to three particular concerns that have been articulated throughout this chapter. First, in line with Eady J's judgment in *Author of a Blog*, anonymity and pseudonymity does not allow the audience to assess the veracity of the speaker. Secondly, it encourages irresponsible and damaging expression. This is animated in the context of citizen journalists by Saul Levmore, who points to the distinction

---

[149] Although the print press has long held archives, both physically and, more recently, online.

[150] See generally V. Mayer-Schönberger, *Delete: The Virtue of Forgetting in the Digital Age* (Princeton University Press, 2009).

[151] J. Van Dijck, *The Culture of Connectivity: A Critical History of Social Media* (Oxford University Press, 2013) 6–7; Coe (n 18) 25; Rowbottom (n 17) 366–377.

[152] Leiter (n 98) 155.

[153] See sections 2.1 and 2.2.

[154] See the discussion above.

[155] Examples include sites such as Social Number, Gaia Online, Evsum and Anonyming. See Barendt (n 1) 134.

Anonymous and pseudonymous speech 231

between the traditional and online media.[156] He states that, with the traditional media, the danger posed by anonymity is mitigated by the presence of an active intermediary[157] in the form of a separation between the journalistic, editorial and publication functions. In this context the journalist, editor or publisher can vouch for the integrity and reliability of their source or speaker. They can also check the story prior to publication or broadcast and, if need be, refer it to their legal team to prevent the dissemination of any material that may present disproportionate legal risks. To the contrary, it is usual for citizen journalists to fulfil all three functions without access to these pre-publication resources, which provide checks and balances on the material and, in turn, aid responsible journalism. Thus, because of citizen journalism's symbiotic relationship with the traditional media, for the reasons advanced in Chapter 3,[158] this can contribute to the proliferation of false news. Thirdly, anonymous and pseudonymous expression prevents, or at the very least makes it difficult (and very expensive), for a victim of, for example, defamation or an invasion of privacy to identify the origin of the material, which in turn can create an insurmountable barrier to remedial action and/or prosecution. Moreover, the fact that a victim is unaware of the perpetrator, and their proximity to them, can make the harm suffered more acute.[159]

These issues serve to support the argument that a constitutionally protected speaker interest-orientated right to anonymous and pseudonymous speech could be claimed by anybody, including those disseminating false news, or engaging in, for example, defamation or privacy-invading expression. Consequently, such a right could inadvertently protect speakers engaging in unwanted and damaging speech. However, despite this, it is submitted that for the reasons set out above in favour of a speaker interest approach it is a non sequitur that an exclusively audience interest approach prevails. This is because the ability to speak anonymously or under a pseudonym encourages free speech by enabling more people to communicate and exchange ideas and information. As a result, it fuels greater participation in public discourse and facilitates self-fulfilment. In doing this, it aids the democratic process by facilitating self-governance. If this type of speech is restricted or prohibited then these tangible advantages will be lost. Consequently, and paradoxically, this can damage the interests of the audience as it may dissuade people from engaging with this form of media and contributing to valuable citizen journalism, which, in turn, could limit the number of people able to participate in democratic discourse. Furthermore, the

---

[156] Levmore (n 1) 50, 54–55.
[157] Ibid. See also S. Levmore, 'The Anonymity Tool' (1996) 144 *University of Pennsylvania Law Review* 2191.
[158] See section Chapter 3 5.3.
[159] Barendt (n 1) 132.

benefit gained by the audience from requiring speakers to identify themselves, particularly in respect of online speech, is questionable; it does not necessarily enable the audience to accurately assess the credentials of the speaker and therefore the value of the communication. Rather, this section has demonstrated that to support citizen journalism and modern media speech, a balance needs to be struck between the two interests. The following and concluding section will set out how the media-as-a-constitutional-component concept can help to achieve this harmonisation.

4 CONCLUSION: HARMONISING SPEAKER AND AUDIENCE INTERESTS

As established in Chapter 6, the media-as-a-constitutional-component concept, as underpinned by social responsibility theory and the argument from self-governance, not only provides a new definition of media, but also requires media actors to abide by certain standards of professional behaviour and norms of discourse for them to benefit from the enhanced right to media freedom.[160] Furthermore, it provides the normative and philosophical foundation for the regulatory framework advanced in Chapter 9.[161] This means that for a media actor to be a member of the scheme, and therefore take advantage of the statutory and non-statutory incentives it offers, including significant reputational benefits, they must adhere to the standards and norms.[162] Thus, for the reasons set out below, the concept provides a mechanism that encourages a speaker interest approach by satisfying the audience interests in: (i) being able to effectively assess the veracity of anonymous or pseudonymous speakers; (ii) encouraging responsible journalism and negating the need for a distinction between journalistic, editorial and publication functions; and (iii) if required, enabling the easier identification of the speaker.

First, as explained in Chapter 9, media actors that can demonstrate positive engagement with the standards and norms by, for example, being members of the regulatory scheme would be able to objectively demonstrate that they are part of a group of media that are accountable and value responsible journalism.[163] Secondly, the identity of anonymous and pseudonymous actors that join the scheme would be protected, so long as they abide by these values. Only in extreme cases of misconduct or criminal activity would their identity be divulged.[164] Therefore, from a speaker interest perspective, the actor can join

---

[160] See Chapter 6 section 3.
[161] See Chapter 9 section 4.1.
[162] See Chapter 9 section 6.
[163] See Chapter 9 section 4.4.2.
[164] Ibid.

Anonymous and pseudonymous speech 233

the scheme and take advantage of its benefits, which include access to training and legal support, safe in the knowledge that their identity and ability to publish anonymously or pseudonymously are protected. Conversely, from an audience interest perspective, the standards imposed by the regulatory scheme on its members provide a method for the audience to objectively and rationally assess the veracity of the speaker and their material, and the speaker's adherence to responsible journalistic practice, regardless of whether or not they are publishing material anonymously or under a pseudonym. Furthermore, even if a citizen journalist member is fulfilling all three journalistic, editorial and publication functions, the audience will know that they have access to legal and other support to provide external checks and balances on their material. Finally, to an extent (as it is recognised that not all citizen journalists operating anonymously or pseudonymously are responsible or will join the scheme),[165] it alleviates the audience interest concern regarding identification of the anonymous or pseudonymous speaker. These members of the regulatory framework will not be named unless they engage in harmful, damaging or criminal activity. In these instances the audience interests are protected as, subject to a review from a panel, the speaker will be identified to allow for remedial action or prosecution.[166]

---

[165] Non-members of the regulatory scheme are dealt with in Chapter 9 section 6.7.

[166] As Citron advocates, users who have previously been allowed to communicate anonymously or under a pseudonym, but who have abused that privilege by engaging in harmful speech, should be prevented from doing so in the future by being required to use their real name: Citron (n 77) 239.

8. Contempt of court and defamation

1 INTRODUCTION

This chapter considers the law of contempt of court and defamation. It sets out how they operate and the rationales that underpin them, namely maintaining the integrity and fairness of trials and protecting reputation respectively. As will be discussed, the principles upon which they are founded can be at odds with media freedom, which can create an imbalance between the state or claimants and the media. In this chapter I make the claim that the adoption of the media-as-a-constitutional-component concept, and the standards of professional behaviour and norms of conduct that it imposes on media actors, provides a mechanism that, at the very least, alleviates this imbalance. Thus, the first half of this chapter applies the concept to contempt of court and the principle of open justice. The second half of the chapter does the same in respect of defamation and the defences of truth, honest opinion, and publication on a matter of public interest.

2 MEDIA FREEDOM VERSUS FAIR TRIALS: THE GENESIS OF CONTEMPT OF COURT

This section sets out the development of the law of contempt of court and how the principles that now underpin it accord with the notion of open justice, which, it argues, could be facilitated by citizen journalism, subject to two issues: (i) the current rules on accessing certain court hearings are unfavourable to citizen journalists, thereby creating a democratic deficit; (ii) citizen journalism has the potential to undermine the integrity of legal proceedings to a far greater extent than the institutional press and media generally. Consequently, this section provides the foundation for the discussions that follow in sections 2.1 and 2.2, in which it is considered how the media-as-a-constitutional-component concept offers a mechanism that deals with issues (i) and (ii) by harmonising media freedom and open justice.

The conflict between media freedom and the fairness of legal proceedings has been the subject of much academic and jurisprudential debate, both historically, in relation to the traditional institutional media[1] and, more recently, in respect of online speech and citizen journalism.[2] This debate stems from the rationale that underpins the law of contempt of court in the UK: a fear of 'trial by media' in that prejudicial publications can distort the trial process[3] by undermining its integrity and, ultimately, its fairness. This can, for instance, stigmatise the defendant before, or even in the absence of, a guilty verdict,[4] lead to the abandonment of trials[5] and, in extreme cases, the quashing of convictions.[6] Furthermore, it is arguable that trial by media is inherently unfair as the media is not constrained by the rules of evidence, or subject to any procedural safeguards. According to Jacob Rowbottom, this argument reflects 'a concern with media power, namely that the media should not use its communicative resources to select and interpret evidence and publicise its own conclusions on alleged transgressions of the law'.[7] Rather, pursuant to the argument against trial by media, a person's guilt should be determined by the court rather than public opinion.[8]

---

[1]   For example, see *R v Bolam, ex parte Haigh* (1949) 93 SJ 220; *Attorney-General v The Times Newspapers Ltd* [1974] AC 273 (HL); *Sunday Times v United Kingdom* App. no. 6538/74 (1979–1980) 2 EHRR 245; G. Robertson QC and A. Nicol QC, *Media Law* (4th edn., Penguin Books, 2002) 345–350; J. Rowbottom, *Media Law* (Hart Publishing, 2018) 112–114; H. Fenwick and G. Phillipson, *Media Freedom under the Human Rights Act* (Oxford University Press, 2006) ch. 6.

[2]   For example, see *Attorney-General v Associated Newspapers Limited* [2011] EWHC 418 (Admin); *R v Harwood* [2012] EWHC Misc 27 (CC); D. Grieve, 'Contempt: A Balancing Act' (Speech at City University, London, 1 December 2011); I. Cram, G. Borrie and N. Lowe, *Borrie & Lowe: The Law of Contempt* (4th edn., LexisNexis, 2010) 687; D. Mac Síthigh, 'Contempt of Court and New Media' in D. Mangan and L. Gillies (eds), *The Legal Challenges of Social Media* (Edward Elgar Publishing, 2017) 83, 86–92; Rowbottom (n 1) 151–152.

[3]   Robertson QC and Nicol QC (n 1) 345.

[4]   Rowbottom (n 1) 112, 114.

[5]   *R v Reade, Morris and Woodwiss*, Central Criminal Court, 15 October 1993, Garland J; *R v Knights*, Harrow Crown Court, 3 October 1995. However, to the contrary, see *R v West* [1996] 2 Cr. App. R. 374, 386 in which Lord Taylor CJ said that it would be ludicrous if heinous crimes could not be tried because of the extensive publicity they inevitably attracted. In the Court's view, all that is required is that the trial judge takes particular care to warn the jury to try the case only on the evidence. See also *R v Michael Stone* [2001] Crim. L.R. 265 (CA); *Montgomery v Her Majesty's Advocate* [2001] 2 WLR 779 (PC) per Lord Hope at 673.

[6]   *R v McCann* (1990) 92 Cr. App. R. 239; *R v Taylor (Michelle Ann and Lisa Jane)* (1993) 98 Cr. App. R. 361; *R v Wood, The Times*, 11 July 1995 (CA).

[7]   Rowbottom (n 1) 112.

[8]   Ibid.

In the UK, contempt of court has roots in both common law and statute (the Contempt of Court Act 1981).[9] Before the introduction of the 1981 Act, at common law, contempt of court *was* a strict liability offence.[10] The effect of section 1 of the Act was to place the strict liability rule on a statutory footing.[11] This rule determines that conduct may be treated as a contempt of court when it interferes 'with the course of justice in legal proceedings', regardless of any intention on the part of the media actor to do so.[12] Section 2 of the Act sets out the scope of the rule,[13] stating that it applies to 'a publication which creates a substantial risk that the course of justice in the proceedings in question will be seriously impeded[14] or prejudiced'[15] if 'the proceedings in question are active[16] within the meaning of this section at the time of the publication'.[17] If the proceedings are not 'active', then any contempt of court proceedings must be pursued under the common law, which is preserved by section 6(c), but which is no longer subject to the strict liability rule as it requires a showing of intent to impede or prejudice the administration of justice.[18]

---

[9]   I refer to the 1981 Act as a UK Act as, pursuant to section 21, it largely extends to Scotland and Northern Ireland. Section 21(4) and (5) sets out those provisions that do not apply to Scotland and Northern Ireland respectively.

[10]   Fenwick and Phillipson (n 1) 248–252.

[11]   Albeit, as I explain below, its scope has been more clearly defined by section 2.

[12]   Contempt of Court Act 1981, section 1.

[13]   Pursuant to section 7, in England and Wales, contempt of court proceedings can only be instigated by the Attorney-General or by the court itself (pursuant to section 21(4), section 7 does not extend to Scotland).

[14]   Although contempt is commonly concerned with material that could influence a juror, the strict liability rule applies to publications that can impede the course of justice in other ways, such as where a publication applies pressure that could alter the conduct of a party or witness during the litigation (see *Attorney-General v Unger* 1 Cr. App. R. 308, 315). In *Attorney-General v Mirror Group Newspapers* [2011] EWHC 2074 (Admin); [2012] 1 WLR 2408 it was held that the newspaper articles vilifying Christopher Jeffries, who was wrongly accused of the murder of Joanna Yates, were in contempt because the negative stories may have discouraged people from coming forward to say positive things about Jeffries' character. See Rowbottom (n 1) 119.

[15]   Contempt of Court Act 1981, section 2(2). As the law of contempt aims to deter the risk of prejudice or impediment at the time of publication, the fact that the publication did not cause any actual prejudice to a trial is not relevant to whether it is contempt. See *Attorney-General v English* [1983] 1 AC 116, per Lord Diplock at 141–142; Rowbottom (n 1) 119.

[16]   Pursuant to Schedule 1 of the Act, in respect of crime, 'active' essentially means from arrest to conviction.

[17]   Contempt of Court Act 1981, section 2(3).

[18]   Ibid, section 6(c). For detailed discussion of intentional contempt at common law, see Fenwick and Phillipson (n 1) 284–296.

Perhaps the highest-profile example of the pre-1981 Act common law version of contempt being used to deal with trial by media is the *Sunday Times* litigation, relating to its campaign for victims of the drug Thalidomide, which, for the reasons explained below, acted as a watershed moment for common law contempt of court. *The Sunday Times* had published an article arguing that Chemie Grünenthal, the manufacturer of Thalidomide, should make a more generous offer of compensation to those affected by the drug. The newspaper then proposed to publish a further article, criticising how the drug was tested and marketed, which led to the Attorney-General obtaining an injunction to restrain publication on the grounds that it would be a contempt of court. In *Attorney-General v The Times Newspapers*[19] the House of Lords upheld the injunction on the basis that legal disputes should not be prejudged, and prejudiced, by the media. Specifically, Lord Diplock stated that holding a litigant up to 'public obloquy' could discourage people from pursuing their legal rights[20] and that there is a danger that media discussion could lead to its own determination of the legal dispute, thereby usurping the function of the court.[21] Similarly, Lord Reid warned of the dangers of 'trial by media', which would give rise to 'disrespect for the processes of the law', which would be prejudicial to 'unpopular people and unpopular causes'.[22]

Because of the judgment, the newspaper was not able to publish its full investigation into the testing and marketing of the drug until the injunction was discharged in 1976. Ultimately, the ECtHR determined that the injunction violated Article 10 ECHR. According to the Court, due to the article being 'couched in moderate terms', it did not pose any substantial risk of 'trial by media'.[23] It found that the domestic court had failed to give priority to freedom of expression, especially as the proposed article related to a matter of 'undisputed public concern' and that the role of the media was not confined to discussing the general principles away from specific cases.[24] However, more importantly for media freedom, the Court also took the opportunity to lay down general principles of policy, stating that the 'courts cannot operate in a vacuum' and, although the courts are the final arbiter of legal disputes, 'this does not mean that there can be no prior discussion of disputes elsewhere'.[25]

---

[19] [1974] AC 273 (HL).

[20] Ibid 313.

[21] Ibid 310.

[22] Ibid 300.

[23] *Sunday Times v United Kingdom* App. no. 6538/74 (1979–1980) 2 EHRR 245, [63].

[24] Ibid [66].

[25] Ibid [65]. See also *Axel Springer v Germany (No. 1)* [2012] App. no. 39954/08, [80], [96].

The Strasbourg Court's judgment highlighted the endemic problem with the application of common law contempt of court, which, according to Geoffrey Robertson QC and Andrew Nicol QC, treated '"the public interest" as synonymous with "the interests of those involved in the legal process", imposing secrecy and censorship without regard for the countervailing benefits of a free flow of information about what happens in the courts'.[26] The Court's ruling, along with the *Report of the Committee on Contempt of Court*,[27] ultimately acted as a catalyst for the introduction of the 1981 Act. Although shortly after the Act's introduction, in *Attorney-General v English*,[28] Lord Diplock stated that 'trial by the media, is not to be permitted in this country',[29] the statutory version of contempt is not designed to prevent the public from forming its own judgement on particular matters.[30] Rather, despite the Act's purpose being to preserve the integrity of the legal system and ensure that publicity does not interfere with legal proceedings, its ability to 'guard' against trial by media is limited.[31] Thus, this development of the law reflected a shift in the role of public opinion as it recognised that the public have a right to form their own views on legal proceedings.[32]

This shift in the principles underpinning the operation of contempt of court accords with the notion of open justice which could be facilitated by citizen journalism. However, there are two issues with this. First, the current rules limiting access to the courts, in certain situations for citizen journalists, combined with the traditional media's reluctance to report on legal proceedings, has created a democratic deficit. Secondly, although, on the one hand, citizen journalism has the potential to support open justice, on the other hand, it presents a modern dichotomy as arguably the conflict between media freedom and the fairness of legal proceedings has been amplified by online expression, including citizen journalism, and its libertarian foundations,[33] which, due to its reach and speed of dissemination, has the potential to encourage and facilitate trial by media, and therefore undermine the integrity of the legal process, to a far greater extent than the traditional institutional media.

The following section will set out, first, the open justice principle and how, in theory, it could be supported by citizen journalism, and, secondly, the dichotomy referred to above. In section 2.2 it will be argued that the

---

[26] Robertson QC and Nicol QC (n 1) 345.
[27] *Report of the Committee on Contempt of Court* (Cmnd 5794, 1974).
[28] [1983] 1 AC 116.
[29] Ibid 141–142.
[30] Rowbottom (n 1) 113.
[31] Ibid.
[32] Ibid.
[33] See Chapter 5 section 2.

Contempt of court and defamation 239

media-as-a-constitutional-component concept, and the inherent standards of professional behaviour and norms of discourse it imposes on media actors,[34] offers a mechanism that harmonises media freedom and open justice, thereby dealing with these issues.

2.1 Open Justice and Citizen Journalism: The Democratic Deficit and a Conflict Between Media Freedom and Fair Trials

The principle of open justice[35] is simple: it determines that legal proceedings must be conducted transparently and publicly. It is deeply rooted in the foundations of the common law, as demonstrated by Lord Shaw's remark in *Scott v Scott*[36] that the principle had received 'a constant and most watchful respect' since the end of the Stuart era.[37] In the same case, Lord Shaw also underlined the principle's constitutional importance, stating that the open administration of justice is a 'constitutional right' as opposed to a matter of judicial discretion.[38] Thus, although the principle is not absolute,[39] its requirement that the administration of justice be conducted publicly is enshrined within, and fundamental to, the rule of law[40] and democracy.[41] It has been given more weight in recent years by Article 6 ECHR, which determines that 'everyone is entitled to a fair and public hearing' in relation to their 'civil rights and obligations or of any criminal charge'.

---

[34]   Ibid Sections 4 and 5.

[35]   For analysis of the arguments for, and the limitations placed on, open justice, see E. Barendt, *Freedom of Speech* (2nd edn., Oxford University Press, 2005) 338–351; Rowbottom (n 1) 132–154; Fenwick and Phillipson (n 1) chs. 4 and 5; E. Barendt, L. Hitchens and R. Craufurd Smith, *Media Law: Text, Cases and Materials* (Longman, 2014) ch. 13; Robertson QC and Nicol QC (n 1) 12–18.

[36]   [1913] AC 417. See also *Guardian News and Media Ltd v City of Westminster Magistrates' Court* [2012] EWCA Civ 420; [2013] QB 618 per Toulson LJ at [2].

[37]   *Scott v Scott* [1913] AC 417, 477.

[38]   Ibid.

[39]   For instance, where access to legal proceedings may result in the risk of harm to others, the court will conduct a proportionality test to decide whether access should be granted or denied. See *Guardian News and Media Ltd v City of Westminster Magistrates' Court* [2012] EWCA Civ 420; [2013] QB 618, [85].

[40]   *R (on the application of Ewing) v Cardiff and Newport Crown Court* [2016] EWHC 183 (Admin), [16]. It has also been adopted by other Commonwealth countries and the United States: see Barendt (n 35) 338 and *Richmond Newspapers v Virginia* 448 US 555 (1980) respectively.

[41]   Fenwick and Phillipson (n 1) 167; I. Cram, *A Virtue Less Cloistered: Courts, Speech and Constitutions* (Hart Publishing, 2002) 10–11.

In *Attorney-General v Leveller Magazine Limited*[42] Lord Diplock divided open justice into two elements: (i) that proceedings are 'held in open court to which the press and public are admitted'; and (ii) the freedom to publish 'fair and accurate reports of proceedings that have taken place in court'.[43] The first element essentially refers to the right to sit in the public gallery and hear what is happening in court.[44] The second element is the right to report on court proceedings. Therefore, subject to any reporting restrictions, the media is free to publish what has been said in open court, without legal obstacle.

The important role played by the media in conveying events to the public was emphasised by Lord Reed in *A v BBC*,[45] in which his Lordship stated that as 'the media are the conduit through which most members of the public receive information about court proceedings, it follows that the principle of open justice is inextricably linked to the freedom of the media to report on court proceedings'.[46] Moreover, in *Sunday Times v United Kingdom*[47] the ECtHR held that 'not only do the media have the task of imparting such information and ideas [relating to the settlement of disputes in court]: the public also has a right to receive them'.[48] Consequently, media freedom serves the ends of justice through its facilitation of open justice, by virtue of the informing and scrutinising roles that it plays,[49] the exercise of which enhances the moral authority of the justice system.[50] According to Helen Fenwick and Gavin Phillipson, reporting restrictions that are in place to ensure the fairness of court hearings are intended to secure the integrity of the criminal and civil justice systems. However, the legal significance attached to the principle is also aimed at ensuring such integrity, and a key reason for insisting upon open justice is to allow for media scrutiny of the justice system.[51] Indeed, in *R (on the application of Mohamed) v Secretary of State for Foreign and Commonwealth*

---

[42] [1979] AC 440.

[43] Ibid 450.

[44] Including taking notes. See *R (on the application of Ewing) v Cardiff and Newport Crown Court* [2016] EWHC 183 (Admin).

[45] [2014] UKSC 25; [2015] AC 588.

[46] Ibid [26].

[47] App. no. 6538/74 (1979–1980) 2 EHRR 245.

[48] Ibid [65]. See also *Axel Springer v Germany (No. 1)* [2012] App. no. 39954/08, [80], [96] in which the ECtHR stated that '[i]t is inconceivable that there can be no prior or contemporaneous discussion of the subject matter of trials, be it in specialised journals, in the general press or amongst the public at large: the public have an interest in being informed ... about criminal proceedings'.

[49] Fenwick and Phillipson (n 1) 167–168.

[50] T. Allan, 'Procedural Fairness and the Duty of Respect' (1988) 18 *Oxford Journal of Legal Studies* 507.

[51] Fenwick and Phillipson (n 1) 167–168.

Affairs[52] Lord Judge CJ stated that '[i]n reality very few citizens can scrutinise the judicial process: that scrutiny is performed by the media, whether newspapers or television, acting on behalf of the body of citizens'.[53]

As a general rule, the principle of open justice is available to anybody[54] but, because of the legal privileges bestowed upon media actors by the enhanced right to media freedom, the media is in a particularly strong position to take advantage of the rights that it provides.[55] As set out in Chapter 4, media freedom provides institutional protection for media actors. This includes a positive obligation placed on the state to facilitate media reporting and newsgathering by allowing those acting as media to access court proceedings and documents.[56] Thus, unlike the general public, an application by a member of the media to report on court proceedings where access has been limited and requires permission will be given considerable weight.[57] The media's enhanced right to access legal proceedings in situations that are otherwise unavailable to the general public has been enshrined within various pieces of legislation,[58] and, more recently, has found its way into Practice Guidance relating to the use

---

[52]   [2010] EWCA Civ 158; [2011] QB 218.

[53]   Ibid [38]. See also *R v Felixstowe Justices, ex parte Leigh* [1987] QB 582 in which Watkins LJ stated at 591: 'no-one nowadays surely can doubt that [the journalist's] presence in court for the purpose of reporting proceedings conducted therein is indispensable. Without him, how is the public to be informed of how justice is being administered in our courts?'

[54]   *Attorney-General v Leveller Magazine Limited* [1979] AC 440, per Lord Diplock at 449–450; *R v Re Crook (Tim)* (1991) 93 Cr. App. R. 17, 24. The same applies to public meetings, as illustrated by Regulation 4(6) of the Local Authorities (Executive Arrangements) (Meetings and Access to Information) (England) Regulations 2012, which provides a right for anyone wanting to report proceedings to be 'afforded reasonable facilities for taking their report'. See also *Cape Intermediate Holdings Limited v Dring (for and on behalf of Asbestos Victims Support Groups Forum UK)* [2019] UKSC 38 in which the Supreme Court held that the public should be allowed access not only to parties' submissions and arguments, but also to documents which have been placed before the court and referred to during the hearing. Thus, even if the judge has not been asked to read the document and/or has not done so, provided the document has been referred to during the hearing, there is a prima facie right of access (albeit this is subject to an application by the party seeking access to the document).

[55]   Rowbottom (n 1) 131.

[56]   See Chapter 4 section 3.3.4.

[57]   Rowbottom (n 1) 131.

[58]   For example, see section 37 of the Children and Young Persons Act 1933, which allows the media access to the court when a child or young person is giving evidence in cases involving indecency; section 25 of the Youth Justice and Criminal Evidence Act 1999, which allows the court to exclude the public and the media, other than one sole representative, from the hearing when children give evidence in cases relating to sexual offences.

242

of 'live forms' of communication: members of the media are able to use social media to report on court proceedings without the court's permission, so long as the proceedings are open to the public and there are no reporting restrictions in place. To the contrary, if a member of the public wanted to live-tweet about a trial they would need to ask the court's permission to activate their laptop, mobile phone or tablet to send the messages.[59]

Despite the constitutional importance attached to the media's role in reporting on court proceedings, in recent years there has been a decline in the traditional institutional media performing this task due to it no longer being profitable.[60] This accords with the observations made in Chapters 2 and 3 that, in some cases, the traditional institutional press's focus has shifted onto commercially viable stories that sell and/or are aligned to the political agenda of owners, as opposed to reporting on matters of public concern.[61] Arguably, citizen journalists are perfectly placed to fill this gap left by the institutional press. However, as explained above, under the current rules, unless the court recognised the citizen journalist as 'media' they would be afforded the same status as the general public and would, therefore, not be subject to the same advantages in securing access to certain legal proceedings, or being able to report those proceedings in the same way, as the traditional media.[62] Thus, at present, the institutional press's reluctance to report on legal proceedings, combined with the current rules on accessing certain hearings and documents being unfavourable to citizen journalists, creates a democratic deficit as, in situations where access to the court is limited, the public is not able to benefit from its constitutional right to open justice through the conduit of the media.

---

[59] Lord Judge, *Practice Guidance: The Use of Live Text-Based Forms of Communications (Including Twitter) from Court for the Purposes of Fair and Accurate Reporting* [2012] 1 WLR 12.

[60] Rowbottom (n 1) 131, 151–152.

[61] See Chapter 2 section 3.3.2 and Chapter 3 section 4. See also C. Calvert and M. Torres, 'Putting the Shock Value in First Amendment Jurisprudence: When Freedom for the Citizen-Journalist Watchdog Trumps the Right of Informational Privacy on the Internet' (2011) 13(2) *Vanderbilt Journal of Entertainment and Technology Law* 323, 341; J. Curran and J. Seaton, *Power Without Responsibility – Press, Broadcasting and the Internet in Britain* (7th edn., Routledge, 2010) 96–98; J. Curran, 'Mass Media and Democracy' in J. Curran and M. Gurevitch, *Mass Media and Society* (Edward Arnold, 1991) 86; T. Gibbons, 'Building Trust in Press Regulation: Obstacles and Opportunities' (2013) 5(2) *Journal of Media Law* 202, 214; T. Gibbons, 'Freedom of the Press: Ownership and Editorial Values' [1992] *Public Law* 279, 286–287, 296; T. Gibbons, 'Conceptions of the Press and the Functions of Regulation' (2016) 22(5) *Convergence: The International Journal of Research into New Media Technologies* 484, 485; R. McChesney, *Rich Media, Poor Democracy* (University of Illinois Press, 1999) 275.

[62] Rowbottom (n 1) 151–152.

Contempt of court and defamation 243

The adoption of the media-as-a-constitutional-component concept would provide a mechanism to deal with this deficit. However, before discussing this it is appropriate to briefly deal with the second issue that could stem from the intersection of online expression and open justice, namely how this has the potential to undermine the fairness of trials to a far greater extent than the traditional media.

In *Attorney-General v Associated Newspapers Limited*,[63] Moses LJ remarked on the 'viral nature' of online communication, stating that '[o]nce information is published on the internet, it is difficult if not impossible completely to remove it' and, consequently, that there is a 'need to recognise that instant news requires instant and effective protection for the integrity of a criminal trial'.[64] Fuelled by prosecutions for contempt of court arising from the use of social media,[65] Moses LJ's comments were indicative of growing judicial concern over seemingly unstoppable online expression[66] and its impact on criminal trials.[67] Indeed, in 2011, then-Attorney-General Dominic Grieve stated:

Unlike major news organisations, which on the whole act in a responsible and measured manner,[68] the inhabitants of the internet often feel themselves to be unconstrained by the laws of the land. There is a certain belief that so long as something

---

[63] [2011] EWHC 418 (Admin).

[64] Ibid [54]. Similarly, according to Ian Cram et al, there are 'obvious and ... possibly insuperable legal and other obstacles' to the robust enforcement of the law of contempt against non-traditional media. Cram, Borrie and Lowe (n 2) 687. See also Mac Sithigh (n 2) 89.

[65] For example, although coming after *Associated Newspapers*, see *Attorney-General v Harkins and Liddle* [2013] EWHC 1455 (Admin); *Attorney-General v Baines* [2013] EWHC 4326 (Admin). See generally P. Coe, 'The Social Media Paradox: An Intersection with Freedom of Expression and the Criminal Law' (2015) 24(1) *Information & Communications Technology Law* 16.

[66] Mac Sithigh (n 2) 90.

[67] *Attorney-General v Harkins and Liddle* [2013] EWHC 1455 (Admin), [22]. Similar comments were made in Australia in the context of defamation litigation. In *O'Reilly v Edgar* [2019] QSC 24 Justice Bradley, in considering the effects of social media, opined that it can make it 'impossible to track the scandal, to know what quarters the poison may reach'.

[68] As argued throughout this book, this is not always the case. Incidentally, this comment seems to conflict with Grieve's earlier statement in the same speech:
I have been concerned, even before I was appointed Attorney-General, at what I perceived to be the increasing tendency of the press to test the boundaries of what was acceptable over the reporting of criminal cases. At times it appeared to me the press had lost any sense of internal constraint and felt able, indeed entitled, to print what they wished, shielded by the right to 'freedom of expression' without any of the concomitant responsibilities (Grieve (n 2)).

244 *Media freedom in the age of citizen journalism*

is published in cyberspace there is no need to respect the laws of contempt or libel. This is mistaken.[69]

Grieve's statement is echoed by Leveson LJ's comments that bloggers can, if they choose, act with impunity[70] as the internet is a 'Wild West, law free zone',[71] and is indicative of the concerns with, and the problems created by, libertarianism as the de facto communication theory for online speech, which were dealt with in Chapter 5.[72] Clearly, people publishing information online about legal proceedings can detrimentally impact the fairness of trials. However, members of the general public who, for example, publish the name and/or pictures of a complainant in a criminal trial may well be in contempt of court but, in most cases, this will not fatally or even critically affect the trial as, due to their (often relatively) limited following, if dealt with quickly, any damage to the integrity of the trial will be limited. The same cannot be said for many (although not all) citizen journalists, who may enjoy significant follower numbers across a variety of 'immediate, pervasive and accessible' platforms,[73] and who may also be publishing anonymously or pseudonymous-ly.[74] Moreover, as advanced throughout this book, citizen journalists have become trusted sources of news and, in some instances, are more trusted by the public to deliver the news in an unbiased and impartial way than the traditional institutional press and wider media.[75] This trust extends to other media actors, including the traditional institutional media, who increasingly rely on citizen journalists as a source of news. This symbiotic relationship creates a cycle in which material published by citizen journalists is recycled by other forms of media regardless of its accuracy and/or legality.[76] The fact that the material

---

[69] Ibid.

[70] Lord Justice Leveson, *An Inquiry into the Culture, Practices and Ethics of the Press: Report*, HC 780, November 2012, 736, [3.2].

[71] A.C. Yen, 'Western Frontier or Feudal Society? Metaphors and Perceptions of Cyberspace' (2002) 17 *Berkeley Technology Law Journal* 1207.

[72] See Chapter 5 sections 2 and 3 for detailed analysis of libertarianism and why it should be rejected as a normative framework for media speech.

[73] See Chapter 5 section 3.2.

[74] See Chapter 7. See generally P. Coe, 'Anonymity and Pseudonymity: Free Speech's Problem Children' (2018) 22(2) *Media & Arts Law Review* 173.

[75] In particular, see Chapter 2 section 3.3.2. For detailed discussion on the concept of trust and how this relates to regulation, see generally Gibbons, 'Building Trust in Press Regulation' (n 61) 202–219.

[76] As observed by Thomas Gibbons, this is particularly evident in the context of the pressurised 24-hour news environment within which many media actors operate, which gives rise to 'a concomitant incapacity to avoid recycling old material, investigate thoroughly, or check accuracy' ibid 214. See also N. Davies, *Flat Earth News* (Vintage, 2009) 370–371; R.L. Weaver, *From Gutenberg to the Internet: Free Speech,*

Contempt of court and defamation 245

has been republished by a 'trusted' media outlet has a 'halo effect' in that it adds credence to the citizen journalist and the material itself, thereby, in some instances, creating a perpetual cycle of misinformation.[77] Furthermore, the recycling of information means that potentially damaging material, including, in a contempt of court context, material that could undermine the integrity of a trial, is distributed far more widely by virtue of 'support' from other media outlets.

2.2 Citizen Journalism, the Media-as-a-constitutional-component Concept and the Harmonisation of Media Freedom and Open Justice

The previous section has established how citizen journalism could support open justice by filling the gap left by the traditional institutional media, and press in particular, albeit, due to the current rules on accessing certain court hearings being unfavourable to citizen journalists, there exists a democratic deficit. However, with online expression comes an increased risk of the integrity of trials being undermined. This section will consider how the media-as-a-constitutional-component concept provides a normative framework that would overcome these issues, thereby harmonising media freedom and open justice.

First, pursuant to the concept and its functional definition of media set out in Chapter 5,[78] citizen journalists are operating as media so long as they are publishing material of value to the public sphere, while complying with the standards of professional behaviour and norms of discourse introduced in Chapter 5[79] and explored in detail in Chapter 6. The concept and its social responsibility foundations require that the material published by media actors derives from accurate, and the best available, information and that the newsgathering process has been conducted responsibly and ethically.[80] In the context of reporting on court proceedings, adherence to these standards and norms would require the media actor to provide an accurate, balanced and transparent report that complies with any legal obligations laid down by the court.

In principle at least, recognition that citizen journalists are acting as media would give them the same positive rights of access as the traditional insti-

---

Advancing Technology, and the Implications for Democracy (2nd edn., Carolina Academic Press, 2019) 202.

[77] This issue has been discussed throughout this book. However, see, in particular, Chapter 3 section 5.3.

[78] See Chapter 5 sections 4 and 5.

[79] See Chapter 5 sections 4.1 and 4.2.

[80] See Chapter 6 section 3.

246 *Media freedom in the age of citizen journalism*

tutional media to those court proceedings[81] that are off-limits to the public, which could, in theory, help to eliminate, or at least reduce, the democratic deficit. By way of analogy, this recognition would accord with the treatment of citizen journalists by the Court of Justice of the European Union in the context of data protection jurisprudence,[82] which has afforded citizen journalists the same status, and the ability to take advantage of the same exemptions, as the traditional institutional media.[83]

Secondly, a media actor's appetite for engagement with the standards and norms imposed by the concept provides an objective benchmark for a court, or other stakeholders in other contexts, to assess the actor's commitment to responsible journalism. The corollary to this is that citizen journalists who do not adhere to them are not acting as media and are therefore not able to avail themselves of the enhanced right to media freedom and the benefits this bestows upon its beneficiaries, including accessing legal proceedings and documents off limits to the general public.[84]

Finally, it is argued in Chapter 9 that because the concept and its normative and philosophical foundation provide a mechanism for citizen journalists to be classed as media, and therefore benefit from media freedom, as media actors they should be subject to a similar regulatory regime as the traditional institutional press. In that chapter, a framework for a new voluntary regulatory scheme that is highly incentivised and would effectively capture citizen journalists is advanced.[85] Membership of the scheme is dependent on the media actor, whether they be a member of the traditional institutional press or a citizen journalist, publishing material and behaving in accordance with the concept and its inherent standards and norms.[86] Thus, a recommended non-statutory incentive is that membership of the scheme would be a mark of responsibility that would demonstrate to the outside world the media actor's

---

[81] See Chapter 4 section 3.3.4 for a discussion on media freedom and positive rights.

[82] Case C-73/07 *Tietosuojavaltuutettu v Satakunnan Markkinapörssi Oy, Satamedia Oy (Satamedia)* ; Case C-345/17 *Sergejs Buivids v Datu valsts inspekcija*.

[83] The *Satamedia* and *Buivids* cases relate to the applicability of Article 9 of the Data Protection Directive (95/46/EC) to citizen journalists as it provides a special purposes exemption for journalism. A slightly modified version of this exemption was found in section 32 of the now-repealed Data Protection Act 1998 and has subsequently been imported into Article 85 of the General Data Protection Regulation and the Data Protection Act 2018, by virtue of Part 5, paragraph 26 of Schedule 2 to the Act. See Chapter 9 section 3 for a brief discussion on this exemption.

[84] See Chapter 4 for a discussion on how media freedom protects speech and the media as an institution.

[85] See Chapter 9 section 6.

[86] Chapter 9 section 6.1.

Contempt of court and defamation   247

appetite for accountability. This would confer upon them a reputational advantage over non-members as they would be awarded something like a kitemark to demonstrate their compliance with the scheme.[87] A second non-statutory incentive is access to training. This would include providing members with a requisite level of knowledge to report appropriately on court proceedings.[88] A recommended statutory incentive is that members would have access to court proceedings and documents otherwise closed to the public.[89] Therefore, notwithstanding the arguments set out in the previous paragraphs, only members of this new regulatory scheme could access these legal proceedings. This would provide the courts, at the very least, with reassurance that citizen journalists reporting on restricted legal proceedings are adhering to the same objective standards as the traditional institutional press and that they belong to a group that is committed to acting responsibly and ethically.

3   DEFAMATION

In a contempt of court context the previous section has talked a lot about responsible journalism and the benefits of media actors adhering to the standards of professional behaviour and norms of discourse inherent within the media-as-a-constitutional-component concept. As that section established, the concept can play a vital role in supporting citizen journalists' facilitation of open justice, thereby enabling the public to realise a constitutional right. Incidentally, this supports both the rule of law and democracy. This section will argue that the concept can play an equally important role in promoting and protecting media freedom in the context of the law of defamation.

3.1   Serious Harm, Defamation Litigation and Costs

Section 1(1) of the Defamation Act 2013 provides that for a statement to be defamatory it must have caused, or is likely to cause, the claimant's reputation

---

[87]   Chapter 9 section 6.5.
[88]   Ibid.
[89]   Chapter 9 Section 6.4.

248 *Media freedom in the age of citizen journalism*

serious harm.[90] The test is not defined or explained explicitly by the Act.[91] Therefore, it has been left to case law to interpret it, as illustrated by the high-profile judicial scrutiny it received in the *Lachaux v Independent Print Limited* litigation.[92]

Prior to the enactment of the 2013 Act, pursuant to Tugendhat J's judgment in *Thornton v Telegraph Media Group Ltd*,[93] for a statement to be defamatory, it had to cross a 'threshold of seriousness'. Accordingly, the appropriate test was whether a statement had a tendency to cause 'substantial' reputational harm.[94] In the *Lachaux* High Court proceedings[95] Warby J's interpretation of section 1(1) was that it does more than just raise the threshold from a tendency to cause 'substantial' to 'serious' reputational harm and that claimants are required to go beyond showing a tendency to harm reputation.[96] This means that claimants have to adduce extrinsic evidence demonstrating as a fact that either serious harm has occurred or, on the balance of probabilities, that it is more likely than not to occur,[97] unless the meaning of the words complained of

---

[90] For bodies that 'trade for profit' this is qualified by section 1(2), which provides that to meet the serious harm threshold companies need to demonstrate actual or likely serious financial loss. In *Gubarev v Orbis Business Intelligence Limited* [2020] EWHC 2912 (QB) Warby J confirmed that in cases involving bodies trading for profit: (i) The claimant is required to show both serious harm to its reputation and serious financial loss that is consequent on the reputational harm [42]. (ii) Financial loss is not necessarily the same thing as loss of revenue. The court must be concerned with the claimant's overall position, asking itself whether a loss of profit has been established. The loss must be 'serious', which is an ordinary English word requiring no elaboration. However, whether loss is serious depends on context [43]. (iii) Financial loss could be established with something less than strict proof – inference may suffice but it must be based on 'a sound evidential basis' [44]–[45].

[91] For analysis of the uncertainty this has created in relation to both the section 1(1) serious harm test and the section 1(2) serious financial loss test, see P. Coe, 'An Analysis of Three Distinct Approaches to Using Defamation to Protect Corporate Reputation from Australia, England and Wales, and Canada' (2021) 41 *Legal Studies* 111; P. Coe, 'A Comparative Analysis of the Treatment of Corporate Reputation in Australia and the UK' in P. Wragg and A. Koltay (eds), *Research Handbook on Comparative Privacy & Defamation Law* (Edward Elgar Publishing, 2020); P. Coe, 'The Defamation Act 2013: We Need to Talk About Corporate Reputation' (2015) 4 *Journal of Business Law* 313; D. Acheson, 'Corporate Reputation Under the European Convention on Human Rights' (2018) 10(1) *Journal of Media Law* 49; D. Acheson, 'Empirical Insights into Corporate Defamation: An Analysis of Cases Decided 2004–2013' (2016) 8(1) *Journal of Media Law* 32.

[92] [2015] EWHC 2242 (QB); [2017] EWCA Civ 1334 (CA); [2019] UKSC 27.

[93] [2010] EWHC 1414 (QB).

[94] Ibid [90]–[92].

[95] [2015] EWHC 2242 (QB).

[96] Ibid [45].

[97] Ibid.

Contempt of court and defamation

is so serious that serious reputational harm is inevitable and can therefore be inferred.[98] The judgment represented a significant departure from the common law, under which inferences as to the seriousness of the allegations could routinely be drawn from the offending words themselves. Therefore, it presented a situation where libel is not actionable per se, as had long been thought to be the case at common law.[99]

According to the Court of Appeal,[100] Warby J's interpretation of section 1(1) represented a radical shift in the law. Therefore, it was effectively reversed by the Court on the basis that there is no mention in the Act of Parliament's intention to alter the long-held view that libel is actionable per se.[101] Consequently, in conflict with Warby J's judgment, the Court of Appeal's decision determined that, ordinarily, claimants do not need to adduce extrinsic evidence of actual damage in order to show that words complained of are 'likely to cause' serious reputational harm; inferences of a likelihood of serious harm may continue in line with the common law, in that they can be drawn from the words themselves,[102] and not just in the most extreme cases, as was suggested in *Cooke and Midland Heart Limited v MGN Limited and Trinity Mirror Midlands* by Bean J and in *Ames v The Spamhaus Project* and *Lachaux* by Warby J.[103]

Ultimately, the Court held that section 1(1) had merely raised the threshold from one of 'substantiality' to one of 'seriousness', with the latter conveying something 'rather more weighty' than the former,[104] and that the words

---

[98] Ibid [57]. For example, if the words purport to identify an individual as involved in a conspiracy to murder or committing a serious sexual crime. In respect of inferential proof, Warby J relied upon Bean J's judgment in *Cooke and Midland Heart Limited v MGN Limited and Trinity Mirror Midlands Limited* [2014] EWHC 2831 (QB), who limited the doctrine of inferential proof to cases 'so obviously likely to cause harm to a person's reputation.' In these instances 'a claimant could rely on inferential proof' [43]. This was approved by Warby J in *Ames v The Spamhaus Project* [2015] EWHC 127 (QB) and later developed in *Lachaux*, in which Warby J held: 'As recognised in *Cooke* and *Ames* ... the serious harm requirement is capable of being satisfied by an inferential case, based on the gravity of the imputation and the extent and nature of its readership or audience.'

[99] *Ratcliffe v Evans* [1892] 2 QB 524, 528 per Bowen J; *English and Scottish Co-Operative v Odhams Press Ltd* [1940] 1 KB 440, 461 per Goddard LJ.

[100] [2017] EWCA Civ 1334 (CA) per Davis, Sharpe and McFarlane LJJJ. The leading judgment was given by Davis LJ, with which Sharpe and McFarlane LJJ agreed.

[101] Ibid [56]–[63].

[102] Ibid [72].

[103] See n 94.

[104] *Lachaux v Independent Print Limited* [2017] EWCA Civ 1334 (CA), [44] per Davis LJ.

'is likely to cause' should be taken as connoting a tendency to cause.[105] Consequently, by enshrining a modified version of the *Thornton* test within the Act,[106] the judgment also had the effect of raising the bar for bringing a claim.

Perhaps unsurprisingly, the Court of Appeal's decision was the subject of a further appeal to the Supreme Court.[107] The appeal was heard by Lords Sumption, Kerr, Wilson, Hodge and Briggs on 13 and 14 November 2018, and the judgment was handed down in June 2019. The Court unanimously overturned the Court of Appeal's interpretation of 'serious harm', thereby preferring the analysis of Warby J.[108] It held that section 1 not only raises the threshold of seriousness from that in *Jameel v Dow Jones & Co Inc*[109] and *Thornton*,[110] but requires its application to be determined by reference to the actual facts about its impact, not merely the meaning of the words.[111] In doing so, the Court held that the Court of Appeal's analysis gave little or no effect to the language of section 1 and was internally contradictory.[112]

It is clear from the *Lachaux* litigation that mass media publication is likely to be an important factor in determining whether the seriousness threshold has been met.[113] This could have serious repercussions for citizen journalists, who can, and often do, reach mass audiences, either as a primary publisher or as a result of their material being recycled by other media actors. Defending defamation claims can be complex and expensive and, if unsuccessful, can result in the payment of significant damages.[114] Indeed, even determining the meaning

---

[105] Ibid [50].

[106] Ibid [49]–[50].

[107] *Lachaux v Independent Print Ltd* [2019] UKSC 27.

[108] Ibid [20], per Lord Sumption.

[109] [2005] QB 946.

[110] [2010] EWHC 1414 (QB).

[111] *Lachaux v Independent Print Ltd* [2019] UKSC 27, [12] per Lord Sumption.

[112] Ibid [20].

[113] *Lachaux v Independent Print Limited* [2017] EWCA Civ 1334 (CA), [65] per Davis LJ; *Cooke and Midland Heart Limited v MGN Limited and Trinity Mirror Midlands* [2014] EWHC 2831 (QB) per Bean J at [43]; Rowbottom (n 1) 49.

[114] The government has commenced section 44 of the Legal Aid, Sentencing and Punishment of Offenders Act 2012 (LASPO) in respect of 'publication and privacy proceedings'. Section 44 was generally brought into force in April 2013, pursuant to the LASPO (Commencement No. 5 and Saving Provision) Order 2013, SI/2013/77. However, as the 2013 Commencement Order made clear, the government deliberately opted not to bring section 44 into force in respect of 'publication and privacy proceedings'. These proceedings were defined in Article 1 of the 2013 Commencement Order as 'proceedings for (a) defamation (b) malicious falsehood; (c) breach of confidence involving publication to the general public (d) misuse of private information or (e) harassment, where the defendant is a news publisher'. Thus, until 6 April 2019 when, pursuant to Article 2 of the LASPO (Commencement No. 13) Order 2018 SI/2018/1287, section 44 commenced in respect of 'publication and privacy proceedings' (defined in

Contempt of court and defamation

of a defamatory statement can require preliminary hearings before the full trial, which increase costs further.[115] The traditional institutional media tend to have the financial and legal resources at their disposal to prevent defamation litigation from arising in the first place, by virtue of pre-publication advice and, in the event of being sued, to deal with defamation claims and absorb legal costs and awards of damages. To the contrary, most citizen journalists are not going to be in the same position. Thus, citizen journalists are vulnerable to wealthier claimants who may wish to silence them, regardless of the truth of the alleged defamatory statement. As discussed throughout this book, citizen journalists are no longer an outlier of free speech. Rather, they are central to how we receive and impart information and ideas and are, therefore, critical to a functioning and healthy democracy. Consequently, if citizen journalists are prevented from publishing material of value to the public sphere through fear of the costs of litigation, or because they do not have the resources to obtain pre-publication advice, or to appropriately deal with defamation claims, then a vital democratic component is potentially lost. Thus, the following section will consider how the media-as-a-constitutional-component concept can go some way to alleviate these issues through its application to specific defences.

3.2   The Media-as-a-constitutional-component Concept and Defences

The Defamation Act 2013 and cognate legislation[116] provide for a number of defences to defamation claims. This section will argue that the standards of professional behaviour and norms of discourse imposed by the media-as-a-constitutional-component concept support the operation of these defences and, in turn, media freedom, specifically the defences of truth,[117] honest opinion[118] and publication on a matter of public interest.[119]

Article 1(2) of the 2018 Commencement Order in exactly the same terms as Article 1 of the 2013 Commencement Order) claimants could still recover Conditional Fee Agreement success fees from the defendant in these types of proceedings. The decision reflects the ECtHR's decision in *Mirror Group Newspapers Limited v United Kingdom* App. no. 39401/04 (2011) 53 EHRR 5 that success fees violated Article 10 ECHR.

[115]   Robertson QC and Nicol QC (n 1) 82–83.

[116]   Defamation Act 1996.

[117]   Defamation Act 2013, section 2.

[118]   Ibid, section 3.

[119]   Ibid, section 4. Arguably, it can also help with the operation of the defences for secondary publishers pursuant to section 10 of the 2013 Act and section 1 of the Defamation Act 1996, as media actors that are members of the regulatory regime set out in Chapter 9 would be easily identifiable.

3.2.1 Truth

Section 2 of the 2013 Act provides a defence to an action for defamation if the defendant can show that the statement complained of is substantially true. Consequently, the defence applies a reverse burden of proof, which means that unless the defendant can prove that the defamatory statement is true on the balance of probabilities, it is presumed to be false. According to Sir David Eady, powerful institutions such as the media should not benefit from an assumption that 'their allegations, however serious, are true' and, therefore, the imposition of the reverse burden reflects the 'awesome power of the press' to damage individuals' reputations.[120] Thus, according to Rowbottom, 'it is the power of the media to damage a name that invokes the "innocent until proven guilty" principle and it is reasonable to expect the media to take on the risk of any inaccuracies'.[121]

Despite the rationale behind the reverse burden, it has been subject to criticism for chilling media speech and protecting undeserved reputations. For example, in Tony Weir's view '[t]his absurd reversal of the normal burden of proof encourages claimants to sue even if they know that what the defendant said was perfectly correct'.[122] In the context of citizen journalism, and the critical role that citizen journalists now play in free speech and the health of the public sphere, the concern articulated by Weir, and the damage that can flow from this, is arguably more acute. As discussed above, citizen journalists tend not to have the same 'awesome power', at least in financial terms and access to legal resources, at their disposal as the traditional institutional media.[123] As a result they are more vulnerable to an imbalance in power and therefore more susceptible to litigation between themselves and wealthy claimants wishing to silence them. Thus, although in *McVicar v United Kingdom*,[124] in a traditional media setting, the ECtHR found that the reverse burden of proof is compatible with Article 10 ECHR,[125] it is arguable that would not be the outcome if applied to citizen journalism.

Notwithstanding the above, the reverse burden is applicable to any defendant wishing to use the defence. As Robertson QC and Nicol QC suggest,

---

[120] D. Eady, 'Defamation: Some Recent Developments and Non-Developments' in M. Saville and R. Susskind (eds), *Essays in Honour of Sir Brian Neil: The Quintessential Judge* (LexisNexis, 2003) 155.

[121] Rowbottom (n 1) 54.

[122] T. Weir, *Tort Law* (Oxford University Press, 2002) 168.

[123] See section 3.1. However, it has been recognised throughout this book that citizen journalists do have significant power in terms of followers, trust, reach and the dissemination of speech.

[124] App. no. 46311/99 (2002) 35 EHRR 22.

[125] Ibid [83]–[87]. This case concerned the reverse burden under the common law defence of justification, which was abolished by section 2 of the 2013 Act.

Contempt of court and defamation

proving the truth of a defamatory imputation on a balance of probabilities can be challenging[126] for any media actor. Accordingly, for investigative journalism that, for example, requires research into areas lacking transparency, or the use of confidential sources or piecemeal evidence, or evidence that would be inadmissible in court, there is a significant risk of error.[127] Thus, the defence encourages media actors to operate diligently and ethically, to maintain a proper paper trail and to verify the veracity of their sources.[128] Operating in this way accords with the standards of professional behaviour and norms of discourse inherent in the media-as-constitutional-component concept[129] and the jurisprudence of the ECtHR.[130] Adherence to these standards and norms is particularly important for citizen journalists, who do not have the same institutional infrastructure behind them to support them in these activities as the traditional institutional media. By adhering to the behaviours imposed by the concept, they stand a better chance of being able to successfully run the defence by overcoming the reverse burden of proof. Moreover, as explained in section 2.2, membership of the regulatory framework advanced in Chapter 9 is dependent upon the media actor operating in a way that accords with the behaviours required to at least make it possible to run the truth defence successfully. This adherence to the concept's behaviours and norms is 'formalised' through the recognition that the regulatory scheme provides. Additionally, membership of the scheme would give members access to an infrastructure that will provide support, in the form of legal advice and training on how to satisfy the requirements imposed by the various defences to defamation claims, including the section 2 reverse burden of proof, and the section 3 defence of honest opinion and the section 4 defence of publication on a matter of publication interest, both of which are considered below.

3.2.2   Honest opinion

A defendant wishing to run the defence must meet three conditions. First, section 3(2) states that the defendant must show that the defamatory statement was one of opinion rather than fact.[131] A nuance of this condition animates the complexity of the defence. Some statements of fact may be defended as

---

[126]   Robertson QC and Nicol QC (n 1) 114–115.

[127]   Rowbottom (n 1) 54.

[128]   Ibid.

[129]   See Chapter 6 section 3.

[130]   *Alithia Publishing Company Ltd and Constantinides v Cyprus* [2008] App. no. 17550/03, [66]; *Gutiérrez Suárez v Spain* [2010] App. no. 16023/07, [38].

[131]   According to *Telnikoff v Matusevitch* [1992] 2 AC 343, in assessing this, rather than assuming the reader had any particular background knowledge, the court will look at the article in isolation.

expressions of opinion if the respective statement's deductions or conclusions can be inferred by other facts that are sufficiently stated or indicated and it is obvious to the reasonable person that the publisher could not have had direct knowledge of the matter and, therefore, must have been expressing an opinion or inference.[132] Secondly, under section 3(3), the statement must indicate the 'basis of the opinion'. Thirdly, pursuant to section 3(4)(a) and (b) the statement must be one that an honest person could have held on the basis of 'any fact which existed at the time the statement complained of was published'[133] or 'anything asserted to be a fact' contained within a privileged statement 'published before the statement complained of'.[134] Finally, pursuant to section 3(5), the defence is defeated if the claimant can show that the defendant did not hold the opinion.

Section 3(4)(b) concerns the position of the publisher who bases an opinion on facts published by somebody else. If those facts prove to be false, the publisher of the opinion exposes themselves to liability and will effectively be asked to prove the validity of the privilege by proxy,[135] which may prove impossible.[136] According to *Gatley on Libel and Slander* this creates a problem for 'social media commentators' as the way in which section 3(4)(b) is drafted significantly diminishes the utility of the defence for publishers who base their opinions on facts published elsewhere.[137] By extension the same argument applies to citizen journalists and also, in some circumstances, to institutional journalists, by virtue of their symbiotic relationship and its inherent recycling of material. The media-as-a-constitutional-component concept's standards of professional behaviour and norms of discourse require media actors to check their sources thoroughly before publication.[138] Thus, adherence to the concept can go some way to reduce citizen journalists not being able to rely on the defence because they are unable to satisfy this condition, as those conforming to its standards and operating within the regulatory framework advanced in Chapter 9[139] are more likely to have undertaken the necessary checks to ensure the veracity of the source/material they are using and, as discussed below, to

---

[132] M. Collins, *Collins on Defamation* (Oxford University Press, 2014) [9.12]. See also the Defamation Act 2013 Explanatory Notes, [21].

[133] Defamation Act 2013, section 3(4)(a).

[134] Ibid section 3(4)(b).

[135] A. Mullis and R. Parkes QC (eds), *Gatley on Libel and Slander* (12th edn., Sweet & Maxwell, 2013) [12.23].

[136] Ministry of Justice, *Government's Response to the Report of the Joint Committee on the Draft Defamation Bill* (Cm. 8295, 2012), [41].

[137] Mullis and Parkes QC (n 135) [12.23].

[138] See Chapter 6 sections 3.2 and 3.3.

[139] See Chapter 9 section 6.

have undergone appropriate training to help them carry out these checks and understand the requirements of the defence.

Clearly, although the defence of honest opinion is broad, its application is complex.[140] It requires an understanding of its nuances, particularly the difference between fact and opinion, the way in which the court assesses this, and the role that inferences can play in the operation of the defence. For the reasons discussed in the previous section, unlike the traditional media, citizen journalists may not have the training, experience or access to legal support to help them delineate between opinion or fact within their reporting or, for instance, to understand how inferences work, which, ultimately, makes them vulnerable to litigation. As explained above in relation to the defence of truth, membership of the regulatory scheme advanced in Chapter 9 would give members access to legal advice and training, which would help to navigate the section 3 conditions.

3.2.3 Publication on a matter of public interest

Section 4 of the Defamation Act 2013 has enshrined a public interest defence within statute. Prior to this, at common law, a more limited public interest defence could be found in the form of *Reynolds privilege*, which was created in *Reynolds v Times Newspapers Limited*.[141] In order to avail themselves of the defence the defendant needed to show: (i) the publication was on a matter of general interest; (ii) publication of the defamatory statement was justifiable as a contribution to the discussion of the matter concerned; and (iii) they had met the requirements of responsible journalism. To determine whether the defendant had met the 'responsible journalism' condition, Lord Nicholls provided non-exhaustive criteria for judges to consider when making their assessment. These included: (i) the 'seriousness of the allegation'; (ii) the 'source of the information'; (iii) the 'steps taken to verify the information'; (iv) '[w]hether comment was sought from the [claimant]'; and (v) the 'tone of the article'.[142]

Although, like the media-as-a-constitutional-component concept, the defence took a functional approach to defining the media,[143] which meant that it was available to anybody that could demonstrate responsible journalism by

---

[140] Rowbottom (n 1) 56.

[141] [2001] 2 AC 127 (HL). For a detailed summary of the law prior to the 2013 Act, see J. Price QC and F. McMahon (eds), *Blackstone's Guide to The Defamation Act 2013* (Oxford University Press, 2013) [5.02]–[5.49].

[142] *Reynolds v Times Newspapers Limited* [2001] 2 AC 127 (HL) per Lord Nicholls at 204–205.

[143] See Chapter 4 section 5 for the arguments against the adoption of an institutional approach to defining the media, and Chapter 5 section 5 for a functional definition of the media.

fulfilment of Lord Nicholls' criteria, the defence had serious limitations for non-institutional media actors, and even for smaller traditional institutional publishers. This is because the responsible journalism requirements were designed to follow the practices of the established mass media and were, there-fore, in practice most useful for larger members of the institutional press and, as a result, more difficult for other media actors to satisfy.[144] This is illustrated by evidence given to the Culture, Media and Sport Select Committee by Alan Rusbridger, a former editor of *The Guardian*, who described the 'long, drawn out, rather arduous way of processing stories' and the legal oversight required to comply with the *Reynolds* criteria.[145] In Rusbridger's opinion, although national newspapers had the resources to do this, the same was not true for local newspapers.[146] Arguably, if an established local newspaper would strug-gle to meet the *Reynolds* standards and to afford the legal input required, by extension it would be harder, if not impossible, for a citizen journalist to do so. How these limitations have been addressed by the current law is considered next.

The *Reynolds* defence was abolished in 2013 on the enactment of the Defamation Act 2013 and replaced by section 4. According to the Act's Explanatory Notes the intention behind the provision was to largely codify the *Reynolds* criteria and follow a negligence standard.[147] Despite this, prima facie at least, the section 4 test is formulated differently.[148] It contains two elements that the defendant must satisfy: (i) the publication 'was, or formed part of, a statement on a matter of public interest';[149] and (ii) 'the defendant reasonably believed' that it was in the public interest to publish the statement complained of.[150]

---

[144] Accordingly, in Rowbottom's opinion, '[u]nlike a political journalist in a leading newspaper, a blogger or social media commentator should not be expected to phone up a politician for comment before making a defamatory statement': Rowbottom (n 1) 90–91.

[145] House of Commons, Culture, Media and Sport Select Committee, *Press stand-ards, privacy and libel* (HC 2009-10, 362-II) evidence given on 5 May 2009 at [155], Q897.

[146] Ibid.

[147] Defamation Act 2013, Explanatory Notes, [35].

[148] Indeed, according to Lord Wilson in *Serafin v Malkiewicz and others* [2020] UKSC 23, [66], this wording in the Explanatory Notes is 'unfortunate' because it could not be said that 'the terms of the section ultimately enacted went so far as to "codify" the law even as set out in the *Jameel* [v *Wall Street Journal Europe SPRL (No.3)* [2006] UKHL 44] and *Flood* [v *Times Newspapers Ltd* [2012] UKSC 11] cases, let alone as set out in the *Reynolds* case'.

[149] Defamation Act 2013 section 4(1)(a).

[150] Ibid section 4(1)(b).

The effective employment of the defence is largely dependent on the second limb of the test and, specifically, the application of the reasonable belief standard.[151] In assessing whether that standard has been met, pursuant to section 4(2) and (4), the court 'must have regard to all the circumstances of the case' and 'make such allowance for editorial judgment as it considers appropriate' respectively. The Court of Appeal's judgment in *Economou v de Freitas*[152] has provided much-needed clarity on the scope of the reasonable belief standard and how this applies to citizen journalists.[153] First, the Court determined that in assessing the reasonableness of the defendant's belief that publication of the statement was in the public interest, the court should pay close attention to the *Reynolds* criteria set out above.[154] Secondly, when making this assessment, the court should exercise considerable flexibility, taking into account all the circumstances of the case,[155] including an appraisal of the defendant's role.[156] Consequently, the court should not be compelled to hold each defendant to the same high standard of 'responsible journalism'.[157]

The judgment determines that citizen journalists and casual social media users alike may be able to avail themselves of the section 4 defence,[158] so long as they can show that they reasonably believed that publishing the defamatory statement was in the public interest, even if their conduct might fall short of that expected of a trained and experienced journalist.[159] However, the judgment is also clear that this will not afford citizen journalists immu-

---

[151] Rowbottom (n 1) 91.

[152] [2018] EWCA Civ 2591; [2019] EMLR 7.

[153] *Economou* was endorsed by the Supreme Court in *Serafin v Malkiewicz and others* [2020] UKSC 23.

[154] *Economou v de Freitas* [2018] EWCA Civ 2591; [2019] EMLR 7, [76] per Sharp LJ.

[155] Ibid [110]. On this point, Lord Wilson, in *Serafin* (at [69]) disagreed with Sharp LJ's use of the word 'checklist' in *Economou* (at [110]) in relation to the factors identified by Lord Nicholls in *Reynolds*:

> Even if, at the time of the decision in the *Reynolds* case, it was appropriate to describe the factors identified by Lord Nicholls as a check list, it is clearly inappropriate so to regard them in the context of the statutory defence. But, as Sharp LJ proceeded to explain, that is not to deny that one or more of them may well be relevant to whether the defendant's belief was reasonable within the meaning of subsection 1(b).

[156] *Economou v de Freitas* [2018] EWCA Civ 2591; [2019] EMLR 7, [76].

[157] Ibid [104]–[110].

[158] Ibid. Sharp LJ was clear that the 'defence is not confined to the media' and is, therefore, of general application.

[159] This accords with Nicklin J's judgment in *Sooben v Badal* [2017] EWHC 2638 (QB), [32]–[34], pursuant to which the *Reynolds* criteria for responsible journalism should be applied to non-professional journalists. See Chapter 7 section 3.1.

nity to report on contentious subjects without risk, nor the freedom to rely, and fall back on, the professional judgement of others. This caveat to the judgment raises some potential challenges for citizen journalists that the media-as-a-constitutional-component concept can help to meet.

In 'considering all the circumstances of the case' to determine whether the belief was reasonable the court is likely to be influenced by the ECtHR's jurisprudence relating to the Article 10(2) ECHR 'duties and responsibilities' qualification to Article 10(1),[160] in that the media actor is 'acting in good faith in order to provide accurate and reliable information in accordance with the ethics of journalism'[161] and that they are expected to meet 'the tenets of responsible journalism'.[162] In respect of the court making appropriate allowances for 'editorial judgment', if the defendant can demonstrate that they went through the necessary pre-publication 'checks and enquiries' then greater weight is likely to be given to their 'editorial judgment'.[163] However, in line with the Strasbourg Court's decision in *Delfi AS v Estonia*,[164] in which it noted how the 'duties and responsibilities' can vary according to the role of the publisher,[165] under the *Economou* interpretation of the provision the publisher's role is critical to the assessment of the reasonable belief standard.[166] Thus, by way of example, depending on the facts[167] it seems that the experience of a citizen journalist could determine the level of adherence to appropriate journalistic conduct and the quality of the editorial judgement required to satisfy the test.

---

[160] Rowbottom (n 1) 91. According to Lord Wilson in *Serafin v Malkiewicz and others* [2020] UKSC 23 the requirements in section 4(1)(a) and (b) are 'intended, and may generally be assumed, to ensure that operation of the section generates no violation either of the claimant's right under article 8, or of the defendant's right under article 10', [74].

[161] *Bladet Tromsø and Stensaas v Norway* (2000) 29 EHRR 125, [65].

[162] *Bedat v Switzerland* (2016) 63 EHRR 15, [50].

[163] *Economou v de Freitas* [2018] EWCA Civ 2591; [2019] EMLR 7, [240] per Warby J. For example, in *Serafin*, the Supreme Court clarified the implications of a defendant failing to make pre-publication enquiries (in the instant case, in the form of not inviting the claimant to comment prior to the story being published):

> A failure to invite comment from the claimant prior to publication will no doubt always at least be the subject of consideration under subsection (1)(b) and may contribute to, perhaps even form the basis of, a conclusion that the defendant has not established that element of the defence. But it is, with respect, too strong to describe the prior invitation to comment as a 'requirement' ([76] per Lord Wilson).

[164] (2016) 62 EHRR 6.

[165] Ibid [113].

[166] In *Economou* this related to their acting as a 'mere contributor' rather than a professional journalist. *Economou v de Freitas* [2018] EWCA Civ 2591; [2019] EMLR 7, [18] per Sharp LJ.

[167] Ibid [110]. The Court affirmed that this assessment is highly fact sensitive.

Contempt of court and defamation 259

Ultimately, these factors may require the court to make additional findings of fact to determine whether the reasonable standard was met, which can increase the complexity and costs of the litigation. This is compounded by the defence's fact-sensitive approach, which creates a lack of certainty and adds to its complexity. As discussed above, because of the relative lack of legal and financial resources available to citizen journalists compared to the traditional media, this makes them less likely to meet the requirements of the defence and more vulnerable to litigious claimants.

It has been well rehearsed throughout this chapter that to be defined as media the media-as-constitutional-component concept requires actors to conform to certain standards of professional behaviour and norms of discourse, which also provide the conceptual rationale that underpins the regulatory scheme advanced in the following, and final, chapter.[168] These standards and norms are indicative of the conduct required to meet, and exceed, the conditions imposed by section 4. Media actors could go a long way in demonstrating that they are fulfilling those standards and norms, and therefore satisfying the 'reasonable belief' requirement, by virtue of their membership of the proposed regulatory scheme. Of course, the corollary to this is that actors that do not adhere to the standards imposed by the concept are not acting as media and therefore should not be assessed in the same way. Although the defence would still apply, what is required from them to make out the defence would be different, although, importantly, not any less onerous, as it would be unfair for one actor to be subject to a higher level of scrutiny than another because they are demonstrating appropriate journalistic behaviours. Rather, the concept could provide an objective benchmark to help the courts assess what standards need to be applied and whether actors are meeting those standards. It is recognised that this will not solve the problems set out above completely, but it may help to reduce the uncertainty attached to the court's assessment and therefore reduce costs.

4 CONCLUSION

Contempt of court and defamation underpin constitutionally vital principles, namely the integrity and fairness of trials and the protection of reputation. However, as established throughout this chapter, the operation of these principles can be at odds with media freedom for a variety of reasons. The media-as-a-constitutional-component concept is not designed or intended to erode the constitutionally vital functions facilitated by the law of contempt of court and defamation. To the contrary, it accepts and embraces countervailing

---

[168] See Chapter 9 section 6.

principles. Rather, this chapter has explained how the concept supports citizen journalism, and therefore media freedom, and how this can address the imbalance that these principles can create between the state or litigious claimants and the media, which is often more acute in the context of citizen journalists despite their central role in the facilitation of free speech and the democratisation of the public sphere. The role of the concept will be developed further in the following, and final, chapter, which sets out a new regulatory framework that effectively captures citizen journalists.

9. Reimagining regulation

1   INTRODUCTION

Regulation is important because, as we have seen throughout this book, press malfeasance, in relation to both its newsgathering and publication activities, has caused, and continues to cause, what Leveson LJ referred to in his *Inquiry* as 'real harm ... to real people'.[1] As Paul Wragg points out, by this, he meant that press abuses not only affect a small minority, such as celebrities, sports stars or politicians, or a group of people defined by Paul Dacre as 'the rich, the powerful and the pompous',[2] but rather a much larger group, which includes ordinary people. These people do not tend to have the financial resources required to fund litigation, nor do they have access to lawyers or reputation management and public relations advisers to help them respond to and spin negative stories.[3] According to Wragg, 'these are people that the press become fascinated with, often briefly, and whose lives are destroyed or irrevocably damaged for reasons of titillation, curiosity, or prurience'. Consequently, he says, these victims alone are reason enough to seek a satisfactory regulatory solution to the problem.[4] Therefore, the purpose of regulation is not to improve the quality of democratic discourse, rather it is about protecting the rights of 'real people'. As we shall see, however, engaging with regulation may incidentally, and ultimately, improve discourse within the public sphere and protect journalists.[5]

The sole concern of Wragg's book *A Free and Regulated Press: Defending Coercive Independent Press Regulation* is the regulation of the institutional press. However, 'real harm to real people' is no longer being caused exclusively by the institutional press: citizen journalists are just as capable of

---

[1]   Lord Justice Leveson, *An Inquiry into the Culture, Practices and Ethics of the Press: Report*, HC 780, November 2012, 50, [2.2].

[2]   See the full text of Paul Dacre's presentation to the seminar on press standards in 'Paul Dacre's speech at the Leveson inquiry – full text', *The Guardian*, 12 October 2011.

[3]   P. Wragg, *A Free and Regulated Press: Defending Coercive Independent Press Regulation* (Hart Publishing, 2020) 60–61.

[4]   Ibid 61.

[5]   See the discussion at section 6.5 on non-statutory incentives.

261

unjustifiably damaging reputations, invading personal privacy and publishing false news. The Alliance of Independent Press Councils of Europe (AIPCE)[6] is a network of national voluntary self-regulatory media Councils that was formed to deal with complaints from the public about editorial content.[7] AIPCE's Councils have, until relatively recently, only been concerned with the institutional printed press, but in recent years the Alliance's remit has been widened to cover the online iterations of the press and citizen journalists. This is because, according to AIPCE, complaints made by the public against citizen journalists for alleged breaches of journalistic ethical standards to its Councils have increased rapidly.[8] Therefore, any 'satisfactory regulatory solution' must be one which extends to citizen journalists and the institutional press. Indeed, in his *Inquiry* Leveson LJ himself was of the view that it is 'abundantly clear that, for a regulatory regime to be effective, it must be capable of delivering any perceived benefits to online publication as much as to print'[9] and that membership of a regulatory body 'should be open to all publishers on fair, reasonable and non-discriminatory terms, including making membership potentially available on different terms for different publishers'.[10] Yet, despite these statements, perhaps rather short-sightedly, his *Inquiry* was exclusively concerned with the printed press. This is perhaps not surprising when one considers that the institutional press, and mainstream media generally, have historically been the concern and subjects of regulation because of their amplification effect – in other words, their ability to 'control the message' that is received by public. Until the dawn of the internet, and the exponential development of social media platforms, which we saw in Chapter 3 have facilitated citizen journalism, there has not been a need to regulate individuals. But things have changed. As this book has established, because of the internet and social media individual publishers – citizen journalists – are, undoubtedly, exercising their 'control over the message'.

Ultimately, for reasons I discuss in section 3, the current voluntary self-regulatory regime in the UK is not satisfactory for the institutional press, let alone citizen journalists. The media-as-constitutional-component concept offers two solutions to this problem, which, in turn, help to protect 'real people from real harm' caused by the malfeasance of the institutional press and citizen journalists. First, publications that damage reputation and/or invade privacy

---

[6]   http://www.aipce.net.
[7]   The Independent Press Standards Organisation (IPSO) is a member. IMPRESS is not a member. Both regulators are discussed below.
[8]   A. Hulin, 'Citizen journalism and news blogs: why media councils don't care (yet)', *Inforrm*, 16 June 2016.
[9]   Leveson (n 1) 1587, [2.9].
[10]   Ibid 1761, [4.13].

without justification may fall short of the standards of professional behaviour and norms of discourse advanced in Chapter 6[11] as it is unlikely they would be in the public interest. As a result, these publications, in most circumstances, would not qualify for protection under media freedom.[12] Secondly, and which is the concern of this chapter, the concept provides a conceptual framework for a modified regulatory regime which could, if implemented, be attractive to, and provide robust regulation of, citizen journalists and the institutional press.[13] As I mentioned in Chapter 5, social responsibility theory allows for regulation, albeit within a purely voluntary and self-regulatory model. It is at this point that the theory and the media-as-a-constitutional-component concept, to an extent, diverge. Although the regulatory scheme advanced in this chapter draws on social responsibility values, is voluntary and will be overseen by an approved regulator (such as IMPRESS), it differs from the current blunt regulatory regime in that it provides statutory and non-statutory incentives, and has statutory powers to impose sanctions on publishers that not only go well beyond section 34 and the currently inactive section 40 of the Crime and Courts Act 2013,[14] but, significantly, would apply, and be attractive, to citizen journalists. Thus, this chapter reimagines regulation in the form of a modified, and robust, approved self-regulatory framework and in doing so it addresses the question of how citizen journalists could be regulated alongside their institutional counterparts.

The following section provides context for the rest of the chapter by briefly summarising the arguments advanced in earlier chapters that justify the creation of a regulatory framework that would be applicable and attractive to citizen journalists. As alluded to above, section 3 explains why the UK's current regulatory regime is deficient and why it largely excludes citizen journalists. Section 4 explains why mandatory regulation does not provide a viable alternative to this in respect of citizen journalism. The regulatory scheme that I advance in section 6 draws on the state of regulation in other jurisdictions. Thus, section 5 explains the rationale for this multi-jurisdictional approach. Finally, section 6 sets out the nature and scope of the reimaged regulatory scheme. The purpose of that section is not to set out the scheme's precise terms (for instance, I have not drafted a standards code). Rather, my concern is to provide a framework, or blueprint, for the scheme and to set out the principles upon which it is based and the parameters of its nature and scope.

---

[11]   See Chapter 6 section 3.
[12]   P. Coe, '(Re)embracing Social Responsibility Theory as a Basis for Media Speech: Shifting the Normative Paradigm for a Modern Media' (2018) 69(4) *Northern Ireland Legal Quarterly* 403, 418–424.
[13]   See section 6.
[14]   These provisions are discussed in the following section.

264 *Media freedom in the age of citizen journalism*

2 WHY CITIZEN JOURNALISTS SHOULD BE SUBJECT TO REGULATION

There are five main arguments for creating a regulatory scheme that is applicable to citizen journalists that can be distilled from the preceding chapters:

1. In Chapters 2 and 3 we saw how a viable news media that includes the institutional press, wider media and citizen journalists is critical to the health of the public sphere as it provides an important source of information that informs the public's views and decisions on democratic issues, thereby enabling the public to exercise its democratic rights. It is therefore in the public interest to ensure the protection of news media plurality. For the reasons discussed at sections 6.2.1 and 6.2.2, regulation provides a way to protect this interest.

2. The internet has changed the way individuals communicate and exercise their right to freedom of expression. As set out in Chapter 3, this has acted as a stimulus for citizen journalism. Social media, in particular, has facilitated an audience and producer convergence that has circumvented traditional barriers to publication, allowing citizen journalists to easily publish information of value to public discourse. As argued throughout this book, citizen journalism is no longer an outlier of free speech. Rather, it plays a central role in how we communicate and impart information and ideas. Thus, protecting citizen journalists' right to media freedom is of fundamental importance to free speech and democracy. Consequently, there is a strong public interest in ensuring that any regulatory scheme encourages rather than stifles a diversity of voices, meaning that any regulatory regime must adopt a functional approach to determining who or what falls within its remit.

3. To the contrary, as discussed in Chapters 2, 3 and 5, the institutional press, and news media more broadly, has the power and the reach to not only facilitate the democratic process, but also to distort it through unfair, selective, inaccurate or misleading reporting; a situation that we saw in Chapter 3 has been exacerbated in recent years by the role being played in the curation and publication of news by platforms such as Facebook and Google. Arguably, as discussed in Chapter 7, this issue can be amplified by the anonymous and pseudonymous nature of many online publications. This applies equally to citizen journalists and the institutional press. Furthermore, as advanced throughout this book, the emergence of citizen journalism has given rise to a symbiotic relationship with the institutional media, in which citizen journalists increasingly act as a source of news, meaning that information published by citizen journalists is often 'recycled' by the press and other forms of mainstream media. Consequently,

Reimagining regulation 265

due to the respect given to the reputations of some institutional news publishers this can add credence to the citizen journalist and inadvertently perpetuate support for false news.[15] It is therefore in the public interest for there to be an effective mechanism, in the form of an appropriate regulatory framework, for holding publishers to account for the exercise of their power, regardless of whether they are a member of the institutional press or a citizen journalist.[16]

4. The enhanced right to media freedom confers certain benefits on media actors.[17] The enjoyment of this right is contingent upon the fulfilment of certain standards of professional behaviour and norms of media discourse, or concomitant duties and responsibilities.[18] Pursuant to the media-as-a-constitutional-component concept, media freedom, and the duties and responsibilities attached to it, applies to any media actor publishing information of value to the public sphere.[19] Therefore, an appropriate regulatory framework will not only protect media freedom and help to ensure that news publishers fulfil their duties and responsibilities, but should also apply to citizen journalists who are not typically regarded as members of the institutional press.

5. As explained in Chapter 5, actors disseminating information of value to public discourse pursuant to the media-as-a-constitutional-component concept are, essentially, publishing a special type of content that is of democratic importance. Ultimately, this requires a different regulatory approach to 'entertainment' because of its significance to a healthy democracy.[20]

3 REGULATION IN THE UK

In this section I will explain why the UK's current regulatory regime does not offer an adequate solution to the challenges posed by ongoing press malfea-

---

[15] In particular, see Chapter 3 section 5.3.

[16] T. Gibbons, 'Building Trust in Press Regulation: Obstacles and Opportunities' (2013) 5(2) *Journal of Media Law* 202–219, 203, 211, 213.

[17] See Chapter 4 sections 3.2 and 3.3.

[18] See Chapter 6 sections 2, 3.2 and 3.3.

[19] See Chapter 5 section 5.

[20] This view correlates with the view of the New Zealand Law Commission which classifies 'news and current affairs' media as a special type of content that requires a unique regulatory approach to other forms of media, such as entertainment media. See New Zealand Law Commission, *The News Media Meets 'New Media' Rights Responsibilities and Regulation in the Digital Age*, March 2013, Report 128, 158–159, [7.14].

sance and, most importantly for the purposes of this chapter, why it is ill-suited for regulating citizen journalists.

The first reason relates to the current status of the UK's regulatory system. However, before we fix our gaze on why its status is problematic, for context, I will sketch out the regulatory landscape. Among the key recommendations made by Leveson LJ in his *Inquiry* was the creation of a system of voluntary self-regulation that is 'genuinely independent' from the government and the press industry.[21] In the words of the Press Recognition Panel (PRP), Leveson LJ 'proposed independent regulation of the press organised by the press, with processes in place to ensure that required levels of independence and effectiveness were met'.[22] As a result, the Royal Charter on Self-Regulation of the Press (Royal Charter) was granted on 30 October 2013,[23] which subsequently created the PRP,[24] a body corporate empowered to approve press regulators that meet the conditions set out in the Recognition Criteria pursuant to Schedule 3 of the Charter. In line with Leveson LJ's recommendation for genuine independence from the government and the press industry, paragraph 1 of Schedule 3 prescribes that an 'independent self-regulatory body should be governed by an independent Board. In order to ensure the independence of the body, the Chair and members of the Board must be appointed in a genuinely open, transparent and independent way, without any influence from industry or Government.'[25] As things currently stand, the UK has two press regulators: the Independent Press Standards Organisation (IPSO)[26] and IMPRESS. Of the two regulators, IMPRESS[27] is the only one approved by the PRP and therefore

---

[21] Leveson (n 1) 1758, [4.1]. However, although he was clear he was not recommending it at the time, Leveson LJ did leave open the possibility of a statutory backstop regulator being established by the government if self-regulation failed: 1758, [3.34]–[3.35].

[22] Press Recognition Panel, *Annual Report on the Recognition System*, 10 February 2021, 10. Pursuant to paragraph 1 of Schedule 4 of the Royal Charter on Self-Regulation of the Press, a 'Regulator' means 'an independent body formed by or on behalf of relevant publishers for the purpose of conducting regulatory activities in relation to their publications'. See Royal Charter on Self-Regulation of the Press.

[23] Ibid.

[24] The PRP came into existence on 3 November 2014.

[25] Pursuant to paragraph 2, the Chair of the Board must be nominated by an appointment panel that must also be independent of government and industry. Paragraph 3 sets out the composition requirements for the panel, including that a substantial majority of the members are 'demonstrably independent' of the press. Paragraph 5 prescribes the composition of the Board, according to which the majority of the members should be independent of the press; it should not include any serving editor; and members must be independent of government and politics.

[26] https://www.ipso.co.uk.

[27] https://impress.press.

Reimagining regulation 267

regarded as being 'Leveson-compliant'.[28] It has the power to fine members who breach its code, and it offers an arbitration service that settles disputes without the need for litigation. IPSO has the power to fine[29] but it has yet to exercise that power,[30] much to the frustration of commentators, given the press's ongoing tendency for malfeasance.[31] Common to both schemes is their reliance on members of the press to voluntarily join them. We will turn now to why this regime as it currently stands is problematic.

Despite the voluntary self-regulatory nature of IMPRESS and IPSO there is a framework in place for a more incentivised, and arguably more coercive, regime. In light of Leveson LJ's recommendations to 'encourage' press membership of a regulator approved by the PRP (currently IMPRESS), section 34 of the Crime and Courts Act 2013 enables a court to award exemplary damages against any 'relevant publisher'[32] in litigation who is *not* a member of 'an approved regulator'. Among the requirements for approved status that are prescribed by the Royal Charter is that the regulator will have a low-cost arbitration system to reduce legal costs for both claimants and the press.[33] Section 40 *could* be at the core of this 'costs incentives regime' as it empowers the court to award adverse costs against non-members of an 'approved regulator' by forcing the 'relevant publisher' to pay the claimant's legal costs even if the publisher is successful in defending the claim, subject to certain exceptions.[34] However, section 40 is not yet in force, meaning that Leveson LJ's recommendations have only been partially implemented.

Consequently, as stated in the PRP's latest *Annual Report on the Recognition System*, the approved regulation system is frustrated by political involvement in that section 40 is dormant and remains unenforceable until it is activated by

---

[28] IMPRESS was recognised by the PRP as the first 'Leveson-compliant' independent press regulator on 25 October 2016, https://www.impress.press/about-us/faq.html.

[29] https://www.ipso.co.uk/monitoring/standards-investigations/.

[30] Indeed, IPSO's annual reports of 2015 to 2019 show that it has not yet even launched a 'standards investigation' – the process that would lead to the imposition of a fine. The reports are accessible at https://www.ipso.co.uk/monitoring/annual-reports/.

[31] Wragg (n 3) 261–262; P. McGrath, 'Bob the Builder: Can IPSO Fix It?' *Inforrm*, 8 November 2018; B. Cathcart, 'Manchester United, the Sun and that Complaint to the "Press Regulator" IPSO', *Inforrm*, 11 February 2020; B. Cathcart, 'IPSO: The Toothless Puppet Rolls Over for Its Masters (Again)', *Inforrm*, 26 October 2018; B. Cathcart, 'Sam Allardyce, the Telegraph and Another IPSO Failure', *Inforrm*, 3 September 2018.

[32] Section 41 sets out what is meant by 'relevant publisher'. This is qualified by Schedule 15, which excludes certain persons and organisations from this definition and, therefore, from the ambit of sections 34 to 42. The scope of section 41 is discussed below.

[33] Royal Charter (n 22) Schedule 3, [22].

[34] These exceptions are dealt with below.

268   *Media freedom in the age of citizen journalism*

the Secretary of State for Digital, Culture, Media and Sport.[35] The effect of this is that approved regulation becomes a blunt instrument as it disincentivises membership of an approved regulatory scheme and it ultimately, and fundamentally, undermines the purpose of approved regulation. Thus, it effectively inverts approved regulation into a self-serving system. As the PRP states, not only has this contributed to a large number of significant publishers choosing not to join IMPRESS,[36] it can also have serious implications for the press and the public:

> ... the absence of section 40 means there is limited incentive in place for people bringing complaints against its member publishers to use IMPRESS's arbitration scheme to settle disputes. This maintains the chilling effect on free speech (which section 40 would remove) as it means that even IMPRESS publishers may still have to defend costly libel actions through the courts rather than through IMPRESS's arbitration process ... The failure to commence section 40 also means there are limited incentives to encourage publishers to sign up to the recognition system and no low cost way for the public to raise legal complaints against the vast majority of news publishers.[37]

Furthermore, the PRP argues that the fact the recognition system is currently in a state of limbo has, paradoxically, maintained a political presence within press regulation; a situation that undermines a self-regulatory system and Leveson LJ's recommendation that politicians should not be involved in press regulation, other than in legislating for a 'backstop' regulator.[38] In the view of the PRP, '[f]ull implementation of the recognition system would safeguard against ongoing political interference'.[39]

Secondly, despite the reasons in favour of citizen journalists being subject to regulation, they rarely join the various regulatory schemes that exist across Europe.[40] Indeed, in his *Inquiry* Leveson LJ acknowledged that technological changes in the past few decades have led to a fragmentation of the media (and its audience), as they have introduced new actors, such as citizen journalists, that do not tend to engage with voluntary regulation.[41] He states that the internet is an 'ethical vacuum ... [that] does not claim to operate by express ethical standards, so that bloggers and others may, if they choose, act with impunity'[42]

---

[35] PRP (n 22) 9, 19–21. The benefits of approved regulation are discussed in section 6.3.
[36] Ibid 9, [26]–[29].
[37] Ibid 9, [20]–[21].
[38] See Leveson (n 1) 1758, [3.34]–[3.35].
[39] PRP (n 22) 9, [21].
[40] Hulin (n 8).
[41] Leveson (n 1) 165–166, [3.7]–[3.8].
[42] Ibid 736, [3.2].

Reimagining regulation 269

and, specifically, '[b]logs and other such websites are entirely unregulated'.[43] This has led some commentators to describe cyberspace as a 'Wild West, law free zone'.[44] As a result, those Councils that can only deal with complaints against their members are hamstrung when it comes to investigating complaints against non-members.[45]

In the UK, this issue has not been helped by IPSO's Code of Practice[46] and the Crime and Courts Act 2013. In respect of IPSO, which as explained above is not a PRP-approved regulator, citizen journalists are only covered by its code if they submit material to the publishers that it regulates.[47] This requirement would seem to exclude most citizen journalists as the very nature of citizen journalism dictates an inherent tendency to eschew the mainstream media, including members of the institutional press that make up the bulk of IPSO's membership.[48]

As explained above, sections 34 and 40 of the Crime and Courts Act 2013 apply to any 'relevant publisher'. According to section 41(1) a 'relevant publisher' is a person who, in the course of a business,[49] publishes news-related material that is written by different authors and is subject to editorial control. Section 41(2) tells us that this means that a person, who does not have to be the publisher, has editorial or equivalent responsibility for the content and presentation of the material, and the decision to publish it. Crucially, section 41 has the potential to exclude a large number of citizen journalists for two reasons. By definition, many citizen journalists are not publishing news-related material 'in the course of a business'. Moreover, citizen journalists tend to be both the author and publisher of their material, as opposed to publishing material

---

[43] Ibid 171, [4.20]. In the UK Ofcom has been installed as the online harms regulator. See the discussion in Chapter 3 section 3.2.

[44] A. Yen, 'Western Frontier or Feudal Society? Metaphors and Perceptions of Cyberspace' (2002) 17 *Berkeley Technology Law Journal* 1207; D. McGoldrick, 'The Limits of Freedom of Expression on Facebook and Social Networking Sites: A UK Perspective' (2013) 13(1) *Human Rights Law Review* 125, 130; P. Coe, 'The Social Media Paradox: An Intersection with Freedom of Expression and the Criminal Law' (2015) 24(1) *Information & Communications Technology Law* 16, 24; G. Benaim, 'A Future with Social Media: Wild West or Utopia? You Have a Stake in the Outcome', *Inforrm*, 14 May 2014.

[45] For example, the Austrian and Dutch Councils and the French and Flemish Councils in Belgium will investigate complaints about any media content, regardless of the publisher. Norway's Council has recently enacted a rule change to enable it to deal with complaints against non-members.

[46] Although the same cannot be said for IMPRESS' Code which does cover citizen journalists.

[47] https://www.ipso.co.uk/faqs/editors-code/.

[48] https://www.ipso.co.uk/complain/who-ipso-regulates/.

[49] Whether or not carried on with a view to make a profit.

'written by different authors'.[50] Thus, the Act's definition of 'relevant publisher' is fundamentally flawed and seems to go against Leveson LJ's view that greater press regulation is required to prevent 'real harm caused to real people',[51] and that membership of a regulatory body 'should be open to all publishers ... including making membership potentially available on different terms for different publishers':[52] why should a member of the institutional press, whether it publishes material in print, or online, be captured by sections 34 and 40 (if it were enacted), yet a citizen journalist, by virtue of not publishing in the course of a business, and being both the author and publisher of the material, not be? Surely, a citizen journalist who is gathering and publishing news should be eligible to join the same regulatory scheme(s), albeit perhaps on 'different terms', as a member of institutional press? Data protection law demonstrates the inequity of this situation. Pursuant to the jurisprudence of the European Court of Justice (as it then was) and the Court of Justice of the European Union (as it is now),[53] the UK Supreme Court[54] and guidance from the ICO,[55] 'journalism' has been given a very wide meaning. Thus, in *The Law Society and others v Kordowski*[56] Tugendhat J held that bloggers engaging in internet journalism are able to avail themselves of the 'special purposes' exemption for 'journalistic, literary or artistic' purposes found in section 32 of the now repealed Data Protection Act 1998, and subsequently imported into Article 85 of the GDPR and the Data Protection Act 2018.[57] According to the ICO, the purpose of the exemption is to 'safeguard freedom of expression'.[58]

4 IS MANDATORY REGULATION A VIABLE ALTERNATIVE?

In his book, Wragg argues convincingly for mandatory regulation of the institutional press[59] but, if we take into account citizen journalists, is this a viable

---

[50] Coe (n 12) 430.

[51] Leveson (n 1).

[52] Ibid) 1761, [4.13].

[53] Case C-73/07 *Tietosuojavaltuutettu v Satakunnan Markkinapörssi Oy, Satamedia Oy (Satamedia)*; Case C-345/17 *Sergejs Buivids v Datu valsts inspekcija*.

[54] *Sugar (Deceased) v BBC* [2012] UKSC 4.

[55] Information Commissioners' Office, *Data protection and journalism: a guide for the media*, 29–30.

[56] [2014] EMLR 2, [99].

[57] The exemption has been imported into the Data Protection Act 2018 by virtue of Part 5, paragraph 26 of Schedule 2. Both the GDPR and 2018 Act added 'academic purposes' to the list.

[58] ICO (n 55) 28.

[59] Wragg (n 3) ch. 9.

Reimagining regulation 271

alternative to voluntary self-regulation? In my view there are two primary reasons why mandatory regulation would not be appropriate for citizen journalists.

First, Wragg suggests that mandatory regulation should be created by legislation that would 'determine the field of members'.[60] With the institutional press, identifying those members would be easily achievable by virtue of their corporate status. To the contrary, the same cannot be said for citizen journalists because: (i) as discussed in the previous section, citizen journalists do not tend to operate 'in the course of a business', therefore they are not identifiable as corporate entities; (ii) the sheer number of citizen journalists operating at any one time, and the transient nature of citizen journalism, in that they may dip in and out of journalism and may publish in an irregular or ad hoc manner, would arguably make it impossible for a regulator to implement a system of regulation that takes regulation *to* the subject (in other words, imposes mandatory regulation on the citizen journalist) and is able to monitor their journalistic activity; (iii) as alluded to in Chapter 5, citizen journalists may not know that what they are doing is journalistic and that they are, as a result, journalists, and subject to regulation.[61] This is because the traditional institutional approaches used for defining media, and therefore who or what should be subject to regulation, that were discussed and discredited in Chapter 4,[62] have created a definitional barrier to regulation for citizen journalists. Many of them will not have professional journalistic experience, or hold a journalism qualification, meaning that they are unlikely to make the link between their newsgathering and publication activity on, for instance, social media platforms, and journalism, and in turn any mandatory requirement to be regulated.

Secondly, if citizen journalists (perhaps incorrectly) perceive regulation as being restrictive by virtue of it being forced upon them, they are less likely to engage with it, regardless of whether it is mandatory, and irrespective of whether it is, in fact, permissive and beneficial. For the reasons discussed in the previous paragraph, enforcing mandatory regulation on citizen journalists would be at best extremely difficult, and at worst impossible. The combination of these two factors may lead to many citizen journalists falling through the cracks of regulation as it would encourage them to participate in 'underground' and unregulated journalism. This would be detrimental to both the public, in that it would further limit the protection they have against the malfeasance of citizen journalists, and citizen journalists themselves, as they would be denied the opportunity to engage with regulation that, contrary to their perception,

---

[60] Ibid 256.
[61] See Chapter 5 section 6.3.
[62] See Chapter 4 section 5.

may be empowering.[63] Taking this argument a step further, this is a situation that could negatively impact upon the health and prosperity of the public sphere. If citizen journalists feel forced to participate in 'underground' journalism to avoid regulation then, because of the 'risks' associated with practising journalism in this way (I am thinking here, predominantly, of the risk of liability for participating in journalism while not being a member of a mandatory scheme), this, in itself, is likely to reduce the number of citizen journalists and therefore the voices that are able to contribute to the public sphere. It could also impact upon the quality of their journalism by virtue of their not being able to take advantage of the professional development opportunities offered through membership of a regulator,[64] or simply because they cannot conduct their newsgathering and publication activities in the same way, and using similar resources, as their regulated (and 'legal') counterparts. A combination of these factors is likely to limit the size of the audience that journalism, undertaken in this way, can reach. Of course, others may be discouraged entirely from participating in public discourse for fear of being subjected to forced regulation. To the contrary, voluntary regulation that is not forced upon citizen journalists, and which comes with clear benefits for engaging with it, is more likely to encourage participation in the scheme, and consequently, the public sphere. This is a view supported by the citizen journalist, Cameron Slater, who runs the award-winning blog *Whale Oil Beef Hooked*.[65] Slater's view was cited by the New Zealand Law Commission (NZLC) in its report *The News Media Meets 'New Media' Rights Responsibilities and Regulation in the Digital Age*:[66]

> Under this regime so long as I agree to submit to the rules, process and responsibilities as outlined then it is very simple, I will be classified as 'news media' ... It does need to be voluntary though. When I was asked about this by the Law Commission and subsequently by journalists my answer has been the same. By having it voluntary bloggers can choose to seek 'certification', so to speak, and in doing so they are signalling that they are prepared to be responsible news and commentary providers. Likewise a blogger can choose to remain outside of the regime and suffer the impression of a lack of responsibility and the accompanying diminishment of the value of what they have to say. Professionalism and competition will ensure that bloggers and other new media people will voluntarily join the regime. Remaining outside will eventually marginalize those who opt to stay outside of regulation.[67]

---

[63] See section 6.5.
[64] Ibid.
[65] https://www.whaleoil.co.nz/.
[66] NZLC (n 20).
[67] Ibid 191, [7.165].

In the previous section, and in this section, we have seen that the UK's current regulatory scheme is deficient and, in any event, is designed and drafted in such a way to largely exclude citizen journalists. And we have seen that a mandatory scheme would be very difficult, if not impossible, to implement and monitor in respect of citizen journalists. Because of this our attention will, in a short while, at section 6, turn to the alternative, reimagined, voluntary and approved self-regulatory scheme that I have previously referred to. However, before that, the following section explains how the regulatory scheme advanced in this chapter is influenced by the state of regulation in other jurisdictions.

5   A COMPARATIVE RATIONALE

5.1   Introduction: A Comparative Perspective

In the pre-internet era, issues such as identifying who should adhere to news standards and be subject to regulation, and the process of determining the boundaries of intervention, were relatively straightforward matters. As set out in Chapter 4, historically, distinguishing media from non-media actors could be achieved by applying tried and tested approaches, namely the press-as-technology model, the 'mass audience approach' and the 'professionalised publisher approach'.[68] As that chapter established, and for the reasons discussed in the previous section, due to the 'disruption' caused by citizen journalists and online speech, those approaches, which were perhaps once effective, now lack merit and are, at worst, redundant. Consequently, dealing with these issues has now become far more complex as bright line distinctions between media formats and genres, creators, consumers, distributors and, significantly, institutional and non-institutional journalists, have become increasingly blurred. This has forced, across a number of jurisdictions, a re-examination of the fundamental justification for regulatory intervention.[69] From these multi-jurisdictional reviews emerges a spectrum of formulas for oversight of news publishers,[70] from industry self-regulation, not requiring

---

[68]   See Chapter 4 section 5.

[69]   NZLC (n 20) ch. 6, 133, [61]; L. Fielden, *Regulating the Press: A Comparative Study of International Press Councils* (Reuters Institute for the Study of Journalism, 2012).

[70]   NZLC (n 69) ch. 6, 146, [6.47].

any legislative provision or recognition at the one end,[71] through to statutory regulation at the other.[72]

The modified scheme of regulation that is set out in section 6 is informed by reviews, recommendations and regulatory schemes from other countries. It draws on Lara Fielden's *Comparative Study of International Press Councils*[73] and, in particular, pays close attention to three wide-ranging reviews of the press that have been conducted in Australia[74] and New Zealand[75] as they have, to varying extents, considered the impact of online media, including citizen journalism, on their respective regulatory frameworks, while taking into account Leveson LJ's recommendations in his *Inquiry*. Consequently, the following section will briefly outline the rationale for adopting this comparative approach with these particular jurisdictions.

---

[71] Fielden (n 69) 16, [1.3.2]–[1.3.3]. For example, see the German and Finnish models of voluntary regulation.

[72] Ibid 16–17, [1.3.4]–[1.3.5]. For example, as discussed in section 6.3, in Ireland the Defamation Act 2009, although not actually establishing the Irish Press Council, sets out the principal objects of the Council, which include the protection of freedom of expression of the press, the protection of the public interest by ensuring ethical, accurate and truthful reporting, maintaining certain minimum ethical and professional standards, and the protection of privacy and dignity of the individual. The Act also sets out the requirements for independence, the composition of directors, funding, investigations and hearings, and powers to require the publication of a determination in any form and manner directed by the Council. In Denmark, the Danish Press Council is an independent public tribunal established under the Media Liability Act 1998, which sets out the Council's purposes: to deal with complaints about journalistic ethics, to contribute to the development of press ethics and to handle complaints about the legal right of correction. The Act also provides for a right of reply and the sanction of being required to publish the Council's decision where a complaint is upheld, along with the punishment for failing to comply (a fine or imprisonment of up to four months). In his excellent book, Paul Wragg argues for mandatory regulation of the press, created by statute. See Wragg (n 3).

[73] Fielden (n 69).

[74] The *Finkelstein Report* and the *Convergence Review* are reviews of Australia's media and its regulatory framework. Both were published by the Australian government in 2012: Australian Government, *The Report of the Independent Inquiry into the Media and Media Regulation*, 28 February 2012 (*Finkelstein Report*); *Convergence Review* (Final Report to the Minister for Broadband, Communications and the Digital Economy, Sydney, 2012).

[75] NZLC (n 20).

Reimagining regulation 275

5.2   The Rationale for a Comparative Approach

Between 2011 and 2012 Lara Fielden conducted a study of international Press Councils.[76] Her report is illuminative for the purposes of the regulatory scheme I advance below for the following reasons. First, it focussed on six countries which share many of the same characteristics as the UK.[77] According to Fielden, these countries were chosen as

> each is a mature democracy, with a 'free press' according to press freedom indices.[78] Each recognises the importance of the freedom to impart and receive information; of balancing competing rights for example in relation to privacy and reputation; and of wider standards of accountability. Each has a Press Council [Sweden and Ireland also have an Ombudsman working in conjunction with the Press Council]. However, each jurisdiction reveals a different approach to press regulation, for example, in relation to statutory or non-statutory powers; the balancing of industry and independent board members; funding; sanctions; and, whether its remit encompasses broadcasting as well as print and online content.[79]

Secondly, in turn, much like the findings of Australia's *Finkelstein Report* and *Convergence Review*,[80] which are referred to in the following section, Fielden's study was relied upon extensively by the NZLC to inform its recommendations in its *The News Media Meets 'New Media'* report.[81] Unlike Leveson LJ's *Inquiry* and Australia's *Finkelstein Report* and *Convergence Review*, the NZLC systematically considered how online publishers, including citizen journalists, may be regulated and how 'news media' may be defined in a media environment that includes citizen journalists and traditional institutional news publishers.[82] Specifically, the NZLC was tasked with investigating whether the growth of online platforms and their increasing contribution to the curation and publication of news had led to gaps in its regulatory regime that needed to be addressed.[83] In March 2013, after two years of investigating New Zealand's then current state of regulation, and after consultation with the

---

[76]   Fielden (n 69) 14, [1.1].

[77]   Ibid 14–18, [1.2]–[1.3.6]. Sweden, Germany, Finland, Denmark, Ireland and Australia. The regulatory regimes in Canada, Norway and New Zealand also informed Fielden's findings.

[78]   Ibid [1.2]. The indices referred to in the report include The Reporters Without Borders Press Freedom Index and the Freedom House index: https://rsf.org/en and https://freedomhouse.org/.

[79]   Ibid 14, [1.2].

[80]   *Finkelstein Report* and *Convergence Review* (n 74).

[81]   NZLC (n 20).

[82]   Ibid 22–24 and ch. 3.

[83]   Ibid 24.

276 *Media freedom in the age of citizen journalism*

traditional institutional media, online platforms and other stakeholders,[84] the NZLC published its findings. In summary, it recommended that the complex and fragmented system of media regulation that existed at the time, which included a statutory authority for broadcasters, the Broadcasting Standards Authority, and a self-regulatory Press Council for the press, be replaced with one overarching 'Grand Regulator',[85] known as the News Media Standards Authority (NMSA).[86] The NZLC's recommendations for a Grand Regulator were not adopted. Justice Minister Judith Collins commented that the regulatory review was not driven by a crisis of confidence in the institutional media and that New Zealand's media had already made progress in dealing with the challenges posed by the impact of media convergence. Consequently, she concluded that there was no pressing need for statutory or institutional change of the regulatory bodies.[87]

Fielden's study, combined with the Australian and New Zealand reviews, provides comprehensive and overarching comparative views of the multi-jurisdictional regulatory environment. Although the NZLC's vision of a Grand Regulator was not realised and, likewise, I do not propose a single converged regulator for the scheme that I advance, as we shall see in the next section, the principles upon which the Law Commission's recommendations are based are closely aligned with the principles that have been advanced in earlier chapters that underpin the media-as-a-constitutional-component concept. Thus, the NZLC's report provides support for the regulatory scheme that we shall now turn to.

6 A REIMAGINED REGULATORY SCHEME

6.1 Conceptual Principles

The primary objective of the NZLC's report was to determine which publishers of news content should be entitled to the legal rights, and subject to the countervailing responsibilities, which have traditionally applied to the institutional

---

[84] Ibid Appendix B, 384–386. Other stakeholders include, for example, academics and non-media bodies.

[85] U. Cheer, 'Regulatory Responses from a Southern Archipelago' in D. Weisenhaus and S. Young (eds), *Media Law and Policy in the Internet Age* (Hart Publishing, 2017) 196.

[86] NZLC (n 20) ch. 7.

[87] New Zealand Ministry of Justice, *Government Response to Law Commission Report 'News Media meets New Media'* (October 2013) 9–10.

Reimagining regulation   277

news media.[88] Its proposals were founded on the following four principles: (i) some bloggers and citizen journalists are undertaking functions traditionally performed by the institutional media, including holding the various branches of government to account;[89] (ii) there 'is a public interest in recognising the news media as a special type of communicator with access to certain legal privileges and exemptions and in continuing to hold them accountable to ethical standards';[90] (iii) consequently, 'a commitment to basic ethical standards, such as accuracy and fairness, is fundamental to the type of communication the law intended to privilege';[91] (iv) it is in the public's interest to ensure all those who wish to fulfil the news media's functions, and are prepared to accept the associated responsibilities, be entitled to do so, rather than confining these privileges to those who meet certain organisational requirements, such as audience size or commercial purpose.[92] As discussed in section 6.2, principles (i) and (iv) are also relevant to the question of who could be subject to the framework and are, therefore, discussed further in that context.

All four principles are indicative of social responsibility theory. Indeed, as the NZLC states, its recommendations formalise the unwritten social contract that has traditionally existed between the news media and the public it serves, by providing a mechanism to cement the connection between the rights and freedoms of the media and their concomitant duties and responsibilities.[93] Thus, as stated above, the NZLC's report, including the principles underpinning its recommendations, lends credence to the reimagined regulatory scheme as it reflects what it is trying to achieve. Much like principles (ii) and (iii), the foundation of this reimagined scheme dictates that for media actors to take advantage of media freedom and the privileged protection it provides, those actors must abide by certain standards of professional behaviour and norms of discourse which underpin it.[94] Essentially, in respect of behavioural standards, the media's privileged protection is subject to it conducting itself in a particular way. This includes ensuring that it acts ethically and in good faith and that the material it publishes or broadcasts is based on reasonable research to verify the provenance of its sources.[95] Pursuant to the norms of public discourse, the enhanced right to media freedom is available to any media actor disseminating

---

[88] Indeed, a 'key driver' behind the review was the emergence of online platforms. NZLC (n 20) 158, [7.13].

[89] Ibid.

[90] Ibid 156, [7.1].

[91] Ibid [7.2].

[92] Ibid.

[93] Ibid 157–158, [7.7]–[7.8].

[94] See Chapter 5 sections 4.1 and 4.2, and Chapter 6 sections 3.1 to 3.3.

[95] Chapter 6 sections 3.1 to 3.3.

278 *Media freedom in the age of citizen journalism*

speech of value to the public sphere; it rewards media actors for engaging in discourse that is in the public interest.[96] Conversely, expression which is not of public concern is not afforded the same level of protection.

6.2 Who Could Be Subject to the Scheme?

Who could be subject to the regulatory scheme can be broken down into two questions: first, how should a regulatory regime deal with online news publishers? Secondly, what are the eligibility criteria for membership?

6.2.1 Online news publishers

As previously explained, Fielden's study of Press Councils focussed on six countries with similar characteristics to the UK.[97] She makes a general observation that, without exception, all of these countries' Press Councils have, at least to an extent, extended 'their jurisdiction from print publications, and in some cases broadcast journalism, to associated online media including "pure player", i.e. online-only providers'.[98] More specifically, according to her study, the Press Councils in Norway, Finland and Denmark cover print, broadcast and online media platforms.[99] The Norwegian Press Council extended coverage to associated social media platforms, such as Twitter and Facebook. This means that material provided by journalists on social media, including private accounts, is captured by the regulatory framework if it is used in connection with their journalism.[100] Thus, as Fielden states:

> Under such a system a reporter's private Twitter account could be held in breach of the press code if it was used in connection with his or her journalism, for example, to provide additional information about a story that has been excluded from the published version. The registered editor-in-chief could be held responsible for the associated material made available on the journalist's private Twitter, Facebook, or other account, just as s/he is responsible for print or online publications.[101]

Similarly, the Danish press regulator, the Pressenævnets, has registered blogs and Twitter accounts as members of its regulatory framework.[102] The Finnish Press Council has developed rules for media websites and deals with

---

[96] See Chapter 6 section 3.1.
[97] See section 5.1 and n 77.
[98] Ibid 34, [3.2].
[99] Ibid 35–37, [3.2].
[100] By way of contrast see the discussion on the UK's Online Safety Bill in Chapter 3 section 3.2.
[101] Fielden (n 69) 35, [3.2].
[102] Ibid 36–37, [3.2].

user-generated content,[103] whereas Sweden has a cross-platform code, albeit administered by three different regulators.[104] In Australia and New Zealand, the *Convergence Review* and the NZLC's report respectively recommended dealing with convergence in much the same way in that they proposed a single converged regulator.[105] As discussed in the following section, in respect of the *Finkelstein Report* and the NZLC report, this regulator would cover any media entity classed as 'news media', subject to a threshold level.

The scheme that I propose shares conceptual similarities with the principles upon which the NZLC's proposals were founded, which were set out in section 6.1. In line with principles (i) and (iv) this scheme will apply to citizen journalists.[106] However, as explained in the following section, pursuant to the media-as-a-constitutional-component concept, it differs from the *Finkelstein Report* and the recommendations made by the NZLC in respect of their definition of 'news media' and its subsequent eligibility criteria. Further, as I said at the end of section 5, I do not go as far as proposing the adoption of a single converged regulator providing regulatory oversight for the print, broadcast and online media. This is because, first, for the reasons discussed in section 4, and for reasons I will develop below, citizen journalism requires a nuanced approach to regulation that understands the nature of citizen journalists and their journalistic activity. A single converged regulator, overseeing all forms of news media, simply could not offer the expertise and understanding that is needed to not only regulate citizen journalists effectively, but, perhaps most importantly, to attract citizen journalists and encourage their engagement with regulation. Secondly, there is already an approved regulator in place, in the form of IMPRESS, that has the necessary knowledge to work with and regulate citizen journalists.

6.2.2 The definition of media and eligibility criteria

The definition of media and the subsequent question of eligibility have courted significant debate, particularly in Australia in the *Finkelstein Report* and the *Convergence Review*. Because the findings of these respective reviews (in particular the *Finkelstein Report*) influenced the NZLC's recommendations, which, in turn, feed into the scheme I propose, it is important to consider them here.

The *Finkelstein Report* proposed that the News Media Council (NMC) would cover all media that falls within the definition of 'news media'

---

[103] Ibid 36, [3.2].
[104] Ibid 34–35, [3.2].
[105] *Convergence Review* (n 74) 41; NZLC (n 20) 155, [6.71].
[106] See section 2.

280 *Media freedom in the age of citizen journalism*

advanced in the NZLC's 2011 Issues Paper,[107] subject to some changes (as set out below). Pursuant to the definition, any publisher, in any medium, who meets the following criteria, would be subject to the applicable law and regulation: (i) a significant proportion of their publishing activities must involve the generation and/or aggregation of news, information and opinion of current value; (ii) they disseminate this information to a public audience; (iii) publication must be regular; (iv) the publisher must be accountable to a code of ethics and a complaints process.[108] The changes suggested by the *Finkelstein Report* included, for instance, that for online publishers of news the respective site had to receive a minimum of 15,000 'hits' per annum to be subject to the NMC and the regulatory framework. In respect of the press, the recommended threshold was more than 3,000 print copies per issue.[109] If the threshold is met, then it becomes compulsory for the respective media actor to join the regime. However, if the threshold is not met, the media actor could still opt in. The *Finkelstein Report* acknowledged that the threshold figures are 'arbitrary' but that 'the line has to be drawn somewhere'.[110]

Similarly, the *Convergence Review* recommended that major media organisations should be required to participate in any scheme, regardless of platform, and they should not be able to opt out. Media actors falling outside the threshold for mandatory participation would be able to opt in to membership. The *Review* suggested, first, giving the new regulator discretion in determining whether a threshold level of size and influence has been reached,[111] and, secondly, that the threshold level should be 'set at a sufficiently high level so that only the most substantial and influential media groups are categorised as content service enterprises'.[112] However, because of the high threshold level, the *Review* effectively excluded all but the largest providers of professional news content.[113] Indeed, the *Review* itself estimates that, at the time it was written, only around 15 organisations would meet the threshold.[114]

The NZLC's recommendations predominantly mirror those of the *Finkelstein Report*. The NZLC was of the view that it is 'justifiable' to adopt a broad definition of 'news' as including any publication which purports to provide factual

---

[107] New Zealand Law Commission, *The News Media Meets the 'New Media' Rights, Responsibilities and Regulation in the Digital Age* (2011) NZLC IP27.

[108] Ibid, 'Summary and Preliminary Proposals', [29].

[109] *Finkelstein Report* (n 74) [11.67].

[110] Ibid.

[111] *Convergence Review* (n 74) 2.

[112] Ibid 12, 50.

[113] T. Flew and A. Swift, 'Regulating Journalists? The Finkelstein Report, the Convergence Review and the News Media Regulation in Australia' (2013) 2(1) *Journal of Applied Journalism & Media Studies* 181, 193.

[114] *Convergence Review* (n 74) 12.

information and which involves real people as such publications engage journalistic standards.[115] Consequently, to be eligible the media actor must meet a recommended definition of 'news media', which contains three ingredients: (i) a significant element of their publishing activities involves the generation and/or aggregation of news, information and opinion of current value; (ii) they disseminate this information to a public audience; (iii) publication is regular and not occasional.[116]

The threshold figures advanced by the *Finkelstein Report* and the *Convergence Review*, and the requirement that a media actor should publish 'regularly' to be subject to regulation found in the *Finkelstein Report* and NZLC report, conflict, to an extent, with the practice in other jurisdictions. For instance, as observed by Fielden, in Denmark membership of the Pressenævnets is mandatory for all publishers who publish at least twice per year and is voluntary for the online media.[117]

Furthermore, this threshold criterion does not correspond with the definition of media advanced in Chapter 5.[118] Rather, the regulatory scheme proposed in this chapter would apply to those actors falling within that definition. The media-as-a-constitutional-component concept adopts a functional, rather than institutional, approach to defining media as it focusses on the functions that are performed by media actors as opposed to their inherent characteristics. Therefore, media freedom, and its concomitant duties and responsibilities, does not have to exclusively apply to the institutional media; it can apply to any actor that conforms to the definition. The definition of media that has been proposed in this book, which would apply for the purposes of this regulatory scheme, is, therefore, as follows: (1) a natural and legal person, (2) engaged in the process of gathering information of public concern, interest and significance, (3) with the intention, and for the purpose of, disseminating this information to a section of the public, (4) while complying with objective standards governing the research, newsgathering and editorial process.[119]

One of the fundamental requirements for determining that an actor is operating as media pursuant to the concept is that actor's contribution to matters of public interest. The recommendations made in the *Finkelstein Report* and by the NZLC that publication is regular and, in the case of the *Finkelstein Report*,

---

[115] NZLC (n 20) 164, [7.39].

[116] Ibid 182, [7.120].

[117] Fielden (n 69) 16, [1.3.4], 28.

[118] See Chapter 5 section 5.

[119] As explained in Chapter 5 (see section 4) and developed in Chapter 6 (see section 3) these standards would include, for instance, the time spent researching stories and ensuring the provenance and reliability of information.

282 *Media freedom in the age of citizen journalism*

meets threshold figures, is over-exclusive.[120] Actors can fulfil the definition of media that I have advanced and make a valuable contribution to the public sphere, on one-off occasions or on an ad hoc basis.[121] Significantly, this can be the case within a citizen journalism context, in which valuable contributions to public discourse can be made intermittently and via different platforms. Thus, an individual can be acting as media, and therefore subject to the right to media freedom and its duties and responsibilities, even if they are publishing on an irregular basis, so long as what they publish is of value to public discourse.

A further recommendation made by the NZLC is that any actor wishing to join its regulatory scheme must be willing to comply with its code of practice, complaints process and any subsequent rulings from the NMSA.[122] The regulatory scheme that I propose would adopt a similar expectation in that it too would require its members to adhere, and be accountable, to a standards code. In Chapter 1 I posed four broad questions for this inquiry to answer.[123] Three of them are pertinent to the discussion here, albeit applied within the context of regulation: first, because citizen journalists are not necessarily socialised into the norms of professional journalism, should they be subject to the same law and regulation as their institutional counterparts? Secondly, should citizen journalists be subject to the same or similar duties and responsibilities as the institutional press? The functional rather than institutional definition of media that has been advanced throughout this book determines that the answer to these questions is yes, albeit, as I explain below in relation to the fourth question posed in Chapter 1, when law or regulation is applied the nature of citizen journalism should be taken into account.[124] Any actor fulfilling the definition of media under the media-as-a-constitutional-component concept's definition would be expected to adhere to the same standards, or duties and responsibilities, including the same standards code, regardless of whether they are a citizen journalist or a member of the institutional press.

---

[120] See also Jan Oster's argument, dealt with in Chapter 5 at section 5, that for this requirement to be fulfilled it must occur periodically. J. Oster, 'Theory and Doctrine of "Media Freedom" as a Legal Concept' (2013) 5(1) *Journal of Media Law* 57, 74.

[121] *Editions Plon v France* App. no. 58148/00 (ECtHR 18 May 2004), [43]; *Lindon, Otchakovsky-Laurens and July v France* App. no. 21279/02 and 36448/02 (ECtHR 22 October 2007), [47].

[122] NZLC (n 20) 182, [7.121].

[123] See Chapter 1 section 3.

[124] To a large extent, this accords with the Court of Appeal's judgment in *Economou v de Freitas* [2018] EWCA Civ 2591; [2019] EMLR 7 in respect of the application of the Defamation Act 2013 section 4 defence of 'publication on a matter of public interest'. The judgment, and its implications for citizen journalists, is discussed in Chapter 8 section 3.2.2.

Reimagining regulation 283

Thirdly, because citizen journalists should be subject to the same law and regulation as institutional journalists, should the nature of citizen journalism, and the needs of citizen journalists, at least be considered for the purposes of implementing regulation? In respect of the practical operation of a standards code my answer to this question is yes. To encourage participation in the regulatory scheme the standards need to be applicable and accessible to citizen journalists. Significantly, this does not mean that they should be subject to *different* standards from those applicable to institutional journalists, or that they need to be. Rather, and quite simply, the standards should be accompanied with clear guidance on their application to citizen journalists who are predominantly operating in an online environment. If we take the IMPRESS Standards Code[125] as an example, in dealing with privacy, Code 7.1 says that 'publishers must respect people's reasonable expectation of privacy'. Modified standards for the purpose of the scheme I advance here would, for instance, provide further contextual guidance on what a 'reasonable expectation of privacy' means if someone shares information on social media, without privacy settings. Furthermore, in applying regulation there needs to be a degree of contextualisation applied. Similarities between IMPRESS's Standards Code and the IPSO Editors' Code[126] animate this point. In respect of IMPRESS, Code 1.3 requires that '[p]ublishers must always distinguish clearly between statements of fact, conjecture and opinion'. Similarly, IPSO's Code 1 (iv) states that '[t]he Press, while free to editorialise and campaign, must distinguish clearly between comment, conjecture and fact'. Notwithstanding the fact that the IPSO Code does not, in practice at least, apply to citizen journalists,[127] arguably, citizen journalists could not always be expected to apply such clear delineation between opinion or comment, conjecture and fact. Instead, it has to be accepted that, due to the nature of citizen journalism, at times the lines between these types of expression may be more blurred than is the case with the institutional press.[128]

Thus, the scheme that I propose would apply to institutional and citizen journalists alike. It has been argued that supporting media diversity in this way might dilute the 'brand'[129] associated with membership of a regulator.[130]

---

[125] https://www.impress.press/downloads/file/code/the-impress-standards-code.pdf.

[126] https://www.ipso.co.uk/editors-code-of-practice/#Accuracy.

[127] See section 2.

[128] This view reflects the opinion of the NZLC, which acknowledges that '[b]loggers ... could not always be expected to be constrained by any requirement of balance to the extent that mainstream media might ...': NZLC (n 20) 168, [7.60].

[129] The benefits of being part of a recognised regulatory 'brand' are discussed at section 6.5.

[130] NZLC (n 20) 182, [7.123].

284 *Media freedom in the age of citizen journalism*

To the contrary, in such a dynamic media environment, in which citizen journalists can, and regularly do, make valuable contributions to the public sphere, whereas educated and professionally trained journalists, employed by members of the institutional press, do not always publish material that is in the public interest,[131] it is no longer appropriate to take an institutional approach to membership. Indeed, in respect of the professionalised publisher approach[132] to defining media, the NZLC's recommendations support these arguments, and that advanced in Chapter 4,[133] that requiring media actors to be connected with, and remunerated by, a member of the institutional media, and/or to have undertaken formal journalistic education and training to benefit from the privileges attributed to media freedom and to be eligible to join a regulatory scheme is over-exclusive and unmeritorious. In the NZLC's view:

> We are ... reluctant to impose any such requirements. Some members of the new media contribute strongly and responsibly to public debate even though they have no journalistic training or experience. Conversely, some reporters and presenters on 'mainstream' outlets ... are not trained journalists and push the boundaries as much as most bloggers.[134]

Equally, as argued in section 3 in respect of the UK, the Crime and Courts Act 2013's definition of 'relevant publisher' is fundamentally flawed as there is no reason why the accountability of a citizen journalist who gathers and publishes news should be any different from the accountability of an institutional journalist.[135]

Membership of the regulatory scheme would be voluntary, which means that journalists could opt out of it.[136] Despite this, it is submitted that many citizen journalists would, in fact, opt in, including those who chose to operate anonymously and pseudonymously.[137] This is because it would not only formally acknowledge them as media, and therefore beneficiaries of media freedom, but would also enable them to access the incentives attached to mem-

---

[131] See Chapters 2 and 3; P. Coe, 'Redefining "Media" Using a "Media-as-a-constitutional-component" Concept: An Evaluation of the Need for the European Court of Human Rights to Alter Its Understanding of "Media" Within a New Media Landscape' (2017) 37(1) *Legal Studies* 25, 40–41.

[132] The press-as-technology model, mass audience approach and professionalised publisher approach are discussed in Chapter 4 sections 5.1 to 5.3.

[133] Ibid.

[134] NZLC (n 20) 182–183, [7.123]–[7.124].

[135] This view is shared by the NZLC. Ibid 186, [7.137].

[136] Non-membership is dealt with at section 6.7.

[137] As set out in section 6.5, the scheme would offer protection for anonymous and pseudonymous actors.

Reimagining regulation   285

bership outlined in section 6.4. As we saw in section 4, this correlates with the evidence given by the citizen journalist, Cameron Slater, to the NZLC.[138]

6.3   Nature of Membership: A Multi-jurisdictional View of Regulation

Whether regulatory schemes should be voluntary or mandatory has been at the heart of debates on press regulation in jurisdictions across the world.[139] Thus, unsurprisingly, as we saw in section 5.1, there is a diversity of membership models.[140] In this section I will discuss the nature of membership of the regulatory regimes in Denmark and Ireland, and the proposed (although unadopted) regimes in Australia and New Zealand, as they provide something like a cross-section of the regulatory schemes that are common to similar jurisdictions to the UK. And, as we shall see, each model offers something very different to the others, and the current UK system. Rather than attempting to shoehorn a new regulatory scheme into one of these established models, which would fail to recognise the nuances of institutional and non-institutional journalists operating within a diverse media environment, a scheme combining different aspects of these models is preferable. Indeed, according to Fielden, 'it is ... more helpful to see the models of press regulation ... as sitting on a spectrum, in which different aspects bleed into each other' as 'attempts at categorisation are less than straightforward'.[141] Thus, for the purposes of reimagining regulation, the ultimate objective of this exercise is to recognise the failings of each of these distinct systems and to identify, and take, the best elements from them to produce a robust regulatory scheme that is attractive to the institutional press and citizen journalists alike.

As discussed in section 3, the UK's press is subject to a voluntary self-regulatory regime that is currently overseen by two regulators: IPSO and the PRP-approved IMPRESS. By virtue of sections 34 and 40 of the Crime and Courts Act 2013, a framework for a more coercive regime exists, albeit section 40 is not yet enacted. Unfortunately, as explained in section 3, even if section 40 were enacted, citizen journalists are effectively excluded from the regime by the definition of 'relevant publisher' pursuant to section 41. Moreover, and in any event, the IPSO Code does not apply, at least practically, to citizen journal-

---

[138]   See n 66.

[139]   Fielden (n 69) 10, 39; Wragg (n 3) ch. 9.

[140]   See nn 71 and 72. As Fielden states, at one end of the spectrum, there is the Danish co-regulatory model discussed below and, at the other end, is the purely voluntary Canadian model, which 'demonstrates the spectre of wholesale withdrawal of publishers from the Press Council system', Fielden (n 69) 10.

[141]   Fielden (n 69) 39, [4].

ists.[142] Setting these issues aside, as I touched upon in section 3 in the context of the deficiencies in the UK's regulatory system, there are considerable benefits to approved regulation, and to being a member of an approved regulator. First, being a PRP-approved regulator identifies IMPRESS (and any other regulator that meets the Recognition Criteria) as being an ethical regulator, which in turn labels the regulator's members as being ethical publishers. This has the ultimate effect of positively distinguishing members of an approved regulator from those members of non-approved regulators. Secondly, although section 40 has not been enacted, it remains on the statute book. Therefore, members of an approved regulator effectively future-proof themselves in the event that the provision is brought into force by, for example, a future Labour government. Of course, if section 40 is repealed, as the Conservative government has threatened, the value of approved regulation, and the incentive of being a member of an approved regulatory scheme, diminishes even further than it already has (by virtue of section 40's dormancy). However, even if section 40 is never enacted, or is repealed, being a member of an approved regulator is still valuable for its 'ethical label' and because it provides some protection against the award of exemplary damages pursuant to section 34.

Within Europe, Denmark has taken the opposite approach to the UK. It has adopted a co-regulatory system, which consists of a combination of self-regulatory elements and mandatory requirements as the Pressenævnets has coercive powers to penalise non-compliance.[143] Thus, it describes itself as an 'independent public tribunal established under the Media Liability Act',[144] which gives it the power to determine what counts as good press practice (*god presseskik*). Section 34 of the Act requires the Danish press to comply with those standards by stipulating that the 'mass media shall be in conformity with sound press ethics'.[145] Pursuant to section 49 it also has the power to hear complaints based on those rules, and to order newspapers to publish its decisions (or a summary) in an appropriate place. Sections 36 to 40 enable the Pressenævnets to order that successful complainants are given a 'right to reply' where the publication of inaccurate information causes significant harm.[146] As Fielden observes, because Denmark imposes compulsory regulation it does not, prima facie, have to incentivise membership and compliance. In reality, though, the Media Liability Act does provide incentives which encourage the industry's 'acceptance' of the statutory framework and online media's desire

---

[142] As stated in section 3, citizen journalists are covered by the IPSO Editors' Code if they submit material to newspapers and magazines that are regulated by IPSO.

[143] Fielden (n 69) 10.

[144] Ibid 52, [4.3].

[145] http://www.pressenaevnet.dk/media-liability-act/.

[146] Wragg (n 3) 58–59.

Reimagining regulation 287

to join it on a voluntary basis.[147] These incentives include rights in relation to the protection of journalistic sources, the gathering and storing of personal information as part of journalistic research and, perhaps most importantly, access to restricted court files for research purposes and judicial acts otherwise closed to the public.[148] However, despite the Danish system being labelled as mandatory,[149] as Wragg states, it actually only represents 'mandatory regulation in its thinnest sense'.[150] This is because only failure to comply with section 49 is punishable by a fine or up to four months' imprisonment, and the Pressenævnets does not have the power to order its members to compensate complainants. Thus, as Wragg goes on to say:

> ... it cannot be said that the Danish press *must* comply with the rules since the only consequence of non-compliance is an obligation to publish a summary of the adverse adjudication. Moreover, it cannot even be said that the Danish press must admit to wrong-doing. Since it can publish the decision without comment, the whole process can be reduced to a sort of bureaucratic undertaking.[151]

Ireland sits somewhere between the UK and Denmark as it has adopted a system that exemplifies voluntary regulation with statutory incentives. According to Fielden, this system provides an example of 'incentivised, active compliance recognised in statute but not subject to it. It is a system that is accountable to the industry and parliament but independent of both.'[152] The Irish Parliament recognises the Press Council and Press Ombudsman pursuant to section 26(2) of the Defamation Act 2009, which provides that in court proceedings considering publication of an allegedly defamatory statement:

> [T]he court shall, in determining whether it was fair and reasonable to publish the statement concerned, take into account such matters it considers relevant including ... in the case of a statement published in a periodical by a person who, at the time of publication, was a member of the Press Council, the extent to which the person adhered to the code of standards of the Press Council and abided by the Press Ombudsman and determinations of the Press Council.[153]

Consequently, membership of the Press Council is 'incentivised' in two primary ways. First, it allows the member to demonstrate its commitment to ethical standards and accountable journalism and, therefore, run the defence

---

147 Fielden (n 69) 52, [4.3].
148 Ibid.
149 Ibid 10.
150 Wragg (n 3) 59.
151 Ibid (emphasis in the original).
152 Fielden (n 69) 10.
153 http://www.irishstatutebook.ie/eli/2009/act/31/enacted/en/pdf.

of 'fair and reasonable' publication to defamation proceedings. Secondly, section 26(2) 'incentivises' the extent to which the code of standards has been complied with, and Press Council determinations have been abided by. Thus, as Fielden states, a 'track record of compliance, not just the simple fact of membership, becomes important in order for a publication to demonstrate its accountability and responsibility in court'.[154] Ireland's regime is akin to the UK's dormant statutory framework as, under section 40 of the Crime and Courts Act 2015, being a member of a PRP-approved regulator means that the publisher is protected from an adverse costs order, regardless of whether or not they successfully defend the claim against them.

However, it is important not to overstate the 'incentives' for Irish publishers to engage with voluntary regulation. This 'incentive', as Wragg suggests, is 'fairly weak' as it impacts only on a narrow area of press operations in that it applies only to defamation claims, and within that context, its application has been reduced further to the defence of qualified privilege.[155] Consequently, regulatory compliance is only relevant when the defendant runs the defence on the basis that the defamatory statement is a 'fair and reasonable publication on a matter of public interest'. Even when the incentive is engaged in this limited way, pursuant to section 26(2) of the 2009 Act, a good record of compliance is just one of ten factors the court can consider when deciding the case.[156] We must, therefore, exercise caution over Fielden's optimistic view of this incentivised model. Indeed, if we bear in mind the high membership rate amongst Irish publishers, 'that optimism must be tempered by the reality of the incentive'.[157] Furthermore, when Fielden conducted her study, section 26(2) had not been tested in court,[158] meaning no assessment could be made at the time as to its actual efficacy – a situation that has not changed in the years since Fielden published her study. There have been no judgments in which a publication's record of regulatory compliance has had any bearing on the outcome.[159] This does not surprise Wragg, who observes that because the civil law can only compensate the claimant, and not penalise the defendant, any consideration of a defendant's regulatory compliance, as part of an evaluation of the instant case, is only ever going to operate 'at the margins of judicial reasoning' and 'cannot be central' to the resolution of the case. As he says, 'the defendant's general approach to accuracy impacts on whether the report was "fair and

---

[154] Fielden (n 69) 48, [4.2].
[155] Wragg (n 3) 58.
[156] Ibid.
[157] Ibid.
[158] Fielden (n 69) 92.
[159] Wragg (n 3) 58.

reasonable" in the circumstances only if it speaks to an attitude prevalent in the newsgathering exercise for the report itself'.[160]

In Australia, the *Convergence Review* suggested a similar regime to Denmark. It concluded that Australia's content, platform and provider-specific codes were inconsistent, confusing and inflexible. Accordingly, it found that it was unreasonable for news and commentary to be subject to different complaint systems and enforcement depending on the format of the platform on which the news or commentary is delivered.[161] It proposed, inter alia, an industry-led self-regulatory news standards body, independent of government,[162] that would cover print, online, television and radio platforms. Similarly, the *Finkelstein Report* recommended the NMC, which would also replace the Australian Press Council (APC) and apply a substantially uniform set of rules for all news producers, irrespective of the platform.[163] However, unlike the *Convergence Review*, the *Finkelstein Report's* NMC would be an entirely statutory entity.[164] According to Terry Flew and Adam Swift, the NMC would be 'neither a government regulator nor a self-regulatory industry body, but rather a co-regulatory hybrid mechanism that the Report terms "enforced regulation"',[165] meaning that it would set and enforce standards, and participation would be compulsory. However, the recommendations made by both the *Convergence Review* and *Finkelstein Report* were not adopted, meaning that the APC is still in operation.

The NZLC's preference was for an independent converged regulator with oversight for a voluntary, yet incentivised, regime.[166] Accordingly, its recommended model would not require legislation to establish the NMSA, but only to recognise it once it was set up, by conferring legal privileges on its members.[167] Thus, it shares similar characteristics with the Irish model and the UK's currently inactive section 40. In coming to this recommendation, it cited Leveson LJ's acknowledgment in his *Inquiry* that for a voluntary model to work, membership incentives must be both attractive and robust.[168]

From the previous sections, and this brief survey of very different regulatory models, a blueprint for the reimagined scheme is beginning to emerge. The reg-

---

[160] Ibid.
[161] *Convergence Review* (n 74) 49.
[162] Ibid 50–51. Although the *Convergence Review's* recommendations do contain statutory elements, such as mandating membership for larger media entities.
[163] *Finkelstein Report* (n 74) 8–9.
[164] Ibid 9.
[165] Flew and Swift (n 113) 190; *Finkelstein Report* (n 74) 287.
[166] NZLC (n 20) 155, [6.71].
[167] Ibid [6.72].
[168] Ibid [6.71].

ulator with oversight for the scheme would be a PRP-approved regulator that demonstrates, through amended Recognition Criteria, understanding of citizen journalism and the needs of citizen journalists. Meeting this criterion could be achieved by, for instance, providing annual evidence of engagement with citizen journalists in panels, focus groups or networking events, or in running education and outreach events to educate citizen journalists on the benefits and permissiveness of regulation, or citizen journalists being invited to join steering groups. The suitability of the incentives offered by the regulator for citizen journalists, and its citizen journalist-friendly contextualisation of its standards code, would also contribute to it meeting this requirement. Membership of the scheme would be voluntary, albeit legislation would confer statutory incentives on members that surpass the 'weak' Irish example and provide coercive powers for the regulator that remedy the defects of, and go well beyond, the dormant and self-serving UK coercive framework. Furthermore, members would be able to take advantage of other, non-statutory, incentives, such as those recommended by the NZLC, that 'encourage' membership in the same way as the Danish model, albeit the reimagined scheme will take these further. Ultimately, this hybrid approach to regulation – a combination of approved voluntary self-regulation with attractive incentives and robust coercive powers – achieves an appropriate balance between protecting media freedom, protecting the public and safeguarding the public sphere. These statutory coercive powers, and statutory and non-statutory incentives are set out in the following section.

6.4   Statutory Incentives

The reimagined scheme will, first, contain incentives similar to sections 34 and 40 of the Crime and Courts Act 2015.[169] The issues associated with these provisions, explained in section 3, would be remedied, in that the provisions would (i) (in the case of section 40) be enacted and operational; and (ii) unlike the 2015 Act, apply to citizen journalists as they would capture actors that are operating as the author and publisher of material and those that are not publishing in the course of a business, in the same way as those that are. Secondly, much like the Danish system, these incentives would extend to access to court files and being able to attend court proceedings otherwise closed to the public. However, unlike the Danish Media Liability Act, this scheme would not include an incentive that allows for the gathering and storing of personal information as part of journalistic research. This is because this is already covered by the 'special purposes' exemption for journalistic, literary, artistic

---

[169]   Discussed in section 3.

Reimagining regulation

or academic purposes, which, as explained in section 2, is found in Article 85 of the GDPR and Schedule 2 of the Data Protection Act 2018 and has been held to apply to citizen journalists.[170] Finally, the scheme would introduce a provision akin to section 26(2) of the Irish Defamation Act 2009. However, unlike the limited scope of section 26(2), the statutory provision in the reimagined scheme would, as explained in Chapter 8, extend to the operation of the Defamation Act 2013 sections 2, 3 and 4 defences of truth, honest opinion, and publication on a matter of public interest respectively.[171]

6.5   Non-statutory Incentives

As I said at the very beginning of this chapter, the concern of regulation is protecting the public, by preventing 'real harm' being caused to 'real people'. Yet, incidentally, the quality of discourse within the public sphere can be improved, and journalists themselves can, to an extent, be shielded from liability, and even empowered, by virtue of the non-statutory incentives, or 'services', offered by a regulatory scheme. These non-statutory incentives or services, could include the following:

1. The *Cairncross Review* has recommended the introduction of a government innovation fund to develop new approaches and tools to improve the supply of public-interest news.[172] It also recommends the introduction of new forms of tax relief, including extending zero-rated VAT to digital newspapers and magazines, as well as digital-only publications.[173] This scheme would take this one step further. Pursuant to the NZLC report, NMSA members can access public funding for publications and programmes falling within its definition of news and adhering to the NMSA's code.[174] A similar incentive would be available to members of the regulator overseeing this scheme as this would, first, serve to protect standards and, secondly, act as an incentive to join the scheme.

2. A mediation service would be accessible to both complainants and members of the regulator to encourage the cost-effective and efficient settlement of cases which may otherwise proceed to court.

---

[170] *The Law Society and others v Kordowski* [2014] EMLR 2, [99].

[171] See Chapter 8 sections 3.2.1, 3.2.2 and 3.2.3.

[172] Dame F. Cairncross, *The Cairncross Review: A Sustainable Future for Journalism*, Department for Digital, Culture, Media & Sport, 12 February 2019, 90–102. See also T. Gibbons, 'Conceptions of the Press and the Functions of Regulation' (2016) 22(5) *Convergence: The International Journal of Research into New Media Technologies* 484, 487.

[173] Cairncross (n 172) 90–102.

[174] NZLC (n 20) 181, [7.115]–[7.117].

292   *Media freedom in the age of citizen journalism*

3. Members would be able to access training,[175] education resources, law and policy updates, and advice to help them to develop their journalistic practice;[176] apply for funding; understand and comply with the scheme's standards code; and, for instance, provide them with a requisite level of knowledge to report appropriately on court proceedings (and therefore to avoid allegations of contempt of court). This incentive would also help them to meet, for instance, the statutory requirements of Defamation Act 2013 defences and to comply with data protection law. This incentive would be particularly attractive to citizen journalists, who are unlikely to have had any 'formal' journalistic or legal training or have access to a legal team.[177] Although not a complete shield, access to training, education and advice is likely to reduce members' risk of liability. At the same time, a member's engagement with these incentives indicates to the public that they are making every effort to operate professionally and within law, and in doing so that they are trying to insulate themselves from unnecessary litigation risks, which leads on to the following incentive.

4. In its Report the NZLC acknowledged that belonging to a regulator (in its case, the NMSA) would be a mark of responsibility which distinguishes members from non-members and would, therefore, provide a reputational advantage to those that are part of the scheme.[178] Membership of this reimagined scheme would provide similar reputational or brand advantages. It would demonstrate to the outside world that members are part of a group of media that place a high value on responsible journalism and have therefore bound themselves to act responsibly. It says that they will abide by the concept's standards of professional behaviour and norms of discourse and are, ultimately, prepared to be accountable for their actions. Something akin to a 'kitemark' could be awarded to members to enable them to demonstrate membership of, and compliance with, the scheme's standards code. As explained in Chapter 7, this will also enable anonymous actors, discussed further below, to advertise their membership without having to be named.[179]

Moreover, membership of the regulatory scheme would confer non-legal benefits on members. For example, journalists are given preferential access in a wide range of circumstances, including: invitations to attend media conferences of public and private agencies; early embargoed access to media

---

[175] Gibbons (n 172) 487.

[176] For example, members would have the opportunity to complete an 'Ethical Journalism Diploma' in partnership with a university.

[177] See the arguments in Chapter 8 at sections 2.2 and 3.2 respectively.

[178] NZLC (n 20) 180, [7.111]–[7.113].

[179] See Chapter 7 section 4.

Reimagining regulation 293

releases; invitations to meetings (such as shareholder meetings); access to police and emergency services briefings. As the NZLC states in its report, '[p]oliticians and other powerful figures in society are often buffered from the media by advisers who determine which media outlets will have access to them. Most people and organisations prefer to deal with accountable media which whom there is a higher degree of trust.'[180] Membership of this regulatory scheme is a way of demonstrating that trust.[181]

5. As established in Chapter 7, many citizen journalists choose to operate anonymously or pseudonymously. To encourage membership of the scheme by these actors, and to ensure they can continue to publish in this way, it would 'protect' their anonymity and pseudonymity so long as they adhered to its standards. This 'protection' would manifest itself in a number of ways. For instance, these media actors would not be named (or their pseudonym would be used) on the regulator's website and in correspondence, briefings or reports etc, and it would extend to any proceedings relating to alleged breaches of its code. Only in extreme cases, such as in the event of breaches of the code amounting to criminal conduct, would the actors be named.[182] This means that not only can anonymous and pseudonymous citizen journalists join the scheme and take advantage of its incentives, safe in the knowledge that their identities are protected, but the audience will know that these actors are members of a scheme committed to responsible journalism by virtue of the award of a kitemark, as discussed above.

6.6 The Regulator: Powers and Sanctions

In addition to the statutory incentives set out in section 6.4, the regulator with oversight of the scheme would have the power to impose sanctions on members for breaches of its code. These include requirements to: (i) publish an adverse decision in the publication concerned, with the regulator having the power to determine its prominence and positioning (including the placement on a website and the period for which it will be displayed); (ii) take down specified material from a website; (iii) correct incorrect material; (iv) grant a right of reply to a person; and (v) publish an apology, with the regulator having the power to direct its prominence and positioning.

Moreover, in exceptional cases, the regulator would have the power to suspend or terminate the membership of any member. As stated above,

---

[180] NZLC (n 20) 180, [7.112].
[181] See generally Gibbons (n 16) 203, 211, 213.
[182] D.K. Citron, *Hate Crimes in Cyberspace* (Harvard University Press, 2014) 239.

294   *Media freedom in the age of citizen journalism*

membership of the regulator will be a mark of responsibility that will give rise to reputational advantages. Therefore, the ability to suspend or terminate membership of a member serves two purposes. First, serious offending would diminish the brand. Therefore, suspension or termination may be necessary to protect the reputation of the regulator and its other members. Secondly, it 'enforces' this incentive, particularly in respect of citizen journalists, who may rely on the brand advantage conferred on them by membership to support their reputation more than established members of the institutional press. Suspension or termination would not mean that the journalist or publisher concerned would be driven from the market or be required to cease publishing. They, or it, would continue as before, but without the benefit of the privileges accruing to membership of the regulator. The suspension or termination would also need to be proportionate to the breach. It is envisaged that in most cases, the offending actor would be able to seek reinstatement of their membership after a suitable period. It is likely that a decision to terminate or suspend membership (or to decline reinstatement) would be subject to judicial review.[183]

Similarly, as mentioned in Chapter 7, in extreme cases the regulator would have the power to name anonymous and pseudonymous members.[184] In much the same way as described above in relation to termination and suspension, it would help to protect the reputation of the regulator and other anonymous and pseudonymous members by encouraging public confidence in those that do adhere to the standards code, albeit anonymously or pseudonymously. However, it is recognised that, unlike suspension of membership, there is 'no way back' once a member's identity has been revealed.[185] Therefore, an assessment of what is meant by 'extreme' and accompanying guidelines would need to be drafted to assist the regulator in making this decision. By way of example, conduct that has been the subject of a successful criminal prosecution would, in most circumstances, warrant the naming of the offending members.

6.7   Non-members

Finally, it is important to consider the position of non-members. It is accepted that some media actors, and of course all non-media actors, will not be within the jurisdiction of the regulator. This is particularly likely within the context of those operating online and via social media, either because they do not meet the eligibility criteria set out at section 6.2.2 or because they elect not to join. Indeed, this was acknowledged by the NZLC in its report: '[t]here will be

---

[183]   NZLC (n 20) 170–171, [7.70]–[7.72].
[184]   See Chapter 7 section 4.
[185]   Citron (n 182) 239.

Reimagining regulation 295

bloggers, website hosts, Facebook users and a myriad of others ... [who] will continue unregulated and may continue to publish as they wish'.[186]

However, it is important to note that these actors will remain subject to both civil and criminal laws,[187] and that, conversely, they are not without privileges as the law confers certain privileges on them. For instance, as set out in Chapter 4, the protection afforded by the right to freedom of expression pursuant to Article 10(1) ECHR is available, subject to qualification, to everybody, irrespective of whether they are media. Equally, the enhanced right to media freedom can, in theory, apply to all media, regardless of whether an actor is or is not a member of a regulatory scheme. By way of example from an English law perspective, as explored in Chapter 8, the Defamation Act 2013 provides defences, such as 'honest opinion' and 'public interest',[188] which exempt publishers from liability for defamation if certain conditions are satisfied. These 'privileges' are incidental to the free speech rights conferred on everybody. Thus, this reimagined regulatory scheme would not interfere with the fundamental free speech rights of citizens or non-member media actors, nor would it impose unnecessary constraints on private publishing activities. Rather, what it would do is provide clarity for those media actors who want to be considered part of the media-as-a-constitutional-component concept and who therefore choose to abide by the standards of professional behaviour and norms of discourse inherent within this concept of media.

7   CONCLUSION

The reimagined regulatory scheme advanced here could, if adopted, regulate members of the institutional press and citizen journalists without compromising the right to freedom of expression and the enhanced right to media freedom. However, by sketching the contours of this scheme I have exposed new lines of enquiry, beyond the scope of this book, that are, nevertheless, vitally important and worthy of further consideration. For instance, it leaves open questions relating to how these non-statutory incentives, or services, could be offered: does the regulator have the expertise, resources and capacity to offer these services, or would they need to be contracted to a third party? Either way, would this expose the regulator to liability and, if so, how would this risk be

---

[186]   NZLC (n 20) 191–192, [7.167]–[7.169].

[187]   For analysis of criminal sanctions see Coe (n 44); P. Coe, 'National Security and the Fourth Estate in a Brave New Social Media World' in L. Scaife (ed), *Social Networks as the New Frontier of Terrorism #Terror* (Routledge, 2017) 165–192.

[188]   See sections 3 and 4 respectively of the Defamation Act 2013. See Chapter 8 section 3.2 for analysis of the concept's impact on the operation of various defences to defamation.

managed? The composition of the standards code, and its contextualisation for citizen journalists, also need to be determined. More broadly, Chapters 7 and 8 looked at how the media-as-a-constitutional-component concept provides a model for dealing with specific legal problems created by citizen journalism and online speech within the current libertarian paradigm. However, there are other challenges, emanating from, or related to, citizen journalism that I have not been able to deal with in this book. For instance, although touched upon in Chapter 7, whistleblowers are a group of actors that would, in certain situations, fall within the concept's scope and its definition of media. The level of protection they should be afforded, and how their rights are balanced with the individuals and organisations they speak out against is open for discussion. As we saw in Chapters 2 and 3 media ownership generally, and more specifically the influence of online platforms such as Facebook and Google, is a challenge that transcends the institutional press. It is affecting all forms of media and all media actors, and is having a profound impact on the public sphere. The discussion in Chapters 2 and 3 only really scratched the service and, because this is a live issue at the time of writing, which is developing at pace, undoubtedly it is an area that is ripe for further consideration. Although it has been touched upon, data protection law, and its impact on citizen journalists, has not been within the scope of this enquiry. I have also not considered issues around national security that may arise from the activities of citizen journalists. Thus, in many ways this book is a starting point, or a catalyst, for further work in this area. In essence, the media-as-a-constitutional-component concept, as a theory of free speech, is, I hope, a trunk from which more branches of enquiry will emerge.

Index

Abrams v United States 8, 132, 146
academic speech, in relation to
    self-fulfilment 228
ACCC's 'News media and digital
    platforms mandatory bargaining
    code' 83
accountability
    of citizen journalist 284
    of institutional journalist 284
ACLU of Nevada v Heller 220
Adams, John 191–2
administration of justice 236, 239
Adorno, Theodor 48
advertisement financing 47
advertising contracts 48
advertising income 68, 71, 76–7
    sources of 47
*Albert-Engelmann-Gesellschaft mbH v
    Austria* 111
*Alithia Publishing Company Ltd and
    Constantinides v Cyprus* 199
Alliance of Independent Press Councils
    of Europe (AIPCE) 262
*American Civil Liberties Union v Zell
    Miller* 217
American Convention on Human Rights
    (ACHR) 106–8
anonymous and pseudonymous speech,
    right to 206–13, 224, 227
    constitutionally protected speaker
    interest-orientated 231
    protection for 219
anti-libertarian movement 157
antitrust laws 13, 28, 36–7
Apple 59, 74, 78
Arab Spring uprising 5, 128
argument from truth 8, 130–32, 136,
    139–45, 155, 161, 227
Associated Press v United States 28
asylum-seekers 228
Attorney-General

v Associated Newspapers Limited
    243
v English 238
v Leveller Magazine Limited 240
v Mulholland and Foster 117
v The Times Newspapers 237
audience interests
    concept of 204–5
    harmonising of 232–3
    problems associated with relying
    exclusively on 219–32
    speaker *versus* 218–32
Australian Competition and Consumer
    Commission (ACCC) 62, 76, 83
Australian Press Council (APC) 289
*Author of a Blog v Times Newspapers
    Ltd* 4, 208, 218, 220–23, 228, 230
author's publication, credibility of 219
autonomous agency, moral principle of
    136
A v BBC 240
A v B plc 189–91
Axel Springer AG v Germany 75, 109

Bagdikian, Ben 23, 37
Baker, C. Edwin 25, 37, 49, 91, 154, 156,
    225
Balfour, Arthur 34
Barendt, Eric 97, 133, 139, 144, 149,
    164–5, 206, 216, 221, 225, 228
Barlow, John Perry 54
BBC's Editorial Guidelines 186, 200
*Beckley Newspapers v Hanks
    Corporation* 200
beneficiaries of media freedom 7, 9, 105,
    115, 120, 130, 156, 284
    approaches for determining 123–9
    mass audience approach 126–7
    press-as-technology model
    123–6

297

'professionalised' publisher approach 127–9
Berlusconi effect 25
Berlusconi, Silvio 25
Bernal, Paul 75
Bertelsmann 39
Bezanson, Randall 101, 114
Bezos, Jeff 39
bloggers 277
    anonymity of 209
    identity of 209
blogs 4–6, 88, 122, 126–7, 170, 209, 223, 272
Bodrožić v Serbia and Montenegro 106
Bork, Robert 162
Boston Herald American 35
Branzburg v Hayes 118–19, 123
Brendon, Piers 34
British Empire 34
British Sky Broadcasting 31
broadcasting services 27
broadcast journalism 278
Brutus v Cozens 206
Buckley v American Constitutional Law Foundation 220
burden of proof 252–3
Burstyn v Wilson 147
Busuioc v Moldova 98
Buzzfeed 57

Cable, Vince 31
Cairncross Review, The 47, 66, 68–9, 71, 75, 291
Calvert, Clay 179
Cambridge Analytica scandal 58, 142–3
Campbell v Mirror Group Newspapers Ltd 188, 191
capitalism, principle of 146
Carey v Brown 185
celebrity gossip 83, 187–91, 194
Centro Europa 7 Srl v Italy 173
Charter of the Fundamental Rights of the European Union (CFREU) 96, 101, 124, 126
Chicago Tribune 35
China
    censorship of social media 5
    intolerance of a free media 5
Chomsky, Noam 22, 49
churnalism, proliferation of 20

citizen journalism 3–7, 10, 51–2, 89, 128, 149–50, 203, 205, 222, 230, 282, 283, 296
    ascendance of 56
    contribution to the digital public sphere 87–92
    development of 121
    emergence of 57, 121, 264
    facilitation of 57, 126
    findings of 122
    growth of 4, 52, 95, 123
    and media freedom 13
    nature of 8, 224, 283
    online speech and 137, 235
    open justice and 239–45
    origins of 3
    Orwell Prize for 222
    and social media 172
    state censorship of 5
    symbiotic relationship with traditional media 122, 231
citizen journalists 5, 11, 12, 69, 95, 111, 163, 261, 263
    accountability of 284
    disruption caused by 273
    dissemination of false information by 198
    emergence of 42
    facilitation of 10, 50
    functions of 277
    internet and social media, use of 53
    needs of 8, 290
    operating through social media 2
    protection of 219
    regulatory scheme for governing 260, 264–5
    right to media freedom 264
    treatment of 246
citizens participating, in public discourse 164
Citizens United v FEC 102
civic journalism 3
"clickbait" headlines 71
Cohen, Bernard 21
Cohen v California 109
Columbia Broadcasting System 16
Commission on Freedom of the Press *see* Hutchins Commission
communication monopoly 172

Index

Communications Decency Act (1996), US 63
communications technology 16, 33, 102, 123
communicative power, risk of abuse of 25
Compaine, Benjamin 26, 36–8, 54
competition law 24
    press and 27–31
    universal and media-specific 27
Competition & Markets Authority (CMA) 73
competitive duplication 48
contempt of court
    application of common law 238
    genesis of 234–47
    law of 234
        development of 234
    offence of 176
Convergence Review (Australia) 275, 280–81, 289
corporate institutional press 68
corporate journalism 43, 68
corporate owners 52
corporate ownership models 20, 24, 66, 90–91
    newspapers operating within 68
Council of Europe 87, 115, 212
    Committee of Ministers of 127
Court of Justice of the European Union 246, 270
court proceedings, media's role in reporting on 242
Crime and Courts Act 2013 (UK) 177, 263, 284–5
Criminal Justice and Courts Act (2015), England and Wales 144
critique of the political economy of the press (CPEP) 16, 51, 53, 65
cross-media mergers 28
cultural pluralism 160, 172–3, 180
Curran, James 23, 91, 159, 179
cyber-culture 214
cyberspace 86, 133, 218, 228, 244, 269

Dacre, Paul 261
Daily Mail 18, 20, 33–4, 40
Daily Mail and General Trust plc (DMGT) 20
Daily Mirror 33

reporting of the COVID-19 pandemic 71
Daily Post, The 35
Daily Star 44
Daily Telegraph 31, 39, 45–6
Data Protection Act (1998) 192
Data Protection Act (2018) 193–4
data protection jurisprudence 246
Davies, Nick 23, 40
decision-making 133, 175, 229
Declaration of the Rights of Man 28
defamation
    law of 176
        Defamation Act (2013) 193, 208, 251, 255
        litigation and costs of 247–51
        media as a constitutional component concept and defences 251–9
        honest opinion 253–5
        publication on a matter of public interest 255–9
        truth 252–3
    protection against 224
    serious harm and 247–51
Defteros v Google LLC 64
Delfi AS v Estonia 211–12, 258
democracy, participatory theory of 9
democratic discourse, quality of 227–8, 231, 261
democratic distribution, principle of 24, 37
democratic society 97, 106, 109, 135
Dennis v United States 146
Detroit Times 35
digital advertising 70, 72, 73, 76
digital intermediaries for civil liability, immunity for 63
digital literacy 13
digitally democratising, the public sphere 85–92
    contribution of citizen journalism in 87–91
        liberating journalists from the dominant proprietor 90–91
        structure and 'norms' of the institutional media 89–90
        technological and financial barriers 88–9

effect of the internet and social media on 93
media as a constitutional component concept 91–2
modern public sphere 85–7
dominant proprietors 1, 17, 24, 26, 31, 33–4, 39, 42, 50, 90
duty of care 63, 84

economic communication markets 154
economic viability, of the press 65–74
impact on
competition, quality and trust 67–9
media plurality and content diversity 66–7
online advertising and low-quality journalism 70–72
reduction in the number of journalists within the institutional press 67–9
vicious circle for the public sphere 73–4
Economou v de Freitas 257
editorial freedom 41, 104, 108, 113–14, 115
right to 114
editorial judgment 257, 258
English common law 101
English jurisprudence 203
Enterprise Act (2002) 29
entertainment journalism 194
Epstein, Joseph 36
Erskine, John 132, 135, 136
ethics of journalism 180, 200, 258
European Broadcasting Union survey 44
European Commission on Human Rights 112
European Convention on Human Rights (ECHR) 92, 168, 209
Article 6 of 239
Article 8 of 118, 189, 196
Article 10 of 112
European Court of Human Rights (ECtHR) 11–12, 97, 106–7, 109–10, 112, 115, 120, 125, 145, 181, 198, 212, 240
on 'duty and responsibility' of the media 200
judgment in

Delfi AS v Estonia 211–12
Janowski v Poland 98
jurisprudence of 95, 112, 127, 253
stance on anonymous and pseudonymous online expression 213
European Union 41, 45, 124, 246, 270
Executive Order on Preventing Online Censorship 63

Facebook 58, 60, 62, 70, 72, 126, 142, 150, 278, 295
advertising revenue 77
anonymity and pseudonymity policy 222
Cambridge Analytica scandal 58, 143
Facebook Watch 60
journalism project 61
Live 88
News Feed 61, 74, 77, 80, 179
Six4Three v Facebook litigation 61
use of algorithms 75, 78
fairness of trials 179, 234, 243–4, 259
fake news *see* false news
false news 81–5, 142, 174–6, 265
amplification of 52
dissemination of 22, 82, 198
proliferation of 231
published during the COVID-19 pandemic 82
on social media 83
spread of 83, 176
Federal Communications Commission v National Citizens Committee for Broadcasting 28
Fenwick, Helen 119, 139, 189, 240
Ferdinand v Mirror Group Newspapers Limited 190
Ferret, The 57
Fielden, Lara 274–6, 278, 281, 285–8
Fifth Estate 2, 55
Filatenko v Russia 112
filter bubbles, theory of 79–81, 153, 172, 198
Financial Times Ltd and others v United Kingdom 118
Finkelstein Report (Australia) 275, 279–81, 289
Finnish Press Council 278

Index

First Draft 45
First National Bank of Boston v Bellotti 32
First National Bank v Bellotti 185
Fourth Estate 17, 114, 125, 131–2, 137, 163
free consumer markets 146
Freeden, Michael 136
freedom of expression 11, 98, 103, 108, 175, 224
  exercise of 228
  media freedom as a right to 96–103
  nature and operation of 10
  negative 185
  newspaper's 111
  principles of 134
  protection of 125, 193
  provisions for safeguarding 124
  purpose of 161
  right to 7, 9, 96, 103, 108, 113, 129, 162–3, 264
  safeguarding of 193
freedom of speech 96, 132–3, 136, 138, 216–17, 221, 225, 228
freedom to hold opinions 96, 104, 108
free media
  China's intolerance of 5
  role in the democratic process 106
free press 17–24, 125, 275
  concept of 10
free speech 10, 84, 97, 108, 203–4, 231, 264
  authoritarian controls of 134
  categories of 7
  concept of 144–5
  de facto normative paradigm for 132–3
  facilitation of 13
  jurisprudence of 137, 139
  limitation on 182
  media as a constitutional component concept and 164–6
  as natural right 136
  operation of 8
  policy of 12
  principle of 181, 206
  privacy/free speech dichotomy 194
  protection of 158
    Post's theory on 166
  provision of 158

  right to 98, 204
  scholarship 13
  social dimension of 106
  speaker-orientated arguments based on 210
Friedman, Thomas 54–5

Garrison v Louisiana 185
General Data Protection Regulation (GDPR) 193
general public interest, matters of 195
German Basic Law 214
Gibbons, Thomas 154
Gillmor, Dan 6, 93
Gizmodo (technology blog) 77
global media conglomerates 38
Goodwin v United Kingdom 116
Google 45, 70, 72, 75, 78
  advertising revenue 77
  Google+ 221
  News 59, 74–5
  Showcase 77
Great Communities 160, 172–3
Grote, Rainer 183
Gsell v Switzerland 100, 116
Guardian Media Group 49
Guardian, The 5, 18, 49–50, 256
Gutenberg, Johannes 32

Haider v Austria 112
Hale, Baroness 191
Halis Dogan and others v Turkey 100
Handyside v United Kingdom 109, 181
harmful speech, dissemination of 90, 205
hate speech, laws relating to 110, 168, 207
Hearst Corporation 39
Hearst, Randolph 35
Herman, Edward 22
Hindman, Matthew 91
Hitchens, Lesley 41
Hocking, William Ernest 137, 156
Holmes, Oliver Wendell 8, 132
honest opinion 234, 251, 253–5, 291, 295
Horkheimer, Max 48
Horton, Richard 4
Houston Chronicle 35
Huffington Post 57

Human Rights Act 1998 (UK) 144–5, 188, 189, 207, 211
Hunt, Jeremy 31
Hurley v Irish-American Gay 220
Hutchins Commission 137, 156–7, 171–2, 175

ideological neutrality 79
immunity from bad publicity, idea of 46, 49
IMPRESS Standards Code 283, 285–6
incentives
    non-statutory 291–3
    statutory 290–91
Independent 57
individual autonomy, concept of 229
individuals' right to freedom of action 182
'*i*' newspaper 20, 38
informational self-determination, right to 213–14
Information Commissioner's Office (ICO) 186
information gathering 116
    process of 281
information pluralism, value of 27
information, recycling of 43
'in-scope' technology companies 64
Instagram 64, 126
institutional broadcast media 1
institutional mass media 104–5
    structure and norms of 89–90
institutional press 264
    corporate ownership of 1
'institutional professional' journalists 8
    accountability of 284
intellectual freedom 134
Inter-American Court of Human Rights (IACHR) 106, 110
International Brotherhood of Electrical Workers v NLRB 146
International Covenant for Civil and Political Rights (ICCPR) 106–8, 168
    Article 17 of 196
internet 3, 10, 11, 17, 51, 53–6, 121, 148
    effect on democratisation of the public sphere 93
    Kaye's support of anonymous communication on 228

investigative journalism 19, 21, 26, 46–7, 83, 115, 154, 253
IPSO Editors' Code 283, 285
Irish Defamation Act (2009) 291

Jacobellis v Ohio 187
Jameel v Wall Street Journal Europe Sprl (No. 3) 188, 190–91
Janowski v Poland 98
Jefferson, Thomas 132, 136
Jersild v Denmark 147
journalism 1
    education 137
    professional standards 75
    quality of 73
journalistic and non-journalistic staff, reduction of 67–9
journalistic ethics 180, 200
    breaches of 262
journalistic responsibilities 224
journalistic sources, protection of 116
JPI Media Publications Limited (JPI Media) 20
junk news 68, 81–5

Kant, Immanuel 182
Kaye, David 228
Klonick, Kate 79
Koltay, András 81
KU v Finland 211

laissez-faire journalism 135, 146
Lavric v Romania 111
law and jurisprudence, polarisation of 205–18
    England and the European Court of Human Rights views on 206–13
    German and US position on 213–18
    right to anonymous and pseudonymous speech 206–13
Law Society and others v Kordowski 193, 270
Lebedev, Evgeny 39
'legacy' newspapers 71
legal proceedings, fairness of 90, 92, 234, 236, 238–9, 241–2, 244, 246–7

Lesbian and Bisexual Group of Boston 220
libertarianism
  application to modern media 135
  argument from truth 139–45
  classic liberalism 134
  dilemma of 155
  as a flawed normative framework 138–55
  influence on free speech 132–3
  marketplace of ideas 145–55
  meaning of 133–7
  and media freedom 134
  self-righting process, notion of 136
  socialist 134
  theory of 132–3
LJ, Leveson 2, 5, 18, 31, 42, 121, 159, 175, 244, 261–2, 266–8, 270, 274–5, 289
L'Oreal SA v Bellure NV 142, 144
Los Angeles Examiner 35

Mail Online 44
Mail on Sunday 40–41
Malicious Communications Act (1998) 207
Manchester Courier 34
Manole and others v Moldova 115
Marcuse, Herbert 23
Marwick, Alice 81
Marxism 134
mass audience 1, 17, 21, 48–9, 55, 69, 86, 95, 123, 126–7, 250, 273
mass communication 32–3, 55, 160
mass-market
  content 71
  journalism 72
mass media communications 149
McChesney, Robert 37
McClaren v News Group Newspapers 190
McIntyre v Ohio Elections Commission 213–18, 215, 219, 227
McKennit v Ash 190
McVicar v United Kingdom 252
media
  companies 60–65
  definition of 279
  independence 104, 115
  malfeasance, impact of 179

plurality, value of 27
professionals 127
reporting on matters of public concern 242
research and investigation, protection of 115–16
role in reporting on court proceedings 242
media actors
  institutional protection of 114–20
  versus non-media actors 121–2
media as a constitutional component
  concept 8–9, 11, 53, 91–3, 95, 105, 126, 128–9, 139, 156–61, 163, 204, 223, 232, 234, 245–7, 262, 279, 281, 295, 296
  adoption of 234, 243
  for balancing the interests of the state and individuals with the media 176–7
  composition of the standards code 296
  defamation and 251–9
  guiding factors 194–7
  on media acting in good faith 199–201
  on media conduct 197–9
  parameters for media freedom 12, 167–9, 170, 178–82
  philosophical foundation for 131
  problem with rationality 174–6
  relationship with other participatory theories of free speech 164–7
  requirements of 191
  and Robert Post's 'norms of civility' 180–82
  social responsibility of 156–60, 199
  standards attached to media discourse and conduct by 182–91
  'veracity of the statement' component 199
media conduct, concept of 197–9
media ecology 52
  news consumption 57–60
  social media platforms 60–65
media enterprises, mergers of 29
media freedom 98, 181, 224
  balance against conflicting rights and interests 182

beneficiaries of 7, 9, 53, 105, 115, 120, 130, 156
approaches for determining 123–9
beyond speech rights 114–20
citizen journalists' right to 264
concept of 10, 95, 103
as a distinct right to freedom of expression 96–103
editorial freedom 113–14
versus fair trials 234–47
in Germany 113
grounds of 29
harmonisation of 245–7
to hold opinions 108–9
to impart information and ideas 109–14
importance of 104–7
institutional protection of media actors 114–20
law's treatment of 8
limitation on 182
media as a constitutional component concept of 12, 167–9, 170, 178–82
Online Safety Bill 64
operation of 183
positive rights 119–20
privileges attributed to 128
protection of 64, 97
media speech 107–14
right to 7, 95, 100, 107–8, 112, 115–19, 122, 182, 265, 277
role in imparting information and ideas 109
role of 104–7
media hyperactivity, effect of 68
Media Liability Act 286, 290
media mergers, UK's preference for 30
media paradigm 1–3, 7, 52, 57, 86, 164
media power, dispersal of 25
Media Reform Coalition 38
media sources, protection of 116–19
Meredith 39
Merrill, John 135
Metro 40
Metromedia v City of San Diego 147
Miami Herald v Tornillo 113
Mill, John Stuart 8, 130, 136, 191, 192, 227

Milton, John 132, 135
Areopagitica 134
moral scrutiny, application of 200
Mosley v News Group Newspapers 188
Murdoch, Rupert 26, 31, 39, 42
News Corporation 38

Negroponte, Nicholas 54
Neil, Andrew 40–41, 165
news
commoditisation of 42, 49
consumption 57–60
definition of 280–81
print newspapers as a source of 58
recycling of 43
News Consumption Survey 58–9
News Corporation 31, 38
newsgathering 170
forms of 115–16
monopolisation of 57
process of 7
News Group Newspapers 190
news journalism 10
news media 3, 10, 19, 21–2, 50, 62, 73, 76, 170, 264, 277, 279–81
definition of 279, 281
News Media Council (NMC) 279
News Media Standards Authority (NMSA), New Zealand 276
Newsnight 46
newspaper
decline in sales of 65
journalistic and non-journalistic staff, reduction of 67–9
operating within the corporate ownership model 68
right to freedom of expression 111
newspaper distribution infrastructure, protection of 100
newsprint 230
news reporting 51
News UK story 38
New York
v Duryea 219
v Harris 56
New York Morning Journal, The 35
New York Times v Sullivan 200
New Zealand Evidence Act (2006) 169
Night Jack blog 4–5, 209, 222–4
Northcliffe's 'confederacy' 35

Norwegian Press Council 278
Norwich Pharmacal orders 210–11
Novaya Gazeta and Borodyanskiy v Russia 180

Oborne, Peter 45–6
obscenity, laws relating to 207
Observer, The 33
Ofcom 63
    online harms regulator 63
    Online Nation Report (2020) 81
OhmyNews.com 6
online advertising 47, 70–72
online aggregation and distribution of content, by digital gatekeepers 74–9
online anonymity and pseudonymity, pervasiveness of 203
online communication 12, 149, 214, 217, 220, 226–7, 229–30, 243
online filter bubbles 52
Online Harms White Paper 63, 83
online media 76, 231, 274, 278–9, 281, 286
online news 47
    consumption 53, 72
online news publishers, regulatory scheme for 278–9
Online Safety Bill 64, 84
online speech 149, 203–4, 232
    and citizen journalism 137, 235
    disruption caused by 273
    harm caused by 135
    internet 133
    normative framework for 131
    paradigm for 131
    social responsibility doctrine 137
    within Western democracies 133
online surveillance, protection against 212
open justice
    and citizen journalism 239–45
    constitutional right to 242
    elements of 240
    harmonisation of 245–7
    intersection of online expression and 243
    for media scrutiny of the justice system 240
    principle of 179, 234, 239, 241

ownership of media
    arguments for opposing 24–6
    common ownership 28
    concentration of 24
    corporate ownership models 24, 66, 90–91
        newspapers operating within 68
    in cross-media mergers 28
    dispersal of 24–5
    models of 31–50
        corporate ownership model and advertising 36–50
        early press barons and the dominant proprietor model 32–6
    press and competition law 27–31
    and promotion of plurality 24–6
    significance of 24–6
Oxford Internet Institute 83

Packingham v North Carolina 86
participatory democracy 37, 165
Pell v Procunier 120
Perrin v United Kingdom 127
personalisation of news feeds, effect of 79, 81
person's identity, protection of 210
Pew Research Centre 58
Phillipson, Gavin 119, 139, 189, 240
phone hacking 30
Piechota, Greg 75–6
pluralism, concept of 27–8, 30, 67, 96, 100, 109, 135, 159–60, 172–3, 180
police power, abuse of 195
political autonomy, notion of 166
political egalitarianism 24
political equality, idea of 49, 121, 154, 166
political minorities 165
political speech 195, 209, 216
Post, Robert 9, 227
    norms of civility 180–82
    participatory theory of democracy 9, 131, 166
press-as-technology model 96
press-as-technology movement 11, 95–6, 101, 103, 120, 123–6, 273
press barons 26, 32–6, 39, 42

press behaviour and speech, laissez-faire
    principles of 23
Press Council 275–6, 278, 287
    Fielden's study of 278
press freedom
    curtailment of 10, 51
    protection of 116
press industry, theoretical origins of 17
Press Ombudsman 287
print circulation 47, 51, 65, 73
printing press 33
    invention of 32
print journalism 6
print newspapers, as a source of news 58
Print Zeitungsverlag v Austria 111
privacy/free speech dichotomy 194
privacy rights, of individuals 189, 194,
    210
privacy violation, protection of 224
probabilities, balance of 252
professional behaviour, standards of
    156–60, 176, 232, 234, 265
professional journalism 43, 282
    norms of 7, 9
ProPublica 57
Protection from Harassment Act (1997)
    207
pseudo-public sphere, media's creation
    of 192
public broadcasters 114
public communication, philosophy of
    158
public concern, matters of 195
public discourse 1, 229, 231, 277
    citizens participating in 164
    norms of 161–9
    paradox of 181
    Post's thesis on 166
    quality of 112
public discussion, notion of 162
public interest
    and creation of artificial supply and
        demand 191–2
    definition of 188, 190–92
    intervention 29
    journalism 66, 69
    need for guidance on 192–4
    publication on a matter of 255–9
    tyranny of
        majority 191

prevailing opinion and feeling
    191
public-interest news 83
    publication of 7
    supply of 291
public interest/privacy dichotomy
    187–91
public journalism, reform movement of
    1980s 3
public media, programming policy of
    196
public order laws 207
public safety rules, violation of 116
public sphere 121
    digitally democratising 85–92
    digitally distorting 74–85
    health and prosperity of 191
    polarisation of communities 172–4
    resistance to social change 172–4
    vicious circle for 73–4
public watchdog 114, 163
    media's role as 104, 117
    role of 97
publish information, right to 111
publishing industry 123

Rawls, John 182
Raz, Joseph 27
real people, rights of 261
Redmond-Bate v DPP 206
regulatory scheme, for governing citizen
    journalists
    comparative rationale of 273–6
        comparative approach 275–6
        perspective of 273–4
    Convergence Review 275
    Finkelstein Report 275
    impact of media convergence on 276
    incentives
        non-statutory 291–3
        statutory 290–91
    for mandatory regulation of the
        institutional press 270–73
    mass audience approach for 273
    membership of reimagined scheme
        292
    models of press regulation 285
    multi-jurisdictional view of 285–90
    in New Zealand 275–6
    non-members, position of 294–5

for online news publishers 278–9
powers and sanctions under 293–4
press-as-technology model 273
professionalised publisher approach
273
purposes of 275
the regulator 293–4
reimagined regulatory scheme
conceptual principles 276–8
multi-jurisdictional view of
regulation 285–90
nature of membership 285–90
non-members 294–5
non-statutory incentives 291–3
powers and sanctions under
293–4
statutory incentives 290–91
subject of 278–85
significance of 264–5
statutory 290–91
statutory incentives 290–91
in UK 265–70
reimaged regulatory scheme, nature and
scope of 263
relevant publisher, definition of 284–5
Reno v American Civil Liberties Union
86, 148, 211, 217
responsible journalism
concept of 224, 257
principles of 200
requirements of 255
tenets of 258
revolutionary socialism 134
Reynolds v Times Newspapers Limited
255–6
right of citizens, protection of 161
Roeman and Schmit v Luxembourg 118
'role model' principle 12, 178, 189
Romenesko, Jim 6
Roo Moo Hyun 6
Rooney, Martin 105
Rothermere, Lord 20, 33–4, 38, 40, 42
Rowbottom, Jacob 30–31, 41, 235, 252
Royal Commission on the Press (1962),
UK 29, 136, 156–7, 171
*R v Secretary of State for the Home
Department, ex parte Simms* 138,
144
*R (on the application of Ullah) v Special
Adjudicator* 145

San Francisco Examiner 35
SARS-CoV-2 (COVID-19) pandemic 5,
21, 43, 142
Daily Mirror's reporting of 71
false content published during 82
misinformation on 45
origin of 44
Wuhan Institute of Virology, China
44
Saxbe v Washington Post 120
Scanlon, Thomas 139, 229
Schauer, Frederick 139–40, 143, 185,
221
*Schweizerische Radio-und
Fernsehgesellschaft SRG v
Switzerland* 120
Scott Trust 49
Scott v Scott 239
Seaton, Jean 179
seditious libel, prosecutions for 32
self-governance, democratic 9, 12, 97,
105, 131, 144, 156, 161, 165, 169,
227
self-righting process, notion of 132,
134–6, 146, 157
Selistö v Finland 109
sensationalised stories, publication of
174–6
Siebert, Fred 133–5
Six4Three v Facebook 61
Slater v Blomfield 169
Smith, Adam 146
Snapchat 148
socialist libertarianism 134
social media 10, 51, 53–6, 60–65, 85,
121, 131, 150
advent of 17
citizen journalists operating through
2, 172
duty of care 63
Facebook *see* Facebook
growth of 3
Instagram 64
news aggregation and editing
practices of 60
online harms regulator 63
process of news distribution by 75
sourcing news from 59
state censorship in China 5
TikTok 64

Twitter 58, 62–4
social networking platforms 143
social responsibility theory 9, 10, 11, 12,
    105, 133, 137, 155–69, 263, 277
  argument from democratic
      self-governance 161–9
  definition of 'the media' based on
      169–71
  emergence of 171
  media as a constitutional component
      concept 156–60, 199
  values of 173
social sharing, impacts of 81
Sooben v Badal 224
speaker
  versus audience interests 218–32
  concept of 204–5
  constitutionally protected 231
  harmonising of 232–3
  right to contribute to public life 227
speech of constitutional value,
    dissemination of 105
Spickmich case 213–18
state repression, of the press 32
Stocker v Stocker 150
Stunt v Associated Newspapers Ltd 194
Sunday Times, The 33, 40, 237
Sunday Times v United Kingdom 240
Sunstein, Cass 185
Sun, The 40, 42

Talley v California 216
*Társaság a Szabadságjogokért v
    Hungary* 115
technology companies 60–65, 74, 78
Telemedia Act (2007) 214
TikTok 64
Times Higher Education 226
Times, The 33–4
tobacco advertising, issues relating to
    196
Torres, Mirelis 179
Totalise plc v The Motley Fool Ltd 210
'traditional institutional' media 10
'traditional professional' press 57

Trending Topics 77–8
trends, creation of 79–81
Trump, Donald 63
truth, of a defamatory imputation 252–3
Twitter 58, 62–4, 103, 126, 278
  fact-check links 63

United Nations Human Rights
    Committee (HRC) 106
United States v Dennis 146
universal law of freedom 182
user preferences 79–81, 172

Vejdeland and others v Sweden 99
ViacomCBS 39
Volokh, Eugene 101–2, 185
voluntary self-regulation 12, 137, 159,
    171, 176–7, 266, 271, 290
Von Hannover v Germany (No 1) 187–91

Walt Disney Company, The 39
WarnerMedia Group 38
Washington Herald, The 35
Washington Times-Herald 35–6
Washington Times, The 35–6, 44
*Watchtower Bible and Tract Society of
    New York v Stratton* 220
Weaver, Russell 33
Weinberg, Jonathan 152
Welles,Orson 16, 35
Wenzel, Nicola 183
WhatsApp 148
Whitney v California 146
Willem v France 127
Wojtas-Kaleta v Poland 98
World Economic Forum 100
Wragg, Paul 25, 188, 261
Wuhan Institute of Virology, China 44

YouTube 58, 126, 148, 150

Zuckerberg, Mark 60–61
ZXC v Bloomberg LP 194